# THE WAR FOR ENGLAND'S SHORES

# THE WAR FOR ENGLAND'S SHORES

S-Boats and the Fight against British Coastal Convoys

G. H. BENNETT

**Seaforth**
PUBLISHING

Copyright © G H Bennett 2023

First published in Great Britain in 2023 by
Seaforth Publishing,
A division of Pen & Sword Books Ltd,
George House, Beevor Street, Barnsley S71 1HN
www.seaforthpublishing.com

British Library Cataloguing in Publication Data
A catalogue record for this book is available from the British Library

ISBN 978 1 3990 7791 0

First published in the United States 2023 by The Naval Institute Press, Annapolis

All rights reserved. No part of this publication may be reproduced or transmitted in any form or by any means, electronic or mechanical, including photocopying, recording, or any information storage and retrieval system, without prior permission in writing of both the copyright owner and the above publisher.

The right of G H Bennett to be identified as the author of this work has been asserted by him in accordance with the Copyright, Designs and Patents Act 1988.

Pen & Sword Books Limited incorporates the imprints of After the Battle, Atlas, Archaeology, Aviation, Discovery, Family History, Fiction, History, Maritime, Military, Military Classics, Politics, Select, Transport, True Crime, Air World, Frontline Publishing, Leo Cooper, Remember When, Seaforth Publishing, The Praetorian Press, Wharncliffe Local History, Wharncliffe Transport, Wharncliffe True Crime and White Owl.

Printed and bound in Great Britain by CPI Group (UK) Ltd, Croydon, CR0 4YY

*For Buster*

*The enemy holds every trump card, covering all areas with long-range air patrols and using location methods against which we still have no warning. . . . The enemy knows all our secrets and we know none of his.*

—**KARL DÖNITZ**, 1943 diary

*A wooden boat is not simply a boat. It has an identity, a personality, a life: Its every frame, timber and fastening are inscribed by the lives of those who built it, by those who maintain it, and by those who crew it. When you part from it the feeling of loss, of absence, is palpable and the sense of longing, eternal. You wouldn't understand unless you'd experienced it. You just wouldn't understand.*

—**MIKE GIRONA**

# CONTENTS

List of Maps and Tables . . . . . . . . . viii
List of Acronyms and Abbreviations . . . . . . . ix
Preface . . . . . . . . . . . . . . xi
Acknowledgments . . . . . . . . . . . . xix

Introduction . . . . . . . . . . . . . 1

**CHAPTER 1** German Naval Strategy, 1870–1940 . . . . . . 11
**CHAPTER 2** The Rise of the S-Boat, 1940–1941 . . . . . . 24
**CHAPTER 3** The Campaign in the Balance, 1941–1942 . . . . 43
**CHAPTER 4** The Human Dimension . . . . . . . . 53
**CHAPTER 5** Dönitz Replaces Raeder . . . . . . . . 74
**CHAPTER 6** The 1943 Turning Point: The Emergence of a Multilayered System of Defense . . . . . . 87
**CHAPTER 7** The 1943 Turning Point: The Role of Intelligence . . 101
**CHAPTER 8** The 1943 Turning Point: German Failure to Respond Effectively . . . . . . . . . 127
**CHAPTER 9** S-Boats and the Shift to the Defensive, 1943–1944 . 144
**CHAPTER 10** D-Day for the Kriegsmarine . . . . . . . 155
**CHAPTER 11** The Long Retreat, 1944–1945 . . . . . . . 168

Conclusion . . . . . . . . . . . . . 185

Appendix: Vessels in English Waters Lost to Torpedo Attacks by S-Boats, 1940–1945 . . . . 197

Notes . . . . . . . . . . . . . . 221
Selected Bibliography . . . . . . . . . . 249
Index . . . . . . . . . . . . . . 263

# MAPS AND TABLES

**MAPS**

MAP 1. Principal Ports along Western Europe and the East Coast of England . . . . . . . . . . xxi

MAP 2. Principal Royal Navy Commands and S-Boat Operating Bases along the Channel Coast . . . . . xxii

**TABLES**

TABLE 1. British Coastal Convoys in Late 1943 . . . . . . . . . 28

TABLE 2. S-Boat Torpedo Successes against Merchant Ships . . . 88

TABLE 3. Destroyers Available on the East Coast, 1941–1943 . . . . 91

TABLE 4. Escort Forces Available for Coastal Convoys in Late 1943 . . . . . . . . . . . . . . . . 92

TABLE 5. Average S-Boat Torpedo Firing Distances . . . . . 132

# ACRONYMS AND ABBREVIATIONS

| | |
|---|---|
| ABCA | Army Bureau of Current Affairs |
| bhp | break horsepower |
| C-in-C | commander-in-chief |
| DEMS | defensively equipped merchant ship |
| FdS | Führer der Schnellboote |
| FdT | Führer der Torpedoboote |
| FN | Forth-North Convoy Designation |
| FS | Forth-South Convoy Designation |
| GRT | gross registered tons |
| HFDF | high-frequency direction finding |
| HMS | His/Her Majesty's Ship |
| HMT | His/Her Majesty's Trawler |
| LCT | landing craft tank |
| MAS | Motoscafo Armato Silurante (Italian motor torpedo boat) |
| MB | Mercedes Benz |
| MGB | motor gunboat |
| ML | motor launch |
| MTB | motor torpedo boat |
| PW | Portland-West Convoy Designation |
| RN | Royal Navy |
| RNVR | Royal Navy Volunteer Reserve |
| SGB | steam gunboat |
| WP | West-Portland Convoy Designation |
| W/T | wireless telegraphy |

# PREFACE

This book frames its subject matter, the German S-boat offensive against Britain's coastal convoys, in three distinct ways:

1. As occupying an overlooked, and yet critical, aspect of the Battle of the Atlantic on which Britain's survival depended during World War II. The battle is generally accepted as one of the defining factors in that war, but in reality it was a campaign rather than a battle lasting from 1939 to 1945, and that campaign extended well beyond the borders of the Atlantic to the adjacent oceans, and to areas such as the English Channel and North Sea.
2. As occupying a geographical and cultural space—the coastal, the traditionally "English" (and European), rather than the oceanic (and global) part of the national identity of Britain/England as a maritime nation—that ensured that it would be neglected in popular memory and historical writing after 1945. For Imperial Britain, for Cold War Britain, and for Global Britain, naval thinking, history writing, and popular memory have been framed by the Atlantic and the connection to the United States instead of the narrow seas between the British Isles and a Europe, toward which British attitudes were frequently ambivalent.
3. As occupying a significant moment in the development of coastal warfare that is not properly understood by the practitioners of naval warfare in a twenty-first century in which, once again, there is a renewed emphasis on military operations in the coastal zone. The development of intelligence and information networks; the connections by 1943 between ship, shore, and aircraft; the integration of strategy, naval tactics, scientific developments, and shipbuilding; and their impact on naval operations in English waters to thwart the German navy prefigures many of the features of what might

be called "sea denial" and networked warfare in the twenty-first century. It also highlights the efficiency and effectiveness of the wartime British state, its flexibility of thinking, and the increasingly technocratic nature of the British way of war. In terms of history in its broadest sense, and in ways of thinking about coastal warfare in the twenty-first century for naval practitioners, what happened in "English" waters between 1940 and 1945 is deeply significant even if it has been neglected and misunderstood.

These ways of thinking constitute a new way of considering and evaluating the German S-boat offensive, highlighting the hidden (coastal/English) "other" in Britain's maritime story. Neglect of that "other" has fed into the writing of Britain's maritime history and into the politics of an island nation trying to understand its past and its future place as a global or continental trading nation. These frameworks also reveal a British way of waging coastal warfare in which combined arms operations, and information-centric warfare involving the processing of data from multiple sources (including intelligence), evolved to a level of effectiveness in sea denial to the enemy that was sharply at odds with Nelsonian traditions and that, from the perspective of the history of warfare, seem almost impossible before the advent of the computer. If we factor in the British defense of coastal convoys from 1940 to 1945, we have to rethink the British approach to maritime operations during World War II and to challenge some of the conceptions of the older maritime history in which ships, admirals, and decisive battles appear preeminent. In the battle of the little ships in the coastal campaign in the English Channel from 1940 to 1945, especially between 1940 and 1944, what did not happen was more important to the Admiralty than what did happen in the form of naval engagements between British and German forces. In line with the teachings of Julian Corbett, if you command the sea, you have little need to demonstrate naval supremacy through victories in combat. A lack of engagements—keeping the enemy port-bound—is better than winning battles and stands as a testament to the effectiveness of a nation's navy. This book, then, is a contribution to thinking about the history of World War II, Britain's maritime identity, and the evolution of naval warfare in the mid-twentieth century.

Wars in modernity are temporary and fleeting events. They despoil the peace that we take as international normality. Historians rarely seek to draw comparisons between wars, as technological, social, economic, and political changes appear to make them radically different animals even though they might be separated, as in the case of the two world wars, by as little as twenty years. Nations might pursue similar goals and strategies in their wars, but other changes limit comparative analysis. One thing, however, changes very slowly indeed: geography. From Alfred Thayer Mahan's analysis of the prerequisites of sea power, to Halford Mackinder's heartland theory and beyond, theoreticians have recognized the importance of geography in shaping the outlook and strategy of states.[1] Beyond Thayer Mahan's analysis, in part written for the benefit of a United States with a very different strategic outlook from that of Great Britain, the strategic position of the British Isles (as opposed to the wider British Empire) has not received much attention from analysts. This is unfortunate, since Britain's maritime identity is split, with the dominant sector (the oceanic) eclipsing the other and older (coastal) identity in the sixteenth century as Tudor England gave way to Jacobean Britain. The implications for perceptions about that identity and the writing of Britain's maritime history have been profound, and that split identity continues to play a role in shaping the national outlook. In 2017 (at a Society for Nautical Research conference on the state of the discipline), Cathryn Pearce drew attention to the fact that "coastal topics are not well represented in maritime history journals" and that the discipline has largely ignored calls by cultural historians, such as John Gillis, to explore island histories and the transitional zones between sea and shore.[2]

This book aims to highlight the eclipsed half of Britain's maritime identity (the coastal/English/continental) and to answer Pearce's call for more exploration of coastal history. It will do so by examining the efforts of the German navy (Kriegsmarine) between 1940 and 1945 to use its small force of motor torpedo boats (S-boats—referred to as E-boats by Allied forces) to disrupt the convoys that ran along the southern and eastern coasts of the United Kingdom. It will do so by utilizing material drawn from public and private archives in Britain, the United States, Germany, and beyond, as well as complete hands-on access for more than fifteen years to S-130, the last surviving S-boat.

That these coastal convoys have had little purchase in the historiographical debate and popular narratives of World War II highlights the extent to which the Battle of the Atlantic and the narrative of an Empire at War (the oceanic) has obscured, in the modern period, the coastal aspects of Britain's maritime history. This is not, however, to suggest that the coastal deserves privilege over the oceanic. They are part of the same maritime identity, the same history, and, in the case of the United Kingdom, part of the same coastline and trading networks. The coastal is not separate, and it certainly should not be overlooked as a facet of the modern maritime history of the United Kingdom. To that end, this book constitutes a call for joined-up thinking and research on Britain's maritime identity and past, especially for the sake of a future in which the coastal region has reemerged as a critical zone of state interaction and an area likely to see military operations between the major powers.

From the eighteenth century onward, the British Empire was a global seaborne power. The British Isles sat at the heart of a spider's web of trading networks that necessitated a Royal Navy capable of plying the world's oceans: a deepwater force with a network of support bases, coaling ports, and safe harbors. That empire was defended across the oceans of the world in wars against the French in the long eighteenth century, and against Germany in the world wars of the twentieth. This narrative of Britain as an oceanic power remains dominant into the twenty-first century and finds expression in post-Brexit referendum references to "Global Britain" and "Empire 2.0." In the days of empire, Britain, an island nation sitting on the edge of the European coastal shelf, was oceanic in its outlook, but it was also continental facing. Bar the eighteen miles of the English Channel and the shallows of the North Sea, Britain continued to be part of the continental landmass that had shaped its identity before the development of the global Empire. Indeed, until the end of the last ice age and the drowning of Doggerland, Britain was physically connected to Europe: a continuation thereof. The ports of the English Channel faced Europe while at the same time connecting to the Atlantic and the global sea-lanes of world trade. The ports of the East Coast linked Britain to the Netherlands, to Belgium and northern France, and to the Baltic. From the eighteenth century onward, Britain, as a maritime nation, was both oceanic and coastal in its trade and national security considerations. Culturally, however, the oceanic predominated over the coastal in the national narrative of a maritime nation. The "romance" of empire in far foreign waters was easier to sell than short, humdrum sea crossings and the work of the fishing fleets from St. Ives to Peterhead.

In the twentieth century, in the defense of the British Empire, oceanic trade and security was emphasized over the coastal. The implications of this were considerable both in terms of the security of the British Isles and the writing of history. Except for the two world wars, in which Britain's ability to import the food necessary to feed its populace was endangered by the German navy, the primary threat to the security of the British Isles has come through the possibility that another power might gain control of the short sea approaches to the British Isles to launch amphibious landings. The Roman military managed a successful invasion of the British Isles in AD43, as did Duke William's forces in 1066. In the wars that followed Britain's split with Catholic Europe in the early 1500s, it was apparent that the principal danger facing Britain involved a Franco-Spanish invasion. Even though the politics of the Franco-Spanish-British conflict evolved after the failure of the Spanish Armada in 1588, the geographies of the resulting naval struggle remained the same. The English Channel formed a critical focus of naval operations, with the possibility that a Franco-Spanish landing in Wales or Ireland might serve as a move to work around the flanks of the strong British forces in the Channel. In 1940 the Channel would again become, for a few short months, the critical focus of British strategic thinking.

From the Romans' construction of the Saxon forts along the southern and eastern coasts in the third century, through the development of Tudor coastal bastions, Martello towers to guard against landings by Napoleon's troops, Palmerston's forts to protect Plymouth and Portsmouth in the mid-nineteenth century, and airfields in World War I to support antisubmarine patrols against the Kaiser's U-boats, there has been ongoing innovation to support the units of the Royal Navy in guarding the short sea approaches to the United Kingdom. Underpinning this infrastructure, and control of the shipping in the Channel, were complex intelligence and signals networks. In the 1500s, fire beacons to warn of the Armada were supplemented by the spy network of Francis Walsingham, by royal couriers who conveyed orders, by networks of merchants and travelers on the continent monitoring military preparations from Spain to the Low Countries, by fishing and commercial vessels keeping a watch on the approaches to the Channel, and by the militia on land maintaining a watch out to sea. In the eighteenth century, a network of semaphore stations was established along the coast to convey to the principal naval bases news of enemy sightings, their strength and location. By the late nineteenth century, semaphore had been replaced by telegraph, which was later augmented by the telephone and wireless. Throughout the history of the British Isles, the English Channel has had enormous importance as a strategically vital waterway. As a tactical environment it has been complex and difficult for an opponent to operate in because of the investment in infrastructure, intelligence, command and control systems, naval assets, and land defenses by the British state.

This long history was to some extent obscured by World War II even though the prospect of invasion in 1940 witnessed a return to many of the practices of coastal defense that had served Britain so well in the past. The "Dad's Army" of "Local Defence Volunteers" and the development of a network of pillboxes to guard landing beaches and to form inland stop lines harked back to the defense against invasion of earlier centuries. Radar, the agents of the "Double Cross" system, and code breaking recalled the monitoring of enemy preparations by Walsingham's intelligence network. But in the popular imagination, thanks to the rhetoric of Winston Churchill, it was the Fighter Command of the Royal Air Force (RAF) that received principal credit for maintaining the security of the English Channel in 1940. Later, the Atlantic lifeline, carrying the food and weapons of war from North America to a beleaguered Britain, eclipsed the Channel as the critical zone of naval operations. In the popular narrative of "World War II at sea," it would be another four years before the English Channel would again assume, with the Normandy landings, a brief strategic importance.

Obscured from the popular narrative, in which the oceanic (in the form of the Battle of the Atlantic) has predominated since 1940, was a no less vital campaign that had the capacity to cause severe disruption to Britain's sea-lines of communication and ability to import the goods necessary to continue the war. From 1939 to 1945 the armed forces of Nazi Germany attempted to disrupt the flow of trade along the short sea-lines of communication around Britain's coast. Convoys of merchant ships running along the coast of the United Kingdom, together with independently routed vessels and fishing boats, were targeted by the aircraft of the Luftwaffe and the small surface ships and submarines of the Kriegsmarine. Both the German navy and air force set mines along the routes used by these vessels. From 1940 until 1943 the motor torpedo boats (S-boats) of the Kriegsmarine served as a particular threat to the maintenance of the coastal convoys.

It was a new development in naval warfare, as the motor torpedo boat had only started to show its potential toward the end of World War I, with Italian Motoscafo Armato Silurante (MAS) boats in the Adriatic, and British use of coastal motorboats (CMB) in the short Anglo-Russian Baltic naval campaign. The Germans would later master the technology and tactics of torpedo boat warfare, which meant that the British from 1940 onward would be required to adapt and improvise to meet the challenge. Such was the success of the Royal Navy that from 1944 until 1945 the strategic balance in the English Channel shifted: the S-boat campaign became more defensive in nature, with the Royal Navy waging its own successful campaign against German shipping in the Channel and North Sea.

The S-boat campaign is the primary focus of this book. What was the nature of the threat posed to British coastal shipping by German motor torpedo boats, and how did the S-boat campaign fit into the wider assault on Britain's sea-lines of communication involving the Luftwaffe and the vessels (surface and subsurface) of the Kriegsmarine? How did the British combat the emergence of a new threat in a zone that for hundreds of years had been critical to their naval operations and security? Why did the Germans fail to make the most of the qualitative superiority of the S-boat over similar British vessels to cause fundamental disruption to British coastal convoy operations? Why was the Kriegsmarine unable to respond effectively to British countermeasures to the S-boat? In answering these questions, the book contributes new understandings about the Kriegsmarine's war against British commerce from 1939 to 1945 and serves as a reminder of the vital, if overlooked, realm of coastal history. While the war on the coastal convoy routes finds minimal acknowledgment in the major texts on the history of World War II, during that conflict the military professionals of both sides were extremely aware of its criticality. By exploring the evolution of the British response to the S-boat threat, this book seeks to contribute to history, and to understandings and debates from a professional military standpoint, about the evolution, nature, and lessons of coastal warfare for an increasingly troubled twenty-first century.

# ACKNOWLEDGMENTS

This book represents the culmination of more than twenty years' worth of research on the Merchant Navy, the Royal Navy, the German Kriegsmarine, and, in particular, the German S-boat. In this endeavor there are many people and institutions that have assisted my research over the past twenty years. My colleagues at Plymouth University (those still active, those who are retired, and those who are no longer with us) have invariably been a great help. The staff at libraries and archives great and small have never been less than outstandingly helpful, including those at the National Archives U.K.; the U.S. National Archives (College Park, Maryland), Stadtarchiv (Kiel), and Bundesarchiv Militärarchiv (Freiburg); the National Maritime Museum (London), British Library (London), and Britannia Royal Naval College Library (Dartmouth); and the Plymouth, Exeter, and Bristol University Libraries. In utilizing German sources, I have placed a particular emphasis on copies of the German Naval Archive seized by the British at Tambach and subsequently filmed by the United States Navy in London before its return to the Federal German authorities. The originals of those documents now sit in the Bundesarchiv Militärarchiv (BA/MA) in Freiburg. For most naval historians the copies held by the National Archives and Records Administration (NARA II) in College Park, Maryland, remain the more "user friendly" and accessible, and file references are given to the NARA copies where possible. (The bibliography also lists the BA/MA file groups against specific groups of documents.)

In researching this book it has not been possible to trace the holders of copyright in every case. Publishers in particular seem noticeably less interested in responding to author queries than they were twenty years ago. In the case of any omission, if the copyright holder would like to contact me, care of the publisher, we will see that due acknowledgment is given in any future edition of the book.

On the personal side I would like to thank Hans Kolbe and Henriette Schlesinger for sharing with me the memoirs of their father, Ulrich Kolbe, along with photographs and family memories (translations from the German by author). They were invaluable for understanding the complex lives of some of those who served in S-boats during World War II and in providing powerful insights into the human side of the war at sea in the English Channel.

Finally, I would like to express particular thanks to the Schlichting family, especially to Peter, and to Kevin Wheatcroft, owner of S-130, the last surviving S-boat of World War II. Built by the Schlichting family in 1943, S-130 is a remarkable survival whose fabric can tell us much about how these vessels were built. The archive of the Schlichting family, which Peter generously allowed me to access, constitutes an incredibly extensive record of one family firm of boatbuilders caught up in World War II. The fabric of S-130 together with the archive have given this historian an insight into his subject that money simply could not buy. Thank you!

G. H. BENNETT
*Plymouth*
*January 2023*

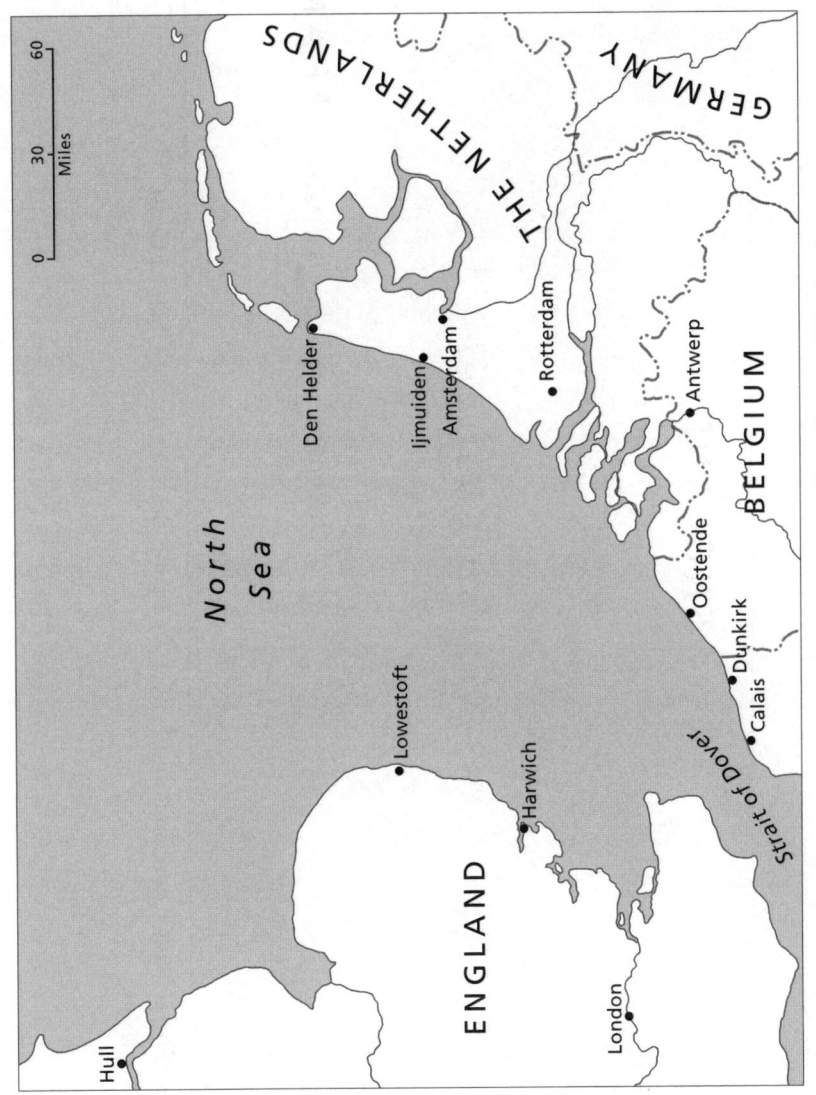

MAP 1. Principal Ports along Western Europe and the East Coast of England
*Created by Chris Robinson*

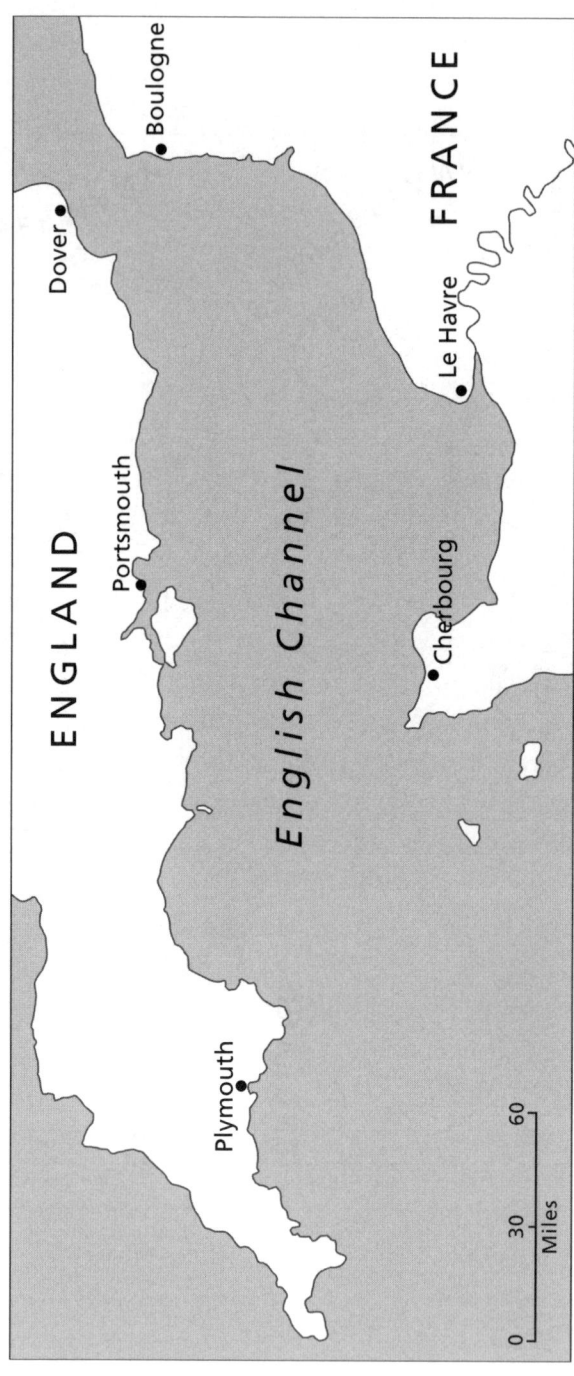

MAP 2. Principal Royal Navy Commands and S-Boat Operating Bases along the Channel Coast
*Created by Chris Robinson*

# INTRODUCTION

IF HISTORY IS WRITTEN BY THE VICTORS, then nowhere should this be truer than in the field of military history. The history of a particular war, campaign, or battle is constructed backward from its denouement, and in the process of defeat the voice, intentions, and hopes of the loser are too easily silenced or overlooked. The concerns of the victor dominate the historical accounts that surface immediately after conflicts, and usually for some time thereafter. "Official histories," those involving specially selected historians with privileged access to sources, make an important contribution to framing the historical debate. The destruction of the records of the loser, and the death of key personnel either in combat or during the postwar period, further diminishes the ability of later historians to reconstruct and understand the operation of the defeated power. By this process, history is skewed toward a particular set of perspectives, and easily overlooked are those possible turning points, ideas, and technologies where different outcomes might have been realized. In these dark corners can sometimes be found instructive lessons relevant to later debates on military strategy, technology, and defense policy.

This book constitutes an inquiry into one of these dark areas of history. It is an assessment of the campaign waged by the fast motor torpedo boats of the Kriegsmarine from 1940 to 1945 against Allied merchant shipping in the English Channel, and off the East Coast of the United Kingdom. These vessels were known to the Allies as E-boats ("E" for "enemy") and to the Germans as *Schnellboote* (S-boats). Armed with torpedo and cannon, the S-boats were just over 100 feet long and capable of speeds in excess of forty knots. They were, in many ways, ideal weapons to deploy against the coastal convoys off the southern and eastern coasts of the United Kingdom. The S-boat campaign in those waters lasted from the summer of 1940 until the closing days of the war, in two distinct phases. With just twelve to sixteen S-boats operational at any one time against Britain's inshore lines of communication, their campaign in Western European waters has been overlooked by successive waves of postwar historians.

There are several reasons an analysis of this campaign is necessary and worthwhile. First, comparatively little has been written about German efforts to disrupt inshore British shipping. The quality of what has been written leaves something to be desired from an academic and military perspective. Little was written during the war. Stanley Rodgers' *Enemy in Sight* contained a single chapter titled "E-Boat Alley and the Channel," and instead of examining S-boat operations from 1940 onward, it was almost completely dominated by the "Channel Dash of 1942" involving the three German heavy ships. Early postwar accounts were written without the benefit of archival sources and were firmly aimed at the market for popular history. Later accounts benefited from the opening up of British archives in the 1970s (under the old thirty-year rule) but are still dogged by quality issues relating to the market for popular history. Such popular accounts, however, are not without their uses. For one thing, they do point to the extent to which the inshore campaign against British shipping had been overlooked even while the war was raging. For example, in the foreword to *The Coal Scuttle Brigade* (written in the 1950s), Alexander McKee complained that "some of the fiercest convoy battles of the war could take place literally on England's doorstep . . . and yet remain almost unknown."[1] Indeed, James A. Williamson in *The English Channel: A History* (1959) gave no mention to the coastal convoy battles.[2] Later accounts, such as Smith's 1984 book *Hold the Narrow Sea: Naval Warfare in the English Channel, 1939–1945*, documented key events in the German attack on coastal shipping but provided insufficient analysis.[3] Likewise, the *Battle of the East Coast* by J. P. Foynes in 1994 was rich in detail but light on interpretation.[4] Similarly, Robert Jackson's 1995 study, *Churchill's Moat: The Channel War, 1939–1945*, offered useful insights but was very much targeted at the "general reader."[5] Alan Burn's 1999 monograph, *The Fighting Commodores: The Convoy Commanders in the Second World War*, offered some interesting insights into the coastal campaign, but only in a solitary chapter devoted to the commodores commanding British coastal convoys.[6] The most recent work on the subject, Nick Hewitt's *Coastal Convoys 1939–1945* (2008), is a history that offers new insights, great material, and a good overview in the process of unpicking some of the complexities that lie at the heart of an understanding of the S-boat campaign.[7]

Beyond such writings, coastal actions have been examined within the pages of histories of British and German forces. Many of the earlier works from the 1940s to the 1970s, such as *The Battle of the Narrow Seas*, by Peter Scott, and *Night Action*, by Captain Peter Dickens, relied on the memories and viewpoints of participants in the battles.[8] In Scott's case there were elements of deliberate deceit for reasons that will become apparent later in this book. The availability of British naval records from the 1970s onward has seen some interesting work, such as Bryan Cooper's *The E-Boat Threat* (1976), Donald Graves' work on the motor torpedo boats of the Royal Canadian Navy, and James Foster Tent's *E-Boat Alert* (1996).[9] Since the publication of Tent's book, new work has almost invariably taken the form of attractively illustrated books on British and German coastal forces by authors such as Gordon Williamson.[10] Such works tend to display a particular fascination with the technical aspects of the weapons of war that were used to wage the coastal campaign. Jac J. Baart's *Schnellboote: Operaties vanuit Holland, Vlaanderen en Frankrijk, 1940–1945* (2006) contains a wealth of detail and relevant analysis, but its impact has been limited by the fact that it is only available in Dutch.[11] Slightly later, Lawrence Paterson's *Schnellboote: A Complete Operational History* (2015) uses secondary sources, including some of the major German sources, to provide an excellent narrative account of the S-boat in action.[12] It does not, however, make significant use of British or American archives to broaden out the source base, and just thirty-one books are listed in the "Select Bibliography." Thus, it remains fair to conclude, as Richard Woodman notes, that the Channel battles remain "one of the many disregarded elements in Britain's maritime struggle."[13] Such comments find support among surviving veterans, one of whom commented in 2005, "These Coastal Convoys have 'slipped through the net' of History."[14]

This charge of "slipping through the net of history" supposes that Britain's coastal convoys and the S-boat campaign against them had some importance. As we shall see in chapter 1, the coastal convoys along the southern and eastern coasts of the United Kingdom constituted a vital part of the British logistical network. The coastal campaign was a key element in the struggle to maintain Britain's war economy after the German victory in France in 1940. Cargoes and ships that had crossed the Atlantic in the teeth of the U-boat threat were at risk from S-boat and aerial attack as they joined the convoys along the coastal routes. From 1940 to 1943, the S-boats of the German navy were the primary means by which the Kriegsmarine attempted to disrupt the flow of British coastal shipping, and an extension of the tonnage war being waged by the U-boats and commerce raiders in the Atlantic and beyond. By the end of 1943 the strategy of the Kriegsmarine began to shift from the offensive to the defensive, as coastal convoys became the primary means by which the Allied powers could make a landing on the coast of Europe. S-boats and the stopping of the coastal convoys became a way to defend "Festung Europa." The continuing flow of goods, and shipping movements in 1944 under Operation Neptune, were essential factors in the liberation of Europe. In the historiography of D-Day the role of the coastal convoys, the S-boat arm, and German strategy to defeat Allied amphibious landings has not been an area of major discussion between historians. The land campaign has dominated discussions of Operation Overlord; the sea element of the landings, Operation Neptune, has been taken largely for granted.[15] Until the 2014 publication of Craig Symonds' *Neptune: The Allied Invasion of Europe and the D-Day Landings*, twenty-first-century discussions on the naval phase of Overlord focused on particular points such as Anglo-American amphibious doctrine and gunfire support from ships for the invading forces.[16] Symonds' book provided a good overview based on unpublished sources in the United States but made minimal use of archival material from British, Canadian, and German sources. The success of Allied naval forces in conveying safely to shore the largest amphibious force ever assembled and protecting the flow of supplies from Britain into the bridgehead requires more extensive analysis than it has so far received. During 1943, the importance and nature of the coastal convoys underwent a subtle change from the defensive (keeping Britain in the war) to the offensive (preparing for cross-Channel assault) as goods, invasion craft, and supplies were delivered close to the points of embarkation that would be used in June 1944. The coastal convoys, and the campaign to halt them, are vital (if overlooked) elements in two of the most important struggles of World War II. Unless we understand the struggle to defeat and to defend coastal shipping, our understanding of the war at sea is seriously deficient. The coastal campaign is a missing link in academic understandings of the maritime aspects of World War II and the wider history of coastal Britain.

In addition to popular histories, the campaign waged along Britain's coasts from 1940 to 1945 has been subsumed into wider studies of the war at sea, such as the multivolume official histories of British and American naval operations in World War II by Roskill and Morison.[17] Those histories reflected contemporary understandings and memories of the war at sea in the Atlantic, which were dominated by the image and threat of the U-boat. Fears of communism, the development of a powerful Russian navy, and cutbacks and reorganizations added a further level of concern for understanding the threat to trade posed by the submarine. As Admiral Inglis, the chief of U.S. Naval Intelligence, explained in the foreword to a postwar essay by Admiral Dönitz, such histories had value "from the standpoint of naval science" in that they served as a powerful reminder of the danger of "disregarding or underestimating the necessity of sea power as a prerequisite to a major political power engaging successfully in war of any magnitude."[18] The concerns of Admiral Inglis were focused very much on policy makers in Britain and the United States, as defense spending in both countries had been cut dramatically in 1945–46. Such concerns in Anglo-American naval circles ensured that the early historiography of the war at sea had a particularly strong focus on the U-boat war.

The British Naval Staff History *The Defeat of the Enemy Attack on Shipping, 1939–1945* (1957) is a particular case in point.[19] Sixteen of its twenty-five chapters are specifically devoted to the U-boat threat. Five concern mine warfare and the threat of aerial attack. Two discuss merchant shipping and convoying. With the opening chapter involving the lessons of World War I, just one chapter, and the occasional paragraph within some of the other chapters, are left to discuss "the operations of surface commerce raiders." Inevitably, it is the larger warships operating as commerce raiders, together with the auxiliary cruisers of the Kriegsmarine, that dominate this lone chapter (S-boats receive just a couple of paragraphs in one of the chapters on mine warfare). That the Naval Staff History was primarily concerned with the submarine threat is further underlined in its opening sentences: "Forty-two years have passed since the outbreak of the First World War and seventeen since the beginning of the Second World War. From the naval viewpoint both titanic struggles were marked by protracted and bitter warfare in which our very survival depended on the outcome of the contest between our anti-submarine forces and the U-Boats."[20] The call to action to meet the new submarine menace delivered in such histories helped to skew Anglo-American accounts of World War II at sea.

German scholarship was affected by such histories and by other forces that served to emphasize the role and importance of the U-boat. In writing the history of the Kriegsmarine, German writers have favored the U-boats. The German Naval Archives remained closed until the 1970s, ensuring that Anglo-American official histories, based on privileged access to British, American, and German sources, were highly influential. Grand Admiral Dönitz, after his release from prison in 1956, continued to have a major influence on German writing on the war at sea. The publication of his memoirs in 1958, and his generosity in giving interviews, ensured a guiding hand on the shoulders of postwar authors.[21] A submariner in World War I, and head of the U-boat arm for the majority of the war, his focus on the U-boat campaign did not waver after he became head of the German navy as a whole in 1943. As Theodore Ropp noted in 1961, that focus continued even after Germany's defeat and is fully reflected in his memoirs.[22] Dönitz's strategy in the submarine war has been questioned, but there has been precious little discussion of anything else, including his handling of German naval strategy from 1943 to 1945.[23] In the historiography of the Kriegsmarine, the U-boat continues to dominate, casting a shadow even over the larger surface vessels. Rendered largely invisible from the history of the war at sea are the smaller ships, destroyers, torpedo boats, S-boats, R-boats, and auxiliaries. These are the vessels that fought along the Channel coast and in the North Sea from 1940 to 1945. They occasionally get a walk-on part in dramatic narratives of the larger surface vessels and in the U-boat war, but usually they are simply ignored altogether. Vincent O'Hara's *The German Fleet at War 1939–1945*, for example, confines itself to surface actions fought by ships of over 500 tons.[24] Long-term German naval strategy, what the German navy hoped to achieve against Britain after the outbreak of war in 1939, the missed chances and opportunities not fully explored, were issues rather lost in the early scholarship. That early scholarship continues to frame public understandings, academic debate, and writing on "World War II at sea" in European waters. The flow of books and articles that explore the German U-boat arm has been considerable, and the development of http://uboat.net/ constitutes one of the best historical resources on the web.[25]

Despite these deficiencies, since the 1990s there has been an additional impetus for a reexamination of the campaign in British coastal waters during World War II. The 1990s brought about a period of reassessment in the foreign and defense policies of Western governments that has brought a slightly different focus on national security and its maintenance. A result of this reassessment has been a renewed concern about the coastal (or littoral) zone as a potential focus for future maritime operations, and an interest in the history of naval operations in coastal waters. The end of the Cold War made it seem increasingly unlikely that there would be open ocean clashes between the fleets of the major powers. However, Russian and Chinese expansionism, terrorist plots, environmental issues, the failure of states, and the activities of organized crime (e.g., drug and people smuggling, piracy) increased the likelihood that navies would be called on to operate in restricted coastal waters. At the end of the twentieth century, definitions of national security extended to port operations, offshore oil and gas fields, undersea pipelines, and fishing grounds: elements at the heart of the "new coastal maritime history" that would begin to emerge following the 1990s.

In recognition of the increased importance of coastal zones, the U.S. Navy on November 1, 2001, announced that it would build a class of vessel known as the littoral combat ship (LCS) that was fast, small, stealthy, and cheap to produce.[26] Specifically designed to operate in coastal waters, these vessels could be configured for a variety of different missions. The first vessel of the class (USS *Freedom*) was commissioned on November 8, 2008. Highly controversial, the LCS concept came under attack for a variety of reasons, including questions about just what it was supposed to do and how it was supposed to do it. To a significant extent the questions remain.

The criticisms of the LCS program focused attention on operations in coastal waters and the need to conduct historical studies to help formulate doctrine and practice. A direct response to this need was the establishment of a Littoral Operations Center at the U.S. Navy's Postgraduate School at Monterey in January 2013 to foster "research into the operational and strategic complexities of the near-shore environment."[27]

Thus, since the turn of the twenty-first century there has been a renewed interest in understanding the complexities and the history of naval operations in coastal waters, dramatically underlined by the sinking of the Russian cruiser *Moskva* in the Black Sea on April 14, 2022, in the Russo-Ukrainian war. While open ocean naval operations have been the subject of considerable attention from naval theorists, operations in coastal and restricted waters, with their very different set of strategic and tactical problems, remained seriously underresearched and undertheorized. This was recognized in 1999 with the publication of Milan Vego's study *Naval Strategy and Operations in Narrow Seas.* Drawing heavily on historical examples, Vego pointed to the growing emphasis on coastal zones as a place for future maritime combat operations.[28] He also pointed out that operations in narrow seas are one of the least researched and most misunderstood aspects of naval strategy and history: "The problem of fighting wars in narrow seas has not been given the serious consideration it deserves by many blue-water navies. There is a widely held but erroneous view that a fleet capable of defeating an adversary on the open ocean could successfully operate in narrow seas."[29] Interestingly, in providing a series of historical case studies to illustrate his points, Vego paid little attention to the significance of the S-boat campaign against British coastal convoys from 1940 to 1945. The changing nature of maritime operations means that in the twenty-first century there is an added emphasis on the need to understand military operations in the English Channel and North Sea during World War II, and in his 2015 *Naval War College Review* article "On Littoral Warfare," Vego devoted more space to the S-boat campaign, while confirming that understandings of coastal warfare had to be historically grounded.[30] Significantly, this article also highlighted some of the fundamental differences between the combat environment in coastal and oceanic operations, including the impact of shallow water on weapons systems and tactics, and the complications of electronic land and sea clutter, caused by the interaction of coast, waves, and weather.[31] The coastal zone is an enormously complicated combat space, and the period from 1940 to 1945 marked its transformation into the most challenging environment in which navies have to operate.

From the point of view of both the historian and the naval strategist and tactician, there is a need for a detailed examination of the Kriegsmarine's S-boat campaign against British coastal convoys from 1940 to 1945 and the reasons for its defeat by Allied (principally British) forces. This book is offered up in response, and it will utilize primary sources from private and public archives in Britain, Germany, and the United States. It was particularly fortunate that in 1944 most of the archival holdings of the German naval staff were evacuated from Berlin to Schloss Tambach in Bavaria to escape Allied bombing. Shortly thereafter, an Allied bombing raid on Berlin destroyed most of the remaining working files, together with the buildings that housed them. The archive at Tambach later fell into Allied hands, giving the British and Americans excellent insight into German naval policy up to October–November 1944.[32] Those documents were subsequently translated by both the British and the Americans, and the originals were eventually returned to Germany. The Tambach archive provides the essential source base for this study, and it will be supplemented by documents and recordings from the Imperial War Museum and other repositories. Regrettably, the passing of years, and a certain reluctance to talk about wartime matters, has prevented extensive gathering and utilization of oral accounts from German veterans. The few survivors now wait to "cross the bar" and join their crewmates on the other side.

But the source base for this book has benefited from access to the last surviving S-boat of World War II, S-130, which forms part of the Wheatcroft collection. It is one thing to read accounts, inspect documents, and hear oral history interviews with veterans. It is quite another to watch and indeed help the work on the last surviving example of a weapons system while its secrets, inner life, and story are laid bare as it is stripped for the purposes of restoration. That process, and the writing of this book, has further benefited from access to the archive of the Schlichting family, who built S-130 and tens of other S-boats during World War II. That archive is an incredibly rich source of material: it contains photographs, 16-mm home movie footage, private papers, and the works magazine. It offers a rare glimpse into the world of German shipbuilding during World War II, and the interconnections between the home front and the campaigns being waged far away. I am indebted to the Schlichting family (and especially to Peter) for their hospitality and the access they have given me to the archive they so carefully built up in the 1930s and 1940s and maintained into the postwar period.

## CHAPTER 1

# GERMAN NAVAL STRATEGY, 1870–1940

THE S-BOAT CAMPAIGN against Britain's coastal convoys in World War II was part of a wider German attack on Britain's commerce from a nation that had struggled with its own maritime identity and strategy since unification in the 1870s. Was Germany a land power requiring a strategy of coastal defense in the Baltic, or was the new German state a world power pursuing a global role with a fleet to match? The debate on that national maritime identity shaped strategy and the evolution of the German fleet. In World Wars I and II, the German navy was forced into a strategy of commerce war because it did not have a fleet strong enough to secure naval superiority. Instead of a battle of annihilation in a fleet-to-fleet action, the navy would be left to contribute to Germany's hoped-for victory through a campaign against Britain's capacity to import and export. The S-boats that fought in the English Channel and North Sea from 1940 to 1945 were the result of an intersection between the long-term naval strategy of the unified German state, the military clauses of the Treaty of Versailles imposed on that state in 1919, developments in naval technologies and marine propulsion, and the build standards and design work of the luxury motor yacht yards of northern Germany. They were the product and expression of a German naval and maritime identity that was shaped, reshaped, and shaped again by domestic and external forces from the late nineteenth century onward. The S-boat provides a means to read the negotiated and shifting identity of maritime Germany, the impact of changing technologies, the development of particular businesses and changes to Germany's position on the world stage. Much of the most recent work on the S-boat remains obsessed with understanding it in narrow technological terms, in line with "traditional" naval history. In terms of the "new, new maritime history," the emergence of the S-boat as a weapon of war also needs to be understood in terms of cultural, political, international, and business history.

In 1929 the Reichsmarine ordered the first S-boat from the German luxury yacht builder Lürssen, based in Bremen. It was 26.5 meters long, with a beam of 4.2 meters and a draft of 1.1 meter. Powered by three Daimler Benz gasoline engines, with a Maybach auxiliary engine, it was capable of speeds up to 34.2 knots. With a crew of twelve, its principal weapons were two torpedo tubes and 20-mm machine guns. The basis of the design was a motor yacht built by Lürssen for an American banker and philanthropist, Otto Hermann Kahn. He approached the company in 1926 to build a yacht. While most accounts indicate that Kahn asked the company to build a fast motor yacht for use on holidays on the Rhine and off the coast of northern Europe, he also seems to have had in mind creating an attention-grabbing boat that would allow him to commute between New York City and his Cold Spring Harbor estate on the North Shore of Long Island.[1] During the "Roaring Twenties," the elite of New York Society competed with each other to build ever-faster motor yachts as status symbols of their wealth and importance.[2] The requirement for high speed in different marine environments, from rivers to seas, created some interesting design difficulties for Lürssen, which had established a strong reputation for design innovation in the building of motorboats since the founding of the company by Friedrich Lürssen in 1875. In 1886 the Lürssen yard turned out the world's first motorboat using a Daimler engine, and in 1905 they produced the Donnerwetter, a motorboat capable of speeds in excess of thirty-four knots using a 40-break-horsepower (bhp) engine.[3] In 1911 and 1912 Lürssen built boats with Daimler engines that won the unofficial world speedboat championship in the Mediterranean. During 1917, Lürssen began to use its speedboat expertise to develop military designs for the German navy.

Following Germany's defeat in World War I, Lürssen turned back toward the luxury yacht market, and in 1926, in trying to meet the requirements of Otto Kahn, the yard struggled to overcome some basic problems with hull design. The round-bottomed displacement hulls used for cruising boats on the Rhine created a smooth ride but resulted in greater drag than the planing boats traditionally favored by the builders of high-speed motor launches. To overcome the drag issue, and to enable the boat to reach high speeds, Lürssen's designers went in the direction of increasing power, shaping the hull, and decreasing weight. This was unsurprising given the history of design in the company. In the early years of the yard, Lürssen had specialized in fast racing rowboats. Minimizing weight and ensuring optimal hydrodynamic flow along the hull were prerequisites to success. To that early tradition was added expertise in the application of motor power to wooden hulls. For Kahn's new build, the weight was limited by developing a hull that was a composite of traditional wooden planking with internal aluminum alloy framing. Power was provided by three VL2 V12 Maybach engines each producing 500 bhp. With engines sited in the middle of the 22.5-meter boat, and with a hull form flattened toward the stern, the boat was nicely balanced to prevent the dropping of the stern at high speed. Realizing speeds of thirty-four knots in trials, Oheka II was the fastest craft in its class in the world: another triumph for Lürssen. In the world of motor yachts that achievement underlined Lürssen's reputation for luxury, cutting-edge design/engineering, and traditional craftsmanship in wooden boat building. It also suggested the military potential of a reworked version of the same design, and in 1927 the yard produced a concept patrol vessel: the 21-meter Luer, capable of speeds of 33.5 knots. The German navy was sufficiently impressed, and in 1929 the government placed an order for S-1, a motor torpedo boat designed as an upscale version of Luer/Oheka II.[4]

The vessel had considerable potential as a flexible but cheap weapons platform—and as a politically useful "wolf in sheep's clothing." It could certainly serve a role as a coastal defense vessel, but perhaps it also had the potential to play a greater strategic role. The unified German state after 1870 had a small coastline that was potentially easy to defend with coastal guns and light units. Despite this, the Kaiser's goal of a large German navy capable of securing an overseas empire, and Tirpitz's embrace of the writings of Alfred Thayer Mahan, had resulted in the pursuit of a fleet and strategy based on offensive oceanic warfare.[5] Though the High Seas Fleet did not perform as well in World War I as some of its protagonists had hoped, German naval thinking and performance was not tied solely to the battleships and battle cruisers. In the straitened circumstances of post-1918 Germany, with a navy limited by the restrictions of the Treaty of Versailles, German naval culture was sufficiently flexible to embrace the potential of a vessel that might be considered otherwise less than ideal in terms of traditional naval engagements in wartime.

The offensive spirit of the Kaiser's navy from 1914 to 1918 had, in part, been maintained by the torpedo boats, submarines, and destroyers deployed in the North Sea and beyond. It was a desperate torpedo attack by the smaller ships at the Battle of Jutland/Skagerrak in 1916 that had allowed the High Seas Fleet to turn away from the British Grand Fleet and escape into the night. In 1929, as the order for the first S-boat was placed with Lürssen, German naval strategists could read in Jellicoe's *The Grand Fleet, 1914–16* of his long-held fears of the German torpedo that, during the battle, had led him to order the turn away from the German attack, mirroring the High Seas Fleet's turn away.[6] In 1916, torpedo-firing fast craft had saved the bigger ships of the Kaiser's navy. In thinking about possibilities of future conflict, the potential for torpedo craft to exercise a critical role could not be ignored.

Their potential was further underlined later in the war, as the Belgian ports had become the focus of a *Kleinkrieg* campaign involving small naval and air units based in Flanders. As Mark Karau has argued, the potential advantages of Belgian and French Channel ports as bases from which to wage war against the Royal Navy had been recognized before World War I.[7] The formation of MarineKorps Flandern in 1914–15 realized some of that potential, despite problems such as insufficient cooperation between naval and air forces. With the realization that the submarine was not simply a coastal defense weapon but a "flexible reconnaissance and torpedo unit" capable of targeting enemy warships or carrying out a sustained attack on commerce, the wartime effectiveness of the Kaiser's fleet extended well beyond the lines of capital ships.[8] The Flanders *Kleinkrieg* and submarine campaigns to some extent overlapped. While the destroyers and torpedo boats of MarineKorps Flandern had two very notable operational successes in 1916 and 1918, tying down Royal Navy units in the Channel throughout the war, the Belgian-based submarines accounted for around 25 percent of the sinkings of the submarine arm as a whole.[9]

During World War I, the U-boat arm did more than the bigger ships to damage Britain's war economy, and came closer to strategic victory, than the High Seas Fleet aiming to defeat the Royal Navy in a large-scale battle. After the war, getting rid of the submarine and forcing Germany to accept a fleet capable only of coastal defense were two of the principal goals of the peacemakers. The German navy, however, continued to harbor ambitions of one day returning to a global strategy with the fleet (and the submarines) to match. In the short term the S-boat (which perhaps offered similar kinds of flexibility as the U-boat in terms of the roles it could play) would help to fulfill some of Germany's defensive needs, and in the longer term it might augment the development of a fleet that could strike at the British, French, or Russians. As Guntram Schulze-Wegener has shown, prewar German naval thinking on the primacy of the battle fleet continued to influence the navy until well into World War II.[10] This may represent a failure of imagination and strategy, as Holger Herwig has argued, but the development of a powerful surface fleet capable of defeating the Royal Navy in battle had a powerful allure for successive generations of German naval officers.[11] Success in World War I had also convinced the German navy as to the value of the U-boat. What was perhaps missing from "lessons of World War" for the German navy was the effectiveness of *Kleinkrieg* based on the Channel ports, and how war in the narrow seas might interact with use of the major units of the German navy, or the operations of its submarine forces.

While coping with the humiliations of the Treaty of Versailles and the frustrations of a navy prevented from possessing battleships and submarines, the German navy continued to pursue the goals of Admiral Tirpitz. Preparations were put in motion for the day when the Treaty of Versailles would be overturned and German shipyards could turn out the new designs of a powerful fleet capable of at least threatening the British. After the Treaty of Versailles was signed, a secret fund was established under Kapitän-zur-See Walter Lohmann, head of the Reichsmarine's Naval Transport Division.[12] To the $25 million placed at his disposal in 1920 from the sale of warships and other materials came a further $2.5 million from Reichstag funds allocated to strengthen Germany's defenses after the French occupation of the Ruhr in 1923. Another $2.25 million would later be diverted to Lohmann from other sources. With the funds under his control, Lohmann funded research and development into a variety of naval weapons systems.[13] In Holland the Ingenieurskantoor voor Scheepsbouw was established with Lohmann's funds to work on future designs of submarine for the Reichsmarine. Money was also pumped into new designs of military aircraft and into the evaluation of fast motorboats for naval purposes. To this end the Travemünder Yachthafen AG was established in 1924 in the small northern German port of Travemünde to build and test motorboats. The following year a High Sea Sports Association was established as a cover for training additional seamen for the Reichsmarine in motor and sail yachting and radio communications. Also, in 1925 Neustädter Slip-GmbH was established to repair motorboats and as a training facility.[14] In 1926 Lohmann gave 60,000 Reichsmarks to the Motor Yacht Club of Germany to help them test out some of the designs coming out of Travemünder Yachthafen AG.[15] By the late 1920s, with dwindling funds, Lohmann embarked on a series of commercial ventures to try and generate additional funds for defense projects. These were spectacularly unsuccessful leading to the exhaustion of the Lohmann funds, a public scandal, and government action to regulate the secret activities of the Reichsmarine. Nevertheless, government support for the clandestine activities of the Reichsmarine continued after the exposure of the Lohmann affair.

During the late 1920s, with the development of the pocket battleship class of heavy cruisers, the German navy took an important step in the process of breaking free from the shackles of Versailles. It would start the process by which Germany would develop a fleet capable of global power projection. Such navies take time to build, and under Plan Z, formed in the 1930s, the German navy was ordered to be prepared for war in 1945 or later. In the meantime, German naval strategy focused on the possibility of defensive action in the Baltic against Poland, Russia, and France.[16] Interim designs of surface ships would provide Germany with a means of naval defense before the emergence of a new High Seas Fleet signaled that Germany was once again ready to assert itself on the world's oceans. With the advent of Hitler in 1933, the new Kriegsmarine under Admiral Erich Raeder commenced rapid expansion, and designs of new vessels (long in preparation) could proceed to fruition.

If the pocket battleship was a stopgap design before a powerful fleet could be ready, then so was the S-boat. Like the U-boat before 1914, the S-boat could be represented as a weapon of coastal defense, but the offensive striking power of the torpedo lay at the heart of both systems. The S-boat could lay defensive minefields and carry out antisubmarine operations, but it could also use its superior speed and sea-keeping qualities to conduct long-range sweeps to hunt for enemy naval units or merchant ships. The battleship remained the capital ship (the primary weapons system) of navies, but the pace of technological change in the period 1860 to 1918 had raised questions about its potential obsolescence.

Developments in naval technologies in the late nineteenth century had led to new naval thinking encapsulated by Admiral Aube and the Jeune Ecole (Young School) in France.[17] With the Royal Navy predominant, the Jeune Ecole had advocated thinking about commerce raiding against Britain's supply lines, and the use of small and heavily armed vessels against British battleships, as a means to tilt the strategic balance at sea toward France. In this they drew inspiration from early experiments in the American Civil War using spar torpedoes (essentially an explosive device on the end of a long pole or spar) on steam-driven launches. The development in the late 1860s of the Whitehead torpedo by British inventor Robert Whitehead, building on the work of Giovanni Luppis, and the increasing efficiency of steam to power small fast boats had led to the creation of a new class of vessel, the torpedo boat, that could be useful in coastal waters. In 1873 HMS *Vesuvius* had become the first vessel to be equipped with the Whitehead torpedo; HMS *Lightning* (designed specifically for the purpose of launching the torpedo) followed three years later. The success of French torpedo boats in the Sino-French war of 1883–85, and the Russians and Japanese in the Russo-Japanese War of 1904–5, had led other navies to begin their own experiments in the field. The dangers posed by the torpedo boat were so obvious, especially after a Chilean ironclad (*Blanco Encalada*) was sunk by a torpedo boat in the Chilean Civil War of 1891, that a new class of vessel had been developed as a countermeasure. The "torpedo boat destroyer" (later shortened to just "destroyer") had become an essential element in fleet protection by World War I. The success of Italian MAS boats in the Adriatic in 1917 and 1918 (the sinking of SMS

*Wien* and SMS *Szent István*) prompted navies to make best use of the mature technology that was the torpedo.

The success of the torpedo and mine, and the emergence of airpower as threats to fleet security, raised questions in the postwar period about whether the battleship was already obsolete or merely obsolescent. The British, whose Royal Navy remained the most powerful force afloat in 1919, would expend considerable time and effort in the immediate postwar period analyzing and debating a question in government and in public that was critical to their maritime security.[18] For the Germans after World War I, like the Jeune Ecole in nineteenth-century France, the torpedo offered an interesting means to offset strategic weakness. If the battleship was vulnerable to the torpedo, then it could help to offset the weakness of German naval arms made through treaty law at Versailles. If the submarine was also forbidden to the German navy by the same treaty, then a fast motor launch could make a good and cheap substitute as a weapons delivery platform for a torpedo and/or mine. Such weapons, and a combination of speed and potency, meant that the S-boat would have the speed of a lightweight and the reach and power of a heavyweight. One writer compared the S-boat to a panther with "a savagery out of all proportion to its size. . . . Leaping forward it could slay a victim twenty times in weight if its fangs [the torpedoes] found a vital mark."[19] The S-boat was a good solution to the naval problems facing Germany after 1919, the state of naval technology, and the long-term ambitions of senior German naval officers. Within the scope of emerging technologies, the restrictions of the Treaty of Versailles, and ambitions for a balanced surface fleet, the S-boat made sense, but at no point does there appear to have been a recognition that, with important question marks after 1918 over the potential obsolescence of the battleship, lighter naval vessels might make more sense than a return to building heavy ships. German naval thinking remained focused on the idea of a blue-water navy and the concept of a decisive battle that would determine the outcome of a war against the British. In the minds of Raeder and others, as Plan Z was slowly realized and the new German naval identity was reborn, S-boats and other "interim" naval vessels would be relegated to the strategic margins. The idea of a commerce war, conducted by surface units, U-boats, and aircraft, was the dream of only a handful of German naval officers, even though such a strategy against the British had proved highly effective during World War I.

Following delivery of the S-1 prototype, the S-boat continued to evolve throughout the years of peace as the design was refined. In practice, the next four vessels to be produced (S-2 to S-5) differed little from S-1 except that they were 27.9 meters long to accommodate three Daimler-Benz 12-cylinder gasoline engines instead of the Maybachs. With the building of S-6, MAN four-stroke diesel engines (a considerable improvement in terms of fire safety) were installed instead of the gasoline engines previously used in the class. That in turn meant that the boat had to be even longer. With the building of S-7 to S-13, the S-boat reached a length of 32.36 meters, and after S-9 the MAN marine diesels gave way to Mercedes Benz MB502 engines producing 1,300 bhp. The growing technical complexity of the design resulted in an increase in crew complement to between seventeen and twenty-one officers and men. The purpose of the steady evolution of the design was to secure the maximum balance between speed and performance through the water. In the early 1930s the Reichsmarine was also not wholly confident that the development of an S-boat arm would not meet with political complications. On February 10, 1932, Admiral Raeder, the head of the Reichsmarine, gave orders that in view of the disarmament conference that had opened in Geneva, the gaps in the decks and deck scoops for the torpedo tubes of S-2 to S-5 (then under construction) would be given light cover plates ("leichte abdeckbleche") to hide the true purpose of these vessels as torpedo carriers.[20] Their initial complement of machine guns/cannons would consist of a relatively unimpressive mix of MG08/15 (belt-fed World War I vintage) and newer MG30 machine guns (made in Switzerland to get around the military clauses of the Treaty of Versailles).[21]

In October 1932, Rear Admiral Hans Kolbe, Befehlshaber der Aufklärungsstreitkräfte (Commander of Reconnaissance Forces, or BdA), oversaw the trials of the first group of boats at Eckernförde in fleet maneuvers. The commander of the 1st S-boat Half Flotilla commented that the trials demonstrated that, with issues around maintenance, the number of boats was simply inadequate to the military tasks assigned to the unit ("zu klein ist, um die gestellten kriegsmässigen Aufgaben mit Sicherheit lösen zu können'").[22] Despite the problems, Rear Admiral Kolbe was favorably impressed with the S-boat and its potential to augment the strength of German naval forces. He believed the S-boat was "a particularly promising weapon" (*eine besonders erfolgversprechende Waffe*) that could be developed "without significant costs" (*ohne erhebliche Kosten*).[23] Of course, Kolbe's assessment must be recognized for what it is. He did not view the S-boat as a revolutionary wonder weapon, a great leap forward in terms of naval warfare and technology: rather, he viewed it as a cost-effective response to the tasks and difficulties facing a German navy forced to observe, at least notionally, the strictures of the Treaty of Versailles. However, the political envelope (both domestic and international) in which the German navy was operating was about to undergo rapid change.

Hitler became chancellor of Germany in January 1933, and in October the new Nazi government withdrew from the disarmament conference. The need for any subterfuge on naval armaments rapidly dwindled, and on June 12, 1935, shortly after Hitler had renounced the military clauses of the Treaty of Versailles, the 1st Flotilla was formed with nine S-boats. A further three boats would join it shortly thereafter. With more than a dozen S-boats in operation, the Kriegsmarine was able to fully evaluate the S-boat in flotilla actions against potential enemy units.

Unlike Kolbe's assessment in 1933, initial trials of the full flotilla in fleet maneuvers were not positive. The performance of the 1st Flotilla of *Schnellboote* was "dogged by bad luck—especially by bad weather and by constructional defects."[24] The S-boat was no easy build; it required craftsmanship of the highest order and a huge investment in terms of man-hours. In heavy seas the design was vulnerable to damage and mechanical breakdown. The 1935 maneuvers led the fleet's commander-in-chief, Vice Admiral Carls, to conclude that S-boats were not a "reliable weapon." He therefore asked the High Command to cancel further orders.[25] The request was overruled by the High Command, but there was a recognition that some things had to change.

One outcome appears to be the decision in December 1936 to sell the gasoline boats S-1 to S-5 to the Spanish nationalists to support their fight in the civil war raging in Spain. A small team of volunteers from the S-boat arm went out to help train Franco's forces. The sale of the S-boats made political sense and was valuable in terms of fleet standardization.

Disposing of the older S-boats made for a more reliable and modern fleet. And the Spanish Civil War demonstrated the potential effectiveness of the S-boat as a minelayer (mines from an S-boat resulted in the accidental crippling of British destroyer HMS *Hunter* on May 13, 1937), even if Franco's seamen proved to be less-than-willing students of the volunteers from the Kriegsmarine.[26]

Increases in length to accommodate more powerful engines continued in the late 1930s. S-14 to S-17 (ordered 1935) used MAN four-stroke diesels (2,050 bhp), and S-18 to S-25 (ordered 1937–38 and delivered 1938–39) MB501 engines (2,000 bhp). By this stage the S-boats produced by the Lürssen yard had grown to 34.62 meters long and were capable of speeds up to 39.5 knots. The growing numbers of S-boats in service saw the formation of the 2nd Flotilla on August 1, 1938, as the crisis over Hitler's ambitions in Czechoslovakia was reaching its height. The threat and reality of war in 1939 led to fresh S-boat orders (S-26 to S-29) that saw a change to the design whereby the torpedo tubes were incorporated in a fairing over the forward part of the hull (they had previously stood alone on either side of the deck). This change increased buoyancy and improved weather protection for the torpedo tubes. The bridge of the S-boat was redesigned at the same time. With just fifteen S-boats available in September 1939, the number of available units was further increased by the commissioning of eight boats (S-30 to S-37) to be built for the Chinese government. They were based on the old S-10 design and were smaller than the S-26 to S-29 type. Entering service from late 1939 through the summer of 1940, they provided badly needed reinforcements for the German navy.

The outbreak of war in 1939 (for a navy planning on the basis of war in 1945–46) was unwelcome. On coming to power in 1933, Hitler had impressed on Raeder, the head of the German navy, that he was determined to avoid war with Britain.[27] Signature of an Anglo-German Naval Agreement in 1935 (by which Germany agreed to build up to no more than 35 percent of Royal Navy tonnage) had been designed to allay British fears.[28] In Raeder's mind, the target of the German naval buildup was France, not Great Britain. The revival of German naval power after 1919, which, as Keith W. Bird has argued, effectively amounted to Raeder's life's work as a senior German naval officer, was about to be undone by the politicians. The outbreak of war with Britain was, to put it simply, a disaster in Raeder's view. The strategic assessment was bleak, to say the least.[29]

Developing a naval force powerful enough to take on the Royal Navy would inevitably take time, and it had only been four years since Germany had renounced the military clauses of the Treaty of Versailles.[30] The outbreak of war in 1939 left the admiral wondering what the German navy could do, with a fleet very much in transition, to confront the British: "No one was in any doubt that as things stood there was little chance of winning any decisive success in a naval war with Britain. . . . The present Fleet would be able to do little more than fight and go down to an honorable defeat."[31] Despite his gloom, the Kriegsmarine scored a series of impressive successes in the early part of the war. S-boats were active, albeit in a supporting role, during the 1939 campaign against Poland (they were involved in the sinking of one small steamer), and in 1940 the German invasion of Norway saw most of the German navy employed in a stunning coup de main against the British and French. In the attack on Norway, both the 1st and 2nd Flotillas of S-boats were engaged in small-scale actions and in escort and reconnaissance duties and in ferrying German troops to landing sites.[32]

More widely in the war at sea, during 1939 and early 1940 Germany's submarines took a great toll on Allied merchant shipping. Both Raeder and the head of the German submarine service, Karl Dönitz, understood that the Kriegsmarine's primary contribution to victory in the West would be a war against British commerce. Despite the success in Norway and plans for a seaborne invasion of Britain, they saw Britain's sea-lines of communication as the Achilles' heel of their enemy, the place they could most effectively target. The emphasis on commerce warfare after 1939 marked a return to pre-1890s thinking in the German navy.[33] Britain's need, as a densely populated island nation, to import a substantial percentage of its food and industrial requirements constituted a significant vulnerability. By the middle of 1940, with the launch of the German offensive in France and the Low Countries, S-boats were ready to contribute to the war on commerce being waged by the Kriegsmarine's U-boats. The S-boats would operate in the shallow waters of the English Channel and North Sea, where shallow depths and closeness to land offered U-boats little seaway and made them vulnerable to escort vessels and aircraft operating from airbases in the British Isles. Their target would be the convoys running along the southern and eastern coasts of England.

Developed as a response to Germany's strategic position after World War I, and embodying much of German maritime culture from strategic ambition, to the craftsmanship of the northern German yacht builders, the evolution of the S-boat had been problematic. No doubt, in the evolution of the German fleet planned by the German naval staff (Plan Z), the S-boat, like the pocket battleship, was set to dwindle in importance by the 1940s, as new designs and bigger ships went down the slipways of German shipbuilders to form an expanded and modernized fleet. By May 1940, however, the S-boat was proving its worth as a valuable maid of all work and as a capable weapon of war, especially in coastal waters. Earlier issues with reliability had been addressed and, in the circumstances of a German fleet inadequate to the tasks facing the Third Reich, commanders were showing some ingenuity in utilizing the qualities of a capable, fast, and heavily armed vessel. With the opening of the campaign in the West, new opportunities for the S-boat would emerge along the coasts of the North Sea and English Channel.

## CHAPTER 2

# THE RISE OF THE S-BOAT, 1940–1941

IN 1939 THERE WAS CONSIDERABLE national pride bound up in both the size and strength of the Royal Navy and the extent and profitability of Britain's Merchant Navy. Over 144,000 seafarers crewed the British registered merchant fleet, which included some of the largest and most prestigious ships in the world. The fleet of coasters and other small vessels operating along Britain's coasts in 1939 (employing over 21,000 seamen) made up a small but significant proportion of the wider whole.[1] In contemporary cultural narratives, which emphasized the oceanic over the coastal, the work of the collier and the coastal carriers was overlooked in favor of the more glamorous shipping companies carrying the goods of empire around the globe. P&O, Union Castle, and Blue Funnel, with their fine cargo liners and house uniforms, acted as the "poster boys" for the peacetime Merchant Navy, while the small utility ships of William Cory, Everards, and others represented the bottom end of the market for the employment of merchant seamen. Mainstream British culture, in which the maritime was celebrated, recognized the economic value and contribution to imperial unity of the foreign trades while almost entirely overlooking the contribution of the coastal fleet. The foreign and home trades represented a cultural divide in more ways than one, and that divide echoes through into the historiography of the war at sea. The struggle to maintain the foreign trades during World War II has received considerable attention, while the home trades have been almost entirely overlooked. This chapter examines the importance of the coastal trade to the British economy, the emergence of a serious threat to the coastal routes in 1940–41 following the fall of France, and initial British steps to protect trade along those routes.

In peacetime, coastal shipping—carrying goods to and from the continent and between the port cities and towns of Britain—was vital. It was more efficient and cheaper to move bulk cargoes of grain, coal, and aggregates by coaster and by barge than by road and rail. In war the coastal convoys fulfilled two vital strategic roles: first, they brought coal from northern England and southern Wales to ports along the southern and eastern coast; and second, coastal shipping facilitated the transshipment of cargoes that had already crossed the oceans to arrive in U.K. waters. Both functions were vital: without coal, homes would go cold and the power needs of war industries could not be maintained. William Cory's use of steam colliers from the 1850s onward to bring coal into the port of London had facilitated the growth of power-hungry industries along the Thames, from engineering and shipbuilding to the production of chemicals.[2] London's power stations had an unceasing demand for coal and required whole fleets of colliers to sustain them. With the transshipment of cargoes, sometimes ships that had made the long ocean crossing were incorporated into a coastal convoy to bring the cargoes closer to the point of use. Otherwise, cargoes could be transshipped from larger vessels to their smaller cousins either in port or in some sheltered location using the cargo-handling derricks of the larger vessels. The deliveries of coal and the transshipment of cargoes played a major role in relieving some of the burden that would otherwise have fallen on ports subject to wartime dislocations and, from early 1940 onward, the danger of aerial attack. If the flow of trade could be disrupted at any point from oceanic and coastal routes, through to off-loading in port, the British war economy would be seriously impacted. To damage one node of the network was to damage the system as a whole.

The vessels that made up the coastal convoys were very different from the larger vessels typical of the foreign trade. That in turn created a different culture, a different mindset, and ultimately a very different kind of inshore war. The coasters operated in different ways and ran to a very different timetable, and their construction and cargo made them particularly vulnerable to enemy attack. They were basic and small, with a handful of crew and a small number of holds. In terms of design, the emphasis was on minimalism, and function in coastal waters would sometimes dictate their layout. For example, the SS *Fulham*, one of the fleet of colliers delivering coal to the Thames power stations, had been launched in 1935 by a less-than-household-name shipping company, the Fulham Borough Council. She was designed with a "flat-iron configuration" (very little superstructure, and a hinged funnel to enable her to pass under Thames bridges) to deliver coal to Fulham Borough Council's Battersea Reach power station. Although she was capable of 10.5 knots laden, the vessel had a draft of just 16 feet to enable her to discharge at Battersea.[3]

The challenges of operating in coastal waters also limited the size of the majority of coasters. For example, 1,597 gross registered tons (GRT) was the average size of the coasters operated by the London Power Company during the war, and the twenty-one colliers of William Cory and Company averaged 2,184 GRT. In any kind of seaway, small, heavily laden vessels with only a shallow draft and low freeboard were potentially difficult to handle and unpleasant in terms of living accommodation.

The convoying of coastal traffic along the East Coast began soon after the outbreak of war. To further try and contain the threat to British merchant shipping, a mine barrage was set across the English Channel at Dover to restrict the potential movement of German submarines that might seek to attack convoy traffic. A start was also made on setting a defensive minefield down the length of the East Coast to create a barrier to protect the north–south convoy coastal route from any attempt at interdiction from the direction of the continent. Small defensive belts were also set to guard the Thames Estuary from operations by small minelaying U-boats. The value of such mine barrages in defense of trade in the North Sea and English Channel had been demonstrated in World War I. The East Coast mine belt developed steadily during 1940 as minelayers became available, and the fortunes of war made it imperative to deny the enemy easy access to the coastal convoy routes and the British coast. The mine belt, the need for convoys, changes to the navigational channels, and the removal of some navigational buoys and extinguishing of some navigational lights, not to mention mining operations carried out by the Germans, made the task of transiting East Coast inshore waters a difficult proposition by the end of 1939 to mid-1940.

Safeguarding the transit of the eclectic collection of ships that made up a coastal convoy was no easy task. A fleet of minesweepers was required on the East Coast to regularly sweep for mines, often just ahead of the convoys plying their way north and south. Finding enough minesweepers and escort vessels to accompany the convoys, given the myriad of other demands, presented another difficulty. In 1939 just twenty-one vessels were ready for minesweeping in home waters, which resulted in hundreds of other vessels ranging from trawlers to paddle steamers being taken up from trade to use as makeshift minesweepers.[4] Even without serious disruption to the flow of coal, the growing needs of the war industries in the South meant that it was difficult to meet demand in the winter of 1939–40. On January 4, First Lord of the Admiralty Winston Churchill initiated an investigation into whether inland waterways might be used to relieve some of the pressure on coastal collier shipping.[5] The dangers to East Coast traffic were underlined on January 29–30, when aerial attacks accounted for the loss of thirty-four thousand tons of British and nine thousand tons of neutral shipping.[6] The success of the German offensive launched against the Low Countries on May 10 made it inevitable that the threat to U.K. coastal shipping would increase dramatically. The fall of France in June made the situation still worse. With Britain seemingly on the brink of defeat as a result of either invasion or the strangulation of her maritime trade, the coastal convoys took on an even greater significance.

From bases along the coast of Europe, German forces would be ideally placed to disrupt the coastal trade. At the same time, the British faced an acute scarcity of resources to meet the threat. Destroyer losses in the Norwegian campaign and in the Dunkirk evacuation had been heavy. Italy's entry into the war meant that the Mediterranean Fleet could not be denuded of its destroyers, and the gathering U-boat campaign in the Atlantic created a further priority for the allocation of available escort vessels. Convoys along the East Coast were considered particularly vulnerable, and the practice of bringing convoys through the Dover–Calais narrows, where they could come under attack from land-based artillery, was abandoned. Despite the dangers, the constant heavy demand for coal in the Southeast (40,000 tons per week) meant that convoys would have to run on six days out of seven along the East Coast from the coalfields of the North to the capital.[7] On an annual basis, the capital needed 10.25 million tons of coal to maintain "gas, electricity, water, sewerage, transportation and hydraulic power."[8] Failure to maintain the flow of coal would mean major disruption to the British war economy. Those convoys varied in size but routinely constituted a large target. For example, by 1943 the PW and WP series of convoys (Bristol Channel to Portsmouth and back again) typically ran one day in two and usually constituted of sixteen to eighteen ships (see table 1). The East Coast convoys, Forth-North (FN) and Forth-South (FS), running six days out of seven, usually involved twice this number of ships and the voyage would take approximately fifty-four hours, giving ample time for attack by German forces. The point at which FN and FS convoys passed each other along the East Coast offered a particularly target-rich environment for German forces. The importance of the coastal convoys was recognized on both sides of the Atlantic, especially their role in carrying "the coal on which London absolutely depended."[9]

The S-boats of the Kriegsmarine made a dramatic debut in the North Sea following the launching of the German offensive in the Low Countries on May 10, 1940.[10] The evacuations from Dunkirk and Calais provided rich pickings for the Luftwaffe and the handful of S-boats that were able to make their way into Dutch and Franco-Belgian waters.[11] As Hans Franks has noted, "The sinking of two destroyers, severe damage to a third, together with three steamers sunk, showed the capabilities of the S-boats despite there only ever being two or three out of a total of

**TABLE 1.** BRITISH COASTAL CONVOYS IN LATE 1943

| ROUTE | CODE ID | FREQUENCY | AVG. NO. SHIPS | NO. HOURS ON PASSAGE |
|---|---|---|---|---|
| Nore–Methil | FN | 6 days in 7 | 33 | 54 |
| Methil–Nore | FS | every 4 days | 33 | 54 |
| Southend–Portsmouth | CW | every 4 days | 20 | 24 |
| Portsmouth–Southend | CE | every 4 days | 20 | 24 |
| Portsmouth–Bristol Channel | PW | 1 day in 2 | 16 | 48 |
| Bristol Channel–Portsmouth | WP | 1 day in 2 | 16 | 48 |

SOURCE: Figures from "Coastal Convoys: An Appreciation," October 11, 1943, TNA: ADM 1/15815.

nine operational at a time because of engine troubles."[12] The loss of over a thousand soldiers killed when their ships were sunk by S-boats during the evacuation process underlined the threat posed by the vessel, even if their successes were dwarfed by the number of kills the Luftwaffe scored during the Dunkirk evacuation. The Admiralty Trade Division got a particularly vivid impression of the impact of a S-boat attack from Second Officer V. P. Wills-Rust, senior survivor of the SS *Abukir*, which was sunk by S-34 on May 28, 1940, after leaving Ostend.[13] A single torpedo hit the ship and sank it in seconds, resulting in the deaths of many of the two hundred or so passengers on board. Willis-Rust later recounted, "Although I was trapped, I could see everything over my head. The stern burst into flames and I saw flames forward. I could see the water coming up and over my head. The ship hit bottom and turned over, the debris was thrown off me and I was released and I came to the surface."[14] S-boat attacks during the Dunkirk evacuation—especially the destruction of the *Chacal*-class destroyer *Jaguar* (France) by S-23 on May 23, HMS *Wakeful* (British W-class destroyer) by S-30 on May 29, and the *Bourrasque*-class destroyer *Siroco* (France) by S-23 and S-26 on May 31—demonstrated the potency of the S-boat as a weapon against even the most modern and heavily armed opponents.[15] To some extent the potential threat to coastal traffic in U.K. waters, and the role of the S-boat as the spearhead of that threat, was lost as the British reeled from the collapse of France and the withdrawals from Dunkirk and western France. The Ju-87 Stuka dive-bomber looked like an even more formidable threat to vessels operating by day in the narrow confines of the North Sea and English Channel.

The Kriegsmarine, however, was very much encouraged by the success of the S-boat in the close confines of the North Sea and English Channel. A radio broadcast on May 29, 1940, by Rear Admiral Lützow, head of the Kriegsmarine's propaganda unit (one of his regular Wednesday night broadcasts on naval warfare and naval power), stressed the threat that the S-boat posed to British trade. He argued that the campaign was "of the greatest strategic and economic importance" and had the potential to "dislocate British trade around the UK and to throttle the flow of trade into the port of London."[16] Such was the importance of the coastal trade routes, and the restricted spaces in which they operated, that the British would have no alternative than to fight for them in a space that left them highly vulnerable to attack by the Kriegsmarine's S-boats.

German victory in the West by the third week of June 1940 was surprising and deeply unwelcome for the British. Unlike in 1914, Franco-British land forces had not been able to hold the line against the German army. The strategic balance between Britain and Germany was transformed, even though the British were able to evacuate most of their forces from the continent. This left the German navy with a dilemma. The strategy envisaged in 1939—that of trying to defeat, or at least contain, Britain by naval blockade—remained the only practical option in the minds of Raeder and most of his immediate subordinates. Meanwhile, Hitler favored an invasion of Britain, or at least (as Walter Ansel concluded in 1960) the threat of it, in order to force the British into a negotiated peace.[17] The collapse of France forced the German Naval High Command to revisit a 1939 study regarding the possibilities for an invasion of Britain drawn up by Commander Reinicke, while his commanding officer, Admiral Fricke, carried out his own evaluation.[18] Fricke's rushed study, completed as the Germans were consolidating their hold on France, Belgium, and the Netherlands, suggested that an invasion might be feasible.[19] With pressure from above, the German navy was left to prepare the groundwork for an invasion, which involved a buildup of troops and invasion craft and the development of detailed plans, while at the same time bringing back into use the naval and other port facilities required for a long-term siege of Britain. Working out how to seize control of the short sea crossings across the English Channel in order to effect an invasion of the British Isles, while at the same time strangling British trade, was a mammoth task.

The size of the U.K. population had exceeded the ability of British agriculture to feed it in the nineteenth century. Maintaining the demands of a complex war economy put further pressure on Britain's sea-lines of communication, which the Kriegsmarine could exploit even as the bulk of Germany's armed forces turned east. At the outbreak of war in 1939, President Franklin D. Roosevelt had called Congress into special session to repeal the Neutrality Acts passed from 1935 onward. Those acts had threatened to cut off all trade between the democracies and the United States. Roosevelt had been sufficiently persuasive to get Congress to pass revised legislation permitting trade on a cash-and-carry basis. The defeat of France, and the loss of much of the British army's heavy equipment in the evacuations from the continent, meant that the sea-lanes across the Atlantic became a vital lifeline for the British and the means by which some of the critical losses of 1940 could be made good. Disrupting the flow of U.K. trade would be the principal task of the Kriegsmarine with the assistance of the Luftwaffe, and on July 2, 1940, as the Battle of Britain had developed, the Oberkommando der Wehrmacht (OKW) had issued an operational instruction to the Luftwaffe that it had two basic tasks before it:

1. The interdiction of the Channel to merchant shipping, to be carried out in conjunction with German naval forces, by means of attacks on convoys, the destruction of harbor facilities, and the sowing of mines in harbor areas and the approaches thereto.
2. The destruction of the Royal Air Force.[20]

This instruction is worth reflecting on given the layers of myth that have built up over the Battle of Britain. The first task of the Luftwaffe was to assist the Kriegsmarine in the war against British maritime commerce as a means to bring Churchill to the negotiating table. The second task was "the destruction of the Royal Air Force," which was considered an important precondition for the invasion of Britain (Hitler's plan B to secure a peace deal with the British). Only in August was the Luftwaffe directed against invasion targets. If German objectives in the Battle of Britain shifted during the course of it, then there is virtual unanimity among historians that the Battle of Britain had undoubtedly started with Luftwaffe attacks on coastal convoys from May 1940. These attacks necessitated a response by the RAF, which had quickly escalated into the developing air campaign over southern England in 1940.

Luftwaffe attacks on coastal shipping were dramatic and dangerous, as pilot Werner Kreipe (Kampfgeschwader 2, Cambrai) later recalled:

> The Channel was bathed in brilliant sunshine. The sea and the sky were contrasting shades of blue that merged at the horizon. A light haze hung over the English coast and there, far below us, was the convoy, like so many toy ships with wispy wakes fanning out behind.

As soon as we were observed, the ships of the convoy dispersed, the merchantmen maneuvering violently and the escorting warships moving out at full speed. Anti-aircraft shells peppered the sky. Our fighters appeared. We made our first bomb run, and fountains leaped up around the ships. The anti-aircraft batteries stationed on the English Coast added their fire to that coming from the ships.[21]

Despite such dramas sinking the colliers and other small ships on a coastal convoy was a difficult task, but what mattered was the overall disruption to the flow of trade. A damaged ship took time to repair, and a disorganized coastal convoy could offer the chance for other forces to attack.

Aerial attacks against coastal convoys was just one means by which British trade could be targeted. German heavy ships based in northern waters could traverse the Greenland-Iceland gap in order to range into the North Atlantic and beyond. The standard German medium submarine, the Type VIIC, could hunt the Atlantic once bases on the western coast of France were ready to support operations (replenishment at sea from German warships, merchant ships or specially developed "Milch Cow" submarines offered a further potential means to increase the reach into the Atlantic of the medium submarine). Closer to occupied France, and in shallow waters not favorable to submarine operations, the smaller vessels of the German navy (destroyers, torpedo boats, R-boats, and S-boats) would maintain the offensive. The Luftwaffe would provide aerial reconnaissance to assist surface and submarine forces, carry out bombing, strafing, and mining missions against British shipping where possible, and attack port cities and railways in the United Kingdom in order to disrupt, as far possible, Britain's ability to secure, transport, and deliver supplies to their point of use. In effect, and despite popular perceptions, the S-boat campaign against the coastal convoys was one element in a multipronged attack against Britain's sea-lines of communication.

**GERMAN SUBMARINE BASES:** Brest; Lorient; St. Nazaire; La Rochelle; Bordeaux.
**S-BOAT PRINCIPAL OPERATING PORTS:** St. Peter Port (Guernsey), Cherbourg, Le Havre, Dieppe, Boulogne, Ostend, Zeebrugge, Rotterdam, Ijmuiden

In managing the campaign against Britain's sea-lines of communication German forces were beset by a number of command and control issues. Sea and Air Forces came under the respective command of the Kriegsmarine and Luftwaffe, with overall control by the Oberkommando der Wehrmacht (OKW), the supreme command of the armed forces. Partly as a result, Kriegsmarine/Luftwaffe cooperation was problematic, and it remained so throughout the war. In the Third Reich, personalities mattered greatly, and the command structure left the navy reliant on the personal whim of Hermann Göring, the egotistical, glory-hunting, self-aggrandizing career Nazi and ex–fighter pilot head of the German air force. He was more interested in making himself and the Luftwaffe look good than in enabling Germany to win the war. He saw little reason to assist the navy or to allow it to develop its own air element. Without a naval air arm, the Kriegsmarine lacked effective aerial reconnaissance for much of the war. Even within the Kriegsmarine there were command and control issues. As Lawrence Paterson has pointed out, the surface fleet and the S-boat flotillas differed sharply from their U-boat counterparts.[22] Whereas U-boat flotillas were subject to the centralized control of Befehlshaber der U-Boote (BdU), surface ships and S-boat flotillas came under the command of regional Kriegsmarine commanders. Such administrative divisions made cooperation difficult, and the differences extended to the operational level. While U-boat flotilla commanders were shore-based, S-boat flotilla commanders routinely planned and were involved in the execution of patrols. The command and control issue hampered the development and execution of the campaign against Britain's transoceanic and coastal convoys.

In the aftermath of the evacuation of Dunkirk and of British forces in western France in May–June 1940, S-boats, with assistance from the Luftwaffe, enjoyed some dramatic successes against the coastal convoys. This was especially remarkable given the small number of operational boats (ten to fifteen) already given hard service in the Baltic and Norwegian waters. Britain was experiencing a critical shortage of escort vessels. Auxiliary escort vessels, such as converted trawlers and whalers, crewed by men from the Royal Navy Patrol Service, were rushed into service. They did not have the firepower or the speed to cope with the S-boats. Not until 1941–42 would greater numbers of escort vessels become available as British boatyards delivered a steady stream of motor launches, motor gunboats, and motor torpedo boats. Shortages of destroyers and other escorts, which the 1941 construction program proposed building, meant that Royal Navy Patrol Service vessels were often all that was available for the coastal runs in late 1940 and early 1941.

Even when destroyers were available, the degree to which they could protect long, straggling convoys was questionable. Destroyers had the firepower to destroy an S-boat, but hitting an S-boat was no easy matter for the heavy guns of a destroyer. In the Royal Navy's official history of the war at sea, gunnery specialist Captain S. W. Roskill noted, "They were difficult targets to deal with, for not only were they hard to sight while lying in wait on the convoy routes by night, but our escort vessels were too slow to catch and destroy them."[23] One destroyer officer noted that S-boats "presented us with new problems in tactics and gunnery. We often heard and saw them as they strove to close our convoys, but to take a damaging shot at the ghostly shadows while they shimmered fleetingly in and out of our ken seemed beyond the capability of our ponderous [fire] control system."[24] Initial British reactions to the emergence of the S-boat threat expressed both concern and a lack of intelligence on the threat they might pose. On July 16 the First Lord of the Admiralty expressed his concerns to fellow ministers: "The First Lord said that there was a source of some anxiety. Like other shallow draft vessels, they might enjoy a high degree of immunity from minefields at certain states of the water. We knew Germany was producing them in numbers and might at the moment possess anything from 50 to 100. In the view of the Naval Staff, destroyers would not be of great use against these craft."[25] This was as close an admission of serious concern as was ever likely to be found in the quietly understated official language of the British government.

In the six months after June 1940, S-boat torpedo attacks accounted for twenty-three merchant ships (47,985 tons) in coastal waters. With other vessels being lost to bombing and mines laid by the Kriegsmarine and Luftwaffe, the coastal campaign was highly destructive and troubling.[26] For example, on July 25, 1940, the twenty-one-ship convoy CW8, passing westbound from the Straits of Dover, was engaged by Luftwaffe bombers.

Five of the merchant ships were sunk, and four were damaged. The dispatch of the destroyers HMS *Brilliant* and HMS *Boreas* drove the S-boats back, but the destroyers were engaged by batteries on the French coast. As Captain Eric Bush recounted in his memoirs, "While returning to Dover, both destroyers were attacked by waves of dive-bombers and put out of action, with heavy casualties in *Boreas*, but they managed to somehow struggle into harbor."[27] The surviving vessels of the convoy were attacked by S-boats (S-19, S-20, and S-27), which claimed three further victims.[28] Overestimating the number and tonnage of the ships sunk, there was satisfaction at Torpedo Boat Command that three S-boats had sunk four ships totaling around 34,000 tons. S-boats and Luftwaffe reduced the convoy to just eleven ships as CW8 passed Dungeness.[29] The twenty-five-ship convoy that followed it (CW9) was attacked after passing through the Straits of Dover on the afternoon of August 7, 1940. S-20, S-21, and S-27 each claimed one ship sunk as a result of the action (and three ships had indeed been sunk as a result of S-boat torpedoes).[30] With the convoy straggling out over ten miles after the attack, the Luftwaffe mounted bombing attacks, which fortunately were interrupted by the arrival of fighter aircraft from No. 145 Squadron.[31]

The attacks on CW8 and CW9 in the summer of 1940 gave the British considerable cause for concern. Stocks of coal at some gasworks were sufficient for less than two weeks of operation, and most coal merchants held significantly lower stocks than they had during the summer of 1939.[32] This left the United Kingdom highly vulnerable to any disruption of the East Coast convoys. Despite this vulnerability and the successes of combined Luftwaffe-Kriegsmarine attacks on coastal convoys in July, Hermann Göring, the head of the Luftwaffe, was not interested in cooperating with the Kriegsmarine.[33] He wanted to build the prestige of the Luftwaffe by gaining air supremacy in the Battle of Britain. The level to which he was willing to pursue the agenda of his own service, at the expense of the Kriegsmarine, was quite striking. Aircraft would not collaborate with ships on joint operations or fleet reconnaissance or provide combat air patrols above units operating at sea. Out of a desire to capitalize on their large explosive yield, one-third of the sea mines available for use in U.K. coastal waters were not used against the shipping lanes; instead, they were dropped on British cities.³⁴ For the war at sea, this was a waste of precious resources.

From September 1939 to the start of March 1940, German mines sank eighty-nine ships around the British Isles.³⁵ While traditional minesweeping gear fitted hurriedly to makeshift minesweepers could deal with old-fashioned moored mines, in 1939, during the second week of the war, ships had begun to be lost to a new kind of mine. It wasn't until November, when one was located on the mudflats at Shoeburyness and successfully defused, that British personnel realized that the new type of mine was magnetic and was being set off by the magnetic field of a steel ship. The British initially had no answer to the magnetic mine, and dropping contact sea mines on blazing cities was a lesser return on their cost. By early 1940 the British had developed degaussing (neutralizing the magnetic field of a ship) as an effective countermeasure to the magnetic mine. Failure on the part of the Luftwaffe to realize that the magnetic mine could paralyze British coastal shipping and cause heavy losses, and wasting contact mines on urban targets, meant that a significant opportunity was squandered in that year of the war to strike a devastating blow against British trade. A lesser opportunity was squandered in August 1940 as the Germans deployed the first acoustic mines, which again were not introduced in overwhelming numbers, giving the British time to introduce countermeasures.

The head of the Luftwaffe was simply not interested in campaigns that might politically advantage the Kriegsmarine. Even with the development of degaussing, and countermeasures for acoustic mines, British shipping losses due to mines did not fall significantly until early 1941. The period from June 1940 to early 1941 represented a vital window of opportunity for the Luftwaffe and Kriegsmarine to attack the coastal convoys in combination. As Sönke Neitzel has argued, "If the Luftwaffe and the navy had agreed on a common strategy it could have weakened Great Britain to a considerable extent in 1940/41 when the Luftwaffe still had large resources available."³⁶ A strategic opportunity was squandered because of interservice difficulties.

In late 1940, British defenses were still dogged by the impact of the lean years of the 1920s and 1930s. Rearmament had begun in the 1930s, but it was by no means complete in 1940. Moreover, the problems had been exacerbated by the disarray caused by the speed of German advances in the West in May and June 1940. It was unsurprising that German naval forces found that they were able to operate in the Channel with some degree of security, and the Luftwaffe could conduct anti-ship operations with similar assurance. Aircraft and fast motor torpedo boats could attack coastal convoys with relative ease. With the Royal Air Force fully engaged against a Luftwaffe that was striving for air superiority, the S-boats faced little danger of aerial attack. S-boats continued to enjoy successes against British coastal shipping throughout 1940.

In the early autumn of 1940, things began to change. It was apparent that the damage done to the heavy units of the Kriegsmarine, the continued strength of the Royal Navy, the inability of the Luftwaffe to defeat the RAF in the skies above the English Channel, and Hitler's desire to attack the Soviet Union precluded any attempt at an invasion of the British Isles. The weather also took a turn for the worse, limiting operations in August and early September, but on September 4, the 1st S-boat Flotilla (S-18, S-20, S-21, S-22, and S-27, with S-54 on attachment) engaged convoy FS271, which contained thirty-five ships.[37] S-18 claimed two steamers, S-21 two steamers, S-22 one tanker, and S-54 damaged a destroyer (a German estimate of 39,000 tons).[38] In reality, five coasters totaling 9,996 tons had been sunk: the circumstances of a night attack accounting for the inaccuracies in types and tonnage of ships attacked. The arrival of the 3rd S-boat Flotilla in Vlissingen on September 10 meant the welcome arrival of additional forces (even if the boats of that flotilla were the aging S-1, S-10, S-11, and S-13), especially as the boats of the 1st Flotilla put into Cherbourg for overhaul. Unfortunately, in the process of moving from Brunsbüttel to Vlissingen, S-1 and S-13 collided, causing severe damage to the stern of S-1. Later a barge collided with S-10, which sustained significant levels of damage. The 3rd Flotilla was thus down to two boats before it had begun operations. An anti-invasion bombing raid by the RAF on Vlissingen then resulted in damage to S-13, along with the wounding of flotilla leader Friedrich Kemnade and seven men.[39] The remaining boats and personnel of the flotilla were thus placed under the temporary command of the 2nd S-boat Flotilla in Rotterdam.[40] On October 18, 1st S-boat Flotilla (having moved from Cherbourg to Rotterdam) engaged convoy FN311. S-27 claimed one steamer, S-24 a tanker, and S-18 one steamer and one tanker.[41] Again, there was a sharp difference between reality and the tonnages of ships claimed as sunk. For example, the 8,000-ton vessel claimed by S-24 was the 3,754-ton French ship *PLM14* traveling in ballast.

Despite these rather disappointing returns, the late summer and autumn of 1940 represented a moment of ascendancy for the S-boats in the English Channel and North Sea. Torpedo, mine, and bomb continued to take a steady, if unspectacular, toll on the coastal convoys. Just as importantly, Luftwaffe attacks against London, and the difficulties of convoying, further hampered the ability to get coal supplies into the capital. In September 1940 (the blitz began on September 7), just 670,000 tons of coal arrived in London (around 60 percent of average for the summer months of that year).[42] However, the scaling back of the aerial effort in the West was a blow, and it was quickly exacerbated by the high command, even though S-boats would continue to operate effectively in the English Channel for the rest of 1940. October 1940 marked the pivotal moment. On October 12, Hitler had issued an order giving permission to release the forces assembled for Operation Sea Lion.[43] The appearance of invasion preparations would continue until after the last suitable big spring tides of 1940, October 30–November 1; but following the decision of October 12, the head of Germany's torpedo boat arm (Führer der Torpedoboote, or FdT) was already planning a redeployment of most of his available forces eastward in preparation for the invasion of the Soviet Union (Operation Barbarossa) on June 22, 1941. The Luftwaffe, badly mauled in the Battle of Britain, began to plan a similar redeployment that would be preceded by a period for reequipment and training. With preparations for the invasion of the Soviet Union, the intensity of the German campaign in British coastal waters was compromised, just at the point where the forces of the Kriegsmarine were enjoying some successes against the British. These successes were in the Channel and North Sea, but, critically, they extended to the North Atlantic, where the U-boats were enjoying considerable success. U-boats, Luftwaffe, and S-boats had proven to be a deadly combination against the convoy network on which the British relied.

S-boat sinkings were particularly useful in that they targeted the short sea traffic that was hard to attack with U-boats and large surface ships.

With some satisfaction, FdT had noted on July 5, 1940, "England is forced to carry on the traffic to London in order to keep Southern England going. This will be done regardless of results."[44] The narrow and shallow confines of the English Channel placed this traffic largely beyond the reach of U-boats and major surface warships; equally, though, it created a hunting zone for light forces.[45] The question was which side would commit the necessary resources to successfully defend or sever the vital lines of communication that ran through this zone. The impact of the Battle of Britain on the Luftwaffe, and the lack of cooperation with the Kriegsmarine, partly answered that question, and by November 1940, with winter approaching, stocks of coal at power stations and elsewhere had increased to 28,155,000 tons from the low of 19,829,000 tons at the end of July.[46] Similarly, stocks of coke had improved from 2,750,000 to 4,000,000 tons.

Führer Directive 21 on December 18, 1940, ordered German forces to prepare for the invasion of Russia in the summer of 1941. All preparations were to be complete by May 15, 1941.[47] Even though he was determined to attack the Soviet Union in the summer of 1941, there appears to have been a belated recognition by Hitler that the winter of 1940–41 represented a vital opportunity to disrupt Britain's convoy system. On February 6, 1941, Hitler issued Directive 23 ("Directions for Operations against the British Economy").[48] It established aerial attack on Britain's port system as a top priority for the Luftwaffe, and it marked a further shifting of the aerial campaign against Britain, which had moved its attacks from the airfields of Fighter Command in the summer of 1940 to the blitz against London, and then to a series of attacks against Britain's industrial cities. Directive 23 was a triumph for the Kriegsmarine, which for several months had been signaling its dissatisfaction with the Luftwaffe in the conduct of the war at sea. Admiral Raeder, the head of the Kriegsmarine, had impressed on Hitler the need for the Luftwaffe to do more to support the war at sea. With Germany's submarines enjoying considerable successes against Britain's merchant fleet in 1940–41, Raeder argued that the war against Britain might be won through siege methods rather than by the targeting of civilians by the German bomber force.

The head of the Luftwaffe for once was willing to go along with the Kriegsmarine's request. Targeting ports represented an easy way for the

Luftwaffe to demonstrate that it was causing serious damage to the British war economy as part of the effort to rebuild the reputation of the service after failure in the Battle of Britain. Attacking London night after night was an exercise in diminishing returns, especially with Britain's aerial defenses improving all the time. Even attacking the coastal convoys themselves was increasingly problematic. The growing strength of RAF Fighter Command ensured by late 1940 that combat air patrols were routinely mounted over coastal convoys. A simple "friend or foe" identification system largely ensured that approaching enemy aircraft would be identified before they came into range. Indeed, the pilots of even friendly aircraft still found it an unnerving experience to be faced with every gun in the convoy trained toward them as they made their approach to the convoy.[49] By late 1940, after the Battle of Britain, coastal convoys were rather harder targets to attack than they had been at the start. With Barbarossa in preparation, ports represented relatively easy pickings in terms of locating and attacking them. This could offer a valuable training experience before the bomber force turned eastward.[50]

The drawing away of Luftwaffe units from west to east in preparation for Operation Barbarossa was mirrored within the Kriegsmarine. In May 1941, the 1st, 2nd, and 3rd S-boat Flotillas were sent to the Baltic to prepare for the attack.[51] It was left to the 4th Flotilla, which was using the older class of S-boat (S-19, S-24, and S-25, later joined by S-20 and S-22), to maintain the campaign off the East Coast and into the English Channel. Given that the older boats were subject to more frequent mechanical problems, the 4th Flotilla could do little more than hope to tie down forces in the West rather than to press home the advantage that S-boats had enjoyed in late 1940 and early 1941. Operating from Rotterdam, the 4th Flotilla did their best to spread the defenses as far as they could. The flotilla's operations were further disrupted in the third week of May by the foray into the Atlantic of the Battleship *Bismarck* and her cruiser consort *Prinz Eugen*. Damage to *Bismarck*, and the need to provide potential cover for her arrival at Brest, resulted in orders for the 4th Flotilla to proceed to Lorient. Poor weather and the loss of *Bismarck* on May 27 prevented the departure of the flotilla, but the episode was still disruptive. During the rest of May and throughout June, with the long hours of summer daylight providing little cover, and with preparations under way for Operation Barbarossa, the boats made just a handful of sorties and sank few ships. It also perhaps did not help that, to try and maintain the appearance of several S-boat flotillas operational in the Channel and the North Sea, the 4th Flotilla spread its operations between Rotterdam, Boulogne, and Cherbourg (thereby further tiring the aging boats). By July, newer boats reached the 4th Flotilla, operating from Cherbourg, to begin replacing the older S-boats, which were no longer fit for frontline service. By July 7, four boats were ready and available for operations (an improvement on the earlier operational state of the flotilla). The development of hardened bunkers at Oostende (first stage opened June 10) and Boulogne (first stage opened June 21), to complement the vaulted basin at Cherbourg (completed in January), also helped to underpin a campaign designed to tie down forces rather than deal significant blows to the British coastal convoy system.[52] Work was also under way at Rotterdam (first stage opened October 11) and Ijmuiden (opened February 1942) to provide additional bunkers and to further develop the infrastructure to support the campaign along the southern and eastern coasts.[53] By August 18, as the Naval High Command was pressing for an early release of the S-boat flotillas sent into the Baltic, the 4th Flotilla arrived back in Rotterdam to continue mining and torpedo operations. It was in this port on October 3 that several of the flotilla's boats were damaged in an air raid and rendered temporarily unserviceable. It was not until the arrival of the 2nd Flotilla on October 9 that operations could be resumed with a joint 2nd Flotilla and 4th Flotilla attack on the East Coast convoy routes on October 12.

Despite the disruptions caused by Operation Barbarossa, the total of S-boat sinkings in 1941 was impressive—twenty-nine ships totaling 58,854 GRT.[54] The Royal Navy was worried enough to ask the Royal Air Force if it could help combat the S-boat menace using Coastal Command aircraft.[55] Despite such evidence of rising concerns on the part of the British, the reality was that a strategic opportunity had been missed. The war in the West had been left to the navy as Hitler had turned east. Even within the navy, given the emphasis on the tonnage war, there was an impression that Germany's submarines, with contributions from the surface ships, might just force the British to the point of surrender. At the senior levels in the Kriegsmarine there was scant recognition of the potential importance of the coastal convoys, as perhaps the weakest link in Britain's supply chain network. In the vast North Atlantic, with U-boats forced to operate miles from base, it was hard to find, fix, and attack convoys with devastating results. Indeed, most of the U-boat victories of "the first happy time" involved the interception and sinking of stragglers or independently routed vessels. In the Channel and the East Coast, geography, which offered friendly bases and air cover, favored the attacking power. Coastal convoys were easy to find and easy to attack, posing significant risks to the functioning of the British war economy.

By May 1941, however, instead of increasing the strike potential of light German naval vessels in the West, Germany's military leaders were leaving the 4th S-boat Flotilla to somehow maintain the appearance that the campaign was ongoing. Rather than exploiting the moment of strategic opportunity through a concentration of existing S-boat forces while growing numbers of new vessels were coming through construction, the Kriegsmarine was fighting a holding action in the English Channel, while perhaps buying too wholeheartedly into the propaganda rhetoric surrounding the war-winning capabilities of the submarine service. Indeed, as the opportunity was being squandered in the English Channel, German submarines were hunting ever farther afield in the North Atlantic in the hope of exploiting some weakness in the convoy system. That in turn would lead to growing antagonisms with the United States that had serious consequences. There was a weakness in the convoy system, but the best way to exploit it was in English waters, and with S-boats rather than submarines.

## CHAPTER 3

# THE CAMPAIGN IN THE BALANCE, 1941–1942

AS 1941 GAVE WAY TO 1942, the S-boat campaign rose to new heights as the flotillas returned from the East. With this second opportunity to paralyze the British coastal trade, the Germans and British initially matched each other's pace in trying to get ahead in the convoy battles on the southern and eastern coasts. Crucially, the German High Command showed little awareness of the opportunity before them in English waters, and the S-boat campaign failed to gain adequate resources or momentum. Instead, it was the British who seized the opportunity before them to find increasingly effective ways of combating the German campaign. In 1940 Germany enjoyed a head start in the coastal campaign, but once that had been squandered, the British were not about to allow them the opportunity to regain the upper hand.

The 2nd S-boat Flotilla took up residence at Ijmuiden on January 6, at Boulogne on January 4, and at Oostende on January 6. Limited operations against British coastal shipping were interrupted in early February by Operation Cerberus, the transit through the English Channel of the German heavy ships *Scharnhorst*, *Gneisenau*, and *Prinz Eugen*. All the German light forces in the English Channel were required to provide support to the operation as the heavy units departed Brest shortly after 2100 hours on February 11. That support ranged from diversionary operations by 6th Flotilla, to escort duty by 4th Flotilla, while the 2nd Flotilla waited at instant readiness to sortie if required. In the event the three heavy ships, with some damage, completed the transit, leading to soul searching in Britain as to how the Kriegsmarine had safely transited the Channel—a feat that had proved to be beyond the Spanish Armada.

For the S-boat flotillas Cerberus was followed almost immediately by mining operations off the East Coast, and S-53 was lost on one such operation on February 19. Mining and torpedo missions continued during February and March 1942, although the 6th Flotilla was relocated to Narvik in mid-February. While the mining operations took a steady toll on Allied shipping, the torpedo actions were unsuccessful, which provided evidence of the growing efficiency of British defenses: growing numbers of escort vessels were being backed by increasingly sophisticated intelligence and detection systems. Likewise, the containment of the threat from contact and magnetic mines was testament to the provision of greater numbers, under emergency war contracts of purpose-built wooden motor minesweepers to replace the trawlers and other vessels taken up from trade in 1939.[1] Nevertheless, the British remained painfully aware of the ongoing threat posed by the S-boat. A sortie by the 2nd Flotilla on March 11 resulted in the torpedoing of the collier SS *Horseferry* (11 fatalities). Four days later S-104 (2nd Flotilla), attacking convoy FS749, sank the escorting destroyer HMS *Vortigern* (110 fatalities). On the run home to Oostende, S-111 was lost after an engagement with British Coastal Forces. During April and May, the S-boats operating against the East Coast experienced repeated contacts with British Coastal Forces that frustrated attempts to intercept convoys. The shorter nights of summer, in addition to strengthening defenses, forced the flotillas to operate farther west in the Channel. But maintenance and supply issues meant that just five boats remained operational between the 2nd and 4th Flotillas.

The weather added a further complication to the operational availability of the S-boat flotillas. Rough weather limited the scope for torpedo operations, and sea state 5 was really at the limit of what S-boat crews could tolerate even for mining operations. The frustration of Admiral Saalwächter (the head of Naval Command West) with the operational impact of the weather on S-boat operations for May 1942 can be glimpsed in the command war diary. There are several references to this effect: "FdS reports no S-boat use due to weather conditions" (meldet kein S-booteinsatz wegen Wetterlage).[2] By the middle of the month he was complaining about the limited seaworthiness ("beschraenkter Seefähigkeit") of the S-boat and that the weather had shut down operations for three weeks.[3] May 1942 eventually yielded five mining operations (one of which had to be broken off due to fog), with an average eight boats in operation at any one time. Admiral Saalwächter, the head of Naval Command West, reflected that for torpedo operations this was a completely inadequate number. He believed that, with enemy resistance in the Channel hardening, a larger number of boats ("gröesser Bootszahlen") was required, preferably to allow attacks in multiple waves ("möeglichst in mehreren Wellen, erfolgsversprechend").[4] Although improved weather in June allowed an increase to twelve operations, the difficulties facing the S-boat campaign were apparent, especially when S-boats had to undertake more defensive operations, such as supporting German coastal convoys along the Franco-Belgian-Dutch coasts that were themselves targets for British motor torpedo boats and the aircraft of RAF Coastal Command.

The first half of 1942 had appeared to demonstrate that British countermeasures against the S-boat campaign (allied with the weather) were highly efficient and that the worst of the campaign might be over. Reaching the Royal Navy were the outputs from the 1941–42 construction program agreed to in April 1941 by the War Cabinet, which envisaged the building of 32 motor torpedo boats, 32 Fairmile "B" launches, 40 Fairmile "D" launches, 72 smaller motor launches, 40 destroyers, 15 coastal minesweepers, and 14 sloops.[5] The Royal Navy also benefited in 1942 from the arrival of 20 Elco 77-foot motor torpedo boats (MTBs 307–26), which Secretary of the U.S. Navy Frank Knox had taken the liberty of ordering for the British in March 1941. The British preferred their own design by Vosper (although in reality there was little to choose between them) and it was with some reluctance that the Royal Navy was persuaded to take them.[6] The impact of all these vessels was very quickly felt on the campaign in the Channel, not just in terms of numbers and firepower but also in terms of the relentlessness with which they were prepared to press home their attacks against German coastal forces, and the supply convoys that the Germans equally needed to pass along close to the shores of occupied Europe. The war diary for German Naval Command West noted one engagement in June 1942 between British and German coastal forces that had closed to a range of just ten meters, with 20-mm cannon, MG34 machine guns, and hand grenades being used at point-blank range.

There was some surprise that one British boat had tried to ram a German counterpart ("Gunboot versuchte zu rammen").[7]

Despite the increasing ferociousness of British Coastal Forces, an attack on convoy WP183 (Milford Haven to Portsmouth) on July 8 served as a powerful reminder of the defenselessness of coasters if S-boats got in among them. Five merchant ships and an escorting trawler were sunk. The contact had been assisted by Luftwaffe aerial reconnaissance, and the following day German bombers attacked the convoy, sinking another six ships. The disaster of convoy WP183 brought back the worst fears of 1940, when S-boats, working in tandem with the Luftwaffe, had proved so effective. With the 5th Flotilla deploying to Boulogne in July, it seemed as though the tide of battle in the coastal campaign might be about to turn in Germany's favor once more despite the meager pickings of torpedo operations in early 1942. The outbreak of war with Japan naval operations in the Far East meant that in early 1942, as the First Lord of the Admiralty commented in April, "the navy is now bearing a far greater strain than at any time since the war began."[8]

The relocation of the 6th Flotilla to Dutch waters in September suggested that with the approach of longer winter nights the Kriegsmarine was about to redouble its efforts. Both sides were concerned about the future evolution of the campaign. For the British it was apparent that if the Germans could get to grips with a convoy, the slaughter could be considerable. On the other side, the growing effectiveness and number of Allied escort vessels was increasingly troubling, and during the summer of 1942, FdS, the head of the S-boat Service (recently separated from the previous FdT command), initiated several programs (discussed later) to enhance the effectiveness of S-boat operations. Those programs did mean that during the late summer and autumn of 1942 some S-boats would be out of service as work was carried out on them in the dockyards of occupied Europe.

## COASTAL CONVOYS: ORGANIZATION AND DEFENSE

By this stage of the war the level of protection that could be afforded to the coastal convoys had improved significantly since the days of 1940. The East Coast mine belt now ran from the Thames Estuary to the Moray Firth, and convoying close to the coast ensured minimal losses.[9] The defensive belt of mines, consisting of over 35,000 contact mines, kept German minelayers (submarines and surface vessels) at arm's distance from the coast.[10] Despite the convoying, some ships were still sent independently around the coasts of Britain, and mines continued to take a steady toll on the independents: "Of ships sunk by mine in UK coastal waters, three out of every four were sailing independently although the bulk of our shipping was in convoy."[11]

The growing number of wrecks, particularly on the East Coast, added to the difficulties of navigating the convoy routes. At each new sinking, one of the Trinity House vessels stationed along the East Coast would come out to "survey and buoy a diversion from the shallow swept channel."[12] The growing number of wrecks along the East Coast held a particular fascination for the seamen who had to navigate around them. Veteran Captain J. O. Rowlands later recounted: "We were passing new wrecks every passage, some of them having sunk in strange positions; one wreck north of Cromer had gone down with only her stern in the water, with her bows as far as the bridge out of the water, sitting quite upright on her stern, and visible a long way off. Another wreck we were passing appeared like a submarine on the surface, and was often fired at by some of the foreign going vessels, who were strange on the coast, being misled by its appearance."[13] The growing collection of East Coast wrecks posed a growing obstacle to the navigation of routes in addition to difficult currents and shoals, and war-related dangers. The difficulties of the route, and the regularity with which it was plied created considerable strain on the part of those serving aboard the ships and left very little opportunity to address problems such as buoys that had dragged their anchors or wrecks in hazardous places. The channels and navigational hazards meant a gauntlet of dangers and potential ambush spots for every passage. Churchill noted, "As it was impossible to vary the East Coast route, the passage of each convoy between the Forth and London became almost every day an action in itself."[14] Tragedies resulted: for example, on the night of August 5, 1941, seven merchant ships from FS559 missed a marker buoy and were lost on Haisborough Sands (a ten-mile-long shoal); lifeboats from Cromer and Great Yarmouth rescued the crews.[15] The loss of over ten thousand tons of merchant shipping as a result of a navigational error was hard to stomach even though the crews had been saved.

If convoying and navigation was the key to the security of the coastal convoys, then their organization and management remained difficult. At the start of the war, it was hoped that convoys along the East Coast could be kept down to a maximum of thirty-five ships, because the narrowness of the marked and swept channel meant that a formation of just two columns could be utilized. In practice by 1942 coastal convoys numbered over sixty vessels, meaning that a convoy spread out over miles of sea.[16] This, in turn, as Peter Gretton noted, made for difficulties in station-keeping as the columns of ships navigated "the tides and the bends in the narrow channels which twisted their way through the sand banks of the East Coast route."[17] These factors, together with the diverse nature of coastal craft and the differing skill levels of their deck officers, convoy commodores faced considerable managerial difficulties. Indeed, as Alan Burn has pointed out, commodores on coastal convoys were very different from their counterparts on the Atlantic convoys:

> Most of the commodores on the coastal convoys were either Commanders or Lieutenant Commanders in the Royal Naval Reserve. In some ways they did not have so much freedom of action as the Ocean Commodores, because their ships were restricted to narrow corridors and the tails of the columns of their convoys were many miles astern, usually out of sight. Whereas the ocean commodore had sea room and could dispose his convoy over a wide front and exercise his charges before entering the danger zones and had some chance to maneuver and take evasive action when attacked, the coastal convoy commodore had no such options.[18]

Against the torpedo, cannon, and mine of the Kriegsmarine and Luftwaffe, coaster crews were largely defenseless. The mild steel and wood of ships' bridges could be augmented with sandbags and, from 1940, with "plastic armor" comprising bitumen and aggregate. Small ships could not mount the kind of weapons, or provide the crews, that oceangoing ships might carry. Equipping coasters with defensive weapons presented greater problems.[19] Stripped down and minimalist in design, they did not have the mounting places for heavy weapons or possess the accommodation space for gunners. One merchant seaman later recalled an exchange as he waited to leave port: "I was standing on the Dock corner at Amble when a young man, packed with gear on his back and a .303 rifle from the Great War, came up to me and said, 'Can you tell me where the *Bandicar* is mister?' I said, 'You're looking at her son.' 'Thanks' he said, 'I'm your gunner' and that was our armament."[20]

Weapons such as the Bofors 40-mm and 4-inch gun required deck areas to be stiffened to absorb the recoil. Mounting machine guns (usually of World War I vintage) was less of a difficulty, but they were unlikely to be effective against most forms of attack.[21] Such weapons were augmented by other "innovative" weapons. The Holman projector, which used steam or compressed air to fire a hand grenade into the air against low-flying aircraft, was considered particularly dangerous. Adjusting the steam or compressed air pressure, and the fuse on the grenade, to control the timings of an explosion against a low-flying aircraft was a tricky business, and to get it wrong would result in a live grenade landing on the deck. At best an exploding grenade might force an aircraft to break off a bomb run. At worst it would kill the crew manning the projector.

The Royal Navy placed an order for one thousand of the Mark 1 Holman projectors in February 1940, and they were deployed quite widely. With the Mark 1, compressed air bottles could supply enough pressure to launch fifty projectiles, with up to thirty grenades a minute being launched into the air. One unexpected feature of the Holman projector was that a grenade bursting in the air gave out a puff of black smoke, making any barrage appear far more formidable and potentially deadly than was in fact the case. Development of the Mark II projector, using steam power, followed quickly after the initial order for the Mark I, as a weapon suitable for vessels such as steam trawlers that had abundant steam power. A final, Mark III version of the projector was developed in 1941 that could launch a projectile one thousand feet in the air, but this only seems to have been fitted to certain craft (e.g., some motor gunboats). For coasters the Holman projector had the advantages that there was little recoil (hence strengthening of decks was not an issue) and that it required little technical skill for basic operation. The coastal convoys were also the ones most likely to suffer from low-level aerial attack, making the weapon suited for deployment on ships in those waters.

Anti-aircraft balloons were similarly problematic for coaster crews. During the summer of 1940, balloons were introduced on the coastal convoys. Handled by the Mobile Balloon Barrage Flotilla, they were intended to make life difficult for Luftwaffe pilots seeking to attack the coastal convoys.[22] Controlling the balloons was very difficult, however, and they were generally despised as more trouble than they were worth.[23] The Royal Navy on whose minesweepers they were also introduced rapidly came to the same conclusion and dropped their use on its vessels, even though they had proved effective on at least one occasion.[24] One photograph of a balloon deployed off a coaster that was released to the American press on April 24 did, however, make some interesting claims about their effectiveness: "Kite balloons, little sisters of the barrage variety, have accounted for at least six enemy aircraft, and have saved over 200 ships during air attacks on coastal traffic around Britain. Merchant skippers, at first distrustful, now appreciate the value of the balloons, and the majority would not sail without them. Dive-bombing and mast-high attacks are now hazardous, and even if the enemy tries to destroy the balloons by firing bullets, he himself offers a target to the ships gunners while doing so."[25]

Having sufficient personnel to man machine guns and handle balloons was always going to be a problem on board coasters. The provision of gunners under the Defensively Equipped Merchant Ship (DEMS) scheme was always problematic for coasters with small crews and Spartan accommodation. Some companies, such as Coast Lines, might have surplus accommodation, since their ships had been designed to carry a few passengers. Most coasters, however, had no such capacity. A working solution of a kind was found on February 27, 1940, when the War Office agreed to supply army gunners and machine guns to East Coast vessels that could accommodate them. Typically, a machine gun team might embark at Southend and leave the ship when it reached its destination on Tyneside or at the Firth of Forth. The gun team could then return home by joining a southbound convoy. Even with the addition of trained gun teams, coasters simply did not possess the firepower to engage and deter attacking S-boats.

## THE CONVOY ACTIONS OF LATE 1942

Once an S-boat Gruppe had closed with a convoy, the losses were likely to be significant, and by the end of autumn 1942 the S-boat flotillas were ready and equipped to press home their attack on the convoy lanes. Until the longer days of summer drew to a close, however, the early results were not wholly encouraging. The number of operations they managed in August was modest: three torpedo and six mining operations.[26] In the next month, however, this dropped away substantially, so that Admiral Wilhelm Marschall, who had taken over from Admiral Saalwächter as head of Naval Command West on September 20, could only report abandoned and inconclusive S-boat operations in the command roundup for that month.[27] The precise circumstances of Saalwächter's replacement are rather mysterious, and it would not be unreasonable to speculate that it might have something to do with perceptions about how the campaign in the Channel was going after substantial investments had been made. If German Naval High Command was hoping that new leadership might lead to improved results, then on October 7, on the East Coast, convoy FN832 was attacked by a force of seventeen S-boats. Five merchant ships were lost, along with an escorting motor launch (ML339). Over the next month, operations against convoys would yield the occasional victim, but nothing like the destruction handed out to FN832. There was general satisfaction, though, at the sense of renewed momentum in the campaign. In the monthly roundup in the war diary for Naval Group Command West, Admiral Marschall reflected that nine torpedo and three mining operations had been staged during October, including, for the first time ever, an operation staged with twenty-six S-boats ("erstmalig ein S-Booteinsatz mit 26 Booten gefahren").[28] There would be one further devastating convoy action before the end of the year. On November 19, 1942, the Cherbourg-based 5th S-boat Flotilla closed with convoy PW250 off the coast of Cornwall. The action led to the sinking of four ships (one Royal Naval Patrol Service whaler and three merchant ships) and the death of fifty-four seamen from Britain, Norway, Estonia, and Belgium.

Despite the losses, 1942 revealed that British defenses had improved considerably since 1940. The withdrawal of German forces to the East in 1941 had given British forces a breathing space in which to make good some obvious deficiencies. The tide of the Battle in the Atlantic had started to turn against German forces in 1942, even if the Kriegsmarine was still able to launch effective attacks on coastal convoys and to take the fight to areas where British defenses were not so developed. During 1942, some twenty-three ships (71,156 tons) had been sunk by torpedoes fired from S-boats, in addition to the steady toll of victims resulting from mining operations. By the end of the year, sufficient S-boats were available to swamp local defenses, as happened with FN832. The question was whether the resources were available to routinely repeat this success. During 1942 the campaign had hung in the balance, and the British were building momentum faster than the Germans. With the U-boat campaign in the Atlantic also reaching a crescendo, it was clear that 1943 might be the decisive moment in the campaign against British shipping.[29]

## CHAPTER 4

# THE HUMAN DIMENSION

THE LOSSES OF SIX VESSELS on convoy FN832 in October 1942 was a salient reminder to the authorities not to lose sight of the human dimension in a campaign that was being played out within sight of shore. Sometimes in military history there is a tendency to downplay the human elements of a campaign in which abstract notions of strategy and tactics, the impact of new technologies, and the faceless movements of task forces, battle groups, and escort groups can mask the human dramas playing out within them. For the mariners on the coastal runs (the merchant seamen of various nations, those charged with escorting them, and those whose duty it was to sink them), there was a very human side to maintaining the flow of coal and other goods; likewise for the coastal communities that provided the sailors and the vessels for the campaign. The government relied on the cooperation and patriotism of those communities, and it was necessary to acknowledge, at least to some extent, the struggles taking place in Britain's coastal waters. The coastal trade was an intrinsic element in the British maritime identify. To the groups that fought the coastal campaign, the merchant seamen and the Coastal Forces of the Royal Navy, the war in the Channel and the East Coast became an important part of their identity and fed back into their attitudes toward a postwar Britain. On both the British and the German side there was a feeling that their war was overshadowed by other facets of the war at sea. This chapter explores the human dimension of the bitter struggles taking place close to the British shore.

### BRITISH WAR REPORTS ON "E-BOAT ALLEY"

From various perspectives, early reporting in the British media of the East Coast and Channel battles left much to be desired, with censorship playing a role in limiting the public's understanding of the threat to U.K. coastal convoys. Attacks by S-boats on cross-Channel traffic involved in the Dunkirk evacuation in May–June 1940 found little place in accounts by the British press shaped of the "miracle of deliverance." By July 1940, British Pathé newsreels covered the Luftwaffe's *Kanalkampf*, but the emphasis was on the skill of the Spitfire pilots rather than on the efforts of the coaster crews to fight through their ships.[1] In August 1940 a Pathé report on convoys under fire from German coastal artillery did at least refer to the "superb seamanship and indomitable courage" of the merchant seamen bringing their ships through under fire.[2] The devastating attacks on convoys CW8 and CW9 in July and August 1940 found little space in the British press, although the Dublin-based newspaper the *Evening Herald* did carry a graphic account of the latter attack (under the heading "Swarms of E-Boats") from the chief officer of one vessel sunk by torpedo: "It was an awful experience. The attack on the convoy by German motor torpedo boats came without any warning. It was pitch dark, and all we could see of the E-boats was the flashes of their machine-guns as they raked the decks of vessels in the convoy. They seemed to be all around us—swarms of them. My own ship was struck by a torpedo, but the entire crew got away in one lifeboat within 3 minutes."[3]

There was little change even in 1941: the amount of press coverage devoted to the conflict in the English Channel was insignificant compared to coverage of events taking place on other battlefronts. The phrase "E-boat alley" as a description of the East Coast convoys did, however, begin to enter common currency.[4] In November 1941, for example, the *Daily Mirror* ran a feature under the headline "E-Boat Alley Is 100 Miles of Danger."[5] The East Coast convoy route was described as "the most hectic piece of water in the world." For the British press, an East Coast convoy represented a quick means to secure the material to write copy. In November 1940 a column was published by an anonymous Able Seaman describing what it was like to be bombed in a Channel convoy.[6] Likewise, in 1943 Herbert W. Richmond (former admiral and distinguished naval historian) wrote a piece titled "Coastal Trade and Flotilla Warfare" that was published in the *Fortnightly Review*.[7] To provide some assurance to readers and to partly allay fears about the S-boat threat, British newspapers reported on the development of Coastal Forces. On February 9, 1942, the *Yorkshire Post* carried an image of a motor gunboat under the heading "Our Miniature Destroyers."[8] Later that same year, on August 1, the *Yorkshire Post* carried an image on the front page of S-111 briefly captured before she sank after an engagement on March 15, 1942.[9] The delay in publication reflected the Admiralty's caution in releasing information that might be useful to the enemy. Later accounts of actions between Coastal Forces and S-boats would emphasize the Royal Navy's fighting spirit, with British sailors "with clubs and cutlasses" ready to board German vessels in order to seize them.[10] Even peaks in S-boat activity could be turned into positive news stories: for example, the *Lancashire Daily Post* declared in 1943 that S-boat activity was a sign of "Berlin's invasion nerves."[11]

Given the involvement of certain coastal communities in the battles along the East Coast, it was unsurprising that the local newspapers would carry features on "E-Boat Alley" and its heroes. In June 1943, one Tyneside newspaper carried a story on the award of an OBE (Order of the British Empire) to the master of a trawler who had been involved in an engagement with S-boats while in convoy in October 1942.[12] The same paper would also carry detailed accounts of convoy actions against German forces on the East Coast.[13] More remarkably, the perils of E-boat alley were also featured in the international press. Both before and after the United States' entry into the war, the American press took a passing interest in the Channel battles. For example, James Minifie's "An Eastbound Convoy," published in *Harper's* in January 1941, gave American readers an insight into the battles taking place off Britain's East Coast.[14] In March 1941, the *Atlantic Monthly* carried a piece on mine warfare and minesweeping in British coastal waters, and in 1943 *Newsweek* carried an account of life in a coastal convoy.[15]

Such reporting, and occasional references to the coastal battles in books on the war at sea, were at least some reassurances to the sailors engaged on them that the campaign mattered and that their efforts were not going completely unrecognized even as the Battle of the Atlantic, the strategic bombing campaign, and land battles filled the newspapers.[16] But there was always the sense that the work of coaster crews and British Coastal Forces was consistently underreported. During the war, the Ministry of Information brought out a steady stream of pamphlets detailing their work: for example, *Coastal Command, Combined Operations, 1940–42*; *Eighth Army*; *His Majesty's Minesweepers*; and a dozen other titles. Only a couple of them briefly mentioned incidents on the coastal convoys, and it was not until 1947 that the title *British Coaster, 1939–45* was published.[17]

Only very rarely glimpsed in publications, letters, memoirs, diaries, and oral history accounts was the human strain involved in long hours, combat stress, and the fast-paced horror of ambush engagements. The strain of operations inevitably took its toll on many of those involved. Coastal Forces veteran Leading Seaman Ken Forrester later gave a graphic account of the strain of operations for those in coastal operations:

> There had to be some comfort somewhere. I then entered my phase of drinking heavily. People at home and in my home area could not (or should I say did not) understand. I was branded a drunkard by people who were supposed to be friends. When you think of it coolly, there was just no escape—there were mines to sail over—attack by aircraft while at sea—always seemed to be in action—always getting battle damage—at action stations all night—the sight of ambulances waiting as you returned—then straight to the refueling wharf and all power cut because of the fear of explosion. That completed, we could then get our breakfast—not forgetting we were liable at any time to be bombed by planes while at Great Yarmouth. . . . Next, it was clean and dry guns and ammunition, and finally fall asleep for a few hours—then it was the same all over again. There was no future as we next sailed down the river, lined up on deck with music playing over the tannoy system. You saw soldiers and airmen with girlfriends happily walking on the embankments. Together with the bomber crews we thought we were getting a rough deal. . . . Morale was at breaking point. The skipper would send me ashore to the Commander's office to collect the sailing orders, and I wished I could get knocked down and a leg or arm broken, anything to be saved from sailing into the unknown. Drink was our only comfort.[18]

## "WE'RE ALL IN IT TOGETHER"

Despite the lack of press coverage, by late 1942 and early 1943 there was a sense that the campaign in U.K. coastal waters seemed to raise issues relating to the nature of a British identity undergoing radical change because of the impact of war. British society was experiencing a degree of forced egalitarianism as the blitz, wartime rationing, and military service challenged the social boundaries of class. To meet the challenge of total war required commitment across British society, and that was particularly evident in the struggle to maintain the coastal convoys. The upper-middle-class graduates of the Royal Navy's officer training establishments commanding the escort destroyers needed the cooperation of the hard-bitten Merchant Navy professionals of half a dozen nations manning the coasters and other small vessels on the coastal run. They in turn needed the support of army gunners and Royal Air Force pilots to defend them. This sense of diversity within the team that ensured the continued running of the coastal convoys was the subject of a January 1943 edition of *War* produced by the Army Bureau of Current Affairs (ABCA).[19] In a special edition devoted to the Merchant Navy, the journalist Anthony Cotterell took two trips on the East Coast run: one on a destroyer, the other on a coaster.[20] From two very different perspectives he gave vivid accounts of the struggle to maintain the coastal convoys, demonstrating tri-service cooperation and the sense of all elements in a society pulling together in the interests of survival. It was, of course, a propaganda image that bore little resemblance to the realities of life on the coastal run.

The image of a nation united in common struggle was by no means unusual, but within the confines of the totemic struggle for hearth and home, and the security of the British coast, formed by the coastal campaign it was particularly potent. What was also significant is the potential political impacts of such imagery and reporting. *War*, the biweekly bulletin of ABCA, was supposed to be distributed to troops and used as the basis for discussions on current affairs by their commanding officers. The image of coastal convoys as state-planned harmony run for the benefit of all society, instead of for a narrow elite, called into question the prewar social, economic, and political order that had helped to produce the circumstances in which the enemy was once again, as in 1588, close to the shores of England.

Nowhere was this process of radicalization more evident than in the British Coastal Forces, whose job it was to disrupt the S-boat campaign and German coastal convoys off the shores of occupied Europe. The men who crewed the motor gunboats (MGBs) and their smaller cousin, the motor torpedo boats (MTBs), within British Coastal Forces were a combination of career naval officers and men, officers of the Royal Naval Volunteer Reserve (RNVR), volunteers, and draftees serving for the duration of the war. As Farquharson-Roberts notes, within Coastal Forces the men of the RNVR quickly came to dominate its ranks due to wartime expansion, which created an almost insatiable demand for officers with experience.[21] Many RNVR officers were peacetime amateur sailors with considerable experience in small boat handling and navigating coastal waters. They quickly won over the regular officers in Coastal Forces.

In turn the enthusiasm and professionalism of Coastal Forces crews made a favorable impression on both RNVR and regular officers:

> The active service ratings were, many of them, magnificent hands, but some were matelots who thought they would get a slack and easy existence in small boats, far removed from the harsh words and deeds of the petty officer in a battleship. These men needed driving. The "Hostilities Only" crews were truly amazing. They were so keen to do their share in downing the Nazis, that they could be knocked into shape in a matter of weeks. Raw boys, from the machine shops, the lathes, the potteries, the railways, the farms, they put up with that most dreadful of scourges, seasickness in smelly engine rooms and stuffy W/T cabins, and they acquitted themselves like seasoned men in the face of the enemy.[22]

This sense of camaraderie and togetherness was emphasized by the relentless nature of the campaign being waged in Britain's coastal waters. To the strains of a nocturnal existence were added the physical demands of being tossed around in small boats, sometimes at speed. As MTB officer Anthony Law noted, stomach problems, strains, falls on deck, and the odd broken bone were the inevitable consequence.[23] The strain was considerable and the demands unrelenting. The war diaries and other records relating to Coastal Forces highlight the pace of nightly operations. The war diary for 7th MGB Flotilla based at Lowestoft for November 19–20, 1941, is typical:

> MGBs 87 & 89 left harbour 1425 5 Buoy. 1429 Cut engines oil pressure low on 89. Returned to harbour, entered 1529. 1615 89 proceeded to N.Wall, centre engine unbuttoned. 1438 87 proceeded. 1450 54F Buoy. 1557 52 buoy. Cut engines; fired small arms. 1602 Sighted HMS *Mallard*. 1610 52 Buoy. Cut engines, fired small arms. 1639 Contacted HMS *Campbell*. 1650 carried out manoeuvres. 1810 5 buoy. 2135 vicinity of 60 Buoy. Destroyer attacked vessel. Fired .5." Vessel fired two-star cartridge; believed to be ML2220 55A buoy. 2332 ship 8 miles to N.W. Torpedoed. Destroyer sighted E-boat to Port. Tracer observed coming from S-bound convoy. Destroyer fired star-shell; E-boat laid smoke screen visible in star shell. 2340 2 E-boats sighted on easterly course. Leading E-boat engaged on Port hand. Range 1000 yards. Two E-boat sighted on Starboard beam and fired on. 2345 Left destroyer and proceeded to chase first E-boat.... [Thursday, November 20] (MGB87) 0010 lost E-boat. Cut engines. 0015 Proceeded to Brown Ridge. 0116 Stopped at Brown Ridge. 0024 Course S 10 E. 0234 Cut engines. 0605 left Brown Ridge. 0745 Saw HMS *Garth* under tow. 0805 5 Buoy. 0830 entered harbour.[24]

The constant strain, danger, and the process of social mixing generated some interesting thoughts about the future. One wartime account was unusually frank in its comments about the outlook of the men of British Coastal Forces:

> Then someone started on the evergreen subject of our political leaders. These men knew something from personal experience of the state of preparedness of this country at the time of Dunkirk. They remembered how, for a year and a half after Dunkirk, they were expected to seek out . . . and fight . . . [S-]boats with gunboats, armed only with .303s against the [S-]boats 20-mm guns. They observed that, except for Mr. Churchill, and very few others, the same men were still in power. These men, like all the other

fighting services, did their job. But they are damned if they have done it to keep in power the incompetent muddlers who brought the war on through their criminal deception of the public. They have seen friends tabled, and others reprimanded and displaced for small failures of efficiency in difficult and dangerous work (as it must be) and they want to know why incompetence at the top goes unpunished.[25]

## S-BOAT CREWS

The men of the German Coastal Forces came to the Channel battles with a different mindset. While the crews of British Coastal Forces could see themselves as descendants of a tradition running onward from Drake, through Nelson and beyond, the men of the Kriegsmarine had a shorter history on which to draw for their ethos and identity. As Nicolas Wolz points out about World War I, the German navy was the young service of a state that had only come together in the 1870s.[26] A generation later, the Kriegsmarine from 1933 could draw on a Great War legacy of one or two inspirational leaders and the occasional victory, wrapped around by strategic failure, and tainted by the stain of Red revolution in 1918. While the Kriegsmarine would rapidly raise new heroes to which the German sailor could aspire (particularly among the U-boat commanders), the legacies of World War I continued to cast a long shadow. The battle of the River Plate in December 1939, carrying with it echoes of the grand scuttle of the German High Seas fleet in 1919, was an uncomfortable reminder of those legacies to a new generation of war sailors of the Reich. With the war shifting to the Channel Coast in 1940, S-boat crews found themselves in occupied France, facing an enemy buoyed by a successful naval tradition and the knowledge that it was fighting for the survival of its homeland.

The men who commanded and crewed the S-boats cannot be thought of in simplistic terms and reconstructing their beliefs and motivations, perhaps changing over time, through letters, diaries, memoirs, oral history, and family memories is an exceptionally difficult task more than eighty years after the outbreak of World War II.[27] For example, Ulrich Kolbe, who would go on to command S-85, came from a conservative northern German naval background. Hans, his father (1882–1957), had served in the Kaiser's navy, rising to the rank of vice admiral before retirement in 1934. Joining the Nazi Party in that year, he would go on to serve as administrator of the Schleswig and Eckernförde districts. It was no surprise that Ulrich would join the Kriegsmarine in 1935–36 and would follow his father's specialism in torpedoes. According to his private family memoir and to family stories, Ulrich had no great enthusiasm for a naval career, but he was thrilled by the technology and engineering of the S-boats. He would later go on to a career in teaching and have no time for meetings of Alte Kameraden. Disgusted by some aspects of the Nazi regime, in late 1935 he was extensively interrogated over several days by the Gestapo as part of an investigation in Kiel. At least for a while, though, he seems to have believed in the unique greatness of German character and culture and in Germany's civilizing mission. That belief did not sit easily with his outrage at witnessing the destruction of the synagogue in Königstein during Kristallnacht in 1938 during a period of recuperation following a motorbike accident. He had at least one contact inside the German resistance to Hitler and was amazed on being invited to dinner by a close family relation, who was a senior army officer in France, at the defeatist talk of senior officers and their contemptuous references to "the Greatest Commander of all time" (Hitler). As the war developed and turned against Germany, his disillusionment grew steadily. He was kept going by a powerful sense of duty to country, to family, and to shipmates and by a powerful sense of what was right and wrong even if the Nazis suggested that morality had no place in total war. For Kolbe, and for many Germans between 1933 and 1945, there was a complexity of thoughts and emotions and great difficulty in trying to do one's duty, during war, while negotiating private morality and the many evils of the Nazi regime.

While a lack of qualitative data limits our ability to understand the motivations and outlook of most of the men who crewed the S-boats, some limited insights into their identities can be gained from wartime records. Wartime interrogation reports contain useful details about those men of the S-boat arm who fell into Allied hands. For example, the interrogation reports of the crew of S-53 (2nd S-boat Flotilla), lost on February 20, 1942, off Lowestoft, yield details of the age and experience profile of the crew. The average age of the nine crew members interrogated (eighteen total survivors from a crew of twenty-four) was just 20.5.[28] Six of the crew members were from the towns and cities of Germany's industrial heartland in the West (Dortmund, Stuttgart, Gelsenkirchen), along with one man from the eastern provinces (Wintersdorf, Thuringia), one from Austria (Vienna), and one from Hamburg. Three had enlisted in the Kriegsmarine before the outbreak of war. After they joined the navy, their basic training in northern Germany had taken two to three months before they had moved onto specialist instruction on engines, engineering, or gunnery. Several members of the crew had brothers serving in the army, and two had fathers who had been called into the armed forces. As detailed by Jac Baart, once posted to operational flotillas they were billeted in hotels requisitioned by the military.[29] Training would take place at the hotels in the morning, and crews would be collected before being taken to the flotilla bases to work on the boats in prospect of a nighttime operation. In the case of S-53, based at Ijmuiden, the crew were housed in the Hotel Stein at Zandvort, along with the crew of S-104. Other crews from the flotilla lived nearby in the Hotel Pfenning. Crews carried small arms for personal protection, and sentries guarded the buildings.

S-boat officers tended to differ from their men in minor ways. An analysis of twenty-five officers from the S-boat service awarded the Knight's Cross during the war shows that they were an average age of 26.5 years old in late 1940 (even though the list is skewed by the inclusion of the forty-six-year-old Führer der Torpedoboote [FdT] and Kapitän-zur-See von Bütow). S-boat officers were only marginally older than their crewmen. While again there was a considerable number of officers drawn from the cities and towns of Germany's industrial heartland in the West, three were from Berlin and eight from Kiel, Flensburg, and other places on the Baltic. In some cases officers had family connections to the maritime sphere. Of the twenty-five men, one (Bütow) had entered the Kaiser's navy, and two the Reichsmarine before 1933 (Petersen and Kemnade); the rest had entered the Kriegsmarine from 1934 to 1937.

In many ways the S-boat service from top to bottom was a tight-knit family. After entering the Kriegsmarine and undergoing basic training a seamen could apply for service in S-boats. They enjoyed a high reputation, as the nature of their operations offered certain attractions to the long cruises of surface warships and submarines.[30] Training at Swinemünde, followed by life in a flotilla (often based around small dormitories and at bases) and operations within the cramped confines of an S-boat, created close bonds and an intimate understanding of crewmates. A high degree of formality was maintained between officers and men and S-boat crews seem to have retained a keen sense of themselves as seamen. They loved their vessels, with their sleek lines and craftsmanship, and were very aware of their superiority over their British gasoline-powered rivals. Even so, there were frequent periods of boredom, combined with stress induced by operations, aerial bombing, or ground attack by the resistance. The sense of camaraderie among crews was considerable. For example, on one mission S-85 was in such close contact with British Coastal Forces that a grenade landed on the bridge. The helmsman was injured by splinters, while the commanding officer was protected by his heavy clothing. Such was the rush to get the wounded helmsman medical attention that S-85 was damaged in passing over a reef near Guernsey.[31]

The strain of combat operations on S-boat crews was considerable, as Ulrich Kolbe, commanding officer of S-85, later remembered. One day a young lieutenant came to see him and sat down on his bed and cried out his concern that he was not up "to the missions. He is so afraid that he puts himself, his boat, his crew, and the flotilla in danger. So, he asked for his transfer. I was touched by his despair."[32] Kolbe asked the FdS to allow him to send the officer back to Germany to pick up a new S-boat on the grounds that he "was still so inexperienced for our more difficult missions."[33] On the return leg of the journey, the S-boat and a sister boat were attacked by MGBs between Rotterdam and Le Havre, and the sister boat was lost in the action. Kolbe recorded in his private family memoir, "He was then demoted by a court martial and sent to Russia for parole at the front. I never heard from him again."

The stresses of combat operations were sometimes relieved by the occasional funny moment. Minelaying was in some ways a safer operation than a torpedo attack on a convoy, and it could be carried out in worse weather, but there could be complications. Ulrich Kolbe was commanding S-85 on a minelaying operation out of Boulogne with another boat when he became aware of a problem on the other boat, which sent "long red" visual signals asking him to stop. Closing with the other boat, Kolbe could see fevered activity at the stern because a mine had jammed on the rails. The men shouted across, "She's already ticking."[34] Unable to free the mine, both boats raced back to Boulogne, where the crews disembarked in some haste. Mine specialists boarded the boat and inspected the ticking mine before calmly reporting, "'The mines have always ticked. They only become active when they have been in the water for about 15 minutes.'"[35]

On operations there was regret at having to sink ships and a powerful awareness that fellow seamen were dying in the process. S-boat man Karl Heinz Thiele, in an interview in 2014, recalled one incident of watching as torpedoes hit a steamer and watching as the crew abandoned ship. Seeing some of the crew lighting cigarettes before going over the side was a painful reminder of the humanity caught up in a successful S-boat attack. Similarly, he recalled the sinking of a destroyer "without a trace. That bothered us a lot. There were human beings on board—just like us."[36] S-boat crews, like their brothers in U-boats, were ready to fish survivors of merchant ships out of the water when opportunity presented itself, but their modus operandi (hit-and-run attacks) and the steadily tilting strategic balance meant that this happened on only a few occasions during the war.

To maintain morale both among S-boat crews, and as part of wider propaganda efforts, German war reporters routinely reported on operations and the wider patterns of warfare in the English Channel and North Sea. With the convoy actions of the summer of 1940, the war reporters of the Kriegsmarine had quickly come to realize that motor torpedo boat attacks in the Channel could make good copy.[37] In August 1940, propaganda magazine *Die Kriegsmarine*, drawing an analogy between the S-boats and the powerful JU87 (Stuka) dive bomber, proclaimed, "Unsere Schnellboote, die Stukas der See" (Our S-boats, the Stukas of the Sea).[38] Unlike a U-boat patrol, which would take several weeks, an S-boat sortie represented a relatively quick way to secure a potentially good story. The nature of the reports filed by German war reporters can be glimpsed from their titles:

"S-Boat Hits Two British Freighters," February 20, 1941[39]
"November Night of the S-Boats off England," November 15, 1941[40]
"S-Boat Alert in the Channel," January 29, 1942[41]
"S-Boats Have Special Orders," January 31, 1943[42]
"German S-Boats Broke Through," September 18, 1943[43]
"German Speedboats Hunting off the English Coast," December 3, 1943[44]

The stories invariably emphasized the speed and power of the S-boat, and the fact that as a weapon of war it allowed the Kriegsmarine to take the fight to within touching distance of the enemy's coast, forcing the British to invest in booms, coastal artillery, and other defenses to protect some English harbors. Stories of S-boat victories were important to ensure the flow of willing volunteers into the Kriegsmarine and the dedication of the boatyard's workers, those performing the demanding task of turning out the S-boats.

The work of the war reporters fed through into other propaganda forms including radio, and more extended print publications. In *Die Kriegsmarine im Kampf um den Atlantik*, Fregattenkapitän Georg von Hase's 1942 compendium covering stories from across the navy, S-boats got their own (if very brief) chapter. The realities of a campaign turning against the S-boats was not allowed to stand in the way of a story of a successful torpedo boat operation and the poetics of certain victory: "We will have success, we hope, we want and we know."[45] Likewise, the beauty of nighttime operations and an S-boat cruising home to a hero's welcome offered a rather different kind of aesthetic, and an appeal to potential recruits to the S-boat service (my secondhand copy was given to someone as a Christmas present in 1943): "The night is beautiful and endlessly far. Then come in the grey of morning. . . . The engines sing their song as always, you sit and swing with the rhythm of the boat."[46]

The work of the S-boat crews featured in the navy's own publications and into books such as Hugo Bürger's *Schnellboote Vor! Ein Erlebnisbericht vom Einsatz einer Schnellboot-Flottille im Osten* (1943).[47] The 140 pages of the publication focused on S-boat operations in the Baltic against the Russians and were lavishly illustrated with 115 pages (11 in full color). Published in the same year, Peter Paul Möbius' 1943 *Schnellboote* was based in part on his experiences as a war reporter going out on S-boat operations.[48] The book covered both operations against the British and the Russians and featured studio portraits of the S-boat commanders who had been awarded the Knight's Cross because of the volume of shipping that they had sunk. Like their U-boat counterparts, the leading S-boat commanders were the "poster boys" of the Kriegsmarine. Sketches of dramatic action complemented a volume of 312 pages. Möbius was at pains to stress that the success of the S-boat, which "had left all the world astonished," did not rest solely on the quality of the boats.[49] A crew "trained to the smallest detail, excellent leadership" and the "dedication of every soldier on board had an impact." Beyond that their success rested on "the German shipbuilders, the machine builders," designers, and "craftsmen."[50]

Möbius' references to the work of the craftsmen and shipyard workers was a recognition of their importance and the need to maintain the impression that they were playing a key role in the German war effort. Little has been written about the work and morale of German shipyards during the war, but some insights are possible in respect of S-boat construction. For the Schlichting, the monthly works newsletter (which appeared under several names) survives in family hands. It displays ample evidence of the enthusiasm and professionalism of shipyard workers in building S-boats.[51] The newsletter started out as a poorly produced newssheet, but over time it grew into a professionally printed mini-magazine. By 1941 the production values had increased, and the contents had become noticeably more ideological. The newsletter was called *Feldpost Zeitung* and featured reports under titles such as "How Far Does Our Continent Grow" and "We Always Have the Better Weapons."[52] The edition for March 1942 celebrated the achievement of the German heavy ships in making the Channel Dash in February, and carried details of the visit to the yard of S-boat commander and Knight's Cross holder Kapitänleutnant Werner Töniges on February 20.[53] The following year, on February 2 the yard received a visit from another Knight's Cross holder, Kapitänleutnant Hermann Opdenhoff.[54] By speeches, in prose, and by image in the works magazine, shipyard workers were encouraged to see themselves as being in partnership with the men of the S-boat arm in defending the German Empire and striking against England like the Vikings of old (while propaganda in the Dutch shipyards evoked the spirit of 1673 and the Third Anglo-Dutch War).[55] Indeed, at the Schlichting Werft some workers from the yard joined the Kriegsmarine, serving in S-boats, and the works magazine would feature their letters to the Schlichting family. The magazine also carried obituaries of some S-boat men and features on others. For example, the newsletter, renamed *Der Werftbote* by July 1942, carried expressions of regret with photographs for two of the crew of S-111 recently killed in action: "We mourn the loss of these two comrades with the parents and the families of the two. We in Travemünde will not forget either."[56] The works magazine highlighted the victories of some of the boats turned out by the yard, and there were regular visits from S-boat officers. Workers would be decorated for their productivity.[57] The commissioning of each boat leaving the yard was celebrated, even with football matches between crews and shipyard workers.[58] On commissioning commanders would sign a friendship book to thank the yard for their new vessel.

**COASTER CREWS**

Against the dedicated and dashing young crews of the Kriegsmarine's S-boat flotillas, the men who crewed the merchant ships on the coastal runs stood in stark contrast. Aged anywhere from their mid-teens to their seventies, the merchant seamen were drawn from more than a dozen nations. Crews on board coasters were small: two or three officers backed by a similar number of able seamen and an engine room staff of two or three engineers and perhaps a couple of stokers.[59] In the British home trades, life was generally unpleasant and markedly different to that experienced by the merchant seamen working for more glamorous companies in the foreign trades. Bulk cargoes with lower profits, the short nature of voyages, and lower wages (home trades seamen were paid less than the foreign trades) made for the most basic of conditions on board ships renowned for being wet and dirty because of their cargoes and low freeboards. Accommodation was basic, to say the least.[60] One journalist who took a voyage on a coaster was struck by the inadequacy of the accommodation even for the master: "The Master showed me into his cabin, which had a bunk down one side, a tall cupboard, a settee and a desk, a small iron safe under the desk, and a small glass-fronted bookshelf."[61] Such conditions helped owners to make profits in peace, but in the circumstances of a war where every sector of the war time economy was crying out for labor, they made life on board a coasting vessel particularly unappealing. Thus, during the war there was some movement to make life more agreeable on the new vessels entering service in the home trades. For example, with the launch of MV *Supremity* in 1944 for Everards, press attention was given to the improved standards of accommodation "enjoyed" by the crew. While it was an improvement on most prewar vessels, the accommodation on MV *Supremity* was still at best an example of penny-pinching minimalism.[62] Standards of food on board were also often extremely low. At least, though, given their short voyages, supplies of fresh produce were available to the cooks on coastal voyages in ways that they frequently were not to the larger vessels engaged on the foreign trades. In addition, coastal crews did not have to cope with extended absences from home and, if they fell ill, could receive medical attention very much sooner than a merchant seaman on an oceanic voyage.

Given such a small number of crew, everyone could expect to play a variety of roles on board ship, particularly when it came to such things as entering port and discharging cargoes. Cooking duties were typically shared, and men were often required to work the twelve-hour stint of a two-watch system, instead of the less tiring eight hours of the three-watch system in use on larger vessels. Skill levels for watch keepers on coasters were not particularly high (little more than the ability to keep the ship heading in the right direction usually by simply following the coast) while observing the rules of the maritime road. This could be evidenced by the syllabus for Board of Trade's "home trades" certificates of competency for masters and mates. There were significant differences from the syllabus required for the identical qualification for the masters and mates employed on the foreign trades.[63] The latter, for example, placed a much greater emphasis on the ability of masters and mates to navigate by the stars and understand the weather. By contrast, as one merchant seaman put it, the certificate for the home trade mate's certificate required "little more than the ability to read and write, and to distinguish between the sun and the moon and one end of a collier from the other."[64] Within the coasting trade there was an Elizabethan disdain for "technical seamen," as opposed to the more practically oriented mariner.[65]

The question of competency for masters and mates in the coasting trade was settled by oral examination; for the foreign trades there was also a process of written examination. The skill level of coaster crews was sufficiently bad that in 1938 the president of the Board of Trade was on the receiving end of some rather pointed questions about under manning and poorly trained crews in the coastal trade.[66] With the advent of war, the Board of Trade went so far as to relax its already lax requirements for the competency of masters and mates in the home trades. Even among masters, the practice of simply following the coast along a frequently traveled route was the basis of their navigation skills: the ability to recognize landmarks (such as inland church steeples, inlets, and small ports) was an essential skill. The difference between the masters of foreign and home trade vessels was well-known: "They say that when a coaster skipper loses sight of the land, he shits himself. When a deep-sea skipper sees some land, he too shits himself."[67]

What the Board of Trade's syllabus for masters and mates could not define, however, was the sort of expert knowledge about local peculiarities, currents, and features that formed the basis of knowledge to operate in shallow tidal waters around the British coast. Detailed local knowledge that in some cases was handed down by word of mouth from one generation to the next, and otherwise was acquired by years of operating in particular waters, was something that could not be examined under any national syllabus. What invariably went with that local knowledge was a very precise understanding about how to handle their vessels in those waters: how to utilize a particular current to best effect when entering an estuary, or which passages were easily navigable at stages of the tide. Those skills became even more important during the war as navigation got steadily more difficult because of minefields, wrecks, and difficulties sometimes in following marked channels. As one gunner on board the MV *River Trent* observed after the war, "You could see shipwrecks all the way down from Hull to Yarmouth. They said you could swim the whole way and have a wreck to rest on all the way down."[68] Navigating at night, through channels swept by minesweepers, was particularly problematic, as

Alan Burn has argued: "Once a convoy was outside the maze of the channels among the shoals off Norfolk and the mouth of the Thames estuary, the ships crept from one to another of the dimly lit buoys which marked the swept channels, though the buoys were often either missing or out of position."[69] Fog added another danger to the process of navigating these channels, although an answer to station keeping in such conditions was quickly found, as one former commodore remembered: "The method of keeping station in foggy weather was with the 'Fog Buoy'; this was a flat board with a kind of funnel attached to it, and was so constructed that when it was towed through the water it would throw a jet of water to a height of 12 to 15 feet according to the speed of the ship. This was towed astern of the ship with a thin strong wire 600 feet long, the ship following keeping the buoy abreast of its bow."[70]

To some extent the differences between foreign and home trade merchant seamen were overplayed because of a strong rivalry between the two. In reality, there was a long-established crossover between the foreign and home trades. There were, though, fundamental differences in the way in which crews and ships operated. In the foreign trades, masters had considerable responsibility for almost every aspect of the operation of their ship. Distance from home and the controlling hand of the shipping company meant that masters had to be prepared to deal with any number of complications arising from entering foreign ports, negotiating with port authorities and businesses, and dealing with local police forces over the misbehavior of merchant seamen. Local practices, local religions, and the attitudes of local officials had to be understood and traversed by the master of a foreign-going ship. He was the man on the spot, and the efficient and safe operation of the ship was in his hands. Liaising with company headquarters in London or Liverpool on anything but the most important issues would result in costly delays. The master of a coastal vessel, by contrast, was routinely in contact with the company, and once the vessel was in port, a simple phone call could summon help, solicit advice, or request orders. To that extent, coastal masters operated rather like railway trains, running on what amounted to a timetable and a fixed route. One merchant seaman later recalled, "Sailing times were never changed, always seven-thirty pm from Southend, arriving at Smith's Knoll lightship at approximately ten-thirty, every week, regular as clockwork."[71] During the war one member of Parliament (MP) complained that Ministry of War Transport was driving crews and ships hard because of the tendency to think about coastal convoys "in terms of railway trains running on rails with a signal every half-a-mile."[72] Tight turnaround times meant that in the wartime coasting trade there were "not a lot of restful periods."[73]

On shore, all merchant seamen faced similar problems. While the men of the Royal Navy had smart uniforms, the lack of a recognizable uniform for Merchant Navy crews often brought unwelcome comments and actions. As one merchant seaman recounted in his memoirs, "In seaport pubs seemingly healthy young men in civilian clothes would be taunted by others in uniform. The less they reacted to the taunts, the more outrageous they would become, especially if there were women present. The men subjected to the ridicule and accusations of cowardice—merchant seamen who had been torpedoed, mined, bombed, machine-gunned . . . —would be goaded into giving the uniformed 'heroes' their first battle wounds."[74] The introduction of Merchant Navy lapel badges, and a growing volume of wartime propaganda celebrating the contribution and stories of Merchant Navy crews, took time to impact on the public consciousness. Coastal crews who might be seen routinely in particular pubs and streets remained particularly vulnerable to suspicions that they might be failing to "do their bit" by enlisting in HM Armed Forces. A fortunate few might be able to point to the gallantry awards that they received because of actions on the coastal convoys. Eleven merchant seamen received the Lloyds War Medal because of actions by S-boats; most of them involved efforts to rescue trapped or wounded survivors from sinking vessels.[75] By and large the gallantry of the merchant seamen on the coasting trades remained unrecognized.

The strain on coaster crews was further compounded by having to operate on the equivalent of a railway timetable in the confines of coastal waters, while under war conditions. In 1943 one Royal Navy officer, who was also an MP, made public reference to the "signs of strain . . . appearing . . . [among] coastal masters and deck hands."[76] Such public references were rare, but in private comments were more frequent. On November 4, 1943, there was a chorus of complaint from the crews of coasters after convoy

CW221 was attacked. Three vessels were lost from the eighteen that made up the convoy.⁷⁷ On board the SS *Fulham*, the mate complained that with merchant seamen being "sought for the much talked of Second Front [he] personally . . . would be only too pleased to take part, as he would at least get decent and reasonable protection."⁷⁸ Such complaints were a reminder that the morale of coaster crews mattered, and the labels given by them to particular stretches of water as "bomb alley" or "E-boat alley" showed that their morale, and continued willingness to go to sea, could not be taken for granted.

Merchant seaman on the coastal and Atlantic runs faced rather different potential outcomes if their vessels were attacked by the enemy, even though they shared many of the same problems, such as the impossibility of extended working in bulky lifejackets even though they were encouraged to do so.⁷⁹ In any sinking, a mariner sunk on the coastal run wouldn't face the prospect of a lengthy lifeboat voyage to safety as those on the Atlantic run did, but they did have the knowledge that a small ship could be torn apart by any explosion due to mine or torpedo in a way a larger vessel would not. The G7 torpedo used by U-boats and S-boats could sink even the largest vessels, and the damage it could do to a coaster, carrying a bulk cargo, with a small number of holds, a low freeboard, and usually wooden instead of steel hatch covers, was typically catastrophic. A torpedo, mine, or bomb explosion could quite literally tear a small merchant ship apart. The scale of the destruction could leave an impression on those who witnessed it. Nowell Hall, an RNVR officer on HMT *Sea Mist*, recalled in his memoirs the sight of a ship damaged by an S-boat torpedo: "Athwart the ebbtide, with engines shattered and sides buckled and torn, lay the *Ilse*, a merchantman of about 4000 tons. . . . The bulkheads were holding, and her stern rode as well as ever; but forward of that gaping hole near the bridge she listed so heavily to starboard that the rail was under water and the waves lapped the edges of her hatch covers."⁸⁰ With such catastrophic damage to small ships, crew members frequently found themselves trapped. The Free French coaster *Daphne* (1,970 GRT) was in convoy FN434 when she was torpedoed off the Humber estuary by S-102 at 0100 on March 18, 1941. The initial explosion trapped eight men, and despite the best efforts of his fellow crew, the donkeyman could not be freed. As the crew prepared to abandon ship, one "promised to visit his wife and children in France after the war," shaking his hand through an open light.[81] Such sad partings were kept from the public in the interests of public morale.

In the coastal war from 1940 to 1945—indeed, in all war—the human element matters greatly, and in naval strategy it is too easily overlooked as a factor in victory or defeat. The war along the coasts of the United Kingdom from 1940 to 1945 pitted two highly trained and dedicated navies against one another. For the Royal Navy, the service's tradition offensive spirit and the closeness of the fight to home were powerful weapons in their own right. For the coaster crews, dogged determination and bloody-mindedness produced an attitude that might be summed up as "Don't give a damn and carry on," to paraphrase the famous wartime slogan. For the officers and men of the S-boat arm, professionalism and patriotism were as vital to sustaining the campaign, especially as the strategic balance shifted, as the continuing flow of torpedoes and diesel fuel. The human element, though, extended well beyond this to dockyard workers, maritime communities, and families who also played a role in sustaining the campaign in the English Channel. Propaganda could, and did play, a key role in sustaining their morale even when in some ways it failed. For the coaster crews working E-boat alley, the sense that the Battle of the Atlantic got the lion's share of media attention was an encouragement to their bloody-minded determination. Similarly, as the strategic balance began to turn against the Kriegsmarine, the claims of German propaganda produced a certain dark humor on the part of S-boat crews. The coastal war made for very different experiences between the different groups who were forced to fight it, while all sides experienced the sense that the campaign in English waters was overshadowed by the U-boat war in the Atlantic.

# CHAPTER 5

# DÖNITZ REPLACES RAEDER

BY LATE 1942 the S-boat campaign had entered a critical phase: the number of sinkings was being maintained in the face of increasing British countermeasures. That same sense that things were finely balanced could be found in other facets of the war at sea, and this chapter explores the impact on the coastal campaign of the shift in German naval strategy that took place in 1943. Just weeks after taking over from Admiral Raeder as head of the German navy on January 30, Admiral Dönitz, the former head of the U-boat arm, was forced to recognize that his crews would not be able to win victory in the submarine war designed to sink cargoes and throttle the Allied war effort.[1] The "critical convoy battles of March 1943," as Jürgen Rohwer has labeled them, rapidly turned into Black May.[2] In that single month 25 percent of the operational strength of the U-boat command (forty-one U-boats) was lost. Dönitz was forced to suspend the U-boat campaign on May 24 and to withdraw most of his submarines from the Atlantic. Programs of limited modernization would enable the obsolescent type VII and type IX submarines to return to the Atlantic later that year, but Dönitz understood that they were capable of fighting only a holding action in the war at sea. It would take a new generation of submarines (the new type XXI and XXIII electro-boats, which had significantly enhanced performance) to breathe real life into the submarine campaign against the Allies. These boats would not be ready for operational service until 1945, and in the meantime, Dönitz would use his refitted type VII and IX submarines, his S-boats, and remaining surface units to try to hold the Allies back.

The difficulties of 1943 threatened to force Germany away from the naval strategy that had been pursued since the summer of 1940. The war on commerce that had been waged against Britain's sea-lines of communications, with minimal cooperation from the Luftwaffe, was disrupted by the growing effectiveness of Allied convoy defenses, underpinned by a rapidly growing number of escort vessels and the introduction of new technologies that facilitated the location and destruction of German submarines. Under pressure on every front, the German high command increasingly looked on the Allied invasion of Western Europe as a moment of strategic decision. If the Allied invasion could be halted at the water's edge, then the balance of the war might shift back in Germany's favor. In the buildup to D-Day, the coastal convoys had a critical role to play in bringing resources to the ports on the southern coast of England from which the invasion would be launched. If the S-boat flotillas and Luftwaffe could interdict that traffic, they could push back the day when the Allies would feel in a position to launch the invasion. Similarly, on D-Day they might be able to launch devastating attacks against the vessels carrying the troops and tanks that would form the amphibious spearhead of the Allied landings. To undertake both of these critical tasks needed a significant increase in the number of S-boats available for operations in the English Channel and North Sea. That buildup would, however, take time and require a considerable level of resources from German war industries. It was essential, however, if Germany was to secure victory on D-Day and to exploit the strategic opportunity it would create. With its western border secured for at least a year, Germany would be free to concentrate its resources on stopping the advance of the Red Army in the East. The failure of the Allied invasion might destroy the fragile relationship between the Anglo-Americans and the Russians. Others hoped that a German victory in the West might open the way to a negotiated peace between Germany and the Allies. The tilting strategic balance and, in particular, the ineffectiveness of German arms against the convoy routes (both coastal and oceanic) forced Admiral Dönitz and the Kriegsmarine toward an increasingly defensive posture. Unfortunately, though, the shift to the defensive was carried out reluctantly and hesitatingly. Dönitz continued to believe that the setbacks to the U-boat and S-boat campaign were only temporary and that, with the development of a new generation of submarines (type XXI and XXIII), the Kriegsmarine would ultimately prove triumphant in the Battle of the Atlantic. As a result, there was a failure to properly envision and implement a strategy of coastal defense. With a lack of coordination between the three services, the onus on stopping the invasion force would fall on the German army, and on D-Day the tide of battle in the West would turn decisively. Germany would surrender less than a year after the Normandy landings, and the months after June 6, 1944, would turn into a long fighting withdrawal of German naval forces along the coasts of northern France, Belgium, and Holland.

## THE FALL OF RAEDER

The first Führer Naval Conference of 1943 was held on January 6, and its repercussions on the course of German naval strategy were to be deeply significant. In the Battle of the Barents Sea on December 31, 1942, the German cruisers *Admiral Hipper* and *Lützow* and destroyers *Friedrich Eckoldt, Richard Beitzen, Theodor Riedel, Z29, Z30,* and *Z31* had been prevented from attacking the convoy JW51B by the escorting British destroyers. The convoy carried supplies badly needed by the Russians on the Eastern Front, and its destruction would have had a significant material and moral effect. All thirteen merchant vessels of the convoy reached their destinations even though the German surface vessels should have been able to overwhelm the destroyer escort. The outcome of the battle had convinced Hitler that the surface ships had limited value, despite their overwhelming cost and drain on manpower and resources. Their prestige value, their large crew size, and the impossibility of replacing them if lost meant that they could only be risked on relatively safe operations, but that placed obvious limits on their operational use.

That Hitler was deeply exasperated by the failure in the Barents Sea and by the wider failure of the surface fleet to match the strategic effectiveness of the U-boat force was evidenced by the leader's opening monologue on January 6 on the subject of German naval history from 1870.[3] This was a neat reversal from the late 1930s, when Raeder used to lecture Hitler on the evolution of German sea power and the need for a powerful battle fleet to pursue the goals of Tirpitz.[4] At the end of the lecture Hitler demanded that the German heavy ships be decommissioned and their resources deployed elsewhere, especially into U-boats and small ships. In Hitler's eyes the large ships were liabilities rather than assets, and implicitly, with the exception of the U-boat war, Hitler was trying to force the German navy back toward a coastal rather than an oceanic strategy.

The big ships had proven highly vulnerable to Allied air attack, and during 1942 they had mostly been sent to Norwegian waters. Here they could threaten the convoys to northern Russia, with range from British airbases and the topography of the fjords providing a good measure of protection from Allied air power. The Battle of the Barents Sea in December 1942 was, in the depths of the Arctic winter, an opportunity for the Kriegsmarine to make a major contribution to the Russian campaign. In Hitler's eyes, the failure to press home the attack and achieve real results called for a fundamental change. He wanted the big ships decommissioned and their guns used to form new coastal batteries. The crews of the heavy ships could be retrained (where needed) and redeployed into U-boats. The head of the German navy, Grand Admiral Raeder, would not countenance it, and he resigned rather than accept the decommissioning. In his place, on January 20 Hitler appointed Admiral Dönitz, the head of the submarine arm. As Jak Mallmann Showell has argued, Dönitz was a somewhat unlikely replacement as head of the Kriegsmarine.[5] He had little experience of the naval high command, and the U-boat war had kept him far distant from Berlin. It was, perhaps, Dönitz's remoteness from the old regime that Hitler was relying on to secure easy acceptance of strategic change in the navy.

Dönitz was through and through a U-boat man who had served in submarines in World War I before being sunk while in command of UB-68 in the Mediterranean in 1918. It was during his time in a prisoner-of-war camp in Yorkshire in 1918 that he had begun to work out the wolf pack tactics of World War II.[6] Rigid in thought and approach to strategic and tactical issues, as Peter Padfield has noted, Dönitz was "slow in comprehension."[7] Dönitz approved of a singularity of thought in his command, and U-boat high command closely reflected his views. He was certain that the submarine was a war-winning weapon even if it had not triumphed in 1914–18. This unshakeable belief in victory undoubtedly endeared him to Hitler, and the two men established a good working relationship with each other during 1943. As Eric Rust has shown, Dönitz's approach to the navy and Hitler's approach toward Germany mirrored each other: intellectual thought was frowned on, while blind conformity was praised and rewarded.[8] Not only was Dönitz able to persuade Hitler not to decommission the big ships; he was also able to secure additional resources to launch a large-scale building program for 1943 (much of it focused on the next generation of U-boats, but also including ambitious plans to build more small surface combatants).

Even with the reprieve for the big ships, and his love of the U-boats, Dönitz appreciated the worth of the smaller ships: S-boats, torpedo boats, minesweepers, and destroyers based along the coast of Western Europe and Norway. The S-boat campaign against the coastal convoys complemented the U-boat campaign in the Atlantic, and the destroyers and torpedo boats had played a valuable role in defending the coast and German coastal convoys. Just as the big ships could tie down forces that might be used against the U-boats, so too did the little ships. Not only were escort vessels used on coastal convoys, but groups of them had to be maintained at key points along the southern and eastern coasts, such as Plymouth and Portsmouth, to counter any activity by the smaller units of the German navy.

The surviving evidence from Dönitz's memoirs and postwar interviews strongly suggests his inability in mid- to late 1943 to fully accept that the Kriegsmarine was being forced onto the defensive, at least until the electro-boats became operational. While the eclipse of the U-boat campaign meant that the Kriegsmarine would be unable to starve the British into submission, or to reduce their war economy to the point of a collapse of productivity, it could at least support the defense of Fortress Europe, and the German Empire in Europe, by assisting the land battle. It could do this by slowing the buildup of invasion forces in Britain, by disrupting any attempted invasion through attacks on Allied amphibious forces, and by restricting the flow of troops and supplies across the English Channel in the event of a successful lodgment on the coast of France. Dönitz could play a vital role in preparing for the invasion, but in his public pronouncements in 1943–44 (as opposed to his memoirs, in which he describes the submarine campaign after May 1943 as a defensive effort) he appears to have been unwilling to concede, or follow through on, a coordinated strategy of coastal defense. This may be a matter of the internal politics and bitter interservice rivalries within the Third Reich, but equally it might have been down to a personal unwillingness to face facts. With the loss of the lives of so many German sailors in a second war against the British, it was hard to face the grim realities of a tide of war turning steadily against the Kriegsmarine. The death of the admiral's youngest son, Peter Dönitz, on May 19, 1943, in the sinking of U-954 made the fortunes of war particularly hard for him to accept. Acknowledging that hundreds more sailors would have to die just to keep the Allies at arm's distance was professionally and personally very difficult, irrespective of the service's need to continue to impress Hitler. Whatever his motives, the head of the Kriegsmarine remained convinced that the campaign against the sea-lines of communication would have to continue, as he argued in his postwar memoirs.[9] Even so, by 1943 the Allies were demonstrating with successful landings in the Mediterranean that Anglo-American amphibious operations constituted a serious threat to the German Empire. A rethink was badly needed to consider a switch from oceanic war to coastal war.

Whether a serious and detailed reconsideration of strategy took place in the Kriegsmarine in 1943 is impossible to trace from the documentary record, as Peter Padfield notes.[10] In any case, a reconsideration might have produced little disagreement among the naval command. This was both a strength and a weakness, and the naval staff probably agreed with their chief on the need to maintain the U-boat campaign on familiar lines. Thus, postwar historians have found much to criticize in Dönitz's apparent "inertia" or apparent foolishness in "throwing more boats and crews away instead of husbanding them carefully while seeking new types and tactics, and a new strategy."[11]

There were dissenting voices, though, as Clay Blair has noted: "Two of the most highly decorated skippers, Reinhard Suhren and Erich Topp, argued against . . . [continuing the tonnage war] because of the anticipated 'immense losses' and the lack of even the 'slightest prospect of success,' as Topp put it in his later memoir. On the other hand, the even more highly decorated skippers Albrecht Brandi and Wolfgang Lüth thought the campaign should continue 'with the greatest intensity possible.'"[12] Despite the dissenting voices, the Kriegsmarine would remain on the offensive (at least rhetorically), and there would be few public concessions in the direction of coastal defense beyond the building of more small ships and the development of more coastal artillery sites.[13] "Offensive U-boat warfare" would remain the German navy's "foremost task" even as "the defensive duties of the Navy . . . rose in importance" in 1943.[14]

## RESOURCING THE 1943 BUILDING PROGRAM

Delivering the 1943 building program would be no easy matter, as Dönitz knew full well. The Kriegsmarine was in competition with the other services in the allocation of industrial resources, and there was no body charged with overall responsibility for managing the competing demands and overseeing armaments programs.[15] Minister of Armaments Albert Speer had responsibility for producing armaments for the army, while the Kriegsmarine directly managed certain facilities (including shipbuilding yards). Labor supply and raw material allocations (including steel) was handled by a Central Planning Committee under Speer, but no representative of the Kriegsmarine sat on the committee, while representatives of the army and air force did. Sensing that he was unlikely to get the resources he required to complete the 1943 building program, Dönitz went to Hitler with a request for more steel and labor to be allocated to the Kriegsmarine. With Hitler's support Dönitz was able to seek an understanding with Speer by which naval construction would get a greater allocation of resources in return for surrendering control over some production facilities. A new Shipbuilding Commission, which included representatives of the shipbuilding companies, was set up with Rear Admiral Topp at its head to advise on the shipbuilding requirements of the Kriegsmarine. In many ways, these reforms made sense and created a streamlined and more integrated set of structures for the management of the Kriegsmarine's armament requirements, but they were long overdue.

Such was the urgent need for resources in 1943 that even with the arrival of new vessels there was little change in the frontline strength of the Channel/North Sea flotillas. Inevitably, the building of different kinds of vessels under the 1943 program impacted on each other. Competition for steel, skilled labor, and dockyard facilities remained acute. With monthly

U-boat production being lifted to twenty-seven per month by the end of 1943 (and increased to thirty in late 1944), the construction of new destroyers had to be abandoned and torpedo boat construction kept to eighteen vessels each year.[16] While sufficient steel quota was found for the annual production of seventy-four general purpose *Minensuchboote*, in reality difficulties were soon encountered, and only seventeen ships would be built before the end of the war. Given that S-boats were made out of wood, at least increased production would have a fairly limited impact on the other types of ship being built under the 1943 program. The wooden boat builders of northern Germany would be asked to turn out seventy-two *Schnellboote* and seventy-two *Räumboote* (R-boat). These lightly armed vessels could undertake a variety of general purpose roles. The S-boats in particular could both play a valuable role as an anti-invasion craft and maintain the campaign against U.K. coastal convoys. They would not, however, be produced in sufficient quantity in time to meet the Allied invasion of June 1944.

## THE 1943 PRODUCTION PROGRAM FOR *SCHNELLBOOTE*

The failure to have sufficient forces available to meet the Allied landings illustrates the wider failings in the German war machine. Dönitz was unable to balance the competing imperatives within his own command, which were being reported to him by the naval high command: "Chief, Naval Staff states that it is impossible to carry out the construction program without a basic solution of the question of manpower. If naval warfare, previously neglected, is to be carried out to the extent planned, there must be a fundamental, strategic change in the attitude of the Fuehrer and concentration must be shifted to matters of personnel."[17] Eight months after Dönitz had taken over, the 1943 building program came under reexamination as it became plain that Germany's war industries would be unable to turn out the planned number of vessels.[18] Despite the urgency of the situation, it would still be necessary to continue with the building of certain kinds of auxiliary vessels.[19] Raising the construction target for S-boats to seventy-two was hugely ambitious. With their traditional building techniques, and origins in the yacht yards of northern Germany, the S-boat design was not ideally suited to mass production. Building S-boats required shipwright skills that took time to acquire. Building U-boats and working in steel called for skills that could be found elsewhere within German industry.

From the outbreak of war onward, the naval high command believed that an annual build rate of 16 boats would be sufficient to maintain a fleet of 40–50 boats. Considerations after victory in the West in 1940 that a fleet of 160 boats would provide coastal protection from Norway to the Spanish border had come to nothing. In addition to the problem of building in wood, the supply of Mercedes Benz marine diesels was also problematic: demand outmatched supply, especially with the Kriegsmarine's desire to maintain 50 percent surplus capacity in engines for its operational boats. This would allow regular replacement of engines for maintenance purposes every 300–350 hours, with an engine exchange every 500–1,000 hours of service. The overhaul of old engines took priority over the production of new units to support new construction. Critical shortages of metal from 1941 added another problem; the shortage of copper in 1941 meant that some engines could not be supplied with oil coolers. Shortages meant difficulties keeping boats in service, and one calculation done in January 1942 in the 2nd S-boat Flotilla estimated S-boat serviceability rates at 68.7 percent.[20] By late 1942 it had been finally possible to raise the production target for new engines to twenty units a month, but this was impacted by the Marienfelde engine works being transferred to the control of the Luftwaffe control. This left the Daimler Benz works at Untertürkheim as the principal facility for the construction of new S-boat engines.[21] Air attacks later hit production at the facility so badly that in October 1944 only one new engine was produced.[22] An expansion of S-boat building required new facilities. In 1940, to try and improve the supply of new hulls, the Schlichting Werft at Travemünde had begun to build S-boats (starting with S-101), but in the circumstances of the 1943 building program it was clear that Lürssen and the Schlichting Werft would not have the capacity to meet the ambitious construction targets.[23]

The growing effectiveness of British defenses in the English Channel, with increasing numbers of escort and Coastal Forces boats and steady improvements in radar led the FdS to conclude in the middle of 1942 that the S-boat was "no longer master of the situation in the Western area."[24]

The FdS considered that only by increases in the number of S-boats, which would allow him to mount swamping attacks against British convoys, could he assert some measure of control in the English Channel. He argued that it was "vital to increase the number of boats in the West, and to develop new types of boats, mines, torpedoes, gunnery and signal equipment."[25] The S-boat's qualitative superiority of 1940 and 1941 were no longer sufficient for success in anticonvoy operations. By October 1942 a production target of thirty-six S-boats per year had been under consideration by the Hauptamt Kriegsschiffbau (Main Office of Naval Construction).[26]

This was the background against which the 1943 S-boat building program was developed. The limitations on hull production were addressed as the Kriegsmarine looked for new producers. A Danzig-based coach works, Danziger Waggonfabrik, was turned to even though its workers had more experience with railway carriages and trams than vessels of war. Lürssen and the Schlichting Werft would lend their expertise to the works, raising the hopes of the FdS that German industry could supply him with the kind of force that he was hoping for. The FdS noted that "increased . . . [S-boat] production, and further development of the speed, stability, and armament of the existing type, should bring about a great improvement; and should justify the building of more boats in the future."[27]

Inevitably it took time for these improvements to come through, and problems became manifest during 1943. These difficulties were highlighted at a meeting in Berlin in the late summer of 1943. At the three-day meeting in Vegesack were key personnel from the shipyards together with the Konstruktionamt (Construction Department) of the Oberkommando der Marine (Naval High Command). Shipyard management from the Danziger Waggonfabrik and Schlichting Werft arrived on December 16 to discuss the difficulties with the staff at Lürssen.[28] Not until early 1944 would badly needed additional labor begin to arrive from the Netherlands and Denmark and other parts of occupied Europe at the shipyards. In the case of the Schlichting Werft, an old hotel was rented to house the extra workers.[29] Russian laborers would arrive later, resulting in the construction of a work camp.

Such enthusiasm and additional resources allowed an increase in the number of S-boats produced as a result of the 1943 building program, but the process of improvement was slow, and Danziger Waggonfabrik did not start producing units until the end of 1944. Despite all the efforts, only at the very end of the year did the 1943 building program began to bear fruit, and even then the rate of improvement was very slow. By early 1944 only one or two additional boats a month were being produced, and it was not until after the Normandy invasion (in July and August 1944) that production improved to a level in excess of 100 percent improvement on the levels of 1943 figures.[30] In other words, 1943 would prove to be a notable failure in the attempt to produce the numbers of S-boats required to disrupt U.K. coastal convoys and to provide for the coastal defense of Nazi-dominated Europe.

## SMALL BATTLE UNITS (KLEINKAMPFVERBANDE)

The growing danger that an Allied invasion of western France might be launched before substantial numbers of new S-boats had become operational under the 1943 building program led to an openness to innovate despite the conservatism of the naval high command. The effectiveness of the commando frogmen and small speedboats of the Italian Decima Flottiglia MAS (10th Assault Flotilla) in the Mediterranean and the British attack on German battleship *Tirpitz* using midget submarines in 1943 suggested their potential as weapons of war. *Tirpitz* was crippled as a result of the attack, which involved placing charges underneath the ship; eight hundred cubic meters of water poured into the ship within 150 minutes after the attack. Though the ship did not sink, there was serious damage to her electrical systems and power plant.[31] Even though the battleship would eventually be repaired, she was rendered nonoperational for months, and questions remained over her performance and reliability.[32] Given the effectiveness of the attack with minimal resources, there was considerable interest within the Kriegsmarine in these small craft and whether Germany might be able to develop similar weapons. Even before this, in 1942 Kapitänleutnant Hans Bartels, who had taken charge of coastal defense in Norway, had produced a paper suggesting the potential value of midget submarines.[33] To try and circumvent the usual processes and the conservatism of the naval high command, Bartels had the paper placed directly into the briefcase of Dönitz's adjutant. Given the ongoing success of Dönitz's submarines in 1942, there was little interest in the suggestions contained in the paper, but with the attack on *Tirpitz* there was considerably more interest in the idea of small battle units. They could be manufactured well away from the shipyards, which were under increasing Allied aerial attack, and their manufacture would not place a serious draw on the resources and raw materials required for U-boat manufacture. Bartels found himself promoted to Korvettenkapitän, with Vice Admiral Hellmuth Heye being appointed to the new command for *Kleinkampfverbände* (small battle units). Heye found himself charged with the task of developing, and rushing into service, a range of midget submarines and explosive attack boats with which to try and take the fight to the enemy inside the coastal waters of Western Europe. The task was almost impossible. The development of such technologies would inevitably take time to perfect, and Nazi Germany just did not have that time by late 1943. Moreover, the development of the small battle units had implications for the S-boat arm. In the first group of volunteers for the small battle units were junior officers Pettke and Potthast, formerly of the 3rd S-boat Flotilla in the Mediterranean.[34] With the expansion in the number of S-boats, such experienced men should have formed the nucleus of new crews. Indeed, in thinking about the implications of the 1943 S-boat building program, FdS Petersen (the head of the S-boat arm) had warned, "The bottleneck to the building up of the . . . arm is the supply of trained personnel, especially of . . . commanders."[35] Such was the slowness of the buildup and the urgency of the invasion threat that men like Pettke and Potthast would be accepted by the small battle units instead of being held back for the new wave of S-boats under construction on the Baltic Coast.

By 1943 the careful strategic development of the German navy under the prewar Plan Z had given way to desperation, experiment, and ad hoc measures. Hitler could throw long-term naval strategy aside in a fit of pique, as he did in January 1943, along with Raeder as the head of the Kriegsmarine. Dönitz's strategy was, in part, based on his own prejudices in favor of the U-boat (confirmed by a pliant naval high command), and he was unwilling to concede a long-term shift in the posture of the navy toward coastal warfare. While Dönitz produced an ambitious building plan for 1943, within the corridors of power of the Nazi state, it took time to negotiate the resources necessary to deliver it. Even as he triumphed, he allowed Hans Bartels to short-cut the command hierarchy within the Kriegsmarine to make a successful pitch for the small battle units. That program drew material resources, and potentially critical personnel, away from the conventional weapons programs of the Kriegsmarine, including the S-boats. New and experimental was effectively privileged at the expense of tried and trusted systems, and it would inevitably take time for new programs to produce results in the form of reliable and effective weapons of war.

## CHAPTER 6

# THE 1943 TURNING POINT
## The Emergence of a Multilayered System of Defense

WHILE KEY POLITICAL BATTLES were being fought in Berlin, in the waters along the southern and eastern coasts of the United Kingdom the tide of battle was turning more firmly against the S-boats. This chapter and the ones that follow it examine specific aspects of the shift in the strategic balance that took place in 1943. Oberleutnant-zur-See Ulrich Kolbe, commanding S-85, later reflected in a private family memoir that "during the winter of 1942 to 1943 the missions from Cherbourg along the English coast were becoming increasingly difficult. Instead of the convoys, which our control center had always predicted quite accurately, so that we could expect that after about 1 1/2 hours of march from Cherbourg we would meet the ships of the convoy, we were now more and more often meeting English destroyers or MGBs (motor gun boats) instead of freighters at our sites in the Lyme Bay."[1] The same difficulties were increasingly being experienced by S-boat crews operating from bases along the English Channel from France to the Netherlands. The reasons for this turning of the tide in the S-boat campaign have received very little analysis from historians, in contrast to the turning point of the U-boat war in March 1943. From 1940 to 1942, coastal convoys had been vulnerable to attack by S-boats, and the Royal Navy had slowly developed the resources and tactics to minimize their effectiveness. During 1943 these resources and tactics would combine to produce dramatic effects in the S-boat campaign.

By the end of 1942 there was little reason to anticipate such a reversal of fortune in the Channel battles. Over a thirty-month period, up until December 1942, there had been a growth in the tonnage of British coastal shipping sunk by S-boats despite rising confidence within the Royal Navy

**TABLE 2.** S–BOAT TORPEDO SUCCESSES AGAINST MERCHANT SHIPS

| YEAR | TONNAGE | NUMBER OF SHIPS |
| --- | --- | --- |
| 1940 | 47,985 | 23 |
| 1941 | 58,854 | 29 |
| 1942 | 71,156 | 23 |
| 1943 | 15,138 | 6 |
| 1944 | 26,321 | 13 |
| 1945 | 10,222 | 5 |

SOURCE: Roskill, *War at Sea*, vol. 3, pt. 2, 479.

about their ability to defend the coastal routes. At the end of 1942, C-in-C Nore had reported on the progress of the campaign up to that point. He estimated that between September 1939 and November 14, 63,350 transits of the East Coast passage had been made by merchant ships. Some 157 of those vessels had been lost to enemy action (0.24 percent of the total number of sailings). His satisfaction at these figures was evident: "These losses cannot, in my opinion, be regarded as excessive, and compare, I believe, favorably with other convoys sailing through dangerous waters."[2]

During 1943 the S-boat campaign against coastal shipping went into marked decline: just six merchant vessels were sunk by the S-boats. Despite a small revival of the numbers of merchant ships being sunk in 1944, as the Allied invasion of Europe meant increasing number of vessels for attack and forced the Kriegsmarine into more risky engagements, the decline of the S-boat campaign in 1943 proved decisive. Not only did it ensure the security of British coastal trade; it also hastened the invasion of Europe. During 1943, the requirements of Operation Bolero (the buildup to D-Day) required more and more cargoes to be moved to points of use/embarkation around the coasts of the United Kingdom. The size of coastal convoys more than doubled during 1943, and larger and larger vessels were incorporated into them. The safe arrival of cargoes around the coastal network was as vital to D-Day as the security of the convoy lines across the North Atlantic. Understanding why the S-boat campaign went into decline is important to our understanding of World War II at sea, and it is also important from the standpoint of understanding the nature of warfare in the coastal zone. This chapter and the two that follow it analyze this collapse across three key aspects. Historians and students of naval warfare have accorded insufficient importance to the fact that between 1940 and 1943 the British were able to create a highly sophisticated, multiweapon defense network (sea, air, and land), capable of harvesting and using real-time intelligence and electronic information, along the sections of the U.K. coast vulnerable to S-boat attack. It is the success of this network, and a German failure to take appropriate countermeasures, that resulted in the collapse of the S-boat campaign. In what might be described as the consensus narrative of the defeat of the S-boat, insofar as the collapse of the S-boat campaign has been analyzed at all, the emergence of the motor gunboat and the growing strength of British Coastal Forces are identified as the key factors. That narrative has been shaped by the memories and writing of Coastal Forces veterans not ideally placed to see the full breadth of the networks developed against the S-boat. It also reflects the primacy of battle narratives in memory and popular history, as opposed to more academic instincts to pursue an understanding of the ideas and practices of sea denial. The reality is that it was not one weapons system but a wider set of tactical, intelligence, and other issues that resulted in the collapse of the S-boat campaign in 1943. Information networking to discern and respond to S-boat sorties from the coast of occupied Europe was particularly key. Those networks would grow in effectiveness during 1944 and 1945, but even in the last days of the war the Royal Navy was still working hard to minimize the threat to coastal convoys.

## BRITAIN'S ANSWER TO THE S-BOAT

To begin with the conventional narrative that it was improvements to escorting forces that resulted in the collapse of the S-boat campaign, the availability and quality of escort vessels for coastal convoys did remain a critical factor affecting their security. The shortage of destroyers of 1940 improved in 1941, and by 1942 British shipyards were turning out a steady stream of escort vessels, including corvettes, frigates, and destroyers. Under the Lend-Lease scheme, passed by Congress in March 1941, American shipyards were building warships and commercial vessels for British use. There was a slow improvement in the quality of the vessels available for coastal defense, and some of the older vessels were modified to improve their effectiveness. Experience had shown that the heavy-caliber guns of a destroyer might sink an S-boat with a direct hit, but training a gun and hitting a fast-moving small target at night was no easy matter. One response was to adapt to shipboard use twin 6-pounder quick-firing guns previously developed for use as coastal artillery. The twin 6-pounder mounting was installed in a forward turret mounting on eight southern and eastern coast destroyers.[3] The eighteen rounds a minute from the twin 6-pounders gave both a volume and a weight of fire, although it would not be until December 1944 that the twin 6-pounder was the principal weapon in the sinking of an S-boat. The report from the commanding officer on that occasion evidenced just how effective the twin 6-pounder was against S-boats and R-boats: "This is the first time that a kill has been made by a six pounder and in my opinion at short ranges (that is below 3,000 yards) one cannot ask for a better weapon."[4]

Despite the steady improvement in the number of available escort vessels, Allied amphibious operations in the Mediterranean led to a dip in the number of destroyers available for the East Coast run. Moreover, by 1943 the stress of wartime operations meant that some of the older escort vessels were increasingly seen as tired and prone to breakdown. For example, in 1943 the aging four Town-class destroyers allocated to the Rosyth Command were declared to be "virtually useless" and "subject to continual breakdowns and minor defects."[5] However, thanks to the increasing strength of Coastal Forces the availability of destroyers was not the issue that it could have been.

During early months of 1941 the Admiralty's emergency boatbuilding program of 1940 began to bear fruit, with a growing number of light vessels available for coastal convoy duty. Qualitatively they were inferior to the S-boats, which were faster, more heavily armed, more capable in rough seas, and better able to survive major damage. In part these disadvantages could be offset by teaming Coastal Forces vessels with destroyers. In the

**TABLE 3.** DESTROYERS AVAILABLE ON THE EAST COAST, 1941–1943

|  | OCTOBER 1941 | OCTOBER 1942 | OCTOBER 1943 |
| --- | --- | --- | --- |
| Rosyth | 25 | 24 | 14 |
| Nore | 21 | 24 | 19 |

SOURCE: Figures contained in Commander-in-Chief Note to Secretary of the Admiralty, October 16, 1943, TNA: ADM 1/15815.

early months of the war, motor torpedo boats (MTB) had been few in number. With the fall of France in June 1940 and the growing attack on Britain's trading network, Britain's boatbuilders had taken on emergency contracts for the construction of MTBs and fast motor launches (MLs). Further orders had followed, with refinements to existing designs and the introduction of new ones. In March 1941 came contracts for the construction of a new design: the motor gunboat (MGB). Within weeks orders had been placed for forty boats.

S-boats, MTBs, and MGBs were, in some senses, evenly matched: they lacked the weapons to deal with each other decisively in the kind of fast-moving ambush warfare that developed in the English Channel and North Sea. From 1940 to 1945 only 6 (out of 82) MTBs and MGBs were sunk by S-boats. Likewise, less than 10 percent of S-boat losses (8 out of 93) came from attacks by MTBs and MGBs. Torpedoes could sink even a battleship, but a hit from one torpedo boat on another was unlikely given the small size and fast speeds. Cannons and machine guns, relying on the sharp shooting skills of their gunners, could pepper the hull and superstructure of an opposing vessel. However, with limited scope for fire control to secure concentration (lateral convergence) and coordination of firing, it was possible to hit an enemy repeatedly before causing serious levels of damage.[6] Firing torpedoes in a fast-moving engagement was unlikely to result in a kill, but a depth charge (shallow set and dropped in the path of a fast-approaching enemy unit) could make a very handy weapon against light craft. The underwater pressure bubble alone resulting from an underwater explosion could open up seams, destroy the fastenings that connected hull planks to major structural members, or stove

**TABLE 4.** ESCORT FORCES AVAILABLE FOR COASTAL CONVOYS IN LATE 1943

| COMMAND | DESTROYERS | ML | MGB | MTB | CORVETTES |
|---|---|---|---|---|---|
| Nore | 12 | 12 | 15 | 10 | 6 |
| Portsmouth | 4 | 12 | 6 | 3 | — |
| Dover | — | 6 | — | — | — |
| Plymouth | 3 | 6 | 3 | 2 | — |
| Rosyth | 15 | — | — | — | — |

SOURCE: Figures from "Coastal Convoys: An Appreciation," October 11, 1943, TNA: ADM 1/15815.

in planks. Ramming was also considered not just a viable option but an effective tactic. A crippled S-boat was unlikely to make it to port, and the imbalance in numbers between German and British coastal forces, and the qualitative inferiority of Allied MTBs and MGBs from 1940 to 1943, opened up interesting possibilities so far as the tactic of ramming was concerned. In April 1942, FdS Petersen had calculated that, despite their qualitative inferiority, British Coastal Forces were now "superior in force" to his S-boat arm ranged against them.[7] Willingness to ram, and a constantly aggressive spirit on the part of the British, fostered a defensive mentality on the part of Petersen and the S-boat flotillas. By 1943, the aggression, efficiency, and numbers of British Coastal Forces could offset a temporary decline in the number of destroyers available for Channel/East Coast escort duty.

## ROBERT HICHENS AND THE DEVELOPMENT OF ANTI-S-BOAT CAMPAIGN

If the growing strength of British Coastal Forces in 1941–43 was helping to tilt the balance, then their effectiveness was increased by the development of tactics that minimized their qualitative limitations. Lieutenant Commander Robert Peverell Hichens took the lead in developing those tactics. He became the leading figure in British Coastal Forces. Before the war he was a sportsman and amateur sailor while practicing law in Falmouth

(Cornwall). In 1936 he joined the Royal Naval Volunteer Supplementary Reserve, becoming a sublieutenant in 1939. The Royal Naval Reserve would later provide the backbone of Coastal Forces, and the thinking of its officers was less fettered by tradition and the confines of officer training. Many, like Hichens, were keen yachtsmen whose boat-handling skills, reflexes, and instincts for the movement of an opposing vessel were shaped in the heat of prewar competition at regattas such as Cowes.[8] In minesweepers in 1940 Hichens was awarded a Distinguished Service Cross for his conduct during the Dunkirk evacuations. Following this, Hichens volunteered for Coastal Forces. By January 1941 Hichens was given command of his own motor gunboat (MGB 64). Widely known by his boat's call sign, "Hitch," Robert Hichens quickly established a reputation as an effective leader and gunboat skipper. As a result, in September 1941, he was given command of 6th MGB Flotilla.[9] He later commanded the 8th MGB Flotilla, and by April 1943 he had become the RNVR's most decorated member, with two Distinguished Service Orders, three Distinguished Service Crosses, and two Mentions in Dispatches.

Following the war, several commentators likened Hichens to Nelson because of an apparent similarity of tactics favored by the two men: relentless pursuit of the enemy and close-quarter engagement irrespective of the damage to British vessels.[10] Both believed that "no captain could do very wrong if he places his ship alongside that of the enemy." This may have been in the best traditions of the service, but more recent history also underlined the utility of such tactics. HMS *Broke* and HMS *Swift* in the Battle of the Dover Strait (April 20–21, 1917) had shown the effectiveness of close-quarter action in modern naval warfare, using torpedo and ramming tactics to deal with a group of six German destroyers. There were other occasions during World War I when the direct approach paid dividends, and the battles waged between British and German coastal forces after 1940 were not that different in tactical terms. At night each side hoped to achieve tactical surprise. S-boats would wait along the convoy route to attack the merchant ships plying the coastal routes, and British Coastal Forces would attempt to ambush the S-boats as they moved into position. In this game of shadows, the S-boats enjoyed the advantage of a lower silhouette than the vessels of British Coastal Forces, and occasionally boats would fire on their own side.¹¹ The odd beauty of fast boats moving at night, chased by pluming white wakes catching the moonlight, or lying eerily still listening for the enemy, impressed itself on many of the participants. Artist and Coastal Forces skipper Peter Scott painted several scenes of S-boat/gunboat clashes at night that are reproduced in his 1945 *The Battle of the Narrow Seas*. Similarly, Hichens wrote in his memoirs, "I think one of the most lovely sights I have ever seen is a gunboat unit at speed in moonlight, with the white pluming wakes, the cascading bow waves, the thin black outlines of the guns starkly silhouetted, the figures of gunners motionless at their positions as though carved out of black rock, all against the beautiful setting of the moon-path on the water."¹² At any moment this scene could be transformed by bright arcs of tracer fire (differently colored between German and British units), the flash of an explosion, or an eruption of flame.

In such engagements what mattered most was not accuracy but weight of firepower. Delivering the twentieth-century equivalent of broadsides at close range was the most likely means of destroying the enemy. As Dudley Pope has observed, any engagement where the ranges opened up to five hundred or more yards was unlikely to result in the destruction of fast-moving motorboats.¹³ Maintaining accurate fire at speeds of twenty-five or more knots in any sort of seaway, with boats bouncily crisscrossing each other's wakes, was all but impossible. Even where a devastating ambush could not be laid, any engagement or detection, even at range, robbed the S-boats of the tactical surprise necessary for a successful torpedo attack or the quiet execution of a mission to lay mines.

In developing these tactics, Hichens had the advantage that a crippled S-boat was unlikely to be able to reach home port. Come the dawn any S-boat limping for home was highly vulnerable to aerial attack. In any case a damaged enemy, even if it managed to reach home, would take time to repair. With German boatyards unable to build S-boats as fast as MGBs and MTBs could be produced in Britain, relative levels of production would hand the advantage in the English Channel and North Sea to the Royal Navy. British and American boats would, however, remain qualitatively inferior. Compared to the S-boat's 108-foot length and speed of more than forty knots, the Fairmile D motor gunboats came in slightly longer, with a speed of around thirty knots. The typical American PT boat, by contrast, could manage speeds just over forty knots but was shorter, only 80 feet long. Both American and British boats relied on planing hull designs, which limited their ability to operate in rough seas, while the substantially more robust S-boats simply cut through the waves. Anglo-American reliance on gasoline engines such as the Packard 4m 2500 put them at considerable risk of catching fire in any gun exchange with the diesel-driven S-boats. The relative superiority of the S-boat in terms of build quality, speed, and firepower over MGBs and MTBs was effectively negated by the daytime control of British coastal waters by the Royal Navy and Royal Air Force. If British Coastal Forces could damage an opponent sufficiently, then it was almost certainly going to be destroyed. In such circumstances S-boats were highly reluctant to engage in a "battle of broadsides" with their British opponents, and in most engagements German skippers preferred to make the most of their advantage in speed and escape from the area as quickly as possible.[14] Likewise, Hichens was happy to encourage his skippers to ram and, if possible, board German vessels when the opportunity presented itself.[15]

Hichens may also have been influenced by infantry tactics of the British army. Hichens had served in Magdalen College's Officer Training Corps while at university. In the 1930s he had also been in the Territorial Army as an officer. Based on the experience of World War I, British Infantry tactics called for units to gain tactical and moral ascendancy over their enemy by regular and aggressive patrolling of no-man's-land. In some respects, the Channel/North Sea constituted a kind of no-man's-land, with the two opposite coasts representing the equivalent of trench lines.

The importance of Hichens in pressing tactical innovation, and the extent to which it percolated throughout Coastal Forces, can be gauged from the later writing of Captain Peter Dickens. After the war, he recounted a conversation he had had with Nore command in 1942 after taking over an MTB flotilla. When he asked for permission to follow the Hichens model and engage the enemy more closely by lying in wait off the Dutch ports, the response from Nore command was less than wholehearted: "'Oh, yes?' they replied. 'Why not? I mean splendid! Where were you thinking of going?'"[16] In Coastal Forces tactical innovation came from below, although the Royal Navy was quick to learn from success. So influential was Hichens in transforming the tactical approach of British Coastal Forces that Peter Scott would confirm on the BBC in 1943 following the death of "Hitch" that "most of the tactical theory [of British Coastal Forces] was first developed and practiced by him."[17]

An action of November 1941 involving an engagement between units of 2nd S-boat Flotilla and MGB 67 and MGB 64 (Hichens commanding) can serve as an exemplar of the tactics of engaging the enemy as closely as possible. After a successful attack on an East Coast convoy, a group of S-boats turned for home. In the darkness and confusion of attack, S-41 and S-47 collided, leaving the former disabled.[18] Taken in tow, S-41 was attacked by MGBs 67 and 64 even though the British vessels were outnumbered by five S-boats in the group. The result was a running engagement in which neither side had the tactical advantage necessary to inflict fatal damage on the other. Given the need to maintain speed, S-41 was abandoned with her seacocks open after her crew had been transferred to other S-boats. The S-boat was located and boarded by the MGB crews before it sank.[19] This resulted in a substantial intelligence haul of "large quantities of equipment—charts, log-books" and other trophies of war.[20] The retreating S-boats later came under attack by RAF fighters.[21] Despite being outnumbered, the MGBs had driven off the Germans who could not be sure in the dark about the number of opponents facing them. Damage to S-41 had resulted in its destruction, and the air power had demonstrated that it could pose a threat to retreating fast units before they reached the safety of port. Such engagements demonstrated the efficacy of aggressive tactics in attacking S-boats at every turn.

During the war from 1942 onward, as the strategic balance in coastal waters tipped more heavily in favor of British forces, Hichens and the Royal Navy had carefully refined their tactics. During 1942 C-in-C Nore had introduced the idea of a standing patrol line offshore to run along the East Coast. Known as the Z-line, it ran approximately thirty miles offshore between Harwich and Cromer (a distance of around one hundred miles).[22] This would serve as a protective screen for the convoys operating inshore of the line. On arriving at the Z-line, Coastal Forces vessels would cut engines and wait while listening for approaching vessels using hydrophones.[23] This did not prevent S-boats from slipping through gaps in the patrol line, but it was an important restriction on their operational use, and a factor in the thinking of S-boat crews, who had to anticipate contact with British Coastal Forces at some point in their journey to or from the convoy route.

Further restrictions on the freedom of movement of S-boats (reinforcing the laying of the East Coast minefields at the start of the war) came with the improvements to fixed coastal defenses with arcs of fire over the approaches to the convoy channels. Seven Maunsell army and navy forts were constructed in the approaches to the Thames Estuary.[24] Constructed in prefabricated sections and equipped with radios, searchlights, and 40-mm and 3.7-inch guns, they were towed into position before they were settled. Although their primary purpose was anti-aircraft defense for the Thames and London, they could also engage any S-boat straying into the area to lay mines or to search for torpedo targets. They also carried radar projecting out to sea to a distance of 8.7 miles (Sunk Head) or even 9.9 miles (Knock John) and interlocking with shore-based sites.[25]

To further supplement the fixed defenses of the Maunsell forts, close escort of convoys and the mid-Channel Z-line, Hichens, and Coastal Forces during 1942 began distant patrols off the coasts of occupied Europe to catch the S-boats as they left or entered port. The impact of such patrols was almost immediate, with the 7th MGB Flotilla making an interception off the Belgian-Dutch coast in the darkness of March 14–15. Their target was the S-boats of the 2nd Flotilla based at Oostende. One S-boat (S-111) was engaged by MGBs 87, 88, and 91 and captured; most of its crew were killed or wounded.[26] Aware from radio signals that S-111 had been engaged by British forces, S-104, S-62, and S-29 of the 2nd Flotilla encountered the British MGBs towing the badly damaged S-boat. The British MGBs dropped the tow to make their escape from the superior German force. The S-boats in turn took S-111 in tow as two more boats (S-105 and S-108) arrived to support the group. The retreating S-boats were subsequently attacked by RAF Spitfires, and all five sustained damage.[27] S-111 was abandoned in a sinking condition. The damage sustained by the five S-boats was sufficient to put them out of operation for a month. The battle was a good propaganda victory for the British and was reported in the *New York Times*.[28] Such engagements, which caused considerable excitement among the MGB and MTB flotillas, helped Coastal Forces turn the balance of the fight in the Channel and North Sea.[29]

During 1942, British Coastal Forces had expanded to the point where they enjoyed numerical superiority over their German counterparts even if, in qualitative terms, the S-boat remained far superior to the MGBs, MTBs, and MLs that made up British Coastal Forces. The increasing ascendancy of Allied forces in the English Channel was important because in the Atlantic the Kriegsmarine appeared to hold the upper hand strategically. The war at sea would, however, remain attritional. The campaign in Britain's coastal waters would be long and drawn out, with enemy attacks prevented, blunted, or contained by aggressive patrolling, ambush, and attack. In turn the German war effort would be hurt by attacks by Coastal Forces and the RAF on German coastal shipping. Hichens explained the role of Coastal Forces within the campaign in his memoirs:

> I am convinced that the steady hard work of patrols, apart from the engagements, trip after trip without making contact often in appalling weather, was not without its value. The . . . [S-]Boats became aware that they were being hunted by small fast boats that might pounce on them at any time and any place, and they did not like it. It made them cautious and ultimately caused them to cut down their operations considerably. This was basically the value of gunboats, rather than the extent of destruction wrought on the . . . [S-]Boats.[30]

During 1943 Hichens' tactics began to bear fruit, as British Coastal Forces established tactical superiority in the English Channel and North Sea. As one side's morale rose, the other's fell. One Coastal Forces officer commented,

> At this stage of the war [1943] a very interesting psychological influence was making itself felt in the naval war of the North Sea and the English Channel. . . . Air power was still the major limiting factor and almost all operations of surface forces were confined to the dark hours because of the vulnerability of ships to air attack.

> The German . . . [S-]boats came across to our convoy routes under strict and very Teutonic orders. Their business was to fire torpedoes or to lay mines. If they were disturbed, they were to make a smoke-screen and run for it. Materially this was eminently sensible, for even superficial damage meant boats out of operations. . . . [Thus] In almost every encounter between our coastal forces and their German opposite numbers, we turned towards, and the Germans turned away; we were the hounds, and they were the hare. I do not for one instant believe that the young Germans who manned the . . . [S-]boats and R-boats and Channel escort vessels were any less brave or determined than the boys in the British boats, but this curious directive which had been given to them gave to us, at the same time, an incontestable moral ascendancy in all our battles and must, I believe, have played a significant part in the eventual outcome.[31]

Hichens would not live to see the full success of his ideas. In 1943 Hichens refused a shore appointment to command a training base.[32] Commanding MGB 77, he was killed at the end of a night action off the Dutch coast on April 12–13, 1943. Reactions within British Coastal Forces to Hichens' death were considerable. Commanding a steam gunboat in the English Channel, Peter Scott later wrote,

> Four days later we were half-way across the Channel listening to the nine o'clock news from the BBC on our way to the German convoy lane when a shattering announcement came over the air. "Hitch" had been killed in action off the Dutch coast. . . . I remember that we stopped, as was our wont, to compare positions at the entrance to the swept channel through the minefield, and at the same time passed the news to the other boats. There was a shocked incredulity in their tone as they answered. Surely there must be some mistake, they seemed to say. Others could be killed in action, but not Hitch.[33]

Scott later recorded an eight-minute eulogy to him in which he spoke of the nature of the engagements taking place in the English Channel and the steady campaign against the S-boats. It concluded in terms that placed Coastal Forces in the Nelsonian tradition: "He was killed instantaneously on April 13th. The country lost a great man. And those who were lucky enough to know him lost an inspiring friend."[34]

Even after his death, Hichens provided an inspirational legacy for British Coastal Forces as they continued to prosecute the attritional tactics against the S-boats that he had helped to develop. The year of 1943 would see a disappointing return of sunk merchant ships in the Channel and off the East Coast for the S-boat flotillas. Beyond the effectiveness of the convoying operations and tactical innovations, other factors were also playing a role in delivering this turning point. The case of Hichens does, however, illustrate the inspirational quality of effective leadership in navies, especially on small vessels, where that leadership can be felt on a regular basis. In both the S-boat arm and British Coastal Forces there was a considerable sense of camaraderie between officers and men, which was reinforced by the sense that officers provided leadership from the front. In motor torpedo boats, launches, and gunboats, dangers and hardships were very much shared, and on both the German and British sides there was a keen understanding that the men opposing them were not so very different from themselves.

While the numerical balance tipped firmly against Germany in 1943, German coastal forces still retained a qualitative superiority in terms of speed, firepower, and the tactical advantage in choosing when and where to fight. They also had the benefit of knowing, more or less, when and where to find the convoys that the British were forced to run with clockwork regularity on the PW-WP/FS-FN routes. The deployment of British Coastal Forces on Z-line and ambush patrols was a luxury born of the productivity of Allied industry, but there were plenty of opportunities for German forces to give them the slip. What would maximize the effectiveness of the greater number of hulls in the water for British Coastal Forces was the ability to know their enemy and to detect and respond to the S-boats as they approached the convoy lanes, vectoring to intercept and cut off German coastal forces.

CHAPTER 7

# THE 1943 TURNING POINT
## The Role of Intelligence

SINCE THE 1970S the pivotal role of intelligence in supporting the Royal Navy's defense of British trade against the Kriegsmarine has been extensively explored.[1] High-frequency direction finding (HFDF) allowed the tracking and interception of U-boats, aerial reconnaissance monitored the preparations and movements of major surface units, and Ultra decrypts could give some warning of impending attack on convoys. Despite variations in the flow of Ultra-derived intelligence (with a blackout on deciphering U-boat traffic from February to December 1942), overall the British Admiralty had detailed insights into enemy intentions from 1940 onward. However, the role of intelligence in combating the S-boat campaign against Britain's coastal convoys has barely been touched by historians. This chapter explores the role of "intelligence" in its broadest sense in combating the S-boat threat to British coastal trade as a contribution to the evolution of thinking on narrow sea naval operations, and the naval and intelligence histories of World War II.

As early as March 1938, the Committee of Imperial Defence had accepted the need for a more integrated approach to national defense at the operational level.[2] Military exercises held in both home and foreign commands had suggested the need to create new integrated bomb-proof headquarters at Plymouth, Portsmouth, and Chatham (Rosyth was subsequently added to the list). At these headquarters Royal Navy, RAF, and army officers would take operational decisions based on available resources and intelligence estimates as to the disposition of enemy forces and their intentions. In World War II they would play a vital role in maintaining British sea control in U.K. coastal areas, although most historians haven't recognized their true significance.[3] Wrangling over the costs delayed their development, and the emergence of new priorities meant that their completion would be staggered (Chatham [HMS *Wildfire*] late 1939 through early 1940, Rosyth [Pitreavie Castle] in 1941, and Portsmouth [Fort Southwick] in late 1942), with that at Plymouth remaining unfinished by the end of 1942. In 1943, with the organizational tasks of D-Day becoming fully apparent, the decision was taken to push on with the completion of the complex at Plymouth. Even so, the outfitting of the new headquarters would not be complete until early 1944, given the ever-growing flows of intelligence and the developing operational integration of ships and air and shore units, which meant an ever-greater need for telephone, teleprinter, signaling, and attendant human resources. Headquarters like that at Mount Wise in Plymouth would handle a range of data derived from signals intelligence (Ultra decrypt, traffic analysis, VHF interception, HFDF), image intelligence (radar, photo reconnaissance), and human intelligence (interrogation reports), although they would often not know the precise origin of the intelligence on which they might have to act. As the war at sea entered its critical phase in 1943–44, the combined headquarters at the principal naval commands, working with the Western Approaches Command at Liverpool, the Cabinet War Rooms in London, and subsidiary commands, made for an increasingly integrated command and control network processing and acting on vast amounts of data.

In dealing with the continuing threat from the European continent, headquarters at the principal naval ports made a vital distinction between coastal and oceanic warfare. Threats from mines and aircraft were most acute over the continental shelf, and in the narrow waters of the English Channel and North Seas (especially with the threat from aircraft), operations were more compressed in both speed and geographical extent. By 1943 the oceanic threat came from the U-boat, whereas at the coastal level the Kriegsmarine still possessed a range of effective resources to attack British forces, from S-boats to R-boats to U-boats, torpedo boats, destroyers, and coastal artillery. The S-boat posed a different set of intelligence problems to the other vessels of the Kriegsmarine. Even their name caused difficulties for naval intelligence. Though they were commonly called "E-boats" by the Royal Navy ("E for enemy"), Lieutenant Commander Norman Denning, head of the Operational Intelligence Centre in the Admiralty (later vice admiral and director of naval intelligence), took a personal dislike to the label, since all enemy vessels were essentially "E-boats."[4] He pressed for them to be called "S-boats," but without success. The label "E-boat" continued to be used by the Royal Navy and the U.S. Navy.

Throughout the war, strenuous efforts had been made to capture an intact S-boat to learn the secrets of its construction and systems. It would be to no avail, though, until after D-Day, when a sunken S-boat was discovered amid the wreckage of a dock basin in Le Havre. The irony was that trade adverts for S-boats could be found in the German and international maritime press during the 1930s.[5] Up until 1939 the Royal Navy could have simply purchased an example direct from the builder, thereby saving a lot of effort during the war and accruing a considerable amount of technical intelligence about the weapons system. That is not to say that before this point the Admiralty did not have some detailed understandings of the weapons system that they were up against. In the June 20, 1940, edition of the Admiralty's weekly intelligence summary, the S-boat was the focus of one of the articles, complete with photographs.[6] Within a month, and obviously impelled by the early successes of the S-boat against British shipping, a three-page detailed technical description appeared with significant details on construction, armament, and propulsion.[7] It was useful technical detail against which to assess other sources of information for use at the operational level.

At the operational level, intelligence was handled by the Admiralty's Operational Intelligence Centre (OPIC), which collated information from various sources before advising tactical commands. However, the sources available to OPIC in respect of S-boat operations were problematic in several respects. HFDF gave good indication of the movements and likely intercept points of slow-moving submarines and heavy warships, but it was of limited value in trying to predict the movements of fast-moving S-boats, especially under the conditions of radio silence that prevailed as they crossed the English Channel.[8] Aerial reconnaissance was similarly of limited value against boats sortieing at night, especially after the development of special S-boat pens, which protected them against aerial observation and attack. With S-boat operations ordered at short notice, and notification between bases usually taking place by telephone rather than encrypted radio message, for much of the war Ultra was of little use at the tactical level in predicting attacks on the coastal convoys. In any case, in the narrow waters of the English Channel, evasive routing was out of the question. The only possible countermeasures to protect a convoy at sea involved either strengthening the escort or bringing it into port.

## OPERATIONAL INTELLIGENCE: ULTRA

Even though Enigma-derived intelligence was of limited value at the tactical level because of delays in decryption, the use of telephones, and the short notice given of S-boat sorties, it still allowed detailed insights into enemy capabilities, procedures, and levels of preparation. It was significant in three main respects. First, low-key traffic (of which there was a substantial amount) revealed details of units, base locations, personalities, procedures, technical issues (such as engine overhaul hourages), and changes to armaments. This facilitated the buildup of a detailed understanding of the S-boat service, its personnel, and the boats on which it relied. While the documentary record is fragmentary, some idea can be gained on the role of Ultra intelligence in providing a picture of the German S-boat arm. The British National Archives contains two very full files on S-boats in the Mediterranean that provide a useful measure.[9] One file contains information sheets, seemingly included by accident, that record the amount of collated information. For example, the file contains collected details on S-153 (build, length, beam, draft, height of superstructure, engines, horsepower, maximum and cruising speed, endurance, crew size, and commanding officer). It also contains a detailed history of the 7th S-boat Flotilla.[10] Such files presumably existed on the boats of other flotillas, but these seemingly have not survived as part of the public record.

Ultra decrypts also gave very significant insights into the nature of the German naval intelligence effort against the coastal convoys, especially the efforts of the highly efficient surveillance service, Beobachtungsdienst (B-dienst). By the end of 1942 the Naval Intelligence Department knew the location of the B-dienst's intercept and direction-finding facilities, the identities of key personnel, and the service's capabilities. For example, the intercepted B-dienst weekly report for October 12–19 revealed a service remarkably adept at picking up signals from Allied vessels, allowing the B-dienst to form accurate impressions of the Royal Navy's order of battle on the East Coast, together with anti-S-boat procedures and likely countermeasures:

> Grimsby informed ships in that area at 0227/14/10 that German S-Boat activity was to be reckoned with in the Cromer sea area. The same message was passed to 2 units and 1 unknown vessel by C. in C. the Nore at 0247 hours. At 0245 hours ML498 and 499 were informed that at 2349 hours presumably German S-Boats had been in 85 degrees, 115 sea miles from Spurn Point, course West. At 0255 hours a unit reported 3 German S-Boats (2nd, 4th, and 6th S. Flotilla) 30 degrees, 10 sea miles from Cromer. Two formation leaders . . . were informed at 0321 hours that coastal warships were to proceed from Yarmouth (?) to unknown positions "RB23" and "RB24" also to 5315 N. 0300 E. (sea area 50–60 sea miles W. of Den Helder).[11]

Ultra traffic also demonstrated that B-dienst was a highly effective service in terms of monitoring the successes of the S-boat campaign.

> The following information is available on the success of the German S-Boats. SS *Lysland* (Norwegian 1335 tons) and *George Balfour* (British 1570 tons) were very badly damaged. At 0720 hours ML197 reported that she had 31 survivors on board from both these steamships, and put into port towards 1015 hours. SS *Lysland* was reported at this time on fire. Position about 30 sea miles NNW of Cromer. At 0839 hours a vessel in 5258N 0302E (62 miles E of Cromer) requested permission from Yarmouth to return to port. In the course of the day 4 tugs and 1 minesweeper were endeavouring to bring both ships in.[12]

The usefulness of Ultra in combating the S-boat threat increased dramatically following the invasion of France in 1944. As Allied forces expanded their lodgment on the coast of Normandy, forcing the abandonment of S-boat bases such as Cherbourg and Le Havre, S-boat command increasingly had to resort to radio to communicate with the flotillas. With increases in the speed of decryption, Ultra intelligence provided enhanced insights into the S-boat arm of the Kriegsmarine. As F. H. Hinsley has noted, "The Enigma decrypts regularly disclosed not merely the number of... S-Boats present at the various bases, but how many were leaving for what kind of operation, in what area and (if the operation was minelaying) with how many mines; and frequently, if not invariably, they did so a few hours before the stated time of departure. The O[perational] I[ntelligence] C[entre] telephoned this intelligence to the operational Commands."[13] The operational commands could make their dispositions accordingly to block off lines of advance across the North Sea and English Channel, to defend vulnerable convoys, and to close off routes of return for homeward-bound S-boats. Hinsley notes that evaluating the precise use of this information at the tactical level is impossible to gauge. The flow of information increased to such a point that "it became a physical impossibility" (and unwise in security terms) to signal every piece of potentially significant information to commanders at the tactical level.[14] Problems with managing the flow of intelligence information and the speed of the decryption process could open the door to successful S-boat operations. For example, attacks on convoys off Dungeness on July 26–27 and 30–31, 1944, proved effective (three ships sunk and four ships damaged) because "decrypts announcing their departure and intentions were not received in time to help the Allied Commands."[15] Likewise, an attempt to intercept an S-boat operation off Cromer on September 16–17, 1944, failed because the decrypts gave "inadequate notice."[16] By early 1945, as the surviving S-boats in the Channel concentrated in Dutch waters, the usefulness of Ultra in providing tactical information declined. Operations in the Scheldt Estuary and approaches to Antwerp provided minute windows of opportunity to intercept, decode, and relay Ultra intelligence to commanders at the tactical level.

## OPERATIONAL INTELLIGENCE: PRISONERS OF WAR

In the early stages of the war, S-boats rescued a number of Allied merchant seamen from the water, for example, two wounded men from the SS *Cordruff* were taken prisoner during the attack on FN426 on March 7–8. Whatever intelligence was derived as a result of such captures appears to have been very limited, and the practice was almost completely abandoned during 1941. But the same was not true of the intelligence derived

S-boat with early war steel wheelhouse. (*Peter Schlichting Archive*)

S-9, showing early model S-boat. (*Peter Schlichting Archive*)

Karl Erhard-Karcher, Knight's Cross Holder. (*Peter Schlichting Archive*)

Kurt Fimmen, Knight's Cross Holder. (*Peter Schlichting Archive*)

S-89 wrecked at Crackington Haven (Cornwall), 1946, showing hull form bow. (*Author's collection*)

S-89 wrecked at Crackington Haven (Cornwall), 1946, showing hull form amidships. (*Author's collection*)

Works cartoon: "Buy a Schlichting's S-boat and Stay Healthy". (*Peter Schlichting Archive*)

S-104, front part of the boat torn off by mine hit January 9, 1943, as part of an East Coast convoy operation. It appears that the aft end of the boat was towed back for parts. (*Peter Schlichting Archive*)

S-130 engine interior showing engine bed and hull construction. (*Author's collection*)

Unknown S-boat showing armored bridge. (*Peter Schlichting Archive*)

Armored bridge close-up. (*Peter Schlichting Archive*)

Gunther Rabe, Commander S-130.
(*Peter Schlichting Archive*)

Cover of Schlichting Werft magazine.
(*Peter Schlichting Archive*)

Cover of Schlichting Werft magazine. (*Peter Schlichting Archive*)

*Die Kriegsmarine*, August 1944, featuring FdS Rudolf Petersen. (*Author's collection*)

Kapitänleutnant Hermann Opdenhoff on a visit to the Schlichting Werft Archive. (*Peter Schlichting Archive*)

Kapitänleutnant Kurt Fimmen on a visit to the Schlicting Werft Archive in August 1944. (*Peter Schlichting Archive*)

from captures of S-boat personnel. Alongside Ultra, prisoners of war from S-boats provided a considerable amount of information to British Naval Intelligence. The issue has a wider significance than the history of World War II at sea. As Simona Tobia and Kent Fedorowich have observed, British interrogation has "thus far attracted little academic attention," and the role of prisoner of war–derived intelligence is little explored.[17] Its place in the history of British intelligence in World War II is only just emerging. The first S-boat personnel to fall into British hands were taken on November 20, 1940, with the sinking of S-38. Five of the crew had been killed, and ten men seriously wounded (including the three surviving officers), in an engagement with HMS *Campbell* and HMS *Garth*. Extensive interrogation of the eight unwounded men yielded much valuable information on S-boats, their equipment, weapons, and operational practices.[18] Information was also gathered on other S-boats, depot ships, tactics, and the organization of the service. With crews transferring between S-boats, the amount of information acquired was considerable, including details of their operational histories and personnel. For example, the information on S-24, which had operated in Norwegian waters and the English Channel, ran to 1.5 pages. The crew of S-38 proved remarkably talkative, suggesting that they had received limited training in behavior under interrogation. The Naval Intelligence Department's summary of the interrogations ran to twenty-four pages, and much of the information was accurate and significant. For example, all the prisoners identified the Lürssen Werft at Vegesack (Bremen) as the primary constructor of S-boats, and one also (correctly) suggested that production was starting up at Travemünde near Lübeck (Schlichting Werft).

The interrogation of the second S-boat crew to fall into British hands showed the extent to which lessons had been learned in the capture of the men from S-38 and in dealing with U-boat crews. Eighteen survivors from S-53 were landed at Sheerness at noon on February 20, 1942, and taken straight to the Combined Services Detailed Interrogation Centre (CSDIC). Their interrogation began at around 0400 hours on the morning of February 21. Suffering sleep deprivation (their mission had begun on February 19, and they had been able to sleep only a few hours before landing), and without any surviving officers, the crew of S-53 provided valuable additional information to support that provided by the men of S-38. In view of postwar revelations about the treatment of prisoners at CSDIC, it is interesting to note that sleep deprivation was singled out in the report of the Naval Intelligence Department as one reason for the success of the interrogation.[19] The youth of the crew (the average age was twenty-two years) was considered a further key factor, as was the nature of the action in which they had been captured (S-53 had been disabled after colliding with S-39 while on a mining operation with 2nd S-boat Flotilla).[20] The vessel was eventually blown up as a boarding party from HMS *Holderness* arrived on board in an attempt to seize the boat. Accounts of the precise circumstances range from the commanding officer of the S-boat, Oberleutnant-zur-See Peter Block, blowing himself up to atone for his perceived disgrace, to the same officer giving his life in an attempt to prevent S-53 being taken by the enemy (but not before he had rather sportingly warned the British boarding party that the boat was about to explode).[21] Either way, the sinking of S-53, along with the condition of some of the other survivors of S-53, suggested to the British that morale in the S-boat service was low. One survivor, a veteran of fifty-five operations in the English Channel, stated that of the original complement of two hundred men who made up 2nd S-boat Flotilla in 1940, only twenty now remained.[22] The depth of technical detail yielded by the interrogation of the crew of S-53 was considerable. This treasure trove of information included the capacity of fuel and oil storage tanks, for example, and the number of engine revolutions at each telegraph position. Maintenance schedules and the suppliers of specific key systems installed in S-53 were established. As with the interrogation of the crew of S-38, each survivor was questioned about the operational histories of other S-boats, and additionally the deployment of S-boats to other theaters of operation, including the Mediterranean. Information was solicited about S-boat bases and crews' housing facilities.

The interrogation of the crew of S-53 demonstrated the way in which British interrogation techniques were evolving and becoming increasingly more effective. On only one small matter, that S-106 was built by Schlichting Werft rather than the Lürssen Werft, did the interrogators appear to have received less than entirely accurate information. The interrogation also demonstrated the extent to which interrogators knew the right questions to ask and the perceived importance of morale. The interrogation also seems to have served as a potential check on information on S-boats being derived from other sources. For example, the crew of S-53 was unable to substantiate information derived from another source (presumably Ultra) that S-boats were conducting trial firings of G-7e electric torpedoes.

Satisfaction with the information derived from the crew of S-53 was further reflected in the interrogation of ten survivors from S-111. Sunk on March 15, 1942, after an action with British MGBs, survivors arrived at CSDIC on March 16. The interrogation team concluded that they were "not so well informed and were more guarded in their replies than the survivors from S-53."[23] The former statement is highly questionable, since the interrogators also concluded that several of the crew of S-111 were veterans who had been serving together since 1940 on S-33 and S-41 under the command of Oberleutnant-zur-see Paul Popp. It is likely that S-111's English Channel veterans were more security conscious and less shocked than the crews of either S-38 or S-53. Survivors were again questioned on the G-7e torpedo, and one of them stated that other flotillas were using it. The crew were also closely questioned on S-111's engines (Mercedes Benz 502s as opposed to S-53's MB501s).

Interestingly, there was no evidence in the Naval Intelligence Department's report that survivor statements were evaluated in the light of seizures of documents or equipment from S-111 (the vessel was successfully boarded by the crews of the MGBs, and the White Ensign was hoisted, before other S-boats arrived to reclaim the prize). British Coastal Forces had already proved highly acquisitive when it came to boarding enemy vessels. For example, when two MGBs from the 6th MGB Flotilla encountered the sinking wreck of S-41 on the night of November 19–20, 1941, they had appropriated everything they could. As Lieutenant Commander Robert Hichens, in command of MGB 64, later wrote, "The order was given to gut the boat. Sailors swarmed all over her, appearing from all the hatches with arms full of equipment. Roberts removed all the W/T equipment, gunners took what guns they could detach and pans of ammunition. Charts, books, log, compasses, searchlights, revolvers, even pictures of Hitler were bundled into the gunboats."[24] S-111 presumably yielded similar intelligence material and trophies. Throughout the war, following engagements with

S-boats, Royal Navy operations were distinguished by the acquisitiveness of crews in the search for intelligence.

Boarding actions were not relegated to the Royal Navy. S-boat crews were ready to board vessels where opportunity presented itself. On February 27, 1944, LCT 381 was in a convoy of ships in Lyme Bay when it was attacked by the 5th S-boat Flotilla from Cherbourg. One cargo vessel (SS *Modavia*) and two armed trawlers (HMT *Lord Hailsham* and HMT *Harstad*) were sunk, and a tank landing craft (LCT 381) was torpedoed by S-85. Ulrich Kolbe, in command, received permission to close with the damaged vessel and finish her off. He later recounted in a private family memoir,

> At a distance of about 50 meters . . . one could see that the ship was up to the deck in the water and that the railing was torn open. A man with a glowing flashlight stumbled aft to the deckhouse. I asked the helmsman . . . to illuminate the deck . . . with the hand light. He started at the bow, then illuminated the man and the torn railing. When he then lit up the deckhouse aft, we looked into the mouths of a 2 cm quadruple cannon . . . with behind it the flat English steel helmets facing us. I didn't need to say anything more. My people gave a short burst of fire from all the barrels we had. There was an MG on the bridge and a 2 cm cannon on the bow. The English lay down on the deckhouse behind the cannon. Then there was complete silence again. . . . My people held our boat with boat hooks. I now asked the chief machinist, armed with my pistol, to climb over. He moaned and didn't want to. Another circumstance came to our aid: the detonation had opened a large hole at the back of the deckhouse, and in the light of the handlight you could see bacon sides, sausages, and butter buckets. That broke all restraint. Now many of our people rushed over. . . . Twelve Englishmen also came on board. They brought a wounded man. All were accommodated in our crew room.[25]

The White Ensign was retrieved from the stricken LCT before the men of the S-boat retired with their collection of goods, and presumably whatever charts, documents, and confidential books could be gathered in the scramble, before LCT 381 was finished off with a torpedo with S-85 retiring to St. Peter Port on Guernsey.

The interrogations of survivors from S-38, S-53, and S-111 set the pattern for interrogations of S-boat crews in 1943 and 1944. During 1943, in part using prisoner-derived intelligence, the Admiralty was able to issue some detailed technical information on the S-boat in a special Book of Reference (BR834) titled *Light Coastal Craft Operating in the North Sea and English Channel* in 1943.[26] The sinkings of 1943–44 yielded increasingly little additional information to what was already known. The interrogation of sixteen survivors from S-96, sunk in action with two British motor launches on September 25, 1943, suggested that S-boat crews were new receiving security training because of the increased chance that they might fall into Allied hands.[27] Among the information the crew ventured was further evidence of the attempt to up-gun/up-armor and improve the systems of S-boats with the introduction of armored bridges, a 40-mm aft-facing gun to defend the boat as it tried to escape pursuers, and the possible fitting of radar onto smaller German warships. Comfortingly, the Naval Intelligence Department recorded that "although one or two boats in each flotilla carry radar little reliance is placed upon it."[28] The most useful information from the crew of S-96 came in the form of a diary kept by one of the engine room ratings who had previously served on S-43. It gave detailed technical information relating to MB501 engines (including cylinder firing order and fuel consumption figures).[29]

Following the interrogation of survivors from S-96, interrogation of captured S-boat personnel became less profitable. The interrogation report for the crew of S-88, sunk on October 25, 1943, off the East Coast by two motor gunboats (MGBs 603 and 607), yielded a report of just nine pages.[30] Likewise, the combined interrogation report for S-141 (sunk May 13, 1944, in action with destroyer) and S-147 (sunk April 26, in action with destroyer) ran to twenty pages.[31] Interrogators maintained their emphasis on the attempts to improve the existing designs of S-boats involving enhanced weaponry, armor, and systems (and learned in the process that S-147 had been used to trial in the Baltic "anti-radar netting" that covered the entire boat).[32] One interesting facet of this was evidence in the report relating to S-141 and S-147 that material recovered from Channel ports after D-Day was now being used to qualify and check assumptions derived from prisoner-of-war intelligence. For example, a suggestion that S-boat torpedo tubes were being used to lay the new family of acoustic mines was discounted by the Naval Intelligence Department on the grounds that "trolleys had been recovered . . . proving that 21-in diameter ground mines have been laid over the sides" of S-boats.[33]

However, in view of the steady collapse of the German naval effort in the West and the concentration of S-boats in Dutch waters, the primary target of interrogators was tactical information that would assist in their location and destruction. In particular, crews gave up detailed information on the light signals in use between S-boats at sea. For example, a short red light indicated that the enemy was in sight. Most importantly, interrogators concentrated on securing information on the codes that had been introduced to disguise orders being given between S-boats on short-range VHF radio. For example, a broadcast command of "Toni Dora 6" would translate into "Boat (Tactical Number 6) carry out torpedo attack."[34] This tactics-level information was exactly what was needed by the operators eavesdropping on S-boat VHF traffic in 1944–45.

## TACTICAL INTELLIGENCE: VHF/RT

Operational intelligence allowed the Naval Intelligence Department to build up a detailed understanding of the S-boat arm, but to translate that into success in the English Channel and North Sea required real-time tactical information. From 1941 onward, British Coastal Forces had four principal sources of tactical information: radio telegraphy (RT) signals in Morse; VHF voice intercepts; seaborne radar; and Air-to-Service Vessel (ASV) radar in the aircraft of RAF Coastal Command. From 1941 onward, VHF/RT intercepts, the latter used very sparingly by S-boats, provided information on the location and movements of S-boats off the British coast. In 1940 the RAF's "Y" service had picked up on the fact that VHF radio was the principal means by which German tanks and aircraft exchanged tactical signals. By August 1940 it was apparent that S-boats in the English Channel were using light signals and VHF radio to coordinate their attacks. As Patrick Beesly has noted, "Commander Sandwith's section, D.S.D./N.I.D.9, responsible for the control and administration of the Navy's 'Y' and D/F sections, very quickly set up a small 'Y' station on the North Foreland manned by the Civilian Wireless Service."[35] This quickly demonstrated the potential to use VHF/RT to monitor the movement and operations of S-boats.

Operating at night, and sometimes at great speed, groups of S-boats used light signals where possible to locate each other and to coordinate their movements. However, once a group of S-boats had been required to break formation, short-range VHF radio was the principal means by which they sought to relocate and reorganize themselves. Especially in the aftermath of an attack, there was an urgent need to establish the location of friendly forces either to come to their aid or to prevent collisions and/or the potential for friendly fire incidents. S-boat commanders appear to have used their VHFs very freely even in the run-in to the convoy lanes giving ample opportunities for the signals to be picked up. Some S-boat flotillas were better than others, but in some cases S-boat skippers would chat to each other over VHF from the point they left harbor. Some of this chatter was of a social rather than a military nature, including details of women whom the officers had encountered the previous evening.[36] This lack of discipline led FdS Petersen in January 1943 to order radio silence on the run-in to the convoy lanes and emergency use only of VHF in close proximity (forty-five miles) to the British coast.[37] The extent to which the order made a difference in practice is hard to establish. For example, in September 1944, eighty-six separate messages were picked up from three S-boats in a seventy-one-minute period during a night action.[38] In December 1944, British warships recorded ninety transmissions in a battle that lasted ninety-eight minutes and resulted in the sinking of S-185 and S-192.[39] Many of these do appear to fall under the label of "emergency use," and they were usually very short (e.g., orders to report). They were frequently broadcast in clear channels, however, giving tactical and positional information. Even without the details of the message, the carrier wave for S-boat VHF radios could be picked up at short ranges by wireless operators on Allied ships, warning that enemy vessels were in the vicinity.[40]

A service to intercept and eavesdrop on S-boat VHF chatter was developed in 1940–41, with listening posts set up on the East Coast and at key Coastal Forces bases. Initially the service relied on the British Army for the provision of the necessary linguists, but it was realized in 1941 that other sources would have to be tapped to provide the number of German speakers to facilitate the expansion of the service. Thus, in October a nationwide hunt was initiated for German speakers who could join British Coastal Forces. From all directions they came, including civilians and members of the armed services, the Merchant Navy, and the Women's Royal Naval Service, and some were less than ideally qualified.[41] Naval officer Alan Peacock, for example, was well schooled in literary German but had never held a conversation in the language, let alone having any familiarity with colloquial German and Kriegsmarine slang.[42] In addition to fluent German, the job called for a keen ear and steady hands "to search slowly and painstakingly over a small area of frequencies listening for, sometimes very faint, 'carrier waves.'"[43]

One German-speaking WREN of the "Y" service who was sent to Sheringham, Norfolk, as part of the watch on the East Coast convoy route recalled,

> The quarters were in a big house on the cliff's edge, and the watch-room, half of which was occupied by WAAF intercept operators, stood on Beeston Hump, the highest piece of cliff in the neighborhood. There was plenty of E-boat traffic, as both convoy routes passed within visual range. It was here that for the first time I saw the whole intercept operation come together. We picked up E-boat signals and identified the boats; together with [other stations at] Trimingham and Hemsby, where signals were also audible, we got a fix on them and quickly telephoned the information to the Intelligence Centre in Chatham. Chatham notified Coastal Forces at Yarmouth and Lowestoft, who sent their MTBs and MGBs racing to the spot.[44]

A base for "headache operators," known after their headphone apparatus, was also established near Dover in a cottage overlooking St. Margaret's Bay. Information derived from intercepts could be telephoned straight through to Dover Castle.[45] Other "Y" stations were established at places such as Trimingham, Hemsby, Southwold, Gorleston, and Felixstowe and staffed by groups of twelve to twenty German speakers from diverse backgrounds. Hilda Hale, for example, had taken German as one of her subjects at school in the 1930s and was staying with a German family before a hurried return home in the late summer of 1939.[46] She later joined the WRENs and served with "Y" service on the East Coast.

The work of the "Y" service was made difficult by the short range of VHF, and then in January 1943 instructions were issued in the S-boat command to maintain radio silence in the approach to the convoy lanes. This meant that shore-based operators could give only minimal warning of the proximity of S-boats.[47] However, there were ways to compensate. While it was difficult for ships at sea—given the speeds involved and the difficulty of triangulating any position, which would involve breaking radio silence and compromising their own position—to direction-find S-boats, value was found in having German-speaking radio operators aboard some Coastal Forces units and destroyers.[48] These headache operators could provide running commentaries on S-boat signals and likely S-boat movements.[49] Given the gender boundaries of the 1940s, these embarked headache operators were all male, despite pressure from a senior and well-placed WREN signals officer.[50] The headache operators on HMS *Westminster*, for example, were two German-speaking Hungarians who could pick up S-boat VHF transmissions fifteen to twenty miles distant.[51] This real-time tactical intelligence had considerable value in the defense of convoys, and it also allowed the British to further develop a detailed picture of their adversaries derived from operational intelligence sources. In 1944 a book was opened at HMS *Hornet* (Gosport) to log every piece of information on S-boat personnel from VHF/RT and other sources. The book became an important source on the opposition facing British Coastal Forces, with one officer later reflecting that it was "a valuable thing."[52] From late 1944 onward, VHF intercepts from S-boats also had another value in terms of the intelligence battle: they helped to protect the Ultra secret by providing a convenient explanation for the number of S-boat operations intercepted by Allied units. As F. H. Hinsley has noted, "In 1944 S-Boat Command believed that the destroyers in the Seine Bay were operating with foreknowledge of German movements derived from Allied exploitation of . . . VHF/RT traffic."[53]

VHF intercepts had value, but it was limited. They could warn of S-boats that were approaching convoys and that, remaining in the vicinity after an engagement, were being missed by their comrades or were in distress themselves. They also provided general intelligence on particular flotillas, and occasionally tactical intelligence as well. Given the speed of S-boat operations, the nature of East Coast convoy operations, and the nature of the war channels on the East Coast, a convoy or individual vessel probably did not have that much scope or space for emergency maneuvers in response to tactical information derived from VHF sources. In particular, responding effectively to a developing torpedo attack relied on cross-referencing VHF data with radar or visual sightings even if a general angle of approach could be assumed. Real-time processing of multiple sources of data at night during an attack remained an extremely difficult process to the end of World War II and beyond.

## TACTICAL INTELLIGENCE: RADAR—SHORE, SHIP, AND AIR

Alongside VHF/RT traffic the development of Allied radar on land, sea, and air had a significant impact on the S-boat campaign at the tactical level. In the mid-1930s, radar direction finding had been developed on the River Deben at Bawdsey Manor.[54] With the emergence of the S-boat threat, type 287 radar towers were rushed into service on the East Coast in early 1941. With a relatively short range they were superseded by later models, but by mid-1941 the proximity of S-boats to the convoy routes on the East Coast was routinely being detected at a range of approximately eighteen miles. For shore-based radar the low-lying nature of the East Coast was a particular difficulty. Between Bawdsey and Cromer the eight radar stations required two-hundred-foot-high towers to allow them to function.[55] The one at Covehithe was typical: a two-hundred-foot tower with a Nissen hut and a nearby house to provide reserve power. At Orford the keep of a medieval castle was used to house some of the radar equipment. There were some gaps and differences in coverage. For example, Bawdsey could detect vessels out to 18.2 miles, while Orford Castle, with slightly less elevation and a greater distance from the coast, had a range of 14.1 miles. Gaps in coverage and breakdowns were considerable, but it did give tactical forces an opportunity to intercept S-boats and also gave convoy escorts forewarning of imminent attack.[56] The opportunity was of limited value, however.

At the extreme range of eighteen miles, an S-boat cruising at twenty knots toward the convoy lanes would be detected thirty-nine minutes before it was able to launch an attack. The radar on some of the sea forts guarding the Thames Estuary would provide just twenty-three minutes' warning of a developing attack even at S-boat cruising speed.[57] What radar did was to prevent S-boats from freely cruising the convoy route or simply lying in wait for the merchant ships to arrive. It also played mind games within S-boat high command, as radar seemed to strip away the element of surprise and the invisibility of night required for successful hunting operations. Rapid technical improvements improved the effectiveness of radar to the point where a successful Coastal Forces night action of April 15–16, 1943, in the Bay of the Seine resulted from the detection of an enemy plot "at a range of seventy miles" by the RDF station at Ventnor.[58]

To try and increase the effectiveness of shore-based radar in providing tactical intelligence on the East Coast, in February 1943 the safe route along the East Coast between Shipwash, Cross Sand, and Hearty Knoll was altered to bring the route farther inshore. This gave better coverage for the radar and VHF intercept stations along the coast.[59] Even so, the intersection between land and sea on the East Coast gave rise to problematic atmospheric conditions, which are a feature of radar use in inshore areas, as is now well understood: "The combined effect of air temperature and proximity of the landmass in a narrow sea frequently causes non-standard propagation of radio waves. This in turn greatly effects the range of radar and radio communications."[60] This was not so well understood in 1943, but the implications were. In October 1943, C-in-C Nore still had to report to their lordships of the Admiralty: "Conditions vary greatly on the East Coast and failures to obtain contacts, even inside the restricted range, are frequent."[61] On the southern coast and in the West, there was also considerable variability in the ability of radar to detect fast-moving vessels approaching the English coast, although the Plymouth Command War Diary for July 2, 1943, does report a radar contact with a group of vessels off Cap de la Hague on the Cotentin Peninsular, a distance of over one hundred nautical miles.[62]

The effectiveness of shore-based radar meant that by mid-1941 it was almost invariably the case that developing S-boat attacks were being detected before contact was made with convoys. S-boat command realized the problem and began to consider countermeasures. Their response was to move S-boat operations away from the areas with the best radar coverage. On the East Coast this meant that operations shifted to the area around Cromer Knoll, "where, it was thought, the risk of detection by the efficient British radar system was less than in any other area."[63] It also resulted in the 2nd and 4th S-boat Flotillas being sent to Cherbourg in June 1942 to operate against convoys routed along the coast of southwestern England. There was limited radar coverage over the seas around that section of the coast, and the flotillas were to try different tactics (e.g., *Stichansatz*; see below), with Luftwaffe or B-dienst intelligence replacing the tactic of simply lying in wait along the convoy routes. The results were dramatic. On July 2, the 2nd S-boat Flotilla sank six ships (12,000 tons) from convoy WP183 after B-dienst had identified that a convoy was at sea.[64] Convoy routes in the West would remain vulnerable to S-boat attacks until the Normandy invasion forced the abandonment of S-boat bases at Cherbourg and Le Havre, but along the East Coast of the United Kingdom, real-time intelligence provided by shore-based radar had taken a decisive step toward the defeat of the enemy attack.

The effect of shore-based radar in providing information to tactical commanders was enhanced by shipborne radar. The type 271 radar was fitted to corvettes, frigates, and destroyers from March 1941 onward and could detect S-boats over six miles distant.[65] While it could give a strong indication of the location of an S-boat, it was not trusted sufficiently for escort vessels to engage without first establishing a visual contact.[66]

By the summer of 1944, radar-equipped escorts could operate in conjunction with MTBs and MGBs (usually around six) vectoring them toward a group of S-boats until close enough to gain a fix on their own radars.[67] Eight *Buckley*-class frigates, built in the United States for the Royal Navy under the Lend-Lease agreement in 1943–44 and named after famous captains, were designated as Coastal Forces Command Frigates.[68] With 40-mm Bofors guns, 2-pounder quick-firing, and 3-inch and Oerlikon cannon, the Captain-class frigates were capable of delivering a significant volume of fire. They also carried the hedgehog antisubmarine mortar and conventional depth charge rails at the stern, giving them good antisubmarine capability. Capable of twenty-four knots and given extensive training with MTBs in the spring of 1944 to prepare them for the fast-moving S-boats, the frigates were based at Plymouth in the run-up to D-Day. In operations in April and May they gained valuable experience that would later be put to good use in defending the invasion fleet.[69] Radar was at the heart of their value as nocturnal hunters as part of a defensive shield against S-boats.

In December 1940, MTB 28 had trialed type 286MY radar, and the following spring type 286MU began to be fitted across British Coastal Forces.[70] The range of type 286 radar was typically around two miles against S-boats and was often combined with the use of a hydrophone to detect approaching vessels. The hydrophones allowed operators to detect and identify vessels by their different engine signatures, together with background natural noises such as passing whales and dolphins.[71] The repercussions of radar intelligence in providing tactical intelligence were considerable. As detailed in the Naval Staff's history *Defeat of the Enemy Attack on Shipping*, "From 1943 onwards E-boats frequently found themselves under fire before they had sighted an enemy."[72] Also, by and large, shore- and ship-based radar removed the element of surprise from S-boat attacks on the eastern and southern coasts. It minimized the time that an S-boat could remain on station prospecting the convoy route for ships. A group of three S-boats could space themselves out and sit along the convoy route watching for signs of coastal convoys. Once sighted, light or VHF/RT signals could be used to reform the group and coordinate an attack. As Gordon Williamson has noted, "By early 1943 it was becoming clear that the previous . . . tactic of lying-in wait on a known convoy route in order to make a night-time ambush was no longer working. This was principally due to the heavy use of radar by both shore stations and Allied aircraft."[73]

Increasingly important in supporting surface operations against the S-boat threat were the radar-equipped aircraft of RAF Coastal Command. Developed during the 1930s Air-to-Surface Vessel (ASV) radar was installed in about half the aircraft of RAF Coastal Command by mid-1941.[74] Issues of reliability and effectiveness plagued the Mark I and II sets, but by the summer of 1941, 16 Group RAF Coastal Command, with an ever-expanding number of squadrons equipped with increasingly diverse types of aircraft, was able to mount reconnaissance flights over known S-boat approaches to the coastal convoy routes. Even without radar an aircraft could, in any case, be effective in detecting S-boats. The wake of an S-boat at night was relatively easy to spot on all but the darkest of nights.[75] One former member of Coastal Command later wrote, "It was . . . their wakes that enabled us to sight them easily in moonlight, rather than the vessels, which were relatively small."[76] In addition, the approach of an aircraft was covered by the noise of the S-boats. In 1940–42, sinking a fast-moving S-boat with bombs or torpedoes was unlikely, but they could at least provide intelligence (course, speed, number) on a developing S-boat attack (this would change later in the war as 16 Group acquired bigger, faster, and more heavily armed aircraft). In October 1941, 16 Group RAF experimented with the use of the home chain radar network to guide aircraft against S-boats and German convoys operating off the coast of the continent.[77] Wing Commander Constable Roberts, air staff officer of Dover Command, was able to report a considerable degree of success: "The information of early approach of enemy light forces by Type 271 10 cm RDF stations has allowed our own [air] forces to intercept before any damage could be done. This fortunate situation has resulted in a complete cessation of enemy . . . minelaying or torpedo attack along our convoy routes in this area."[78] The expansion of 16 Group by 1943 enhanced the levels of airborne electronic surveillance over the approaches to the coastal convoy routes. The group's principal weapon against the S-boats was the radar-equipped, twin-engine Whitley bomber, while the Fleet Air Arm operated Albacore and Fairey Swordfish. Their role was "primarily to give warning" of approaching S-boats.[79] With a cruising speed of 100–120 knots, carrying a full load of 250-pound bombs and flares, the Fairey Albacore struggled to intercept forty-knot S-boats. In the circumstances, they could hope to do little better than "scare them," as one Albacore pilot later put it.[80]

Even where they could give advance warning of a developing S-boat, there was a problem in utilizing the intelligence. Flare or flame floats would have to be used to mark the position of any S-boats detected. While an aircraft could relay information to base, it could not use radio telephony to contact any surface vessel operating in support of the convoys. However, by May 1943 the director of Air Warfare and Flying Training was looking forward to the installation of high-frequency radios in Coastal Command aircraft, which would allow direct radio contact between "convoy escorts, counter attacking force and homing aircraft."[81] This was a belated development; the first trials had taken place in September 1939.[82] By the late summer of 1944, the problems of installing 86-meter-type transmitters in coastal craft still hadn't been resolved; there was still a potential for interference between radar and wireless transmitter.[83] The technical issues were not fully addressed until early 1945.

The flow of electronic intelligence was gathered at three critical points: plot rooms in the three major commands covering the English Channel (Plymouth, Portsmouth, and Dover). Forces at sea in the English Channel would be identified and plotted with a constant flow of information relayed from other commands by telephone and wireless. Some of the subcommands, such as the Coastal Forces base at Dartmouth, also seem to have maintained their own plotting room.[84] The integration of the data streams into the three major operational commands, and the ability to rapidly deploy forces, created what one naval officer would later refer to as a "complete system of naval operating," although the sheer volume of maritime traffic in English coastal waters in 1943–44 with the buildup to D-Day often exceeded the capacities of the systems and network.[85]

## IMPACT OF THE "COMPLETE SYSTEM OF NAVAL OPERATING"

The development of this "complete system of naval operating" with intelligence and information streams feeding into networks of command and control, allied to the growing number of increasingly well-armed escort vessels available for service in English waters (as we saw in the last chapter), began to impact the coastal convoy campaign in late 1943, but it remained anything but "complete" even if its evolution was impressive and rapid. British Forces faced the longer autumn and winter nights of late 1943, with their increased opportunities for S-boat operations, with some trepidation. In October 1943, C-in-C Nore asked the Admiralty for reinforcement. He wrote, "I consider the extraordinarily small losses which have taken place over recent months must be attributed principally to good fortune and lack of enterprise on the part of the enemy."[86] He concluded, "These two factors cannot be expected to continue indefinitely." There was a perception in some quarters that the Royal Navy in the English Channel and on the East Coast was being starved of resources to bolster Allied Forces in the Atlantic. C-in-C Rosyth expressed grave concerns in late 1943 about the shortage of escorts: "While every effort is being made to win the Battle of the Atlantic and considerable success is being attained in bringing convoys safely to West coast ports, I view with alarm their passage up and down the East coast unprotected save by a single destroyer."[87] This was a rather simplistic, if undoubtedly well-meaning, reading of the means by which coastal convoys were protected by 1943, but it underlined perceptions about the threat posed by the ongoing S-boat campaign and the criticality of the English Channel as the battleground for the invasion that was in preparation.

The concerns of senior figures in the Royal Navy can be contrasted with the markedly more negative views in the Kriegsmarine about the likely evolution of the S-boat campaign. In a paper on S-boat operations in 1943, written on the last day of that year, FdS Petersen pictured the campaign against coastal convoys as being in "crisis."[88] Since 1940, British defenses had improved considerably and there had been a corresponding failure to invest in the S-boat campaign either with significant increases in the number of available vessels or with major qualitative improvements in the new vessels being sent to the Channel and North Sea ports. German high command had failed to identify the importance of the coastal convoys to British trade and their significance in Allied preparations for launching a second front in Western Europe. What the report by FdS Petersen did not emphasize was that, with the inadequacies of the German battle fleet, there had been overreliance on the U-boat offensive as the Kriegsmarine's major contribution to the war effort. By the end of 1943, with the U-boat fleet suffering serious reverses in the spring and summer, that overreliance on submarine designs that were dated and inadequate looked like a major strategic failure on the part of the German navy. Failure to integrate the Luftwaffe into joint operations over the Atlantic was another serious failure that the report did not linger on. Instead, Petersen's report preferred to look forward to the renewal of the S-boat campaign, with increased number of vessels scheduled for building under the 1943 building program.

He also looked forward to a renewal of the partnership between Luftwaffe and Kriegsmarine that had proved so effective against a couple of convoys in 1940. The report was a consummate exercise in the politics of high command, but it was also a recognition that the S-boat offensive was shifting from the offensive to the defensive. The destruction of cargoes and the disruption of coastal shipping was no longer about starving Britain into submission. Rather, it was about delaying and damaging the Allied buildup toward the launching of an invasion of Western Europe.

This growing sense of crisis within the S-boat force and the increasing confidence in British Coastal Forces played out in a series of critical coastal convoy battles in late 1943. Those battles were fought against a backdrop of a weakened escort force available in the Channel and North Sea because of withdrawal of destroyers to meet requirements in the Mediterranean and Atlantic (see table 3). In the summer of 1943, concerns had been expressed within the Rosyth command about the security of larger Bolero convoys when longer nights returned in the autumn, in the light of the available escort forces.[89] Convoys had been reduced to operating with just one destroyer as close escort, in addition to lighter forces. For example, convoy CW221, which was attacked on November 4, with the loss of two ships, was protected by just one destroyer as close escort. With two destroyers for escort in 1942, the reduction to one a year later caused concern in Royal Navy and Merchant Navy ranks.[90] On reviewing the engagement, C-in-C Portsmouth concluded, "Although the substance of these reports is from imperfectly informed persons they emphasize once again the necessity for additional escorting destroyers for Channel convoys."[91] Within the Royal Navy, given what was at stake in terms of the buildup toward the invasion, there was a redoubled sense of urgency to beef up the defenses on the East Coast and Channel. Given the ability of the different commands to reinforce threatened convoys, the situation was not perhaps as bad as some senior naval officers feared. Thus, when one FN convoy was attacked by S-boats on October 24–25, 1943, rallying to its defense were HMS *Pytchley* (the escorting destroyer) plus four other destroyers (dispatched in support) and a force of twenty-one motor launches, MGBs, and MTBs.[92] Eventually, after C-in-C Nore had campaigned for the return of some of the Hunt-class destroyers from the Mediterranean, five old Town-class destroyers were additionally allocated to Rosyth.[93] This helped to ensure that the Royal Navy did manage to get away with providing just one destroyer as close escort, while bringing up Bolero requirements to the necessary minimum.

The situation, however, was given added urgency by the discovery that the buildup under the Bolero plan (the buildup toward D-Day) was significantly "behind schedule."[94] Coal stocks were thought to be three weeks below the minimum required for sufficient stocks to launch an invasion in the spring of 1944. Thus, on November 25 the Naval Staff instructed commands in the Channel and North Sea to be ready to start seven-day convoying.[95] The C-in-C Nore command made it clear that he accepted the order only "on the understanding that the situation renders it essential to accept a considerably increased risk."[96] It was a move that was born of desperation but also a certain degree of confidence. The S-boat threat remained serious, but Royal Navy officers felt that they could mitigate the risks of inadequate close escort through the layered defense that had evolved since 1940. Within the Trade Division there was rather less confidence. One person wrote in the minutes, "I hope that our luck with the East Coast convoys will hold until reinforcements are available."[97]

That luck did indeed hold, and despite the worst fears of some, the S-boat campaign proved largely ineffective during the remainder of November and December 1943. The coastal actions that did take place demonstrated that, as in the Atlantic in March 1943, a turning point had been reached. They established that the S-boat flotillas no longer had the ability to cross the Channel undetected; they no longer had the ability to loiter along the convoy lanes and attack with impunity; they could expect to encounter British Coastal Forces; and they could expect the most vigorous response from Coastal Forces skippers ready to lose their vessel to inflict significant damage on the enemy. A crippled S-boat was almost certainly going to be lost to further attacks. Given the inadequate number of S-boats being built and the slowness of the shipyards in building new ones, German commanders had to adopt a strategy of "fleet in being" to preserve the campaign, even if it limited the chances for successful engagements with convoys and escorting. The British, meanwhile, could afford to replace their qualitatively inferior boats with others and thus were prepared to take greater risks. The danger of invasion added a further reason not to take risks with S-boat units, and that in turn led to the development of a defensive mindset. That mindset can be glimpsed in the comments of those who closely observed the coastal campaign and the operations of the S-boat arm. Peter Scott, for example, commented that an S-boat "carried torpedoes and mines against merchant ships. Should it meet anything else it must not become involved but must retire behind a smokescreen. So . . . [S-boat] crews were instructed . . . to flee should any opposition be encountered."[98] One American officer, the executive officer on the USS *Frankford*, noted that S-boat "captains are seldom aggressive in the face of illumination and gunfire."[99]

The battles of late 1943, with the British fine-tuning an increasingly effective way of coastal warfare, were a turning point that decisively affected the confidence levels of the different combatants. Admiral Tovey recognized both the improvement of Coastal Forces and what more might be achieved when he reflected on the successful defense of FN1160 in October:

> This action gives general proof of a great improvement in the efficiency of the Coastal Forces particularly as regards communications and the use of radar. The small number of material breakdowns— also indicates a higher standard of interest and handling by the Commanding Officers and crews of boats and reflects great credit on the maintenance officers and staffs of the bases. Furthermore, it clearly demonstrates the value and essential need of constant training and practice. In addition to the successful defence of the convoy, it is considered permissible to feel a modicum of satisfaction in the number of times the E[nemy] boats were engaged. They were roughly handled six times in or near the convoy route. . . . Had the RAF been able to attack them after daylight it would have been a strong deterrent to E-boats leaving their return to their bases till so late.[100]

By the end of 1943, the British had developed a range of responses to the S-boat campaign that effectively utilized multiple sources of intelligence within a layered defense of aircraft, ships, and artillery- and radar-equipped forts. While the S-boats could still make their way across the Channel, attack a convoy, and return to base, the increasingly frequent contacts between German and British units took a steady toll on the former, sharply limiting their chances of mounting an effective surprise attack. As the war in the Channel turned against the Kriegsmarine, the speed of S-boats and their capacity to absorb considerable punishment were the saving graces for the crews that operated them. The question was whether the Germans could find some means to offset growing Allied strength in the Channel.

**CHAPTER 8**

# THE 1943 TURNING POINT
## German Failure to Respond Effectively

FACED WITH THE growing effectiveness of British efforts to protect the convoys, the inadequacy of the Luftwaffe in the West to provide either protection or reconnaissance, and a strategic balance that was slowly tipping against Germany, during late 1942 and into 1943 the Kriegsmarine struggled to respond to the challenges it faced in the prosecution of the coastal campaign. The Kriegsmarine, and especially its S-boat arm, faced a clear choice of either trying to build and field greater numbers of boats, which probably meant changing their design, or trying to maintain or extend their qualitative superiority over Allied naval forces in the Channel. The German naval high command, sticking to the strategy of what amounted to a holding operation in the coastal waters of Western Europe, chose the latter. The greatest investment would go into U-boat production, particularly at the expense of the larger surface ships. This chapter examines the steps taken by S-boat command to do what it could with the inadequate resources at its disposal in order to maintain the campaign, and to give crews a realistic chance of returning from missions.

### BASE FACILITIES

Trying to secure boats and crews in port against the growing Allied air offensive had been a concern since 1941, and in 1943 the need increased still further. The development of protected base facilities at Oostende, Cherbourg, Rotterdam, Ijmuiden, and Boulogne in 1941–42 had enabled the S-boat force to spread the coastal campaign along the length of England's southern and eastern coasts, while giving S-boats in port some protection from aerial attack. The growing strength of Allied airpower, and hopes for a greater availability of S-boats, led to fresh construction in 1943. New bunkers were planned and existing bunkers extended.[1] A new bunker at Den Helder scheduled for fourteen berths was extended to double that. Ijmuiden, built as a ten-berth bunker, was extended to a twenty-eight-berth facility. The basic vault arrangement at Cherbourg was also extended to twenty-eight, with an additional fourteen berth bunkers planned for L'Aber Wrac'h and Lézardrieux. Even by this stage of the war, as noted by Admiral Saalwächter (head of Marine Command West), labor and material shortages forced a "frugal approach [*Sparsamkeit*] toward the provision of new bomb-proof facilities for S-boats."[2]

In late 1943, planning was undertaken to create a second bunker at Ijmuiden (an extra fourteen berths). Although not all these facilities would be built because of shortages of manpower and materials, other priorities, and the evolving nature of the coastal campaign, the provision of additional bunker facilities was a logical response to the growth of the Allied heavy bombing campaign. The development of R-boat bunkers at Le Havre and Dunkirk created additional facilities that might be used by S-boat flotillas. Unfortunately, the S- and R-boat bunkers were not built to the same standard as those that protected the U-boats. They were vulnerable to the heaviest Allied bombs, such as the tallboy, despite having ten-foot-thick reinforced concrete roofs.

Supplementing the program of building bunkers for the S-boat was the development of an S-boat command headquarters at Scheveningen on the Dutch coast. Construction of a network of command and supporting bunkers began in March and ended in December 1943. The main command bunkers were centrally heated and equipped with powerful wireless transmitters and receiving equipment. At the heart of one sat an illuminated table on which the dispositions of bases and units at sea could be plotted. A network of support bunkers (machine room, personnel, cookhouse) supported the command bunkers, near which were large villas requisitioned by the Germany navy for the FdS and his staff (around 195 officers and men). The headquarters of the FdS was subordinate to Marine Gruppe West, to which it was linked, along with the S-boat bases along the coast, by telephone and wireless. The building of the headquarters, together with the port bunkers, meant that during 1943 significant steps were taken to protect the S-boat force along the Channel coast from the growing threat of aerial attack. What the architects of Organization Todt failed to take into account, however, was the development of heavier bombs capable of piercing even the best-protected bunker.

## IMPROVED WEAPONS ON S-BOATS

While the Royal Navy was busy improving its combat power through the quality and number of its units, there was a failure on the part of the Kriegsmarine to match those improvements on the S-boats. Experience early in the war had led to some changes to the design of S-boats: S-38 to S-53, which entered service between late 1940 and late 1941, were equipped with three MB501 engines. Offensive firepower was also increased with the addition of extra machine guns and cannon (especially a 2-cm flak cannon in front of the wheelhouse). To facilitate the changes, the length of the hull was increased to 39.4 meters. While S-62 to S-66 would be built to the same type 38 design, a further revision was introduced (38b) for S-67 to S-99, S-101 to S-131, and S-137 to S-138. Most of the boats built in the middle of the war were constructed to the 38b classification. The MB501 engine remained the standard for the type 38, 38b, and their successor, the type 100 (S-100, S-134 to S-150). The MB511 engine was introduced for the type 100 boats from S-167 to S-218; this engine would allow S-boats to travel more than forty knots. Further experimentation would take place with S-208, which trialed MB508 engines. With the type 100 the S-boat design appeared to reach some sort of plateau. The basic design had been taken about as far as was possible. To reach higher speeds, a very different design would be required. Improving the effectiveness of the S-boat would be a matter of trying to improve onboard equipment and providing greater firepower.

The need for equipment and firepower improvements was necessary even as the hull design was plateauing. The growing effectiveness of British Coastal Forces during 1941 had led the Führer der Torpedoboote (FdT) to conclude in December that decisive action was required: "German defensive and offensive ability could be increased only by continual improvement of equipment and type, and the present advantage over the enemy could be maintained only if an improved type of S-boat were to be produced."[3] Six months later, with the creation of the post of Führer der Schnellboote (FdS), the new head had concluded that the S-boats were "no longer master of the situation in the Western area."⁴ The seriousness of the situation was underlined by an intelligence windfall that had occurred with an action on September 10, 1942. In that action MGB 335 had been captured virtually intact after a gun action with German forces.⁵ This had given the Kriegsmarine access to her confidential books, her radar, her radio gear, and a set of marked-up maps. At Den Helder the boat was inspected by FdS Petersen and B-dienst.⁶ The capture was kept secret by the Kriegsmarine, with media claims that the boat had been sunk, to keep secret the intelligence derived as a result. The British were apparently convinced enough not to immediately revise the secret codes that had fallen into B-dienst's hands with the capture of the vessel.⁷ Petersen was troubled by his inspection of the MGB, as his notes reveal:

A) Speed less than an S-boat, probably about 30 knots.
B) Gunnery armament far heavier.
C) Seaworthiness . . . not regarded unfavorably.
D) MGB has radar and radio equipment such as has been recommended for the last two years for the S-boats and which is only just beginning to be produced. . . .
E) Has other equipment not yet recognized.
F) Has VHF aerial but no set. Possibly also infra-red signaling.
G) Bridge is armored. . . .
H) Simple construction and engines. Appearances of having been built simply and quickly.⁸

Petersen's initial response was to insist that S-boats remain together on their way to the attack points and to vary their routes to and from port to decrease the chance that they might be ambushed. Petersen also called for programs to upgrade the S-boats. In May 1942 he had concluded that it was "vital to . . . to develop new types of boats, mines, torpedoes, gunnery and signal equipment."⁹ On inspection of the MGB, he thought there was a need to go further and begin the armoring of bridges and the rapid introduction of radar to go with the other upgrades.¹⁰ Petersen believed there was an urgent need to improve the systems of the S-boat to increase both its offensive and defensive capabilities. Tactical changes would also have to be considered.

Such were the demands on the German war economy, especially given the fighting in Russia, the need to combat the Allied heavy bomber offensive, and, in the case of the Kriegsmarine, the need for U-boat production that there was little scope for immediate improvement. The G7a torpedo, standard with S-boats and U-boats at the outbreak of the war, was still the mainstay of the S-boat torpedo arsenal in 1945, even though the torpedo had several drawbacks, including the fact that it left a visible wake because it was powered by compressed air. That wake could give critical warning of the approach of a torpedo and the direction of the attacker. The G7a was principally a weapon designed for use by U-boats at long range (up to 13,700 meters). Most S-boat attacks, meanwhile, typically took place at shorter ranges (less than 3,000 meters).[11] In time many of the torpedo types developed for U-boats were made available to the S-boat flotillas, although the nature of S-boat warfare, and the fact that S-boats could carry only four torpedoes, limited their use. For example, an electric-drive G7e torpedo, first mooted after World War I, was developed for use by U-boats, and it was tried by the S-boat arm.[12] The G7e left no telltale wake, but its use was largely abandoned by the S-boat arm after trials in 1942. Good for silent and long-range use against convoys by submerged U-boats, the torpedo ran too slow for hit-and-run actions against coastal convoys.[13] In particular, against fast-moving enemy destroyers the G7e was a very poor weapon that gave an S-boat little chance of defending itself. But in 1943 the FAT (*Federapparat*) torpedo was introduced into the S-boat arm.[14] It was essentially a G7a torpedo with a programmable course. This torpedo would run until, after a given distance, it would loop back on its own track and continue to do so until it found a target or ran out of fuel and sank to the bottom. With the changing fortunes of war, specialized torpedoes could come into their own. For example, in 1944 Dackel (TIIId) torpedoes, a variant on the G7e torpedo designed for coast defense, were utilized to good effect by the 6th S-boat Flotilla to make long-range attacks on the vast Allied invasion fleet anchored off the Normandy coast. For the most part, however, senior commanders continued to put their faith in the G7a.

The need for better torpedoes was underpinned by the growing effectiveness of Allied defenses in the English Channel. This had meant that torpedo attacks after 1942 had taken place at greater distances than

**TABLE 5.** AVERAGE S-BOAT TORPEDO FIRING DISTANCES

| YEAR | DISTANCE |
|---|---|
| 1940 | 900 meters |
| 1941 | 1,700 meters |
| 1942 | 1,800 meters |
| 1943 | 2,000 meters |
| 1944 | 1,700 meters |

SOURCE: Underwater Weapons Department (Admiralty), German Torpedo Documents, TNA: ADM 292/204.

previously. Many of the new S-boat commanders arriving at the Channel flotillas in 1943 came straight from training in the Baltic, and they would require some time to develop their craft. This can be evidenced from the records of S-boat torpedo firings that were recorded by the Kriegsmarine and later captured by the British (table 5). The ratio hits on enemy vessels versus the number of firings fluctuated considerably during the war, from 1 in 4 in 1940 to 1 in 2 in 1942. During 1943 it fell back to less than 1 in 3. By 1944 only 15 percent of torpedoes found their mark.[15] At least, in part, this may be as a result of problems with the torpedoes. The introduction of newer torpedo types in 1943–44 seems to have coincided with an increase in the number of reports of torpedo misfires and premature detonations.

Although there was only limited improvement in the torpedo weapon for S-boat crews, there was substantial improvement of deck guns. These were the primary means by which an S-boat could defend itself against the increasing numbers of MGBs, MTBs, and MLs. In addition, the early S-boats carried little more than a single 2-cm anti-aircraft gun and some light machine guns. By the S-38 class, things had improved to the point whereby a 2-cm gun turret was sited between the forward torpedo tubes. This gave considerable forward-facing firepower, but even this was considered insufficient by 1942. Thus, the S-100 class brought in during 1943 carried a twin 2-cm cannon amidships and a heavier gun (3.7 cm) facing aft. The latter was particularly important as a means for S-boats to utilize a heavy weapon against pursuing forces. During 1943 older S-boat models were refitted with heavier weaponry, including 4-cm aft-firing guns, as available and according to the preferences of commanding officers.[16] In some cases commanding officers of the older S-boats preferred to mount a lighter weapon aft. The recoil on a 4-cm gun was equivalent to 1.5 tons, which put a considerable strain on the frames of boats weakened by age and length of service.[17] A further complication was caused by the availability of dockyard resources: a weapons refit required up to six weeks of dockyard work, which impacted considerably on the number of operational S-boats during the summer of 1943.[18] By war's end the latest S-boats were being planned with a single aft-firing torpedo tube mounted on the stern, and aft-firing was being taught in specially fitted rooms at the German navy's Torpedo School at Mürwik.[19] Interestingly, a proposal in 1943 from S-boat officers for an all-gun S-boat (*Artillerieschnellboote*) to combat the British MGB seems to have been quashed within the German naval high command.[20] Within the S-boat arm, this was taken as further evidence of a lack of understanding about the nature of the coastal warfare in which they were engaged.[21]

**IMPROVED COMMUNICATION AND SENSOR SYSTEMS**

Increasing the number and caliber of deck weapons was designed to enhance the ability of S-boats to defend themselves as they pursued the offensive goals of staging torpedo and mine attacks against Allied merchant ships, which remained their primary targets. To further improve the defensive and offensive capabilities of S-boats, there were also attempts to improve other shipboard systems. These attempts met with limited success, so Morse signaling, short-range voice VHF radios (type Lo 1 UK 35), and old-fashioned flag semaphore, signal lamps, and lights continued to function as the main way S-boats coordinated their movements at sea. With British Coastal Forces using German VHF signals to warn of the approach of S-boats, and later being able to use headache operators to provide real-time intelligence on the movement of German forces, VHF transmissions from boats operating in the Channel had been turned to the advantage of the Allies. In addition, the ability of S-boats along the southern coast of the United Kingdom to locate their targets continued to rely on good intelligence, a skipper's best guess as to where a convoy might be located, and the execution of good search patterns. Radio direction finding (RDF), facilitated by a direction-finding loop aerial mounted on the wheelhouse, could help to locate enemy ships if they broke radio silence. This was useful for both offensive and defensive purposes, but what was clearly required was the kind of radio equipment being installed in British Coastal Forces.[22] Unfortunately, the S-boats were not considered a priority for such equipment. Adapted from units used by the Luftwaffe night fighter force, the FuMo 71 Lichtenstein B/C radar was inadequate in most respects: it had a range of only 3,000 meters against a merchant ship, and a limited arc (35 degrees ahead of the boat). Fitted to a small number of boats in 1943, even in the hands of the best operators, the performance of the set was disappointing against even the larger potential radar targets. Against the smaller vessels of British Coastal Forces, with their lower profiles and less reflective surfaces, the FuMo 71 was largely useless. It could provide very little warning that an S-boat was about to be ambushed by, for example, a pair of MGBs lying in wait along the convoy route.

S-boat flotillas in the English Channel did try to make the most of FuMo 71 by changing their tactics. For example, in the dark hours of March 7–8, 1943, radar lurking was employed by three S-boat flotillas working together (2nd, 4th, and 6th). The 4th Flotilla maintained a radar watch along the edge of the convoy lanes while the 2nd and 6th Flotillas waited farther out to sea for deployment in the case of a contact. On detecting a convoy, the ready flotillas would deploy in a *Stichansatz* formation in order not to miss the convoy. On the night of March 7–8, low visibility impaired the attack, so only the 6th Flotilla attacked. They were driven off by the destroyer HMS *Mackay* and two MGBs (20 and 21). In the process S-114 and S-119 were involved in a collision, and S-119 was lost as a result (the crew was rescued by S-114).[23]

If the application of an inadequate radar system to S-boat tactics made little difference to their offensive potential, then at least the provision of passive radar detection and ranging equipment could improve their defensive capabilities. Radar emissions could give away the location of Allied warships hunting for S-boats and the FuMB 29 "Bali" multidirectional antenna, and the FuMB 10 "Borkum" signal detector could give warning of an enemy actively seeking their position. Developing effective systems took time, unfortunately, and it wasn't until March 1944 that the first sets were delivered. Even then, S-boat crews had their suspicions about the equipment they were being provided with. For example, the FuMB 10 threat warning device was regarded as practically useless, since it did not provide an indication of what direction the threat was coming from. In any case, as Oberleutnant-zur-See Ulrich Kolbe, commander of S-85 in 1942–44, noted, "Practically we were always 'located,' even when we had just left [port]."[24]

## TACTICAL INNOVATION

In the face of inadequate equipment and delays to production, the S-boats had no choice but to innovate tactically. For example, June 1942 saw the introduction of the *Stichansatz* tactic, whereby a group of S-boats, working from radio intercepts or aerial reconnaissance, would spread itself along a coastal route in the hopes of locating a convoy. In effect, the group's combat power would be temporarily dispersed to enhance its ability to locate enemy ships. As soon as the convoy was located, the dispersed force would come together to carry out the attack. The tactic may also have been combined with an attempt at stealth, as there is some suggestion of S-boats waiting next to some of the buoys along the marked channel. With metal buoys providing a solid radar return, the Germans may have hoped that they would provide a space in which to "hide" an S-boat. In reality the type 287 radar carried on board some of the escort destroyers was good enough to allow an operator to identify any larger-than-expected radar returns.[25] Although the tactic meant a temporary dispersal of the group's combat power, the tactic could be successful. For example, on July 8, 1942, the tactic was used to locate a convoy in which six merchant ships were sunk.[26] Nevertheless, the introduction of *Stichansatz* showed something of the growing difficulties the S-boat arm faced in trying to locate and engage convoys in seas in which the enemy was increasingly dominant. Indeed, on January 20, 1943, FdS Petersen counseled that S-boat flotillas could not be continued in current form because enemy defenses were simply too strong. A single S-boat dispersed along the line was potentially very vulnerable to ambush.[27]

## SIGNALS AND HUMAN INTELLIGENCE

As a means of locating convoys, the *Stichansatz* tactic was supplemented by the work of the naval radio intercept and decoding service (B-dienst), which had, with the fall of France in 1940, been able to expand its operations along the coast of occupied Europe. As Marcus Faulkner notes, during the 1930s B-dienst had become highly efficient at high-frequency direction finding and had routinely been able to report on the maneuvers of the Royal Navy and French fleet.[28] The occupation in 1940 of the French Atlantic coasts, and along the southern shore of the English Channel into Belgium and the Netherlands gave B-dienst great opportunities to exercise a vital influence over the war at sea in U.K. coastal waters. The intensity of convoy operations and the growth of marine signals traffic along the coastal routes (including wireless and radio, both ship-to-ship and ship-to-shore) meant a target-rich environment for B-dienst. As Jak Mallmann Showell notes, radio communications between shore-based radar stations and units at sea resulted in a particularly large volume of traffic.[29] Any intercept could reveal the location of a vessel at sea, and even the most basic analysis of the pattern and nature of traffic could suggest the passage of a convoy along one of the coastal routes. While the B-dienst gained in efficiency and value in terms of the S-boat campaign, the increasing difficulties of operating close to the British coast deprived the S-boat service of the human intelligence that could be derived from the rescue of survivors from sunken ships. In the early phase of the S-boat campaign, those survivors sometimes revealed information of great value. For example, two of them proved very talkative on February 6, 1941, following the sinking of the 501-ton coaster SS *Angularity* in the Shipwash Channel. They provided details on range of confidential matters, from the types of destroyer working along the East Coast, to means of convoy organization, to British perceptions of the threat from German forces.[30] By 1943, the dangers of attack from the ever more numerous British Coastal Forces vessels and, increasingly, from the air made it almost impossible for S-boats to spend any time in the vicinity of a successful attack hunting for survivors to rescue for the purposes of interrogation. The near absence of human intelligence from interrogated survivors and the increasing effectiveness of British forces made it even more important for the Kriegsmarine forces along the Channel coast to have the support of the Luftwaffe, but here too there were significant problems.

## S-BOAT–LUFTWAFFE COOPERATION

The potential for the success of combined Luftwaffe/S-boat operations had been demonstrated in the operations against convoys CW8 and CW9 and in the summer of 1940. The FdT believed that only a combined sea-air offensive would result in the crippling of the convoys around the British coast: "The traffic in the Channel can only be paralyzed by full use of the Luftwaffe by day, and . . . [S-boats] at night."[31] Despite his views, preparations for the attack on Russia in 1941 had meant that Luftwaffe strength in the West was reduced.[32] The evolution of the strategic bombing offensive against Germany's cities in 1942 and 1943 had ensured that Luftwaffe resources could not be transferred westward. Damage to factories, losses of pilots, and a growing shortage of fuel meant a steady decline of the combat power of the German air force. Göring's lack of interest in cooperating with the Kriegsmarine on any aspect of the prosecution of the war at sea, including the U-boat offensive, affected the S-boat offensive in three ways: a shortage of bomber units available for antishipping missions in the English Channel; a shortage of fighter units available to cover S-boats as they returned to port after operations; and, perhaps most critically of all, a shortage of aircraft capable of carrying out reconnaissance to supplement the information. In a year-end review of S-boat campaigns in 1943, the FdS concluded that the lack of Luftwaffe support was the critical factor in the S-boats' declining effectiveness.[33] The sense of frustration with the Luftwaffe felt by many of those in the Kriegsmarine can be glimpsed in a brief comment by the FdS in 1942: "Owing to the relative weakness of the German air force . . . there have been gaps in the reconnaissance network."[34] The *Stichansatz* tactic and the efficiency of B-dienst could only partially offset the lack of effective aerial reconnaissance, and in April 1943 the FdS called for "fighter reconnaissance by aircraft equipped with radar." He considered this the "only reliable method by which aircraft can contact convoys at night."[35] His request was ignored. Likewise, even as S-boats were increasingly subject to aerial attack, the growing bomber offensive against the Reich meant that home defense continued to enjoy absolute priority for Luftwaffe fighter allocation.[36] The scale of the problem was revealed in a May 1943 paper in which the FdS noted that during the early part of the year S-boats had come under aerial attack "16 times during their operations, even though there was no moon, and visibility was bad."[37] The FdS anticipated the day when S-boats would come under attack from night fighters from the moment they left port to the minute they returned. With Coastal Command hunting both S-boats and U-boats, the FdS was concerned that only fighter support could prevent unsustainable losses of boats, as they were routinely hunted by aircraft at night.

## ARMORING

Increased armor was another way to improve the survivability of boat and crew. During 1942, experiments had been conducted with S-67. Armoring the whole vessel threatened to impede the boat's performance. In any case, S-boats had already established a formidable reputation for being able to survive serious amounts of damage from enemy vessels. It did, however, make sense to offer greater protection to the coxswain and senior officers in the S-boat's cockpit. The basic steel wheelhouse fitted to wartime S-boats offered no protection against larger projectiles. The result of the experiments was the development of a design for an armored wheelhouse that could provide protection to critical personnel. New S-boats would be built with the design and existing boats upgraded in a refit program in the shipyards of Rotterdam. Fitting the armored wheelhouse, which was usually referred to as the *Panzerkalotte* (armored skullcap), was first introduced in the new boats of the S-38 class, resulting in a specific variant: the 38b. That, in turn, was superseded by the S-100 class, in which the *Panzerkalotte* was fitted as standard. The S-100 class saw further armoring of the vessel and further up-gunning. These processes did, however, add to the weight of the vessel, necessitating further improvement to systems and power plant.[38]

The up-armoring of the existing S-boat design inevitably raised the issue of whether to introduce a new design of S-boat with a steel, rather than wooden, hull. An S-boat built out of steel was theoretically easier to produce, since it required less-skilled labor and could be subject to industrial methods of production. Even though by 1943 an S-boat could be built in about four months, it remained a bespoke vessel, carefully crafted out of wood. To get the best performance out of a complex design required great skill and precision. Not until after 1945, however, would the idea of a steel S-boat for the German navy be realized, for two principal reasons. First, the boatyards of northern Germany were geared toward the production of wooden vessels, and working in steel would require the reskilling of an existing labor force. Second, with the army and air force in charge of much of Nazi Germany's industry, and especially the production of steel, the Kriegsmarine had encountered considerable political battles in obtaining supplies of metal for shipbuilding purposes, and even the Luftwaffe began to examine new aircraft designs using wood in place of aluminum.[39] The navy's and Dönitz's priority was to use its steel allocation to support U-boat construction; the building of submarines was privileged over that of surface ships. Given the industrial and political difficulties, it was not practicable to move toward building S-boats out of steel during the middle years of World War II.

The British meanwhile continued to innovate in their designs for coastal vessels. The steam gunboat (SGB) class introduced in 1942, with its steel hull, represented a particularly interesting development. Weighing 260 tons, and 137 feet in length, the SGB had two steam turbine engines capable of taking the vessel to thirty knots. They were also heavily armed with "one 3-in, two 6-pdrs, and three twin 20-mm guns, with two 21-inch torpedoes."[40] Leonard Reynolds has described them as "mini-destroyers," and, like the S-boat, they too were subject to up-armoring and revisions to improve the basic design.[41] Those improvements were necessary to improve basic systems that in action had proved insufficiently robust. But problems persisted even after the changes were made, as demonstrated in a report following an action in the Channel on May 28–29, 1943. In command of SGB 4, Lieutenant T. W. Boyd commented, "Gunnery communications, already the subject of frequent correspondence, again proved a failure."[42] Although the SGB design showed the potential of steel-hulled coastal craft, overall the design was not considered a success. Only seven out of a planned sixty were built. Problems with the SGB design perhaps suggest that the Germans might not have been wrong to stick with a tried and trusted design.

The difficulties of improving the S-boat design made it vital to increase the number of available units, especially in the West, where an invasion of France threatened. In December 1941 the FdT had believed that it would take around forty operational S-boats to really threaten the East Coast convoys.[43] Unfortunately, given the boatyards' limitations and the long build times, "this was not a practical possibility."[44] Not until the drawing up of the 1943 building program, which called for the production of seventy-two boats per year, did the Kriegsmarine set itself the task of building a massively increased fleet of S-boats. Inevitably there would be a time lag, and the 1943 program would only begin to deliver the promised numbers in the summer of 1944.

## THE LOGISTICAL BUILDUP IN LATE 1943

The scale and variety of issues facing the S-boat campaign manifested themselves during the late autumn of 1943 as the longer nights gave more opportunities to attack coastal convoys. This was coupled with an increase in the number and size of ships plying the coastal trade routes because of the buildup toward the launching of an Allied invasion of Western Europe. This was a critical phase in the war. On July 6, 1943, the need to increase the pace of the Allied buildup had led to a decision to run convoys every day (instead of six days out of seven) in order to meet the schedules specified in the Bolero plan.[45] The demands on the railways were such that there was no other way to meet the demand, and to fall behind the Bolero plan was to delay the launching of the second front.[46] The need to meet the Bolero plan meant bigger convoys and larger ships for the passage. In September, with the increasingly longer nights facilitating S-boat attacks, the volume of traffic along the southern coast was expected to double because of D-Day requirements. Those convoys, carrying material vital to the invasion buildup, would make significant and tempting targets for the S-boats based along the southern shore of the English Channel. The Admiralty was hesitant to go down the road of seven-day convoying, even though that had been agreed in July. The vulnerability of convoys to attack was the prime concern of the Royal Navy, and while it was appreciated that defenses were much better than in 1940, there was a still a great deal of concern about the potential impact of any attack. The situation was kept under constant review, and the Royal Navy considered augmenting defenses along the coastal route with new minefields (surface and deep set) to counter any attempt to use both S-boats or U-boats in a more vigorous inshore campaign.[47] Plans for more extensive mining were ultimately rejected, however, on grounds that they might impede coastal shipping and cause problems when the invasion was ultimately launched.[48]

On the German side there was a keen awareness of the importance of renewing the coastal campaign. The summer months had been spent in improving the S-boat fleet in the Channel with improvements in both armor and weaponry. By the middle of September the 2, 4, 6, and 8th S-boat Flotillas stood ready in Dutch ports (Ijmuiden and Rotterdam) to again take the attack to the British.[49] During the last week of September they launched the winter campaign of 1943–44 with mining operations coordinated with the Luftwaffe. As part of this effort, on the night of September 24–25, 1943, the S-boat flotillas at Ijmuiden and Rotterdam were sent out on a torpedo and minelaying operation. The latter was a success, but the accompanying torpedo operation had more mixed results. S-96 and S-88 of the 4th Flotilla, encountering two armed trawlers, launched torpedoes that sank HMT *Franc Tireur*.[50] In turn, however, the S-boats were attacked by two motor launches (ML150 and ML145). S-96 was rammed and shot up and began to sink.[51] The commanding officer of ML150 later set down his account of what followed:

> The crunch when I hit him was awful, and threw my crew flat on the deck. Bits of wood & metal flew round my head and the coxswain who was standing beside me on the wheel. We should both have been laid out—but somehow it all missed us. I stopped, being damaged, and it was a glorious feeling to see the enemy slow right down and watch my opposite number fairly wade into him and finish him off. Rescuing the survivors took us at least an hour, due chiefly to the heavy sea that was running.[52]

Sixteen survivors were recovered from the water after S-96 was scuttled, once permission had been obtained from S-boat headquarters.[53] Despite being seriously damaged, ML150 managed to make it back to port. Lieutenant Eric Whitehead, one of those injured in the collision, later recalled their arrival back in port: "We had a royal reception back at Lowestoft. All the base seemed to have turned out to applaud, including my wife Ann. The press was also there. The prisoners, who had been blindfolded, were turned over to the base staff. I was dispatched to the sick bay where a doctor picked some shattered glass out of my head."[54] With six other S-boats being damaged in the action (including three due to crankcase explosions, potentially as a result of sabotage), it had been a costly night's work for the flotillas based in Dutch waters.[55] The British press reported on the night's events in some detail, especially the ramming incident.[56] The losses did not stop the Germans from launching a follow-up minelaying operation on October 7, which was successful (two further S-boats succumbed to engine problems), but on October 10 the Luftwaffe ended their involvement in the campaign as Hitler called for a renewed bombing effort against Britain's cities. FdS Petersen was left to carry on the campaign with the forces at his disposal.

Thus, on the night of October 24–25 another large operation was launched in which thirty-one S-boats (2nd, 4th, 6th, and 8th S-boat Flotillas) were sent against East Coast convoy FN1160.[57] This constituted a maximum effort designed to test British defenses on the East Coast to the fullest extent.[58] The British, by contrast, had over three hundred MGBs, MTBs, and MLs operating in support of the coastal convoys. On the night of October 24–25, the Luftwaffe was, as usual, unable to provide aerial reconnaissance and it was carried out solely on the basis of B-dienst intercepts. The British forces in a position to respond to the attack included five destroyers, eight MGBs, four MLs, and nine MTBs.[59] To some extent the defending force was hampered by a radar breakdown on MGB 610, and it was left to the "new center line hydrophones" to locate the enemy.[60] Combining the information from radar and hydrophone contacts proved highly effective. Radar on the other vessels enabled S-boats to be picked up at 2,000 to 3,000 yards. Hydrophone contact provided the course and speed of the S-boats.[61] The result was a series of contacts between British and German forces with sixteen separate engagements as the S-boats tried to close with the convoy.[62] German attempts to swamp the defenses failed, the only loss being HMT *William Stephen* and damage to one MGB.[63] German forces, meanwhile, lost two S-boats (S-63 and S-88).[64] At least one other S-boat had been crippled, and it probably owed its escape to the radar failure on MGB 610, although in after-action reports there was some speculation as to whether one or more of the German vessels had been equipped with passive radar detection equipment.[65] During the rest of 1943, severe storms limited S-boat operations, although on November 4 convoy CW221 was attacked by the 5th S-boat Flotilla, with the loss of three merchant ships.[66] The following night on the East Coast twenty-four boats carried out a minelaying and torpedo operation. In an attack on FN1170, two merchant were damaged, including one by a (FAT) torpedo (their first use by S-boats).[67] In the operation there were also casualties on the German side. British Beaufighter aircraft attacked Germans forces as they retired toward the coast, and S-74 was destroyed despite a request for Luftwaffe fighter cover. The request was denied on the grounds that all aircraft were needed to intercept a force of Allied bombers heading toward Germany. By the time aircraft were available, the British fighters had left the scene.[68]

Despite the best efforts of the S-boat flotillas, and limited efforts to enhance their armament and equipment, in late 1943 they had made minimal impact on the growing stream of coastal traffic. The victories had been minor and more than offset by the cost in S-boats sunk and damaged. Fifteen boats had been sunk, with eighty-four men killed in action.[69] Yet again cooperation with the Luftwaffe had been noticeable in its absence. Most importantly, in terms of the strategic balance, the flow of equipment and stores required under the Bolero plan had not been disrupted to any meaningful extent. The attempt to relaunch the S-boat offensive with better-protected boats carrying more effective weapons had failed. During 1943 just 26,024 gross registered tons of Allied shipping had been sunk by S-boats off the shores of Britain: a total that was disappointing and completely inadequate to the task of correcting a strategic balance that was tilting against Nazi Germany.[70]

## CHAPTER 9
# S-BOATS AND THE SHIFT TO THE DEFENSIVE, 1943–1944

THE FAILURE TO SUCCESSFULLY relaunch the campaign against the coastal convoy routes placed an increasing emphasis on the S-boats as a defensive weapon that could play a role in defending the coast of Europe against an Allied invasion of Western Europe. This chapter analyzes the gradual strategic shift toward the defensive. The *guerre de course* against Britain by the submarines and surface vessels of the Kriegsmarine would continue, but with German armies under pressure on all fronts, the attention of the German high command increasingly turned to the moment when Allied armies would attempt an amphibious landing on the coast of Western Europe. Strategically Germany had been forced onto the defensive, but Dönitz continued to think in offensive terms. For him the U-boat campaign, with the prospect of a next generation of submarines entering service in late 1944 and early 1945, continued to be the priority for the Kriegsmarine. As a result, the Kriegsmarine failed to implement a strategy of coastal defense in line with Germany's strategic imperatives in 1944. The German army would be left to fight D-Day with little help from either the Kriegsmarine or the Luftwaffe. The failure to embrace a strategy of coastal defense meant that the U-boat campaign continued to receive priority in terms of industrial production. In any case, German industry was not well equipped to turn out significant numbers of vessels suitable for coastal defense. S-boats had considerable potential value against an invasion force, but the design was not well suited to mass production in preparation for the threat of invasion.

The sense of impending catastrophe could not have been lost on the S-boat crews along the Channel coast. They knew that much would depend on them in terms of providing the Kriegsmarine's response to the arrival of the invasion, even if destroyers, larger torpedo boats, minesweepers, R-boats, and other support craft and coastal artillery batteries would act in support. Increasingly outnumbered and with speed frequently their only advantage, the men of the 5th S-boat Flotilla at Cherbourg joked about being willing to "swap Knight's Cross for running shoes."[1] The men of the 5th Flotilla had a sharp understanding of the deteriorating situation and their inability to effect change. Ulrich Kolbe, commander of S-85, later recorded,

> These doubts about the "final victory" made a big impression on me at the time. . . . We were fighting on a secondary theater of war. The smaller freighters that we were able to sink were certainly not the only decisive factor in the war. At that time, the English received almost unlimited help from the USA. The large amount of material was landed in the Irish Sea because the large convoys were not supposed to pass through the Channel. In the ports of the Irish Sea, supplies were transferred to smaller freighters, which had to bring it to the West coast, because the railways alone could not manage the transport. . . . On these routes of the convoys through the Channel lay our "pasture area." And we saw and put it this way: "You can't pump against an enema."[2]

The S-boat crews had a good understanding of the aims and objectives of the campaign in the English Channel, and by 1944 it was clear that the situation was about to take a dramatic turn for the worse.

## WAITING FOR THE INVASION

In early 1944, Kriegsmarine high command struggled to make adequate preparations for a landing that would most likely come in the spring or summer of that year. The buildup of amphibious forces in British waters offered the clearest indications that the Allies were coming and coming in some force. A multidivisional landing across a broad front, and the establishment of a bridgehead from which the Allies would begin a drive on Berlin, would be the objective of the cross-Channel attack. The disastrous Dieppe landings of 1942 had demonstrated the potential for large-scale landings to go wrong; equally, though, the success of Allied amphibious landings in the Mediterranean in 1942 and 1943 had provided evidence of growing Allied capability and capacity. Allied planners could not disguise the fact that a buildup of forces was taking place in southern Britain. Instead, they sought to misdirect German intelligence as to the likely landing site. Operation Fortitude was a multilayered deception plan that, by fake radio signals from nonexistent units in southeastern England, backed by misleading reports from German agents who were in fact working for the British under the Double Cross system, sought to convince Wehrmacht High Command (OKW) that the main Allied landings would take place in the Pas de Calais area.[3]

During the early months of 1944 the English Channel became a strategic no-man's-land that the Allies sought to dominate to protect the coastal convoys, but also to control the space across which invasion forces would be sent by the middle months of the year. Trying to respond to this attempt to dominate the sea space was difficult for Navy Group West. With German naval bases along the Channel under attack from Allied air forces, and German naval units routinely engaged as they left port, maintaining an effective presence in the Channel, let alone maintaining the campaign against the coastal convoys, became hugely difficult. Continuing to attack the coastal convoys was just as important as being able to respond to the invasion fleet once it was at sea. From late 1943 onward the coastal convoys carried increasing amounts of invasion material (vehicles, ammunition, stores) to the ports on the southern coast that would support the landings. The Bolero plan for the logistical buildup to D-Day placed a heavy reliance on coastal convoys. In the context of the Allied invasion, those convoys in early 1944 were carrying a significant proportion of the supplies called for under Operation Bolero. With deliveries under the plan falling behind schedule by late 1943, the Royal Navy, reluctantly agreed to increase the frequency of convoys on the coastal routes and to incorporate larger vessels on the coastal routes.[4] On November 25, orders for the move to seven-day convoying were given to the commands at the Nore, Rosyth, and Portsmouth.[5] Any disruption to the coastal convoys by the S-boat flotillas might have an impact on the buildup to D-Day, and patrolling S-boats in the Channel could provide advance warning of the invasion fleet's departure from the South Coast points. In the circumstances of 1944, however, this was an impossibility.

The head of the Kriegsmarine later noted in his memoirs, "The meagre forces at the disposal of the Commander-in-Chief, Navy Group West, could not be kept permanently at sea as patrols against possible enemy landings.... The losses and damage we sustained were so severe that even the maintenance of a permanent patrol line, let alone any reconnaissance sortie into enemy coastal waters, was out of the question."[6] Undoubtedly, part of the problem was that with the small number of S-boats in commission, the Kriegsmarine was risk averse in its attitude toward operations in the English Channel. Greater availability of S-boats could have transformed this situation, allowing routine nighttime patrolling in the Channel, close reconnaissance of the British coast and the potential invasion ports, and perhaps spoiling attacks against specific targets. Increased minelaying by S-boats would have had more than just nuisance value. Long-range torpedo attacks, using the new generation of torpedoes, into packed anchorages offered another potential opportunity. The type 38 S-boat could carry, in addition to two torpedoes in the tubes, six conventional mines.[7] With ships and aircraft in short supply, only limited mining operations were undertaken against ports rich with potential targets. The strategic importance of these concentrations of shipping was considerable. It was later noted by the British naval staff that "had the [limited mining] attacks been on a more massive scale they might well have caused the Allies serious embarrassment."[8] For the Kriegsmarine, and for Nazi Germany, early 1944 witnessed a series of lost opportunities to affect the outcome of D-Day. Lacking the resources for extensive offensive operations, Kriegsmarine units on the Channel coast could only await the day of the invasion and to respond to developments as best they could.

## THE PROBLEM OF MORALE

The impact on morale within the Kriegsmarine of the approaching challenges was considerable. As Anglo-American industry turned out growing numbers of aircraft and escort vessels, the Kriegsmarine was left to reflect on the material inadequacies of German forces. Across the Kriegsmarine as a whole, morale was in serious decline in the lead-up to the invasion.

One deserter who made his way to Spain and was subsequently interviewed by the U.S. assistant naval attaché argued,

> Morale of practically all petty officers and men who have been in service for several years is at an all-time low ebb. . . . [New arrivals have been indoctrinated and enter] . . . full of enthusiasm and grit. Subject stated . . . that a source of bitter disappointment to German naval personnel is the intense feeling in French ports against the Germans stationed there. He stated that all personnel have rigid orders never to walk on streets alone, but always in groups of at least two or three; that in spite of this precautionary measure, many sailors and soldiers are found strangled or with their throats cut, and others have disappeared without any trace.[9]

Within the German armed forces, by 1944 belief in final victory was rapidly ebbing. The average German soldier, airman, and sailor continued to fight because there appeared to be no other choice. The promise of wonder weapons that would transform the war situation was the subject of an increasing number of jokes in the armed forces, but the will to resist continued at a high level. Saving Germany from annihilation, the possibilities of a dictated peace, a sense of duty to one's country and comrades, and professional pride in the armed forces provided powerful motivations to keep fighting.[10] As one report noted in March 1944, the Germans increasingly advised each other to "enjoy the war. The Peace will be terrible."[11] At every turn, as German forces in France hurriedly tried to prepare for the day of invasion, difficulties were encountered. Labor was always in short supply, as were vital resources such as iron, steel, and concrete. Enhancing the defenses at water's edge, constructing fixed defenses for the army, building coastal batteries (army and navy), and developing the sites from which to fire V-1 flying bombs required enormous resources. Demand invariably outstripped supply, and in the chaotic Nazi state, disagreements between the services often made matters worse. For example, the Kriegsmarine preferred to site its coastal batteries where they could engage enemy naval units with direct fire. The army, meanwhile, preferred them to be sited inland, where they would be less vulnerable but from which only indirect fire would be possible.

## THE CONTINUED POTENTIAL POTENCY OF THE S-BOAT

Despite the difficulties facing the S-boat arm two actions in early 1944 demonstrated the potential for S-boats to cause havoc on D-Day.[12] On the evening of January 5, 1944, the 5th Flotilla under the command of Kapitänleutnant Karl Wilhelm Walter Müller departed Cherbourg to hunt for a coastal convoy. In the early hours of January 6, six S-boats (S-84, S-136, S-138, S-141, S-52, S-142, and S-143) attacked convoy WP457 off the Lizard Peninsula. They had waited close inshore, being mistaken for British torpedo boats, before siting the convoy and commencing their attack. This attack marked the most westerly attack of the S-boats during World War II. The destroyer HMS *Mackay* was unable to defend the convoy against such a mass attack involving the firing of twenty-three torpedoes. Four ships were sunk (HMS *Wallasea*, an armed trawler of the Royal Navy Patrol Service; SS *Solstad*; MV *Polperro*; and MV *Underwood*).[13] The Swedish *Solstad* and Cornish-registered *Polperro* carried coal, while *Underwood* was carrying Bolero cargo, including vehicles. All were small vessels of 2,000 tons or less. Five were killed on the *Solstad*, eleven on the *Polperro* (eight seamen and three gunners), and seventeen on the *Wallasea*. The attack was a powerful reminder that S-boats remained highly dangerous, especially where they could be deployed to the remoter areas where British defenses were weaker.

More dramatically still in April 1944 came an attack by the 5th and 9th S-boat Flotillas on a convoy of tank landing ships (LSTs) taking part in Exercise Tiger: a rehearsal for the landings on Utah Beach.[14] The devastating results of the Exercise Tiger attack, and the security clampdown that followed, have given rise to ongoing debates about whether intelligence operations imperiled the security of the convoy.[15] The attack occurred in the western reaches of the English Channel, where anti-S-boat defenses were not as strong as they were along the East Coast. The convoy carrying a mixture of U.S. Army units had been picked up by B-dienst monitoring its radio signals, and the S-boat flotillas were dispatched from Cherbourg to investigate. Encountering vessels to the west of Portland in Lyme Bay, the S-boats slipped past the patrolling destroyers providing distant protection for the convoy. After a seemingly abortive attack on a convoy of landing barges that were of such shallow draft that torpedoes from S-140 and S-142 simply passed underneath, S-boats attacked the convoy of LSTs, which had just one Flower-class corvette (HMS *Azalea*) as close escort (a second vessel had been unable to sail with the convoy after it suffered damage in an accident). Three LSTs were torpedoed and two of them sank, resulting in the deaths of around 749 U.S. Army and U.S. Navy personnel. Retreating at some speed, the S-boats did not appreciate that they had attacked a landing rehearsal.[16] They did not attempt to rescue or take prisoner any of the many hundreds of survivors in the water, and it was only later, after B-dienst analysis, that the significance of the attack was properly realized. Survivors who landed in the United Kingdom were instructed not to talk about the incident, which was kept secret until after the invasion.

In fact, the German attack came close to much bigger success. S-140 and S-142 had wasted their torpedoes on shallow-draft landing barges, while S-138 and S-136 had fired their torpedoes at two patrolling destroyers and never made contact with the LSTs. Throughout the action there were incidents of unexplained detonation of torpedoes; one torpedo landed on the deck of one of the destroyers it was fired at.[17] With over two hundred vessels at sea for Exercise Tiger, the S-boats were in a target-rich environment, and Royal Navy plotters were unable to identify on radar all the radar echoes in Lyme Bay.[18] In effect, the "complete system of naval operating" broke down under the sheer weight of numbers and extent of the data that needed to be gathered and responded to. Indeed, as the S-boats ran south, they crossed the path of another convoy of LSTs (code-named Obstacle) that was coming round to Portland with cargoes related to the sailing of Force O.[19] The British destroyers attempting to close with the S-boats were completely unaware of the convoy and opened fire (briefly and with light weapons) on the U.S. Navy escorts protecting the convoy.[20] The friendly fire incident ended when the U.S. Navy vessels flashed visual signals. In the ensuing confusion the S-boats, largely out of torpedoes, cut through the convoy and made their escape. With more torpedoes, and presented with another set of targets, further LSTs could have been lost. Indeed, the 5th and 9th Flotillas had approached Lyme Bay with a combined total of thirty-six torpedoes. Perhaps just five torpedoes from the nine S-boats had reached their target, resulting in significant losses.

The episode showed clearly that S-boats had the capacity to inflict serious casualties on the invasion force. If torpedoes found the right targets, the damage inflicted on the D-Day amphibious force could be considerable, perhaps enough to give the German army a chance of defeating the Allied armies on the beaches and in the fields behind. Within the German naval high command there was some satisfaction at the results. Some of this can be glimpsed in one of Admiral Dönitz's postwar interrogations. Asked about Exercise Tiger, he responded with alacrity: "I recall the incident well."[21] The attack on the Exercise Tiger convoy raised to new levels Allied concerns about the S-boat threat to D-Day. As James Foster Tent has argued, senior Allied officers in 1944 were concerned about the S-boat threat even before April 1944.[22] Interestingly, a Royal Navy assessment determined that the main problem for the S-boat arm from 1940 to 1944 was the location of convoys.[23] If they could be located, there was little that could be done to prevent an attack, although the escort might be able to limit its effectiveness. When S-boats located a convoy, they were typically highly effective, sinking an average of 2.4 ships per engagement. It was obvious that S-boats would have little difficulty locating Allied ships in the target-rich environment presented by the launching of the invasion. With screening forces, S-boats could be kept away from the vital troop ships. In the aftermath of the attack on the Exercise Tiger T4 convoy, as inquiries were hurriedly held, the Royal Navy concluded that such countermeasures would prove sufficient, even as some senior officers in the U.S. Navy considered an operation to target the S-boat flotillas at Cherbourg in the hours before the invasion flotilla arrived off the coast of Normandy.[24] Some American vessels, including Destroyer Squadron 18, were put through anti-S-boat drills on the Clyde in May 1944.[25] In addition, limited air operations against S-boat bases were also staged to provide reassurance that the S-boat threat could be contained without staging the kind of operation that might send a very clear signal as to Allied intentions for the second front. A bombing attack on the S-boat base at Boulogne on June 2, for example, caused difficulties for the boats based there as the entrance to two pens were damaged and "one door of the shelter sank."[26]

The Kriegsmarine's failure to mount an effective response to the invasion fleet was particularly unfortunate in that the naval high command had correctly anticipated that the landings would take place on the coast of Normandy: "The naval command considered the area east of the Cotentin Peninsula as far as Boulogne to be the most probable place for a landing. The coast of the Pas de Calais was regarded as the second possibility."[27] It was impossible to miss the increasing number of invasion craft moving around the coast and ports of southwestern England.[28] Indeed, to guard against the threat, a mine barrage was laid along the coast up to Dutch waters. The timing, however, was particularly unfortunate. Because German naval command feared the impact of the barrage on their own coastal convoys, the mines that made up the barrage were set to flood and go to the seabed on May 31.[29] The barrage effectively became nonoperational just as the tides and long daylight hours of summer made an invasion possible and highly likely. In early June the naval high command were investigating a variety of measures, including refitting barges prepared for Operation Sea Lion (the invasion of the United Kingdom), to increase the number of vessels capable of contributing to the minelaying effort.[30] At the same time, Group West and the relevant Luftwaffe command were struggling to come to properly effective agreements to govern aerial and marine minelaying operations to disrupt any invasion force and in the immediate aftermath of any landing.[31] Instructions to French Resistance groups at the start of June to maintain a radio watch on the BBC, through which urgent messages would be relayed, was taken by the naval high command as a very strong indicator that they could expect the invasion between June 5 and 13.[32] Bombing attacks against coastal artillery positions along the French coast were yet another pointer to the imminent nature of the invasion threat. The complete domination of the Allies in the air left no one in any doubt as to the ferocity of the attack when it came. The pages of naval high command's war diary for June 1944 make for grim reading, with German forces along the invasion coast subject to ongoing and heavy aerial attack. The war diary for June 4 offers a good example: "During the day more than 1000 enemy planes entered Belgium, Northern France, and Western France. Attacks were made on the defensive zone in the coastal area and in the areas of Dunkerque, Arras, Amiens, Boulogne, Calais, Chartres, and Conflans. . . . During the night of 4 June, the attacks on the defense zones in the areas of Calais-Boulogne were continued by 250 bombers. Other enemy planes entered the area of Ijmuiden-Cap Griz Nez without attacking, and Western France probably to supply agents, as well as the waters around Brest for mine-dropping."[33] While the Kriegsmarine prepared for an Allied invasion of Western Europe in early June, Rommel, as Commanding General West, concluded on June 5 that while the pattern of air attacks might indicate "the enemy's intentions against . . . Normandy," the invasion was "not immediately imminent judging from the intensity of air attacks."[34]

Despite that conclusion, at 0145 hours the telephone lines between Paris and Cherbourg were cut by the French Resistance. Navy Group West fell back on the use of radios, through which came the first signs that an invasion was potentially under way. At 0200 on June 6, the admiral commanding the Channel coast sent a message to the naval staff that parachutists and gliders were landing on the Cotentin Peninsula. Confirmation of airborne landings was sent out at 0240, and Dönitz canceled his leave to take command of the developing situation. Dönitz's senior officers reported for duty at headquarters as quickly as they could; Chief of Staff Admiral Hoffmann arrived in his dressing gown. The same pattern was repeated at naval and army headquarters across the West. While the army high command speculated that the landings in Normandy were a diversion before a main force landing in the Pas de Calais, the Kriegsmarine was ready to conclude that "the invasion has begun. . . . Once again there is an opportunity to bring about a quick decision of the war by a short but energetic fight."[35]

The reality, however, was that there were simply not enough boats in commission to constitute an effective force against the invasion fleet. The war diary for Schnellboote Command recorded that on June 1 just twenty-nine boats were available for the coastal defense of Western Europe.

**DISPOSITION OF UNITS, JUNE 1, 1944**

| | | |
|---|---|---|
| 1st Flotilla | 8 boats operational | Black Sea |
| 2nd Flotilla | 5 boats operational | Ostend |
| 3rd Flotilla | 2 boats operational | Cattaro |
| 4th Flotilla | 8 boats operational | Boulogne |
| 5th Flotilla | 5 boats operational | Cherbourg |
| 6th Flotilla | 8 boats operational | Gulf of Finland |
| 7th Flotilla | 5 boats operational | Cattaro |
| 8th Flotilla | 4 boats operational | Ijmuiden |
| 9th Flotilla | 7 boats operational | Cherbourg |
| 10th Flotilla | 2 boats operational | Swinemuende[36] |

The boats in the English Channel would simply have to do what they could to meet the invasion force and to contribute to what they hoped would be a victory that would stem the tide running ever more quickly against Germany. The invasion had come too soon for Dönitz, the Kriegsmarine's 1943 building program, and the next generation of U-boats, on which so many hopes had been pinned.

**CHAPTER 10**

# D-DAY FOR THE KRIEGSMARINE

THE DAWN OF D-DAY on June 6, 1944, brought the arrival of Allied amphibious forces to the coast of France. The German naval high command regarded the moment as a decisive opportunity to turn the tide of battle in the West. The S-boats, torpedo boats, and other light naval forces available in the ports along the coast of western France would be committed to the battle. In most accounts of D-Day, the naval struggles off the Normandy coast on June 6 and in the days following are rapidly passed over in narratives that emphasize the crushing weight of Anglo-American forces. This chapter argues that we need to look again at events off the coast of Normandy in June 1944. Most of the emphasis in the varied accounts and more scholarly analyses of D-Day emphasize the battle at the water's edge, and there is little place for the naval aspects of the landings. Volume 11 of Samuel Eliot Morison's history *United States Naval Operations in World War II* contains just five pages on German naval responses to the arrival of the invasion fleet.[1]

Although the first indications of an Allied landing were being received by Kriegsmarine commands along the Channel coast, it was not until 0330 that reports of invasion craft in the Seine Bay were received.[2] At 0348 hours on the morning of June 6, the 8th Destroyer Flotilla was ordered to move from the Gironde to Brest. At the same time, the commander of Group West ordered the 5th and 9th S-boat Flotillas to proceed to sea from their base at Cherbourg. Their mission, with reports of Allied Airborne forces landing on the Cotentin Peninsula, was to carry out inshore patrolling and to potentially intercept any attempt at a landing. Despite the vital nature of this task, the boats of the 5th S-boat Flotilla turned back soon after they left harbor as they came under attack from patrolling Allied aircraft. The 9th Flotilla was similarly attacked and forced to return to port, but not until it had contacted the invasion force approaching the coast. A long-range torpedo attack was mounted before the 9th Flotilla returned to the relative safety of the Cherbourg S-boat bunker. At 0435 Group West submitted further reports to the naval high command about enemy airborne landings across a broad front. Farther to the east, it took almost until dawn for the four vessels of the 5th Torpedo Boat Flotilla (*T28*, *Falke*, *Jaguar*, and *Moewe*) to leave Le Havre to look for targets. When they fired their torpedoes at long range, the Norwegian destroyer *Svenner* was their only victim and the only casualty of the attack, which was assisted by the smokescreen laid by aircraft to cover the eastern assault area. Smoke laid by aircraft over the eastern assault area aided the German vessels in their attack and helped the S-boats in their escape.[3]

The opening battles seemed to set the tone for naval engagements over the next few days. Naval Group West, convinced that the invasion had begun, attempted to move available forces to the landing zone with varying levels of success.[4] The 4th S-boat Flotilla was moved from Boulogne to Le Havre (eight boats starting out at 0510), but heavier German units were not in a position to rush to the scene of the landing.[5] The strength of Allied air and sea power made any movement very difficult, and the situation was complicated by divisions in Group West and the German high command. By 0530 Naval Group West was convinced that the decisive moment was at hand and was doing all in its power to affect the outcome of the invasion. The operations officer at Group West at 0545 informed the naval high command that the commanding general and commanding admiral at Group West disagreed over the nature of the landings. While the latter was certain that the invasion was at hand, the former believed that a large raid or diversion from landings elsewhere was taking place.[6] Between 0730 and 0745, reports of large-scale landings at various beaches on the coast of Normandy appeared to confirm the admiral's assessment of the extent of the landings. Within two hours, and despite confused reports from units along the Normandy coast, Allied radio was reporting that a full-scale invasion was under way and that along the coast the first lines of German defenses had been breached.[7]

Throughout the rest of D-Day, and in the days following, Kriegsmarine units continued to try and take the offensive against the invasion force steadily pouring troops, vehicles, and supplies into the bridgehead. In view of the urgency of the situation, with army and SS units fighting to contain and reduce the Allied bridgehead, and despite concerns about operating in shallow waters, Dönitz ordered into the invasion area as soon as possible seventeen U-boats (eight of which had been retrofitted with the schnorkel device to allow them to recharge their batteries while remaining submerged). As Lawrence Paterson has noted, "within days" the U-boat force operating in the English Channel had been reduced to just five of the schnorkel boats, the rest having been sunk or forced to withdraw in a damaged state.[8] If the operating conditions were extremely difficult for the U-boat crews, then in many ways they were far worse for the surface units, and the heavier vessels found it almost impossible to get into a position from which they might potentially engage the enemy. Dönitz later pointed out that "the German light naval forces found themselves confronted with a vastly superior enemy. We had thirty . . . [S-boats], four destroyers and nine torpedo boats. The British and the Americans, on the other hand, had concentrated between seven and eight hundred warships in the sea area of the invasion. . . . The German naval forces did what they could and managed even to achieve a few successes."[9] To Allied interrogators in July 1945 he put it more succinctly: with the units at their disposal, German forces could only inflict "flea bites."[10] Academic opinion has perhaps, though, been a little too quick to accept Dönitz's analysis. Peter Smith, for example, argues, "The limited German forces found themselves overwhelmed by the huge size of the Allied fleet. They could never hope to make more than a few sorties before destruction, but, in the event, made even less of an impression than had been expected."[11]

The kind of long-range attack mounted by 9th S-boat Flotilla on June 6 set the tone for S-boat operations over the next few days. Facing the danger of aerial attack from the Albacores and Swordfish of 19 and 16 Groups RAF Coastal Command the moment they left port, S-boats were reluctant to close with Allied screening forces, which included the Coastal Forces Command Frigates, with their groups of MTBs and MGBs.[12] So effective was the screen, with its integrated defense, that the S-boats generally fired torpedoes at extreme ranges. At least two potential attacks on the invasion fleet on the night of June 6–7 were checked by the Coastal Forces groups of HMS *Stayner* and HMS *Trollope*.[13] So closely protected was the invasion force, and so closely blockaded was Cherbourg, that only the S-boats operating at Le Havre really stood a chance of making any significant kills.[14]

Although the S-boats were being contained, the threat from the forces at Le Havre brought a devastating response from Allied forces. On June 14 RAF Bomber Command attacked Le Havre in an operation calculated to remove the threat.[15] Le Havre did not have the kind of hardened dockyard facilities to cope with the maintenance demands of the number of vessels that had seen considerable service since June 6. Critically, it also lacked the torpedo-handling facility and stocks needed to support the fleet of S-boats operating from Le Havre. With torpedo stocks running down, the need to conserve reserves had begun to impact on operations.[16] In the attack, three waves of bombers targeted the dock basins and protected pens. It was thought that even if the pens were not penetrated (and they were, to devastating effect), bombs falling into the basins could create a tsunami-like effect that would damage or destroy the vessels sheltering within them.[17] Crews were later congratulated by Air Chief Marshall Harris, the head of Bomber Command.[18] Details of the "mighty blow" struck against the enemy were quickly passed to the British press.[19] Kriegsmarine losses were considerable: "Twenty minesweepers and patrol-boats, nineteen tugs, three torpedo boats . . . and fourteen S-boats [were destroyed and others damaged]. Only one S-boat (S-167) was left operational in Le Havre."[20] One French civilian later reported that as a result of the bombing there had been a mutiny among the sailors at Le Havre, and a substantial number (800) had been shot, in addition to around 3,200 sailors and soldiers killed by the bombing.[21] While these figures cannot be verified, the report does point toward a potentially significant impact that the attack had on the morale of those trying to resist Allied naval forces off the Normandy coast. In demonstrable material terms alone, at a single stroke the S-boat threat to Allied naval units off the coast of Normandy had been neutralized.

The consensus among historians on the Normandy invasion would refute the possibility that better-equipped and more numerous Kriegsmarine light forces on D-Day would have been able to make a stronger and more impactful showing on D-Day. Certainly, Allied forces were very quick to conclude in the hours following the invasion that the S-boat threat had been effectively nullified and that only in exceptional circumstances might they prove effective. As the commander of the USS *Baldwin* concluded, "It is considered unlikely that a group of . . . [S]-boats, unless attacking in overwhelming numbers, and upon an extremely disorganized convoy or task force, could press home their attacks with any success in view of the present equipment and doctrine used by our ships."[22]

Perhaps, though, there is scope for a reevaluation of the effectiveness of the S-boat campaign against the invasion force in June 1944. Dönitz (in his memoirs) and postwar historians have been a little too eager to write off the operations of the 4th, 5th, and 9th S-boat flotillas in June 1944 as an inevitably feeble effort against a vast Allied invasion force. In the immediate aftermath of the invasion, however, Dönitz appears to have recognized that with a larger number of S-boats, the Kriegsmarine might have been able to contest the waters off the Normandy coast more effectively. The war diary of the naval high command on June 8 recorded him as saying, "The most effective methods of preventing the landing by naval operations against the approaching landing fleet is [*sic*] impossible for us because of lack of strength. . . . The situation would be different, if a considerable number of torpedo-carriers, especially . . . [S]-boats, would be at our disposal."[23]

This sense that things could have been very different was shared by FdS Petersen. Fully acknowledging that available Kriegsmarine forces were outmatched by Allied naval units and that long summer days restricted the scope for S-boats to operate by cover of night, Petersen did identify certain operational advantages the S-boat flotillas could count on:

1. Contrary to expectation, the enemy did not attempt to take either the two harbors of CHERBOURG or LE HAVRE, immediately, so that the S-boats had bases close to either flank from which they could operate against the SEINE ESTUARY.
2. The enemy was forced, at least in the early days, to operate with large surface forces and transport units, in a narrow area,

without any regular convoy rhythm, so that there were always worthwhile targets in the area.
3. Enemy defense systems were not fully worked up, so that in the early days they were reasonably easy to break through.
4. The enemy had many new units—especially American units—which were neither used to the area nor to S-boat warfare, and which were therefore easier targets for . . . [S-boats] than the experienced British Channel destroyers.[24]

These advantages suggest that S-boat operations against the Allied invasion force deserve some reassessment. Allied naval and air superiority did not preclude S-boat operations. Did the S-boats enjoy successes against the invasion fleet that have been submerged by the dominant narrative of Operation Neptune as a brief and unimportant precursor to the fight on land? Certainly, Dönitz's rather dismissive analysis in his memoirs of the effectiveness of S-boat operations on and after D-Day do not appear to be wholly justified. V. E. Tarrant has argued that "the S-boats sank three tank landing ships, one tank landing craft, one infantry landing craft, one motor-torpedo boat, one motor gunboat, the US tug *Partridge*, three small merchant ships grossing 1,812 tons, a component of the artificial Mulberry harbor, and the frigate [HMS] *Halsted* . . . written off as a constructional loss."[25] Also damaged were a destroyer and two amphibious craft. Of course, this wasn't enough to change the course of the battle, and in view of the size of the Allied invasion force, the haul of victims by the S-boats was small. Even so, it was a contribution, and its significance can be judged by making a comparison with the U-boat force sent into the Channel to operate against the invasion fleet. In the two months after D-Day, Dönitz's submarines sank four merchant vessels, two amphibious ships, and five escorts.[26] By comparison with the U-boats, the S-boat successes in the week following June 6 were notable. As Clay Blair has commented, sending U-boats to operate against the invasion fleet was a mark of desperation: "Submarines were useless against alert invasion forces."[27] The result was, as John Terraine notes, "a real U-boat fiasco." In particular, the dispatch to the invasion area of U-boats not yet fitted with schnorkel constituted "an abject confession of powerlessness."[28] It was simply sending men to their deaths without any prospect of their survival or likelihood that they could inflict serious damage on Allied naval forces. "The U-boats [as Padfield notes] had been literally overwhelmed by the forces massed to prevent them reaching the transports."[29] For the type VIIc U-boats that had been so effective in the Atlantic from 1940 to 1943, it was a last hurrah. Corelli Barnett argues that it was "a pitiful performance for a weapons-system and a service which had come so near to winning both world wars; the last limp punch of a beaten prizefighter whose legs were already buckling."[30] In the circumstances of the Normandy invasion, the S-boats demonstrated that, in comparison to the obsolete VIIc U-boats, they retained the capacity to inflict significant damage on Allied naval units.

Indeed, on June 10, FdS Petersen expressed his happiness with the effectiveness of the S-boat attacks that had been mounted: "S-boat successes against the invasion fleet first class! . . . Keep at it! Now you have plenty of targets—at them!"[31] This was not simply an overinflated analysis wrapped in an exhortation to exhausted crews to maintain the offensive despite Allied naval supremacy. On June 13, Petersen was awarded the Oak Leaves to the Knight's Cross by Hitler for the success of the S-boats off the coast of Normandy.[32] The same honor was accorded the following day to the head of the 9th S-boat Flotilla, Kapitänleutnant von Mirbach. At the same time, in reports from the battlefront the German press proclaimed "the great hour of the *Schnellboote*."[33] Press claims as to the number of invasion vessels sunk were exaggerated, but they were not wholly without substance.[34] The successes do beg the question of what might have happened in June 1944 if a larger force had been available. The likelihood is that the Kriegsmarine would have been in a position to mount attacks that could have swamped the forces defending the invasion fleet. A larger number of S-boats would have meant that greater risks could have been taken in order to cut through the destroyer screens and to attack the ships carrying troops, ammunition, vehicles, and stores. On June 6, at least on Omaha Beach, a relatively small number of additional sinkings could have made the difference between an insecure or failed lodgment and German defeat. In the days after the Normandy landings, every loss at sea impacted on Allied ability to link the invasion bridgeheads and to move inland. Any delay increased the opportunities for German forces to arrive from the interior and to mount counterattacks against the bridgeheads.

The effectiveness of the S-boat, and thus the potential of a larger S-boat force, was enhanced in June 1944 by the availability to the Luftwaffe and Kriegsmarine of a type of mine. The new kind of pressure mine (usually referred to as the oyster mine by the Allies even though there were three different kinds) had been kept back to ensure the element of surprise.[35] The mines, around 4,500 of them, were being held in Germany with the intention of rushing them to the battle area once the invasion was at hand.[36] A defensive strategy to make the most of the new weapon remained dangerously undeveloped. At Le Mans in the first months of 1944, around 2,000 of the new types of mine were being held at bunkers for rush deployment with the Luftwaffe. In May, however, Göring concluded that in an Allied landing the stocks might be overrun before they could be used. He ordered that the mines be pulled back to depots in Germany. The last mines arrived at their new home in Germany just two days before the Normandy landing.

Conventional mines were available, and at the end of May the Kriegsmarine was ready to lay additional minefields to enhance the security of the Normandy coast. The German minelaying effort on May 23 was disrupted thanks to attacks by RAF aircraft after Ultra decrypts had revealed their intentions.[37] Two fast minelayers were lost in the process, so minelaying efforts in the Seine estuary did not resume until June 5.[38] Using S-boat and R-boats to lay new fields was an option, but Navy Group West wanted to maintain its anti-invasion forces at a high state of readiness. The potential impact of fresh minefields along the Normandy coast in time for the invasion might have been considerable, as Vice Admiral Ruge later observed: "Even a few hundred mines in the Seine Bight could have caused losses and considerable delays."[39] Effective minefields backed by coastal artillery and light forces had the potential to be of more than nuisance value against the Allies. The new oyster mines, once they had been returned from Germany and laid by S-boats and aircraft, as Luftwaffe and Kriegsmarine worked together, proved hugely effective.[40] The commander of U.S. Naval Forces later gave ample testimony of the dangers in June 1944 posed by oyster mines, first encountered on June 7 off Utah Beach: "The field claimed seven casualties including two U.S. destroyers . . . and the U.S. Fleet minesweeper *Tide*. In the eastern area . . . the air mining effort mounted steadily. . . . Fifteen casualties, three vessels sunk and twelve damaged, were suffered in the ETF area by D-plus 16, while some ninety mines had been swept."[41] Unreliable fuses caused some difficulties, and the campaign further suffered from a shortage of aircraft and vehicles to lay them in large numbers.[42] The British Naval Staff later observed, with some sympathy, "[The Germans] found themselves in the exasperating position of possessing weapons of a most formidable nature while deprived of the ability to lay them offensively except on a relatively small scale."[43] Between June 7 and 21, forty-four Allied ships were damaged or sunk by the mining effort, forcing Allied navies to take desperate measures.[44] As a stopgap measure, minesweepers resorted to using hand grenades tossed over the side to try and cause mines to detonate in sympathetic explosion.[45] This practice was later refined into the "X-sweep" with a device to drop a pattern of grenades into the water, but that somewhat rough-and-ready device had flaws that could result in injury to minesweeper and crew.[46] At the same time that the Royal Navy were improvising, the RAF tried to target the airfields where minelaying aircraft operated from, and night fighters flew combat air patrols over the invasion area to keep away aircraft or vessels that might attempt to lay mines by night. Increased sweeping efforts, tight controls over the lanes available to shipping approaches approaching the bridgeheads, and restrictions on maximum speeds further decreased the danger from acoustic and other mines.[47] While the number of mine casualties in June 1944 did not imperil the invasion, it amounted to more than nuisance value. Delays and lost cargo and ships slowed the pace of the Allied advance inland, resulting in problems such as the need to ration daily expenditure of artillery ammunition.[48]

S-boat operations against the invasion fleet, some twenty vessels against more than a thousand Allied ships, did meet with some success between June 6 and 14 even though they were grossly outnumbered. The raid on Le Havre on June 14 effectively ended the threat to the invasion force, at a point where it could make a real contribution to the fighting on the land, leaving surviving German coastal forces to stage a fighting withdrawal up the Channel coast using ports such as Le Havre and St. Malo.[49] The surviving S-boats continued to do what they could against the invasion force: for example, the 6th S-boat Flotilla fired 91 Dackel (TIIId) to make long-range torpedo attacks on the Normandy anchorage from August 4–18. The main job of continuing to engage the invasion force, however, had fallen to the K-Verband even before the S-boats abandoned Le Havre at the end of August.[50] In any event, the K-Verband hadn't been given the time to become effective; as Hellmuth Heye commented, "Trials were, virtually speaking, made against the enemy."[51] Dönitz, however, appears to have had some difficulty in accepting their failure, and his memoirs are replete with references to the "courageous determination" and comments about their sinking "a number of enemy ships."[52] Heye, more honestly, noted after the war that "whatever their nature, small battle weapons can never be a substitute for regular weapons of war."[53] It was a recognition that the Kriegsmarine should have invested more heavily in S-boats, destroyers, and other conventional vessels. Even as the war was drawing toward a close, the Kriegsmarine continued to develop new weapons suitable for coastal warfare, including a new type of four-man (*Hydraboot*) motor torpedo boat capable of thirty-six knots.[54] After initial trials in August 1944, an initial order was placed for 50 on December 4, 1944, with an order for a further 115 placed on February 8, 1945. Some 38 boats were ready by the time of the German surrender, but by that point it was simply too late.

As the experience of the K-Verband and *Hydraboot* demonstrate, 1943 had been the pivotal year for German coastal defense. By the end of that year, the Kriegsmarine had been forced into a coastal war. Dönitz was unwilling to accept it and pinned his hopes on new generations of submarines that would allow him to restart oceanic warfare. The performance of the Kriegsmarine in meeting the invasion on June 6, 1944, left much to be desired, but it was markedly better than has been acknowledged by postwar historians. It serves as an indication of what might have been achieved if a strategy of coastal defense had been thought through and implemented by the German armed forces. In captivity after the war one German general reflected,

> The preparation and organization of the defense was not systematical since the beginning. The defective organization of Army, Navy

and "Todt" caused superfluous work and bad co-operation. There were continuous arguments between the high commands of these three organizations originated by different opinions and sometimes by personal dislike. The requirements of Army and Navy were sometimes opposed to each other. The Navy, insisting on the importance of the Naval war, always demanded full independence for the preparation of the defense. . . . Until the beginning of the invasion there was no organized cooperation between Army and Navy and such cooperation that existed was due only to good relations between the lower commands. The limited experiences of the Navy in modern defensive operations and its belief in the fundamental importance of the naval war made modern warfare impossible.[55]

Nevertheless, the performance of the S-boat against the Allied invasion flotilla in June 1944 was more significant than is acknowledged in subsequent accounts, serving as an indicator of what might have been thought through and embraced by Dönitz in partnership with the other service heads. Even in December 1944, Dönitz still insisted on adding the caveat "with the exception of submarine warfare" to the admission to the Führer that the Kriegsmarine was waging "a purely coastal war."[56] Although the combat power of the German navy was declining markedly as Allied armies marched toward Berlin, Dönitz continued to give the most optimistic assessments of the offensive performance of the Kriegsmarine. He told Hitler on January 3, 1945, that he expected the *Seehund* midget submarine to sink 100,000 tons of Allied shipping.[57] Even after the conclusion of the war, while a prisoner of the British, Dönitz continued to argue that the Kriegsmarine had experienced "considerable success" during 1944 even if that success had not been sufficient to "bring about a change in the situation."[58] He argued that it was entirely due to the numerical and industrial superiority of the Allies that they had triumphed in 1944. Time in Allied captivity, following the Nuremberg Trials, does appear to have shifted his views somewhat. In his memoirs, published after his release from jail, he began to raise issues about German strategy in 1944. The principal targets of his analysis were, however, the Wehrmacht and

Luftwaffe rather than his own direction of the Kriegsmarine. At no point does he invite questions about his pursuit and conduct of the U-boat war.[59] Nor does he take issue with the failure to create a command structure in the West, and a defensive plan, which could have created the circumstances for a more integrated and effective response to the invasion. Instead, the Luftwaffe, Kriegsmarine, and Heer (army) would be left to fight their separate battles on D-Day. There would be "no uniform defense plan. . . . The three services did not co-operate enough in many details. . . . Almost every commander had his own ideas, not always very clear, on how to defend his area."[60] Dönitz's acceptance in 1944 and later of the flaws in the German plan appear to be part of what Vice Admiral Ruge would later describe as a "fatalistic acceptance of the deteriorating situation, and a lack of alertness in looking for possible improvements."[61]

The failure to meet the threat of invasion in 1944 speaks to the failure of leadership in the Third Reich; the failure to reevaluate strategy and to shift from offense to defense at the appropriate moment; the failure to effectively manage production and industrial planning; and the failure of the state to make the most of German science and engineering to secure ongoing weapons and technological innovation. That failure extended even to Dönitz's much-vaunted submarine-building program for the electro-boats on which he placed such great hopes. While some writers, including Cajus Bekker, have argued that in the spring of 1945 the Germans were about to use the electro-boats to restart the U-boat war with a vengeance, their build quality in many cases left much to be desired.[62] These stemmed, Grier maintains, from "simple poor planning," poor coordination, and a failure to meet construction specifications.[63] If a more successful S-boat and U-boat campaign in 1944 had allowed Nazi Germany a few more months of existence, it is still unlikely that the new classes of U-boats would have been able to alter the strategic balance in 1945. A declining number of S-boats would find themselves retreating from port to port in northern Europe as Allied forces took the coast away from them, making it ever more risky to venture out to the old hunting grounds, the English waters of 1940 to 1943.

The level of Allied sea control in 1944 proved not just effective, but decisive, in launching the largest seaborne invasion in history. The long-honed practices of controlling a sea space developed to protect the coastal convoys were utilized to significantly neutralize the S-boat threat on the flanks of the invasion fleet. The operational commands at Portsmouth and Plymouth that had become focal points in the defense of the English coast became critical command and control nodes in the projection of Allied power onto the coast of occupied Europe. In the process they showed remarkable capacity to handle the inflowing and outflowing streams of data in the form of information/intelligence and orders. The Kriegsmarine, by contrast, found itself beset by misinformation and network failure as a result of Allied action and the problematic nature of the hierarchies in the Nazi state. D-Day for the Kriegsmarine was a battle lost in the relative industrial outputs of the two opposing forces compounded by the success of Allied planning, and the efficiency of Allied data networks in handling vast streams of information/intelligence and orders. The invasion worked because the right fleet had been built and assembled, and its combat power deployed to its point of use, without enemy forces causing serious disruption. As the summer of 1944 progressed, the Allies owned not just English waters but also, increasingly, those on the far shore.

**CHAPTER 11**

# THE LONG RETREAT, 1944–1945

THIS CHAPTER ANALYZES the dying months of the S-boat campaign in European waters. Keeping together a force headed toward defeat and experiencing growing shortages, a slow process of retreat, and increasing rates of attrition on its vessels and crews placed a particularly heavy burden on FdS Kapitän-zur-See Rudolf Petersen.[1] Born on June 15, 1905, in Atzerballing on Alsen Island, Petersen's family moved to Berlin at the end of World War I when northern Schleswig was given to Denmark. He joined the Reichsmarine as a cadet in April 1925. Commissioned in 1929, he received the Wehrmacht Long Service medal on April 1, 1937, after spending the intervening years in torpedo boats, a light cruiser, and the Reichsmarine's hydrographic service. Taking over command of the 2nd S-boat Flotilla in 1938, he took part in the German takeover of Memel in 1939 and the assault on Norway in 1940. In 1941 he was declared unfit for sea service following a car accident and was sent as staff officer to the Führer der Torpedoboote. As Hans Frank argues, to the serious and high-minded Petersen (his father had been a minister) it was a profound disappointment that his frontline career in S-boats had effectively been ended by the accident.[2] He did not see himself as an administrator and had little time for paperwork and writing. It is this aversion that makes some of his writing in the period 1944–45 so fascinating.

Fascinated by history, and interested in religious questions, Petersen had taken a pessimistic view of the Kriegsmarine's future on the outbreak of war in 1939, and by late 1944 those fears were being realized. The impressions of the officers who talked to Hans Frank in the 1980s and 1990s suggest a man committed to a strategy of attrition as the only course open to the German navy.[3] He brought this outlook to the post of FdS, to which he was appointed on April 20, 1942. To go with the post, he was promoted to the rank of Korvettenkapitän (the lowest rank for a senior officer). Petersen took over his new post at the height of the S-boat campaign against the British Isles, but from the position of command he had observed the steady eclipse of the S-boat campaign during late 1942–43. Not about to waste boats or the lives of his crews on pointless or hopeless missions, he was prepared to commit them at what he saw was the appropriate moment. In early 1943 he was reprimanded by Commander-in-Chief Group West for sending all available S-boats to assist in the recovery of a damaged boat rather than pressing the attack against the enemy, but on June 13, for the efforts of the S-boats during the D-Day landings, he was awarded the Oak Leaves to the Knight's Cross he had been awarded in 1940 for his leadership in the assault on Norway.[4] Nevertheless, he was still subject to ongoing criticism and suspicion by Commander-in-Chief Group West, even as he did his best to rally his forces in the aftermath of D-Day, the devastating raid on Le Havre, and the start of the retreat to the North.[5]

In September 1944, the surviving S-boats were concentrated in Dutch ports, and U-boats began to relocate to Norwegian waters as their Atlantic bases faced the prospect of encirclement and capture as Allied forces moved into Brittany and along the French Atlantic coast. From their bases in Norway and along the French coast during 1944 and into 1945, the U-boat arm would attempt to mount a campaign against British inshore shipping, in the North Sea, the Western Approaches to the English Channel, even to the Thames Estuary, as well as more distant U.K. waters. The campaign was a belated recognition of the significance of the shipping plying Britain's inshore waters, now made richer by the need to keep supplying the Allied forces advancing in France. As Admiral Godt, tactical head of the Submarine Arm (BdU), confirmed after the war, the idea of an inshore campaign using the schnorkel had not occurred to the Kriegsmarine high command until after the D-Day landing.[6] Launching the campaign was a reluctant move to the defensive: Dönitz hoped to enable the German army to win a stalemate on the battlefield that could buy sufficient time to bring the new generation of submarines into service. The British quickly adopted new technologies, laid new mine barrages, and adapted the anti-U-boat skills learned from the Atlantic campaign to inshore waters as German submariners found that the density layers caused by coastal currents and the proliferation of underwater targets around the United Kingdom did offer them some protection from searching escorts.[7]

The decision to use U-boats against British coastal waters potentially opened up possibilities for the S-boats, but it was effectively too late to turn the tide of battle: in September 1944, Petersen had unsuccessfully suggested that they be withdrawn entirely from the North Sea and Channel. He believed that, given the Russian advances in the East, the S-boats might be better deployed in the Baltic and in coastal defense of the northern German ports.[8] In part, Petersen may well have been trying to keep his command together. During early September, a crisis in the morale of German troops in the Netherlands became apparent as a shortage of war news, and the bedraggled arrival of retreating units from Belgium and France on September 3–4, triggered a sense of panic. The admiral commanding the Netherlands later reported "many an unpleasant manifestation," as positions were abandoned with "ugly rumors" flying "with the speed of lightning" through the country.[9]

S-boat forces in the Netherlands remained considerable. The 8th Flotilla was based at Ijmuiden (five boats operational), the 10th at Amsterdam (five boats operational), and the 9th at Delfzijl (three boats operational). They would move between those ports, Rotterdam, and Den Helder during late 1944. As the high command attempted to restabilize the front in the Netherlands, Petersen's request to relocate to the Baltic would be denied. The S-boats would continue to operate against shipping in the Scheldt Estuary (mining attacks) and against the East Coast convoys (mine and torpedo) until the end of the war. Command was transferred from Naval Command West to Naval Command North. The S-boat had effectively been forced out of the Channel, although there would be one last engagement on September 18–19 as four S-boats (8th and 10th Flotillas) ran a resupply mission to the besieged German garrison at Dunkirk. Commanded by Admiral Friedrich Frisius from September 15 onward, the port was protected by ten thousand German soldiers mostly drawn from five divisions that had retreated there with the collapse of the front in France. It was under siege from Canadian forces who hoped to eject

German forces so that the port could be used to help ease the logistical problems facing the Allied armies.[10]

The planning and execution of this mission indicates the increasing problems facing S-boat command, the steady collapse of German resistance in the West, and growing tensions between FdS Petersen and his superiors. On September 14 Commander-in-Chief Naval Forces Netherlands sent a signal to S-boat command that the ammunition situation in the Dunkirk pocket was critical and that resupply should be attempted by S-boat. Three S-boats based in Rotterdam were quickly loaded with eighteen tons of deck cargo, but the operation was postponed on account of the weather. With each boat carrying six tons of highly explosive deck cargo, and a significant chance of encountering the enemy, the operation was risky in the extreme. An officer like Petersen who had served in S-boats, who knew his commanders, and who had seen the turn of the tide in the Channel battles was probably less than enthusiastic at the invitation to order three crews to their likely deaths. Dunkirk seemingly had little strategic value, and the remaining pockets of resistance along the Channel coast continued to fight on the orders of Hitler, who was unwilling to sanction either withdrawal or surrender. Petersen was only too happy to use the weather as a convenient excuse to delay the operation, as he could legitimately argue that substantial amounts of deck cargo would seriously reduce the sea-keeping qualities of the S-boats.

Petersen was prepared to risk his crews, but only on missions that he thought had military value and a realistic chance of success and survival. Thus, on September 16 nine boats from the 9th and 10th Flotillas (three groups of three in open formation) were sent out to hunt for convoy traffic off Cromer. One group turned back after one of their number developed a rudder problem. The other two groups failed to contact a convoy but did lay mines despite being attacked by aircraft and engaged by a destroyer.

The launching on September 17 of Operation Market Garden, an Allied thrust toward the Rhine through the Netherlands, altered the strategic position in northwestern Europe. The operation left the Dunkirk garrison both more isolated and, at the same time, even more useful in tying down troops that might otherwise be sent into the Netherlands. On the evening of September 17, Commander-in-Chief Naval Forces Netherlands directed that the Dunkirk resupply operation be attempted with a convoy of landing craft and R-boats under escort from Petersen's S-boats. The operation, as envisaged, was near suicidal for the men in the slow-moving landing craft and R-boats, and also for the escorting S-boats, whose speed would be compromised by the slowest-moving vessels in the convoy. Petersen refused the request, which led Commander-in-Chief Naval Command North to step in and order a compromise. Twenty tons of supplies would be sent in on four S-boats.[11] To give them some protection, Petersen sent a covering force of three boats. In the event, the main force was able to execute its mission, landing their supplies and evacuating General Wolfgang von Kluge and the staff of the 226 Infantry Division.[12] But in a confused action with repeated encounters and false identifications, the covering force of three boats from the 10th Flotilla (S-183, S-200, and S-702) was attacked and sunk by Coastal Forces control frigate HMS *Stayner* and her MTB group. All communication between the S-boat group fell apart as S-183 was initially damaged by MTBs and then engaged by HMS *Stayner* at close range.[13] A postaction report by the commander of MTB 724 stated that "the attack was carried out at 75 yards range all guns hitting the enemy with devastating results. . . . The enemy was enveloped by smoke, 3 heavy explosions were heard and seen."[14] Following this, the two other S-boats collided while being pursued by MTBs. They were then finished off by HMS *Stayner* and the MTBs. Following the action, survivors from the three crews were pulled from the water. Reactions within the German naval high command that such losses "must be expected" spoke volumes about the increasing desperation of German forces.[15]

Following the sinkings, Kapitänleutnant Müller, the commander of the 10th S-boat Flotilla, and two commanding officers, along with forty-five men, were taken prisoner by the Royal Navy.[16] Müller was intensively questioned by British Naval Intelligence before being handed over to two Coastal Forces officers (Dreyer and Scott) for them to conduct their own interrogation, which took place on October 6 and 14. Unusually good accounts of this interrogation survive because Dreyer was later interviewed by the Imperial War Museum, and Scott left papers that detail the interrogation and its repercussions. Scott talked to the German officer at the first meeting, and for the second he was joined by Dreyer.

The atmosphere was convivial, and Dreyer noted the fluency and quality of Müller's English.[17] Müller was seemingly good company, and they compared notes with him, in both English and German, on a range of matters. While they did not learn anything particularly surprising, the exchanges confirmed a great deal for the men of British Coastal Forces. The conviviality of the meeting came across in Scott's later written account. He described how Müller was five feet, eight inches tall, with dark hair. Married, and twenty-eight years old, his home was in the Black Forest. There first conversation lasted for three hours, and the second, in Dreyer's company, lasted for four and a half hours as they went for a walk together in nearby parkland.[18]

In their conversation the officers ranged quite widely across subjects ranging from S-boat operations to personalities of the S-boat arm, and even Müller's thoughts on the Nazi high command. FdS Petersen was described as being Viking in type, another flotilla leader (von Mirbach) as like an oak. Feldt was singled out for his popularity, while Klug was clever but rather stiff. Zymalkowski was praised as being extraordinarily efficient.[19] Müller was ready to cooperate so freely because he believed that the war was already lost and that it was better for it to be concluded quickly. His lack of enthusiasm for the war was further evidenced in his descriptions of the Nazi high command. He described meeting Hitler and a conversation with him that was rather disconcerting. Hitler's eyes seemed rather strange and unfocused, and if the leader of Germany came over as great, he also appeared a little crazy.[20] Himmler, meanwhile, was described as pleasant and correct but also dangerously ambitious.[21]

The interrogation report was circulated by the Naval Intelligence Department and was later sent to senior officers in Coastal Forces, at Peter Scott's request, with the proviso that it should be sent only to those officers who had been briefed on the nature of such reports.[22] Scott not only obeyed instructions in sending out around thirty-eight copies of the report but also sent covering letters asking commanders to treat the contents with great care, as he would not want any information to reach Germany that might reveal Müller's level of cooperation.[23] Müller felt that the war was all but over and wished his interrogators to see him as a naval professional rather than as the representative of the Nazi Third Reich.

Indeed, Müller continued to be highly cooperative. Following his interrogation, Scott shared with him the manuscript of the book that he was writing that would be published in 1945 under the title *Battle of the Narrow Seas*. Scott had been writing the book since at least 1943 and had been careful to clear with the Admiralty Press Office details of what he was allowed to release.[24] To gather information for the book, Scott had solicited accounts of actions from MGB and MTB skippers and flotilla commanders.[25] Müller was happy to read the manuscript and sent back a lengthy and supportive response saying that he was impressed by its accuracy and expressing his intention to buy a copy of the book after publication.[26]

A few days after the interrogation, Müller was able to get himself exchanged for British SAS Captain M. R. D. Foot; the exchange took place at the edge of the besieged St. Nazaire pocket. In *Battle of the Narrow Seas*, Scott was very careful not to suggest that Müller had been helpful and cooperative while being interrogated. Indeed, Scott turns the story around to suggest that Müller effectively played them and was able to return to German occupied territory with potentially useful intelligence that had been shared with him while he was being interrogated. One thing that Müller was undoubtedly able to do was to confirm to Petersen what B-dienst had already advised him: that "in bad visibility" the "enemy's great radar advantage over S-boats" had resulted in the destruction of the covering force under Müller's command.[27]

After September 18, efforts to resupply the garrison at Dunkirk by sea were broken off. Instead, limited resupply was attempted from the air using "supply bombs" dropped by HE-111 aircraft.[28] With the opening up of the port of Oostende in late September (it had been captured by the Canadians on September 8), Montgomery was prepared to simply sit back and contain the garrison, which would not surrender until May 9, 1945.[29] By this stage the S-boat flotillas had ceded both strategic and tactical superiority to Allied forces off the coast of Western Europe, but the high command was determined to do what it could to deny Allied forces easy access to the coast. Maximizing the logistical difficulties for Allied forces in order to ease pressure on the land front was the primary goal of the Seekriegsleitung (Maritime Warfare Command). In early October 1944, the Commander-in-Chief of German Forces in the West received a directive emphasizing that "the enemy news have proved again . . . [that] enemy supplies and with that the battle activity are being hampered by a steadfast defense of the ports."[30] Petersen came under pressure to resume resupply operations for Dunkirk, and on November 14 he indicated to Naval Command West that, with the longer nights, he believed that resupply operations for Dunkirk involved a level of risk no greater than a normal torpedo operation ("kein größeres Risiko").[31]

This was despite the outcome of the earlier attempt to resupply the Dunkirk pocket via sea and the growing efficiency of anti-S-boat forces. During the summer of 1944, training for British Coastal Forces had moved up a gear with an emphasis on teamwork, use of initiative, and the highest professional standards. Evidence of this, in the form of Peter Scott's 1944 lecture notes for Coastal Forces papers, lies in Cambridge University.[32] The principal messages emphasized in training were that it was necessary to take the offensive at every turn, that surprise was the greatest weapon of Coastal Forces, and that any weakness of the enemy should be exploited. Scott was at pains to explain the latter to his audiences and to explain just how that might be achieved. Human weaknesses of the enemy were to be exploited, and unexpected lines of attack, such as entering an enemy harbor in daylight, making strange signals, or attacking from an unlikely direction, could prove particularly disconcerting.[33]

The offensive ethos of Coastal Forces, and its tactical manifestations highlighted in Scott's lecture notes, meant that by late 1944, with the deteriorating military situation, British Coastal Forces had established morale superiority over the S-boat arm along with their numerical supremacy. Müller's relaxed attitude toward interrogation provided some useful confirmation of intelligence derived from other sources, but its true significance lay in what it revealed about opinion within the S-boat arm. It took enormous reserves of bravery and professionalism to put to sea with morale being steadily degraded and with the high likelihood of ambush by British Coastal Forces. That S-boats continued to put to sea despite the odds facing them was remarkable testimony to the discipline of the Kriegsmarine.

Behind such discipline lay increasing tensions between officers and men, and between frontline officers and the naval high command. The growing tensions between Petersen and his naval superiors are evident even in the terse sentences of the FdS war diary (*Kriegstagbuch*). The Dunkirk operation had almost brought those tensions to a head, and he was further angered on September 18 by a signal from the Operations Division of the Naval War Staff giving him permission for the destruction of facilities at the ports of Amsterdam and Rotterdam. Petersen intervened, with signals going back and forth from September 21 to 23, to prevent their destruction, which would have meant "the end of all defensive and offensive S-boat operations in the area."[34]

A further glimpse of Petersen's growing exasperation and depression can be glimpsed in a situation report written two days before the Dunkirk resupply fiasco. Prompted by the evacuation of naval forces from Boulogne, Petersen reflected on the ejection of the S-boat flotillas from the English Channel:

> With the evacuation of Naval Forces from Boulogne, the S-boat has lost an important operational area which has been at its disposal without interruption from 1940 until the 10th Flotilla left on the 5th of September. How great a blow was given to further S-boat warfare by this loss, is shown by the fact now the S-boat Command must endeavor to maintain the Dutch Coast as their last remaining operational area, if S-boats are not to lose their purpose as offensive naval striking forces against British supply routes on the enemy coast. If I have been forced, by the immense speed of developments in the war on land in northern France and Belgium, to evacuate (as a matter of foresight) the depots and reserves of personnel and material from Holland to Germany, I have made provision at the same time, for striking power of all operational boats in the remaining ports to be maintained. It was my endeavor primarily, to use every opportunity offered by the weather to carry out offensive operations with torpedo and mine, against the British South-East Coast convoy traffic. Only once, however (12–13.9.44), did an opportunity occur, and even then, the weather was against us. On this occasion it could be seen that the enemy, having his air force free from ties on the Atlantic and Channel Coasts, uses concentrated forces to

watch every movement of our ships in the Hoofden ports, from the moment they pass the pierhead. In practice therefore, the last possibility of a surprise attack by an undetected S-boat advance into the operational area is lost to us.[35]

Petersen's situation report was a reflection of his own dismay at the steady collapse of German forces in the West, his difficulties with his commanders in the Kriegsmarine, and the near impossibility of staging successful S-boat attacks. Ship and airborne radar, and real-time transmission of intelligence data to naval units via VHF wireless, came into its own in late 1944 and early 1945.[36] S-boats could be expected to be detected often by the radar- and VHF-equipped Wellingtons of 16 Group and engaged shortly after leaving their bases, all the way through to the East Coast convoy lanes. The concentration in Dutch waters decreased the operational scope and range of the S-boats, which Petersen defined in late September 1944 as "(A) Minelaying in the Scheldt Estuary, Flemish Coast and Thames Estuary areas. (B) Torpedo attacks on supply convoys in the same areas. (C) Torpedo and minelaying operations off the British South East coast."[37]

The minelaying effort in the Scheldt Estuary went to considerable lengths, as Richard Brooks has noted. Before this point 1,703 ground and contact mines had been laid around the mouth of the river, and following Petersen's orders another 653 would be laid in the estuary or on the approach to Vlissingen.[38] Mining operations continued to meet with some success. On September 28 at 0750, while returning to Harwich, HMS *Duff* hit a mine laid by S-boats the previous evening.[39] One of the Coastal Forces control frigates, HMS *Duff* had been patrolling the waters off Oostende. Hit under the forward boiler room, the vessel was able to reach Harwich despite a low freeboard at the bows. She was later declared a constructive total loss.

To effect the tasks defined by Peterson, the S-boat command on October 1 had a force of just nine operational boats under his command.[40] Even though additional boats would reach Holland from Germany, the S-boat was subject to increasing shortages and problems of repair. Postwar official British estimates placed the number of S-boats (operational and nonoperational) in Dutch waters at 50 in late 1944.[41] On October 24 the *Liverpool*

*Echo* went so far as to ask the question "End of the E-Boat Menace?" when it reported that 143 S-boats had been put out of action since D-Day.[42] Even with the arrival of additional boats, shortages and damage to boats meant that just 16 were operational on November 16, 1944.[43] In addition, the concentration in Dutch waters left the remaining S-boats increasingly vulnerable to aerial attack in their bases and while at sea. Despite the difficulties facing the S-boat arm, the offensive against the coastal convoys continued until the end. From September onward the surviving S-boats were used primarily as fast minelayers. Allied landings on Walcheren Island in the southern Netherlands (Operation Infatuate) on November 1, 1944, briefly offered the targets of opportunity for torpedo attacks but yielded nothing. More importantly, to the German campaign in the West, and the role of S-boat command within it, the capture of Walcheren meant that, once it had been swept, the Scheldt and Antwerp were open to Allied merchant shipping. The minesweeping effort was completed on November 26: two days later a convoy of nineteen merchant ships arrived in Antwerp.[44]

An analysis of S-boat operations in October–November 1944 reveals the lack of opportunity for torpedo operations, and the importance of minelaying as the last offensive action the S-boats were capable of undertaking with a reasonable chance of success.

*Number of operations*: 14 (average number of boats: 12)

*Results claimed in 7 torpedo operations*
   1 ship of 3,000 tons sunk
   1 ship of 2,500 tons torpedoed
   1 LST (3,000 tons) probably torpedoed
   1 MGB heavily damaged

*Results of 7 minelaying operations*
   Number of mines laid: 182
   1 ship of 7,000 tons sunk
   1 ML sunk
   1 LCT (3–5,000 tons) sunk
   1 destroyer heavily damaged
   2 unknown vessels heavily damaged[45]

The offensive potential of the force under Petersen's command was further decreased by an attack on the S-boat pens at Ijmuiden on December 15, 1944. One boat was destroyed and six damaged. Comments in the S-boat Command's war diary displayed the growing sense of despair:

> Air Raid on E-Boat Shelter at Ijmuiden. Shelter penetrated by two "5.6-ton bombs." One boat (S-198) total loss, 2 boats medium damage, 4 boats slightly damaged and out of action, docking desirable. 1 killed, 12 missing, 5 wounded. The entire S-boat maintenance arrangements were disorganized. Six pens unusable, 1 boat trapped in the pen by debris. Whole of 8th Flotilla out of action. 4 boats ready for action by 22.12.44. FdS stated, "This event brings the bitter knowledge that S-boat shelters in Rotterdam and Ijmuiden in their present form no longer afford protection against bombing and have accordingly lost their purpose. I have therefore decided not to fill the pens with S-boats any longer, in view of the character of these shelters as special targets. The boats will be dispersed in the harbours, even at the expense of other advantages. This measure is not an ideal solution, and may be subject to alteration under certain circumstances, according to air situations or the tactics of enemy day-fighter-bombers."[46]

Following the attack on the Ijmuiden bunker, after receiving additional boats from home waters, five flotillas with twenty-six boats were based in Dutch waters at the start of 1945.[47] However, the growing difficulties of repairing damaged S-boats meant that eleven were in a nonoperational condition.[48] According to Hans Frank, at the end of 1944 Petersen was involved in an astonishing but revealing outburst in the ruined bunker at Ijmuiden. Seeing a Christmas service in progress on S-199, Petersen interrupted to object to the siting of a Christmas tree on a gun.[49] He was upset by the juxtaposition of a symbol of peace on a weapon of war.

Even as S-boat numbers increased in late 1944 and early 1945, with the headquarters of the FdS relocating from Scheveningen to Sengwarden near Wilhelmshaven, the war diary of the FdS for early 1945 made grim reading: S-boat operations were spotted on ship or airborne radar almost as soon as they reached open water. Mining operations continued, and from

September 1944 to May 1945 some 600 mines were laid in British coastal waters (the Luftwaffe added a further 750 mines) operating from Ijmuiden and Rotterdam.[50] In mid-January 1945 Petersen appears to have given up any attempt to maintain the war diary of the S-boat force. What prompted this decision is open to question, but it may be because of a protracted attack on his leadership of the S-boat force by Grand Admiral Dönitz. On January 12, as Lawrence Paterson notes, Dönitz wrote to Petersen to ask him why S-boats were engaged on attacks on the eastern convoys rather than intensifying attacks in the Scheldt Estuary.[51] Restricting the access of Allied shipping to Antwerp was a strategic imperative. With Antwerp open, the Allied armies would enjoy short logistical lines as they pushed into Germany from Belgium and the Netherlands. Petersen responded by saying that S-boats required the space to maneuver and that the estuary was a less-than-ideal operational area. Dönitz responded with an attack on overly strict orders that limited the fighting activity of the S-boat arm. A personal letter from the head of the Kriegsmarine followed in which Petersen was admonished for trying to protect his crews while U-boat crews risked all on a daily basis. Petersen was instructed to review various aspects of operational procedure, including the practice of trying to rescue disabled boats. The head of the S-boat arm argued his case, trying to explain the difficulties of surface operations in the face of overwhelming enemy superiority. Rather than removing the head of the S-boat arm, Dönitz issued orders on February 24, during a mining operation, that limited the S-boats' operational area.

While Petersen was fighting battles with high command, the war of attrition in the North Sea continued. Air-to-sea cooperation between British units was increasingly effective, playing a vital role in containing the threat to Allied shipping. Relevant files in the British National Archives and the U.S. National Archives at College Park, Maryland, reveal the volume of information and signal traffic being processed and actioned by Allied units in the Channel, with information gathered from radar, hydrophones, headache, and visual fixes being exchanged between aircraft, destroyers/frigates, MGBs/MTBs, and shore stations. By early 1945 the analogue equivalent of network-centric warfare was in operation in the North Sea, some fifty years before the U.S. Navy reimagined it for the computer age. This was despite difficulties ranging from breakdowns in the technology to the occasional lack of discipline on the part of operators. For example, following an operation in early 1945 one Royal Navy officer complained that lack of radio discipline by airmen made it "difficult to get a word in edge ways."[52]

The tactical edge this gave Allied units in the closing phases of the S-boat offensive was telling, allowing for multiple attacks by different air and sea assets. For example, on March 21, 1945, twenty boats from the 2nd, 5th, 4th, 6th, and 9th S-boat flotillas sortied for an attack on a convoy (*"Torp.-Angriff"*) northeast of Great Yarmouth.[53] On a moonlit and cloudless night ("mondheller wolkenloser Nacht") the 2nd Flotilla was quickly detected leaving Den Helder, was attacked from the air, and lost S-181, shot up, blown up, and left burning before eventually sinking. The four Beaufighters from 236 Squadron had seen the wake of the S-boats and had attacked with cannon "despite intense light flak."[54] The returning S-boats from the other flotillas were further engaged by destroyers and MGBs. The loss was bigger than the destruction of a single boat, as it had been under the command of Hermann Opdenhoff, the 2nd Flotilla leader and a holder of the Knight's Cross of the Iron Cross.[55] He had won that award in May 1940 in actions with the 2nd Flotilla that had initially established the S-boat as a potent weapon of war in the North Sea and English Channel. He was more than just a respected and experienced officer: he symbolized the S-boat campaign in the way that Robert Hitchens had come to represent the spirit and ethos of British Coastal Forces.

Two days later, on March 23, the pattern of early detection and attack was repeated as nine boats from the 4th and 6th Flotillas were "sighted by British aircraft and located by radar from destroyers" before being "attacked and pursued by MGBs."[56] By war's end, it was virtually impossible for the surviving S-boats to put to sea without being detected with British Coastal Forces and RAF Coastal Command aircraft being vectored to interception. The full gravity of the crisis facing the S-boat arm was slightly masked by the growing shortage of diesel, which otherwise placed severe limits on S-boat operations. The threat to Britain's coastal convoys was almost over, but in and around Dutch waters, mines laid by S-boats continued to take their toll. During the first three months of 1945,

S-boats conducted 303 sorties, losing five vessels in the process. They sank 12,972 tons of shipping by torpedo and 67,626 by mine, with 21,577 tons damaged by torpedoes and mine.[57] By comparison, the *Seehunde*s of the small battle units launched 106 sorties; they lost 23 units but managed to sink 9,282 tons of Allied shipping.[58] The other craft of the *Kleinkampfverbände* failed to achieve anything.

The desperate situation facing the remaining S-boats operating from Dutch waters in April 1945 can be glimpsed in some of the final reports reaching German naval command. In a roundup the Naval News Service reported from Berlin on April 8, 1945, as Soviet forces closed on the German capital, that the five S-boat flotillas in Holland had fuel for just five more major operations.[59] The reality was even worse: a major operation was concluding even as the news roundup was being compiled in Berlin. An operation on April 6–7 involving the 2nd, 4th, 6th, and 9th S-boat Flotillas (twenty-four boats) saw the loss of S-176 and S-177 after a mining operation off the Humber Estuary ran into British MTBs, together with two Captain-class Coastal Forces control frigates (HMS *Cubitt* and HMS *Rutherford*). S-176 rammed what it took to be the leading motor gunboat, which in reality was MTB 494, killing most of the crew and capsizing the British vessel. S-177 was also involved in a collision with MTB 493 and had to be abandoned after being heavily shot up, resulting in numerous hits below the waterline.[60] S-174 took on board the crew of S-177, and the British rescued all but five of the crew of S-176. The remaining four boats of the flotilla returned home to Den Helder, but even then, the grim realities of the fortunes facing the last S-boats was apparent. On returning home, Oberleutnant-zur-See Kurt Neugebauer was badly wounded by an accidental discharge from a machine gun as he clambered over the armored bridge. He died in the sick bay later the same day, and that evening RAF Lancasters and Mosquitos carried out a bombing mission on the S-boat bunker at Den Helder.[61] For the men of the S-boat arm, the sense of futility in carrying on the struggle must have been almost unbearable.

The damage sustained by the 2nd S-boat Flotilla put it out of operations for the remainder of the war, but the 4th, 6th, and 9th Flotillas were again in action, and again German forces sustained decisive losses. The boats were shadowed by RAF Wellingtons from 16 Group as they left the

Hook of Holland with good air-to-sea liaison with Coastal Forces MTBs, backed by HMS *Rutherford*, another of the Captain-class Coastal Forces control frigates. Off Oostende one of the groups of S-boats was shot up by British motor torpedo boats (MTBs 482 and 484), causing S-202 and S-703 to collide.[62] Forty men found themselves in the rafts and in the water hoping that rescue would come, which it did from the MTBs. On board MTB 482, Sublieutenant Roderick Timms, who would be mentioned in dispatches because of the action later recorded in his log regarding the tension at encountering the enemy: "I can still see clearly the two dinghies coming alongside the starboard side, feelings were running high and I grabbed the two .303 Browning machine guns mounted in the starboard side and cocked them and trained them on the survivors in case of some possible attack—there were plenty of them, and I thought make one move you bastards and I'll shoot the lot of you. I know at the time I hoped they would so I could kill them. [He later added,] In retrospect what a terrible thought."[63] His initial reaction did not prevent him from helping to haul in survivors from the dinghy, including one German sailor whose binoculars got stuck under the capping. Stripping him of the binoculars to get him on board, Timms later took them as a prize, along with a laundry list, as a war trophy to remember a war that was fast drawing to a close.[64]

On May 8, as the unconditional surrender of German forces came into effect, a final parade of S-boat personnel took place at Geltinger Bay as four boats from 10th S-boat Flotilla and twenty boats from 3rd School Flotilla, along with S-196 from 8th Flotilla and S-227 from 9th Flotilla, gathered with the four depot ships. Petersen, who had arrived from his new headquarters in Flensburg, addressed the men of his command for the last time. The ceremony was repeated the following day as another group of S-boats that had been involved in the Baltic evacuations arrived at Geltinger Bay.[65] Taking the parade was not quite Petersen's last command act. On March 10, he presided over the court-martial of three sailors who had deserted their posts on March 6 in the belief that the war was over. They were caught by the Danish police and handed back to the Kriegsmarine.[66] The legal position was clear, and military law dictated that Petersen convene a court-martial. Following a short trial, the accused were executed by firing squad on May 10, 1945—an almost inexplicable outcome in the context of a leader who had tried to be very economical with the lives of his crews. Petersen may well have been reminded of the collapse of discipline in the German navy at the end of World War I.[67] On the East Coast the final act of the S-boat campaign came on May 13, as two S-boats (S-204 and S-205) crossed the Channel to moor up at HMS *Beehive*, the Coastal Forces base at Felixstowe. On board were Admiral Breuning (commander-in-chief, Naval Forces West) and Kurt Fimmen (commanding the 4th Flotilla). Breuning was swiftly taken to Harwich to negotiate the surrender and handover of remaining German naval forces in the Netherlands. The coastal campaign was over.

Two features above all stand out in this last phase of the coastal campaign. One was the grim determination of German forces to keep doing what they could despite the implausibility of any outcome to the war other than complete German defeat. The second was the near totality of control that Allied forces enjoyed over the waters that were the last refuge of the S-boat in the North Sea. Such was the Allies' level of control that by 1945 every S-boat mission was virtually guaranteed to result in a negative outcome for German forces, as the Allies effectively realized the "complete system of naval operating" that had been coming together since 1940.

# CONCLUSION

THE COASTAL CAMPAIGN as it emerged in 1940 was something neither the British nor the Germans expected or wanted. For the British, that facet of the war was a little too close to home. For the Germans, the war on commerce was forced on the Kriegsmarine, with a fleet still in the process of transitioning toward a battle fleet capable of overwhelming the Royal Navy. Neither navy wanted to be in the business of a commerce war, let alone a campaign in the English Channel. In 1957 Friedrich Ruge, the former Kriegsmarine commander of Naval Group West, now serving as vice admiral in the Bundesmarine, wrote a short history of Germany's war at sea.[1] Contained within were some thoughtful paragraphs about the contemporary Cold War relevance of the conduct of Germany's wartime strategy. The relationship between the three services, the tactical and strategic interaction between them, and the role of the leader were considered by Ruge, along with more detailed consideration of the war at sea. Interestingly, and in apparent recognition that during the war naval high command had not paid sufficient attention to the coastal zone, he singled out coastal waters as a "special theater of war."[2] He commented that "to exercise control over such areas in war raises special problems, which have only recently been examined by military science."[3] Almost ironically, at the point of Ruge's writing several of the Kriegsmarine's S-boats sold before 1939 or surrendered in 1945 were reaching the end of their service lives with the navies of West Germany, Spain, Denmark, and the Soviet Union. In Cold War Europe, and before the ubiquity of the guided missile, the S-boat remained a potent vessel of war and all-round utility craft. Indeed, S-130 (built in 1943, then renamed by the British and later by the Bundesmarine) would continue in West German service until the end of the Cold War.

In 1969, just a decade after Ruge set down his thoughts, Captain P. G. C. Dickens, a distinguished former Royal Navy Coastal Forces officer writing in the *Journal of the Royal United Services Institute*, complained bitterly that the lessons hard learned in World War II about coastal warfare had been all but forgotten. The Royal Navy had abandoned the idea, systems, and vessels necessary to fight Cold War coastal engagements in the English Channel. Dickens put this down to an "inherent [British] distaste" for coastal warfare (and the navy to fight it) over the desire for an oceanic fleet and the strategy to go with it.[4] Within a quarter of a century of the end of the war, the Royal Navy was down to just two fast patrol boats. Ironically, the Bundesmarine during the Cold War continued to invest in successive generations of fast attack craft of the Jaguar, Tiger, Seeadler, Albatros, and Gepard classes (the last ones were decommissioned or sold to foreign navies in 2016) just at the time that a threat from a resurgent Russia in the Baltic and elsewhere was becoming manifest.

The writings of both Dickens and Ruge point toward the fact that in the twenty-first century there is still much to find out, much to relearn, and much to theorize about strategy and tactics in coastal waters. The British remain culturally tied to #GlobalBritain and the oceanic role that it implies, while cuts to public spending present the Royal Navy with a choice between high-end warfighting capacity with an inadequate number of hulls, or lower-end capacity with more hulls. A similar dilemma confronts the U.S. Navy, and the evolution of its littoral combat ship (LCS) program provides a perfect case in point. Arising in the backwash of discussions in the 1990s about a future class of ship capable of operating in coastal waters, the LCS is a world away from some of the ideas put forward, ranging from dreadnoughts capable of withstanding the toughest punishments, to semisubmersible light craft, to well-armed, inexpensive small craft that could be built in large numbers and treated as essentially disposable in the circumstance of war. The resulting LCS, driven by Secretary of Defense Donald Rumsfeld, was a compromise between these radical suggestions for future vessels and a navy wedded to traditional, high-end warship designs. The result has satisfied no one: the LCS is three times the weight of the smaller craft suggested in the 1990s, immeasurably more complex, and challenging to build and operate. As more and more roles were assigned to the LCS using the idea of modularity, it was transformed from a vessel intended for coastal waters into a multimission platform capable of doing several of the jobs of traditional ship types. The LCS is an oceanic ship on the cheap operating under the protection of a balanced fleet (or "Hunter-Killer Surface Action Group" under the concept of "Distributed Lethality," in the management-speak of navies). Significantly, the LCS (or small surface combatant, as it should perhaps be known) lacks survivability in a combat environment (the major perceived objection to the "build it cheap but in large numbers" idea), nor does it carry sufficient firepower to serve as a ship killer, although remedial action may address that issue. By comparison, the S-boat, with its torpedoes, could sink the largest ships afloat, had an enviable ability to evade enemies and, given the naval technologies of the day, could stay afloat despite significant levels of damage. Coastal warships are always going to involve a trade-off between the elements of lethality, stealth/speed and systems, cost/production, and survivability; and the concept of a coastal vessel runs counter to the design principles of the vessels of oceanic navies.

It is unsurprising that in the twenty-first century, with the ongoing development of access-denial weaponry, oceanic navies contend that they are ill equipped for combat in coastal waters. The navies are materially ill equipped because institutionally they have been culturally ill prepared to accept the need for a specialist class of coastal warfare vessels. As Ruge recognized in the 1950s, the lessons of the 1940s were that shallow and narrow waters are problematic for blue-water navies, especially when an enemy-controlled shore provides the means for an enemy to conduct aerial attack, engage with direct fire, and carry out electronic surveillance. The rise of drone technologies, stunningly demonstrated in the sinking of the Russian cruiser *Moskva* in the Black Sea on April 14, 2022, underlines the dangers to large warships of operating in narrow waters. Such waters carry heavy demands on crews and vessels, and the threats are increasing with technological innovation in the twenty-first century. The type of strategy and tactics to secure victory in such waters, and the type of vessel capable of carrying it out, are inevitably specialized. Campaigns of attrition in coastal waters, and the acceptance of high rates of loss of vessels and crews rather than fleet-to-fleet engagements designed to result in decisive victory at minimal cost, are not an "easy sell" to policy makers and the public in democracies, where defense budgets are invariably hard pressed.

In writing about the importance of coastal warfare in 1957, Ruge was reflecting on the Kriegsmarine's operations off the southern and eastern coasts of England during 1940–44. Ruge knew full well that of the 216 S-boats built during the 1930s and 1940s, 140 had been lost in action with 767 personnel being killed, 620 wounded, and 322 taken prisoner. The campaign had, indeed, ended in failure (despite the potential to disrupt the flow of British trade), and from Ruge's perspective, Germany had been too slow in learning the lessons of fighting in coastal waters. As was evident right from the moment that the first S-boat half-flotilla was found wanting in the fleet maneuvers of 1932 S-boats needed to be available in large numbers to handle the tasks that might be assigned to them once combat operations were under way. Germany never developed the capacity to turn out boats in large enough capacity, and the problem was magnified by a failure to concentrate those available in the English Channel. Using the S-boat as a maid of all work to be thrown into the mix of forces, and deployed to whatever theater Hitler's gaze settled on next, represented a strategic failure to maximize the impact of the available military resource. Instead, S-boats could be found in Norway, the Baltic, the Black Sea, and the Mediterranean. At times the available German S-boat force in the Channel was only slightly larger than that found wanting in the fleet maneuvers in the Baltic in 1932.

Beyond the mistakes committed by the German high command, in defeating the German coastal campaign between 1940 and 1945 the Royal Navy had developed a well-rounded and technically literate understanding of the ways and means of warfare in the English Channel and North Sea. The Royal Navy had always been keenly interested, and vastly experienced, in the defense of traditional "English waters," and they would add new volumes to that understanding between 1940 and 1945. In 1945 they set about codifying that new knowledge, but they did so in a rather cursory fashion. A paper written in 1945, just a few weeks after the end of the European war, by the Director of Naval Operational Research (DNOR) attempted to give an overview of the effectiveness of the campaign in British coastal waters by the Kriegsmarine's S-boats. He identified five fundamental features in terms of S-boat operations: "(1) The efficiency of the craft in evading interception and in penetrating to their objective—convoy route or swept channel, (2) Their relative inefficiency in torpedo attacks on protected convoys, (3) The very low level of lethality of gunfire in actions between E-boats and coastal forces, (4) The negligibly low lethality of air attack on these vessels at sea, (5) The low level of activity which could be maintained over a long period."[5] By his estimation only around a third of S-boat attacks were turned back by patrolling vessels, meaning that they got through to their targets two-thirds of the time. He argued that their effectiveness was compromised by the low number of operations mounted in any given month (three to four per boat) and their apparent difficulty in mounting successful torpedo attacks.[6] The latter problem, he suggested, might be down to a combination of the difficulty of getting into firing position and then the challenge of obtaining a hit with a torpedo. The value of mining operations was not quantified and was largely ignored. For the future he suggested that fast motor torpedo boats might best be combated by finding ways to increase the lethality of firepower on Royal Navy vessels. These conclusions were based on some rather rushed and inconclusive research that did not utilize the German records that had recently fallen into Allied hands.[7] It was also a rather one-sided evaluation in that it was focused on the means of defeating a threat in coastal waters, rather than also providing an assessment of the impact of the coastal campaign on the British war economy as a whole, including the loss of cargoes, ships, personnel, the disruption to trade, and the provision of defensive forces, including destroyers, patrol ships, aircraft, and a substantial fleet of minesweepers. While the Royal Navy had interest in winning a future coastal campaign, it had no interest in drawing up a strategic evaluation that might suggest the impact and value of littoral warfare and catch the eye of policy makers.

The paper was one of several drawn up in 1945 as the Royal Navy hurriedly sought to prepare itself for an expanding combat role in the Pacific as the war against Japan was fought to a conclusion. The papers ranged from the very specific "The War against E-Boats, 1945" through to more general studies.[8] One of the specific studies was from the Directorate of Operational Research on the effectiveness of British Coastal Forces. The paper stressed the impact on the efficiency of Coastal Forces in meeting the

S-boat threat of having vessels that were markedly slower than their German counterparts. The author of the report commented, "One is tempted to ask how long the RAF would tolerate operating with a fighter about 50 mph slower than the enemy."[9] The report further suggested that in the defense of coastal convoys it was usually the convoy escort that typically made first contact with, and then succeeded in driving away, attacking S-boats. In their retreat they would then be engaged by Coastal Forces patrolling the Z-line. This was backed up in a report arising from the interrogation of FdS Petersen, who by this time was a prisoner-of-war in northern Germany. He told Royal Navy interrogators that "the constant preoccupation of the E-boats was the Destroyer Patrols, not the MTBs. The E-boats felt that they were 'blind,' having no effective radar, whereas we had shore radar and the destroyers had a radar which could detect the E-boats at a distance at which they could not detect the destroyers."[10] Petersen's interrogators concluded that "he was obsessed by the effectiveness of our use of radar," and the readers of the report failed to take on its central message if they were not convinced of the premise "Big ships good—little ships much less so."

The plethora of investigations was evidence of an urgent desire on the part of the Royal Navy to capture the lessons of the recent coastal campaign before they were lost. For an oceangoing Royal Navy, the battle for U.K. inshore waters between 1940 and 1945 had thrown up a series of challenges, the answer to which required a combination of traditional techniques (convoying) with new technologies (radar) and techniques (air-to-sea cooperation via VHF). For the Germans the English Channel and East Coast of the United Kingdom was an unexpected front on which to fight, but it was one that they had some familiarity with because of the campaign of 1914–18. The lessons of the Flanders *Kleinkrieg*, however, had been quietly forgotten after 1918, while the centrality of the battle fleet and the U-boat arm had not. For the British the English Channel was seemingly a familiar and unavoidable battleground, but one that after the war it was politically convenient to forget. Animated primarily by the need to emphasize the threats posed by the development of the postwar Soviet submarine fleet, Captain S. W. Roskill, writing in 1956 in volume 2 of the official history of the war at sea, took pains to overemphasize the totality of the Royal Navy's command of the seas around the United Kingdom against the S-boats:

> The patrol line of motor gunboats and motor launches . . . [was] established some eight miles to seaward of the shipping lanes. . . . Our short-wave shore radar and the "Very High Frequency" wireless stations now played a big part in keeping the patrol craft informed of enemy movements. By the end of the year [1942] the whole of the Nore Command's coastal area was covered by these radar beams, and the enemy could be detected and plotted while still some twenty miles offshore; and added to this great advantage was the fact that radar sets were now being fitted in the Coastal Force vessels themselves.[11]

While this was true, it was also convenient. As table 5 in chapter 8 shows, faced with the British effort along the East Coast the Kriegsmarine had simply shifted the strategic focus of S-boat torpedo operations to the west, while continuing to mount mining operations against the Forth-North/Forth-South convoys. Interestingly, this shift coincided with the long buildup to D-Day, which meant that it was in the western waters of England and the Channel that the forthcoming Battle for France would be decided. While escorting destroyers were usually good enough to keep the merchant ships safe, on the occasions that S-boats did get to grips with colliers, small steamers, and, increasingly, invasion craft, the results could be devastating. A breakdown of the escort would result in convoys being ravaged, losing a significant proportion of their merchant ships. S-boat command recognized that even on the better-defended East Coast run, the deployment of three or even four S-boat flotillas was sufficient to temporarily overwhelm the escorting forces of a convoy, even when they could be speedily reinforced. Fortunately for the British, the Kriegsmarine lacked the resources to maintain operations in these numbers with any sort of intensity. The Germans simply lacked sufficient combat power, especially with a less-than-ideal relationship between Kriegsmarine and Luftwaffe, and Hitler's roving eye as to the next set of German conquests, to strike critical blows against the coastal convoy routes on the southern or eastern coasts of England.

It was impossible for the Royal Navy to forget that the English Channel, as a vital symbol of British national security, had long been a powerful element in the British national identity. From 1066 onward, potential invaders from Philip II of Spain to Emperor Bonaparte and the Kaiser's army were checked by the English Channel and the Royal Navy's command of the sea. In 1940 the English Channel was again the vital feature preventing the execution of Operation Sea Lion. The Royal Navy's defense of the Channel between 1940 and 1945 might have utilized new technologies and tactics, but the strategy was well worn: use every available source of intelligence, effective signals, standing patrols, and convoys, and relentlessly pursue the offensive. In one sense the men of Coastal Forces had stood as the direct descendants of Drake and Nelson in their battles to maintain control of the Channel.

The familiarity and historicity of the battleground did, however, hide fundamental changes wrought by technology that had transformed the battlespace since the late nineteenth century. The mine, as a weapon of access denial, could augment the natural hazards of coastal waters along the East Coast to leave narrow channels as the only "safe" means of navigating between the Thames Estuary to the Wash to the Humber and beyond. The rise of the submarine and aircraft (turning the two-dimensional battlespace of surface warfare into a three-dimensional space with subsea and air elements) expanded the strategic and tactical possibilities open to powers seeking to disrupt the trade networks running along Britain's eastern and southern coasts. The rise of radar (shore, ship, or air based) and signals intelligence, allied to the mine, compressed both the geographical and virtual/electronic space of the battlefield. The speed with which units could move (S-boat, MGB/MTB/ML, and aircraft) transformed the pace and intensity of naval operations. Increases in the destructive capacity of weapons meant that attacks could be as devastating as they were swift. Technology completely transformed what might be described as the time-space continuum of the battlefield of the English Channel and East Coast. In 1588 the Spanish Armada was sighted off Cornwall on July 19, proceeding up the Channel to anchor at Calais on July 27, harried along the way by English ships that did not possess the weight of firepower to destroy the Spanish vessels. In the later hours of April 28, 1944, a group of S-boats could leave Cherbourg (on SIGINT-derived intelligence), cross the English Channel at one of its widest points, launch a devastating attack against the T4 Exercise Tiger convoy, and be back in time for breakfast despite attempts by Allied forces to engage them. The time-space continuum of the battlespace, to lean perhaps a little uncomfortably on the realm of physics, had been massively compressed by the new technologies of naval warfare introduced from 1850 onward.

On the East Coast this compression, especially given the mine barrage and the natural hazards, was marked to the point where the battlespace was transformed beyond the familiar confines of naval strategy/tactics. The latter assumes a degree of movement and flexibility, and of access, that simply did not exist during the S-boat campaign. The battlespace east of the marked war channels was more like that of land warfare: the space between the coasts of Britain and Europe constituted a sort of World War I no-man's-land to be dominated by aggressive patrolling, observation posts, and defensive belts to deny access. Raids across no-man's-land became the stock-in-trade of both British and German coastal forces. Inside the "British lines," the tactical environment was more reminiscent of an urban warfare environment, with the marked war channels constituting the roads, and the shallows the city blocks of a highly restricted combat space. Room for maneuver in this space was sharply limited, making it ideal for offensive warfare, and meaning that any ambush could be devastating. While the nature of the space meant that an attack could not completely halt the movement of a column of ships in the same way that a wreck or obstacle could obstruct movement in a built-up environment, the effect wasn't so very different. A long column of ships made for easy location and attack, with limited scope for mutually supporting fields of fire from the defenders.

The nature of the combat space off the East Coast of the United Kingdom between 1940 and 1945, as in modern urban warfare, placed an emphasis on speed, firepower, tactics, and armor. In many ways the S-boats and MGBs were ideal weapons for the highly specialized combat environment of coastal warfare. S-boats were largely lacking in armor, but they were nevertheless, with their speed and construction, extremely hard to hit, disable, or kill. The G7a torpedo, fast, simple, and reliable, was well suited to use in these waters, giving an S-boat the ability to destroy even the heaviest vessel it might encounter on the coastal run. S-boat mines, in a variety of types, were deadly, and the vessel was an efficient minelayer. In the S-boat the Kriegsmarine had a hugely effective weapon, operated by capable and experienced crews, but ultimately it was not effective because of, to follow the lessons of urban warfare, failure at the tactical level. The nature of the combat environment in the English Channel and off the East Coast required the deployment of larger groups of S-boats to overwhelm convoy defenses, eliminate the intelligence advantages of the British, and inflict horrendous casualties to break the ability to run convoys along the war channels. Flotilla commanders and senior officers knew that they simply could not run risks with the meager forces at their disposal. By contrast, the MGB, while inferior in several respects, was Britain's "answer" to the S-boats because it could be built and deployed in sufficient numbers to offset the qualitative advantages of the German coastal craft.[12] As Coastal Forces officer Christopher Dreyer later recounted, S-boats were "marvelous boats . . . very fast—comfortable 40 knots" and capable of cruising at 35 knots. However, against the Channel convoys their "results [were] deplorable." They "ought to have slaughtered the East Coast [convoys]." They "didn't operate enough."[13]

If the number of available vessels was critical to the failure of the campaign, then Germany and the Kriegsmarine did have options beyond earlier prioritization (before the 1943 building program) of S-boat construction. Even at the point of capitulation in 1945, the Kriegsmarine had over ninety S-boats spread across nine flotillas. Deployments to the Black Sea (1st Flotilla 1942–45, and 11th Flotilla, using captured Italian boats, in 1943) and the Mediterranean/Aegean (3rd and 7th Flotillas, 1942–45, and 21st, 22nd, and 24th Flotillas, using captured Italian boats, in 1943) drew men and resources away from the area of critical importance in the English Channel (as the eastern continuation of the Battle of the Atlantic). Drawing flotillas away from the English Channel in 1941–42, at the height of the Channel battles, for Operation Barbarossa similarly seems like a strategic mistake because in the theaters beyond the English Channel/North Sea and Baltic, the S-boats could inflict some notable losses on Allied forces, but they could not have significant effect at the strategic level. Likewise, the use of S-boats in a defensive role (usually alongside the slower R-boats) to protect the Kriegsmarine's own coastal convoys running along the coast of Europe further reduced the number of vessels available for offensive operations against British coastal convoys. Other operational requirements, such as the need to support the passage of the German heavy ships through the English Channel in 1942 as part of Operation Cerberus, and the movements of blockade runners and auxiliary cruisers to and from the Atlantic, further conflicted with the S-boats' central goal—to disrupt British coastal convoys.

Despite the failure to stop or seriously disrupt the coastal convoys, the damage inflicted on the British war economy by German attacks against British Coastal shipping was considerable, although the Royal Navy was rather reluctant to admit it. Beyond the official losses in convoy, there was a steady, and largely forgotten, run of casualties involving vessels working the East Coast, usually by mine, outside the defended convoys. Fishing vessels carried on their trade regardless of the risks. By the end of 1941, 219 of them had been lost.[14] Barges similarly continued to move bulk cargoes on the East Coast, and they too sustained steady casualties. For example, a book published by a local newspaper in Essex in 1945 recalled a list of seven local sailing barges sunk or damaged because of enemy action.[15] Mines also took their toll on motor barges made of steel or wood, belonging to small companies such as Horlocks of Mistley (Essex). The losses in terms of ships and crews were not excessive, but they were nevertheless costly. Nick Hewitt has estimated that from all causes 1,431 merchant ships (3,768,599 tons) were lost around the coasts of the United Kingdom between 1939 and 1945.[16] The impact on individual companies was considerable. Of the fourteen vessels operated by the London Power Company during the war, five were lost (three to S-boat torpedoes, one to collision, one to U-boat).[17] Similarly, William Cory and Son lost thirteen of the twenty-one ships it managed between 1939 and 1945 (seven to mines, four to aircraft, two to S-boat torpedoes).[18] The collier company Everards lost sixteen vessels on the East Coast during the war, and France Fenwick, a Tyneside-based company, lost nine ships in U.K. coastal waters.[19] The human casualties of the campaign amounted to something like 3,600 dead among the merchant seamen of perhaps twenty nations.[20] "Not a Battle of the Atlantic [as J. P. Foynes has put it] but a severe campaign by any other standards."[21]

During the war the Royal Navy attached considerable importance to the coastal convoys even though the losses on them in terms of ships, seamen, and cargoes was vastly less than that on the Atlantic run. There was a painful awareness that the convoys remained vulnerable despite the growing number and increasing impact of Coastal Forces. In late 1943 and early 1944 there was a recognition that risks were having to be run and that serious losses were being avoided only because of "good fortune and lack of enterprise on the part of the enemy."[22] That "lack of enterprise" was a Royal Navy reading of the defensive mindset of an enemy trying to keep a fleet in being during effective defenses, inadequate resources, and a strategic balance tilting against Germany. For those organizing the defense of coastal convoys, there was also a painful sense that they were having to make do with inadequate resources, with every effort being "made to win the Battle of the Atlantic."[23] By slow and painful evolution the British found a way to win in coastal warfare. The defeat of the German coastal campaign exemplifies Milan Vego's dictum of the prerequisites for success in coastal warfare: "suitable and diverse platforms, weapons and sensors; robust command organization; close co-operation among friendly forces; air superiority; well-developed theory; and sound doctrine."[24]

In terms of the grand strategy of World War II the successful defense of the coastal convoy routes was essential to victory: just as essential to victory as driving the U-boats from the Atlantic. By war's end, 30 million tons of cargo (9 million tons of general cargo and 21 million tons of coal) had been delivered by coastal convoy.[25] That struggle, though, is now largely forgotten, exactly at the point when the possibility of large-scale combat operations in Europe and Asia has once again become acute, and even as modern navies struggle to understand the emerging combat environments and new naval technologies of the twenty-first century. The lessons of 1940 to 1945 do point toward the need for coastal warfare to be treated as a specialist field, requiring special vessels and special tactics. While modern Western armies formulate their tactics, equipment, and unit structures to operate in the urban environments of the next fifty years, the navies of many of the democracies are perhaps lagging behind in shaping their forces, structures, and doctrine for success in combat operations in the coastal zones. The cost of relearning the lessons of coastal warfare in some future conflict might come at an even higher cost than the butcher's bill of 1939–45.

APPENDIX

*Vessels in English Waters Lost to Torpedo Attacks by S-Boats, 1940–1945*

NOTE: The purpose of this list is to provide an impression of the ebb and flow of S-boat torpedo operations and the nature of the campaign against British coastal convoys. The list only covers vessels lost as a result of S-boat torpedo attacks, or in consequence thereof (e.g., collision).[1] S-boats were also engaged in minelaying, but sinkings by mines cannot be attributed with reasonable certainty to the activities of particular S-boats or aircraft that laid the mine. To these totals, then, can be added a proportion of those vessels lost to mines in English waters from 1940 to 1945. In some cases there are divergences between the German and Allied records that it is not possible to reconcile. German records might attribute a particular sinking to a successful torpedo attack, while British records put the sinking down to a mine. In such cases, where a German claim appears highly likely, it has been given.

## 1940
### DUNKIRK EVACUATION

| DATE | VESSEL | TONS (TYPE, IF WARSHIP) | POSITION | ACCOUNT |
|---|---|---|---|---|
| May 23 | *Jaguar* (Fr) | destroyer | off Dunkirk | Hit by a torpedo by either S-21 or S-23 and beached at Malo-les-Bains and written off—13 crew killed |
| May 28 | SS *Abukir* | 694 | off Dunkirk | Sunk by S-34 while evacuating troops from Dunkirk—16 crew killed together with an unknown number of passengers (200+ UK Armed Forces, plus civilians and Belgian Air Force). Lloyds War Medals awarded to Captain R. M. Woolfendon and 2nd Officer V. P. Wills-Rust. Citation: "Many were killed, including the Chief Officer. The master and second officer, who had remained undismayed by repeated attacks from the air whilst at Ostend and on the way back, had shown great courage in attacking the [E-Boat], and during the six hours they remained in the water before being picked up did their utmost to cheer and support the few survivors who remained afloat." |
| May 29 | HMS *Wakeful* | destroyer | off Dunkirk | Sunk by S-30 while evacuating troops from Dunkirk—97 crew and 639 embarked troops killed |
| May 31 | *Siroco* (Fr) | destroyer | off Dunkirk | Sunk by S-23/S-26—660 crew and embarked French soldiers killed out of 930 on board |
| June 1 | HMT *Argyllshire* | trawler | Dunkirk evacuation | Sunk by S-34—21 crew killed |
| June 1 | HMS *Stella Dorado* | trawler | Dunkirk evacuation | Sunk by S-34—15 crew killed |

## INDEPENDENT SAILING

| DATE | VESSEL | TONS (TYPE, IF WARSHIP) | POSITION | ACCOUNT |
|---|---|---|---|---|
| June 19 | *Roseburn* | 3,103 | off Dungeness | Sunk by S-26 while carrying a cargo of pit props from St. John (New Brunswick) to Hartlepool. Beached and declared a constructive total loss—all crew survived. |

## UNKNOWN CONVOY

| DATE | VESSEL | TONS (TYPE, IF WARSHIP) | POSITION | ACCOUNT |
|---|---|---|---|---|
| June 24 | *Albuera* | 3,477 | 2 m SW of Lydd Light Float | Sunk by S-36 while carrying a cargo of pit props from St. John (New Brunswick) to Hartlepool—7 crew killed |
| June 24 | *Kingfisher* | 276 | off Beachy Head | Sunk by S-19 en route from Milford Haven to London—1 crew killed. Lloyd's War Medal awarded to Second Engineer W. Pybus. Citation: "The ship was torpedoed during the night, and listed to port, settling down by the head. The master mustered his crew, and ordered the port lifeboat lowered. It was known that one man had been killed by the explosion, but another man was not accounted for. Although the ship's decks were awash, the second engineer, taking a torch from the lifeboat, volunteered to search for him. Forcing his way to the forepart of the bridge-deck, he found the man badly cut about the head and unconscious in his bunk. He got him out safely, the two men going straight from the rail to the lifeboat. The ship sank as they pulled away. The rescued man owed his life to the gallant act of the second engineer." |

## FOUR STRAGGLERS FROM OA178 CONVOY ATTACKED

| DATE | VESSEL | TONS (TYPE, IF WARSHIP) | POSITION | ACCOUNT |
|---|---|---|---|---|
| July 4 | *Elmcrest* | 4,343 | S of Portland | Sunk by S-20—en route from Hull to Wabana Canada in ballast—16 crew killed. *British Corporal* (6,972) and *Hartlepool* (5,500) were damaged by S-20, S-24, and S-26, and *British Corporal*—2 crew killed—was later damaged by dive bombing by JU87s. The 14-ship convoy had been attacked by JU87s before the S-boat attack that sank 1 vessel and damaged 4. |

## LONE PATROL BOAT TORPEDOED

| July 8 | HMT *Cayton Wyke* | trawler | near Goodwin Sands | Sunk by S-36—17 crew killed. The trawler was part of the 9th Anti-Submarine Flotilla. |
|---|---|---|---|---|

## LONE VESSEL

| July 11 | *Mallard* | 352 | South of Bognor Regis | British coaster sunk by S-26—6 of 9 crew killed. The survivors were taken prisoner by S-24. |
|---|---|---|---|---|

## ATTACK ON A STEAMER REPATRIATING FRENCH MILITARY PERSONNEL BACK TO FRANCE

| July 24 | *Meknes* (Fr) | 6,127 | English Channel | Sunk by S-27 while repatriating sailors to France—374 crew and embarked troops killed |
|---|---|---|---|---|

## ATTACK ON CW8

| | | | | Twenty-one-ship convoy; nine were sunk by a combination of S-boat and Stuka attacks. |
|---|---|---|---|---|
| July 26 | *Lulonga* | 821 | 10 m S of Shoreham | Sunk by S-27—1 crew killed |
| July 26 | *Broadhurst* | 1,013 | 14 m S by W of Shoreham | Sunk by S-20—4 crew killed |
| July 26 | *London Trader* | 646 | 13 m S by W of Shoreham | Sunk by S-19—1 crew killed |

## ATTACK ON CW9

| DATE | VESSEL | TONS (TYPE, IF WARSHIP) | POSITION | ACCOUNT |
|---|---|---|---|---|
| | | | | Twenty-five-ship convoy; six were sunk by a combination of S-boat and Stuka attacks. |
| Aug 8 | *Holme Force* | 1,216 | off Newhaven | Sunk by S-21—6 crew killed out of a crew of 13 and 4 gunners |
| Aug 8 | *Fife Coast* | 367 | 10–15 m W of Beachy Head | Sunk by S-27 |
| Aug 8 | *Ouse* | 1,004 | off Newhaven | Sunk in collision while avoiding torpedo from S-20. *Polly M* (380) and *John M* (500) attacked by S-25 but did not sink. *Empire Crusader* (1,042), en route from Seaham to Devonport with coal, was sunk in the same incident as a result of enemy bombing—2 crew killed. Lloyd's War Medals awarded to Chief Engineer J. E. Cowper and Able Seaman W. Robson. Citation: "The ship was heavily attacked by E-boats and enemy aircraft. The front of the bridge was blown in, the engine room damaged, and the steam pipes burst. There was a crater in the cargo, which was on fire. The chief engineer stopped the engines and went to the aid of the second mate, who was badly hurt. He and acting able seaman Robson got the wounded man across the skylights and into the partly lowered boat, but in doing so Robson was hit by a machine-gun bullet. The chief engineer returned to look for the master in the chartroom, but he could not find him. The eight or nine uninjured survivors and the wounded whom they had rescued got away from the ship, which was then on fire and seemed about to sink." |

## ATTACK ON FS271

| DATE | VESSEL | TONS (TYPE, IF WARSHIP) | POSITION | ACCOUNT |
|---|---|---|---|---|
| Sept 4 | Corbrook | 1,729 | off Lowestoft | Sunk by S-21 carrying coal from Sunderland to London—no casualties |
| Sept 4 | New Lambton | 2,709 | off Lowestoft | Sunk by S-21 |
| Sept 4 | Nieuwland (Nl) | 1,075 | off Lowestoft | Sunk by S-18 carrying coal from Sunderland to London—8 crew killed |
| Sept 4 | Joseph Swan | 1,571 | off Lowestoft | Sunk by S-18 carrying coal from Sunderland to London—16 crew killed |
| Sept 4 | Fulham V | 1,562 | off Lowestoft | Sunk by S-22. In addition, out of the other 31 merchant ships in the convoy, SS Ewell (1,350) was damaged by a torpedo from S-54. |

## ATTACK ON FS273

| DATE | VESSEL | TONS (TYPE, IF WARSHIP) | POSITION | ACCOUNT |
|---|---|---|---|---|
| Sept 7 | Stad Alkmaar | 5,750 | off Lowestoft | Sunk by S-33 and S-36 en route from Cuba to London via Methil—14 crew killed |

## ATTACK ON FN289

| DATE | VESSEL | TONS (TYPE, IF WARSHIP) | POSITION | ACCOUNT |
|---|---|---|---|---|
| Sept 24 | Continental Coaster | 555 | off Cromer | Sunk by S-30—4 crew killed |

## ATTACK ON FN311

| DATE | VESSEL | TONS (TYPE, IF WARSHIP) | POSITION | ACCOUNT |
|---|---|---|---|---|
| Oct 17 | Hauxley | 1,595 | off Great Yarmouth | Sunk by S-18. PLM14 (Fr) (3,754) and Gasfire (2,972) were damaged in the same attack—11 crew killed on Gasfire. |

## ATTACK ON FS360

| DATE | VESSEL | TONS (TYPE, IF WARSHIP) | POSITION | ACCOUNT |
|---|---|---|---|---|
| Dec 15 | N. C. Monberg (Den) | 2,301 | off Lowestoft | Sunk by S-25 and S-58—9 crew killed |

## ATTACK ON FS366 AND FN367

| DATE | VESSEL | TONS (TYPE, IF WARSHIP) | POSITION | ACCOUNT |
|---|---|---|---|---|
| Dec 23 | Stad Masstricht (Nl) | 6,552 | SE of Clacton on Sea | Sunk by S-59—vessel taken in tow by rescue tugs Kenia, Krooman, and Norman but sank |
| Dec 23 | HMT Pelton | trawler | off Yarmouth | Sunk by S-23—19 crew killed |

## 1941

### ATTACK ON FS379

| DATE | VESSEL | TONS | POSITION | ACCOUNT |
|---|---|---|---|---|
| Jan 7 | H. H. Petersen | 975 | SE of Lowestoft | Sunk by S-101. The attack was so sudden and unexpected that the sinking was put down to a mine. |

### ATTACK ON FN401

| DATE | VESSEL | TONS | POSITION | ACCOUNT |
|---|---|---|---|---|
| Feb 6 | Angularity | 501 | off Ispwich | Sunk by S-30 while straggling from the convoy—8 crew killed, 2 taken prisoner by S-30 and S-34 |

### ATTACK ON FN411

| DATE | VESSEL | TONS | POSITION | ACCOUNT |
|---|---|---|---|---|
| Feb 19 | Algarve | 1,355 | near Sheringham Light Float | Sunk by S-102—all 27 crew killed |

### ATTACK ON FN417

| DATE | VESSEL | TONS | POSITION | ACCOUNT |
|---|---|---|---|---|
| Feb 25 | HMS Exmoor | destroyer | off Lowestoft | Sunk by either S-30 or S-33—104 crew killed (32 survivors rescued) |

### ATTACK ON UNIDENTIFIED CONVOY

| DATE | VESSEL | TONS | POSITION | ACCOUNT |
|---|---|---|---|---|
| Feb 26 | Minorca | 1,123 | N of Cromer | Sunk by S-28 en route from London to Grangemouth with cement—17 crew and 2 passengers killed |

## ATTACK ON FS429 AND FN426

| DATE | VESSEL | TONS (TYPE, IF WARSHIP) | POSITION | ACCOUNT |
|---|---|---|---|---|
| Mar 7 | *Dotterel* | 1,385 | off No. 6 Buoy, Southwold | Sunk by S-29 while part of FN426 |
| Mar 7 | *Kenton* | 1,047 | off Cromer | Sunk by S-31 while part of FS429—4 crew killed |
| Mar 7 | *Corduff* | 2,345 | off Cromer | Sunk by S-28 while part of FN426—master plus one other taken prisoner |
| Mar 7 | *Boulderpool* | 4,805 | off Cromer | Sunk by S-61 while part of FS429—no casualties |
| Mar 7 | *Rye* | 1,048 | off Cromer | Sunk by S-27 in ballast while part of FN426—22 crew and 6 gunners killed |
| Mar 8 | *Norman Queen* | 957 | off Cromer | Sunk by S-101 while part of FN426—12 crew and 2 passengers killed (1 taken prisoner) |
| Mar 8 | *Togston* | 1,547 | 2 m from Smith's Knoll | Sunk by S-102 while part of FN426, en route from Blyth to London with coal—9 crew killed. Lloyd's War Medal awarded to Captain L. Laurenson. Citation: "The ship was torpedoed and began to list to starboard. The starboard lifeboat had disappeared and the master ordered all hands into the port lifeboat. He had to cross the bunker-hatch, but the covers had been blown away and he fell into the hatchway. The boatswain failed to pull him out of the bunker, as he was too heavy. The master then ordered him into the lifeboat, hoping himself to float out when the ship sank. This unlikely event occurred, as another explosion threw him out into the sea as the vessel sank, and he was picked up by the lifeboat. Though there seemed very little chance of escaping, the master courageously refused all help so that the rest of the crew could get safely away." |

## ATTACK ON FS432

| DATE | VESSEL | TONS (TYPE, IF WARSHIP) | POSITION | ACCOUNT |
|---|---|---|---|---|
| Mar 11 | *Trevethoe* | 5,257 | off Orfordness | Sunk by S-28 while carrying wheat—1 crew killed |

## ATTACK ON FN434

| DATE | VESSEL | TONS (TYPE, IF WARSHIP) | POSITION | ACCOUNT |
|---|---|---|---|---|
| Mar 18 | *Daphne II* (Fr) | 1,970 | No. 59 Buoy, off Humber | Sunk by S-102—ship badly damaged and broke up under tow |

## ATTACK ON FS464

| DATE | VESSEL | TONS (TYPE, IF WARSHIP) | POSITION | ACCOUNT |
|---|---|---|---|---|
| Apr 17 | *Effra* | 1,446 | near Cross Sand Light Vessel | Sunk by S-43—2 crew killed |
| Apr 17 | *Nereus* (Nl) | 1,298 | off Great Yarmouth | Sunk by S-104—no fatalities. *Eskburn* (472) damaged by a torpedo from S-55, with 2 crew being killed by machine-gun fire. *Ethel Radcliffe* (5,673) also damaged and beached with no harm to her 40 crew. Attacked by aircraft, she was declared to be beyond salvage on May 20. |

## ATTACK ON EC13

| DATE | VESSEL | TONS (TYPE, IF WARSHIP) | POSITION | ACCOUNT |
|---|---|---|---|---|
| Apr 28 | *Ambrose Fleming* | 1,555 | NNW of Cromer | Sunk by S-29 while sailing in ballast from Southend to the Clyde as part of a 57-ship convoy—10 crew and 1 gunner killed |

## ATTACK ON FLEET TENDER "C"

| DATE | VESSEL | TONS (TYPE, IF WARSHIP) | POSITION | ACCOUNT |
|---|---|---|---|---|
| June 2 | Fleet Tender "C" | tender | off Cromer | Sunk by S-22 and S-24, disguised to resemble HMS *Hermes* |

## ATTACK ON CW45

| DATE | VESSEL | TONS (TYPE, IF WARSHIP) | POSITION | ACCOUNT |
|---|---|---|---|---|
| Aug 11 | *Sir Russell* | 1,548 | off Dungeness | Sunk by S-49—no fatalities |

## ATTACK ON FN507

| DATE | VESSEL | TONS (TYPE, IF WARSHIP) | POSITION | ACCOUNT |
|---|---|---|---|---|
| | *Czestochowa* (Pol) | 1,971 | off Orfordness | Sunk by S-48 while sailing with a cargo of cement for Reykjavik—1 crew killed from 26. SS *Dalewood* (2,774) was damaged in the attack but was towed into the Humber for repair—3 crew and 1 gunner killed. |

## ATTACK ON EC70

| Sept 7 | *Duncarron* | 478 | 3 m E of Sheringham Buoy | Sunk by S-50—9 crew killed |
|---|---|---|---|---|
| Sept 7 | *Eikhaug* (Nor) | 1,436 | 3 m E of Sheringham Buoy | Sunk by S-52 while sailing with a cargo of cement from Southend to Grangemouth—17 crew killed |

## ATTACK ON EC74

| Sept 17 | *Teddington* | 4,762 | off Cromer | Sunk by S-51 while carrying nickel ingots to Calcutta. *Tetela* (5,389) was damaged in same attack. She was beached but refloated the following day. |
|---|---|---|---|---|

## ATTACK ON FN531

| Oct 12 | *Chevington* | 1,537 | NNE of Cromer | Sunk by S-105 while carrying cement from London to Grangemouth—9 crew killed |
|---|---|---|---|---|
| Oct 12 | *Roy* (Nor) | 1,768 | NNE of Cromer | Sunk by S-53—3 crew killed |

## ATTACK ON FS650

| DATE | VESSEL | TONS (TYPE, IF WARSHIP) | POSITION | ACCOUNT |
|---|---|---|---|---|
| Nov 19 | Aruba | 1,159 | off Lowestoft | Sunk by S-105 while carrying coal from Blyth to Cowes—1 gunner killed |
| Nov 19 | Waldinge | 2,462 | off Great Yarmouth | Sunk by S-53 while carrying coal from Tyne to London—1 gunner killed |
| Nov 20 | War Methar | tanker | off Great Yarmouth | Sunk by S-104 while carrying fuel oil from Grangemouth to Harwich |

## ATTACK ON FS654

| DATE | VESSEL | TONS (TYPE, IF WARSHIP) | POSITION | ACCOUNT |
|---|---|---|---|---|
| Nov 24 | Virgilia | 5,723 | 3 m NE of Hearty Knoll | Sunk by S-109—23 crew killed and 21 survived |
| Nov 24 | Groenlo (NL) | 1,984 | 3 m NE of Hearty Knoll | Sunk by S-52—1 crew killed and 9 missing. *Blairnevis* (4,155) damaged in same attack by torpedo from S-51. |

## ATTACK ON FN664

| DATE | VESSEL | TONS (TYPE, IF WARSHIP) | POSITION | ACCOUNT |
|---|---|---|---|---|
| Nov 29 | Asperity | 699 | NW of Cromer | Sunk by S-64—10 crew killed |
| Nov 29 | Cormarsh | 2,848 | NW of Cromer | Sunk by S-51—no casualties |
| Nov 30 | Empire Newcomen | 2,840 | S of Dudgeon Light, off Cromer | Sunk by S-52—11 crew killed |

## 1942
### ATTACK ON LONE DUTCH TRAWLER UNKNOWN

| DATE | VESSEL | TONS (TYPE, IF WARSHIP) | POSITION | ACCOUNT |
|---|---|---|---|---|
| Feb 1 | unknown Dutch vessel out of Ijmuiden | trawler | North Sea | Sunk by S-62 when she failed to stop after shots were put across her bow—11 crew (2 injured) taken on board by S-62 and S-53 |

### ATTACK ON FS746

| Mar 11 | *Horseferry* | 951 | off Sheringham | Sunk by S-70 carrying coal from the Tyne to London—11 crew killed |
|---|---|---|---|---|

### ATTACK ON FS749

| Mar 15 | HMS *Vortigern* | destroyer | off Cromer | Sunk by S-104—110 crew killed |
|---|---|---|---|---|

### ATTACK ON WP183

| July 9 | HMT *Manor* | trawler | off East Devon | Sunk by S-63—20 crew killed |
|---|---|---|---|---|
| July 9 | *Pomella* | 6,766 | off East Devon | Sunk by S-67 while carrying crude oil |
| July 9 | *Kongshaug* (Nor) | 1,156 | off East Devon | Sunk by S-48 while carrying fuel—8 crew killed |
| July 9 | *Røsten* (Nor) | 736 | off East Devon | Sunk by S-109 |
| July 9 | *Bokn* (Nor) | 698 | off East Devon | Sunk by S-70 while carrying coal—12 crew killed |
| July 9 | *Reggestrom* (Nl) | 2,836 | off East Devon | Sunk by S-50 |

### ATTACK ON PW226

| Oct 2 | HMT *Lord Stonehaven* | trawler | off Eddystone Light | Sunk by S-112—18 crew killed |
|---|---|---|---|---|

## ACTION WITH BRITISH TORPEDO BOATS

| DATE | VESSEL | TONS (TYPE, IF WARSHIP) | POSITION | ACCOUNT |
|---|---|---|---|---|
| Oct 6 | MGB 76 | MGB | North Sea | Sunk after collision with S-boat with 2nd, 4th, and 6th S-boat Flotillas at sea |

## ATTACK ON FN832

| DATE | VESSEL | TONS (TYPE, IF WARSHIP) | POSITION | ACCOUNT |
|---|---|---|---|---|
| Oct 7 | HMS *Caroline Møller* | rescue tug | N of Cromer | Sunk by S-80—3 crew killed |
| Oct 7 | ML 339 | ML | N of Cromer | Sunk by S-62—14 survivors |
| Oct 7 | *Sheaf Water* | 2,730 | N of Cromer | Sunk by S-46 |
| Oct 7 | *Ilse* | 2,874 | N of Cromer | Sunk by S-105 |
| Oct 7 | *Jessie Maersk* (Den) | 1,972 | N of Cromer | Sunk by S-117—20 crew killed. HMS *Sheldrake* and HMT *Monimia* also damaged in the attack and SS *Igtham* (1,337) struck mines and was sunk while avoiding S-boat attack—18 crew and 6 gunners saved. |

## ATTACK ON FN838

| DATE | VESSEL | TONS (TYPE, IF WARSHIP) | POSITION | ACCOUNT |
|---|---|---|---|---|
| Oct 14 | *George Balfour* | 1,570 | N of Cromer | Damaged by 6th S-boat Flotilla. Ship broke in two as it was being towed, but both halves were secured and taken into Yarmouth. The ship later returned to service. |
| Oct 14 | *Lysland* (Nor) | [1,335] | N of Cromer | Damaged by torpedo from S-75 and then towed into the Humber—3 crew killed |

## ATTACK ON FN861

| DATE | VESSEL | TONS (TYPE, IF WARSHIP) | POSITION | ACCOUNT |
|---|---|---|---|---|
| Nov 2 | Fidelio (Nor) | 1,843 | off Lowestoft | Twenty-three boats from 2nd, 4th, and 6th S-boat Flotillas sortied, firing multiple torpedoes, so it is unclear which S-boat sank the vessel—6 crew and 1 gunner killed. *Wandle* (1,482) also badly damaged (1 gunner killed) but the ship was towed to safety and then to the Tyne for repair, reaching safety on November 9. |

## ATTACK ON PW250

| Nov 19 | HMS *Ullswater* | trawler | near Eddystone Light | Sunk by S-112—33 crew killed |
|---|---|---|---|---|
| Nov 19 | *Yewforest* | 815 | near Eddystone Light | Sunk by torpedoes fired from S-65, S-81, S-112, and S-115—11 crew killed |
| Nov 19 | *Birgitte* | 1,595 | near Eddystone Light | Sunk by torpedoes fired from S-65, S-81, S-112, and S-115—10 crew killed |
| Nov 19 | *Lab* | 1,118 | near Eddystone Light | Sunk by torpedoes fired from S-65, S-81, S-112, and S-115 |

## ATTACK ON PW256

| Dec 1 | HMT *Jasper* | trawler | off Salcombe | Sunk by S-81—10 crew killed |
|---|---|---|---|---|

## ATTACK ON PW257

| Dec 3 | *Gatinais* | 383 | off Start Point | Sunk by S-81 or S-116 en route from Portsmouth to Llanelly carrying scrap—9 crew killed |
|---|---|---|---|---|
| Dec 3 | HMS *Penylan* | destroyer | off Start Point | Sunk by S-115—37 crew killed |

## ATTACK ON FN889

| DATE | VESSEL | TONS (TYPE, IF WARSHIP) | POSITION | ACCOUNT |
|---|---|---|---|---|
| Dec 12 | Glen Tilt | 871 | off Lowestoft | Sunk by S-110 en route from London to Middlesborough with cement—1 crew killed |
| Dec 12 | Lindisfarne | 999 | off Lowestoft | Sunk by S-63—9 crew killed |
| Dec 12 | Knitsley | 2,272 | off Lowestoft | Sunk by S-117—11 crew and 1 gunner killed |
| Dec 12 | Marianne (Nor) | 1,915 | off Lowestoft | Sunk by S-63—12 crew and 2 gunners killed |
| Dec 12 | Avonwood | 1,056 | off Lowestoft | Sunk by S-48—9 crew killed. Lloyd's War Medal awarded posthumously to Steward W. Hutchinson. Citation: "Steward Hutchinson sacrificed his life in a gallant attempt to save one of the crew. He was a powerful swimmer, and was last seen supporting his shipmate whose leg had been broken by the explosion." |

## 1943
## ATTACK ON WP300

| Feb 27 | HMT Lord Hailsham | trawler | Lyme Bay | Sunk by S-65—18 crew killed |
| Feb 27 | HMT Harstad (Nor) | whaler | Lyme Bay | Sunk by S-68—5 crew killed |
| Feb 27 | Moldavia | 4,858 | Lyme Bay | Sunk by S-68 and S-81 |
| Feb 27 | LCT 381 | LCT | Lyme Bay | Sunk by S-85 and S-65—11 taken prisoner |

## ATTACK ON PW323

| DATE | VESSEL | TONS (TYPE, IF WARSHIP) | POSITION | ACCOUNT |
|---|---|---|---|---|
| Apr 14 | *Stanlake* | 1,742 | off the Lizard | Sunk by S-121 |
| Apr 14 | HMS *Eskdale* | destroyer | off Lizard Head | Sunk by S-65, S-90, and S-111—25 crew killed |

## TORPEDOED ON PATROL DUTIES

| Apr 15 | HMT *Adonis* | trawler | off Lowestoft | Sunk in action with 4th S-boat Flotilla—17 crew killed |
|---|---|---|---|---|

## TORPEDOED ON MINESWEEPING DUTIES

| Aug 5 | HMT *Red Gauntlet* | trawler | North Sea | Sunk by S-86—17 crew killed |
|---|---|---|---|---|

## TORPEDOED ON MINESWEEPING DUTIES

| Sept 25 | HMT *Franc Tireur* | trawler | off Harwich | Sunk by S-96—15 crew killed. HMT *Donna Nook* sunk in the same action as a result of a collision between two of the four minesweeping trawlers. |
|---|---|---|---|---|

## ATTACK ON FN1160

| Oct 25 | HMT *William Stephen* | trawler | off Cromer | Sunk by S-74—15 crew killed |
|---|---|---|---|---|

## ATTACK ON CW221

| Nov 2 | *Dona Isabel* | 1,179 | off Dungeness | Sunk by S-136—torpedo that hit the engine room failed to explode before passing out the other side straight in front of the chief engineer |
|---|---|---|---|---|
| Nov 2 | *Storaa* | 1,967 | off Hastings | Sunk by S-138—22 killed out of a crew of 36 |
| Nov 2 | *Foam Queen* | 811 | off Dungeness | Sunk by S-100—10 killed |

## ATTACK ON FN1170

| DATE | VESSEL | TONS (TYPE, IF WARSHIP) | POSITION | ACCOUNT |
|---|---|---|---|---|
| Nov 4 | British Progress | 4,581 | off Great Yarmouth | Hit by S-62; Firelight (2,841)—hit by S-80 and S-88, which also were damaged in this attack |

## LONE ARMED TRAWLER SUNK

| Dec 1 | HMT Aventurine | trawler | off Beachy Head | Sunk by S-142—lost in action with 5th S-boat Flotilla |
|---|---|---|---|---|

## 1944
### ATTACK ON WP457

| Jan 6 | Polperro | 403 | South of the Lizard | Sunk by S-84 and S-136 while carrying coal—8 crew and 3 gunners killed |
|---|---|---|---|---|
| Jan 6 | Underwood | 1,990 | South of the Lizard | Sunk by S-141 while carrying invasion craft—15 crew and 3 gunners killed |
| Jan 6 | Solstad (Swe) | 1,408 | South of the Lizard | Sunk by S-142 en route to London with coal—5 crew killed |
| Jan 6 | HMT Wallasea | trawler | South of the Lizard | Sunk by S-138—17 crew killed |

### ATTACK ON CW243

| Jan 31 | Emerald | 806 | SE of Beachy Head | Sunk by S-142—12 crew and 3 gunners killed |
|---|---|---|---|---|
| Jan 31 | Caleb Sprague | 1,813 | 10 m SE of Beachy Head | Sunk by S-138—22 crew and 3 gunners killed |
| Jan 31 | HMT Pine | trawler | off Selsey Bill | Sunk by S-142—10 crew killed |

### MINESWEEPING OFF THE EAST COAST

| Feb 13 | HMT Cap d'Antifer | trawler | off the Humber | Sunk by S-65 and S-99—24 crew killed |
|---|---|---|---|---|

## ATTACK ON FS1371

| DATE | VESSEL | TONS (TYPE, IF WARSHIP) | POSITION | ACCOUNT |
|---|---|---|---|---|
| Feb 24 | *Phillip M* | 2,085 | off Great Yarmouth | Sunk by 13 S-boats from 2nd and 8th Flotillas. Survivors rescued by *Lady Olga*, with the Lloyd's War Medal being awarded to Captain L. B. Anderson. Citation: "During an attack by enemy E-boats, two torpedoes were fired at the ship while sailing in a coastal convoy, and they were evaded thanks to the prompt and skillful evasive action taken by Captain Anderson. Another vessel [the *Phillip M*] in the convoy was also torpedoed and sank rapidly. In the midst of the attack, Captain Anderson maneuvered his ship close to the rapidly sinking vessel, and a boat was launched to pick up survivors. After searching for other survivors the ship proceeded at full speed and rejoined the convoy four hours later. Captain Anderson showed outstanding courage and fine seamanship in the face of great danger, and was instrumental in many lives being saved." |

## ATTACK ON CW264

| Apr 24 | HMS *Roode Zee* | tug | off Dungeness | Sunk by S-100 |
|---|---|---|---|---|

## ATTACK ON T-4 CONVOY (EXERCISE TIGER)

| Apr 28 | LST 507 (U.S.) | LST | Lyme Bay | Sunk by S-130 and S-150 |
|---|---|---|---|---|
| Apr 28 | LST 531 (U.S.) | LST | Lyme Bay | Sunk by S-150 and S-138. Around 639 U.S. Navy and Army casualties; LST 289 was also badly damaged by S-145. |

## NORMANDY LANDINGS

| DATE | VESSEL | TONS (TYPE, IF WARSHIP) | POSITION | ACCOUNT |
|---|---|---|---|---|
| June 8 | LCI 105 | LCI | Normandy | Sunk in action with S-boats of the 9th S-boat Flotilla—7 crew killed |
| June 8 | LCT 875 | LCT | Normandy | Sunk in action with S-boats of the 5th S-boat Flotilla—12 crew killed |
| June 9 | LST 376 (U.S.) | LST | Normandy | Sunk in action with S-172, S-174, S-175, and S-187—46 crew killed |
| June 9 | LCT 314 (U.S.) | LCT | Normandy | Sunk in action with S-172, S-174, S-175, and S-187—67 crew killed |

## ATTACK ON ETC4W

| DATE | VESSEL | TONS (TYPE, IF WARSHIP) | POSITION | ACCOUNT |
|---|---|---|---|---|
| June 10 | *Dungrange* | 621 | off Isle of Wight | Sunk by S-177 and S-178—18 crew killed as ammunition cargo exploded |
| June 10 | *Brackenfield* | 657 | off Isle of Wight | Sunk by S-189 while carrying ammunition—10 crew killed |
| June 10 | *Ashanti* | 534 | off Isle of Wight | Sunk by S-179—17 crew killed as cargo of cased octane fuel exploded |

## NORMANDY

| DATE | VESSEL | TONS (TYPE, IF WARSHIP) | POSITION | ACCOUNT |
|---|---|---|---|---|
| June 11 | USS *Partridge* | minesweeper | off Normandy | Sunk in action with 9th S-boat Flotilla |
| June 11 | HMS *Sesame* | tug | off Normandy | Sunk in action with 9th S-boat Flotilla |
| June 11 | MTB 448 | MTB | off Normandy | Sunk in action with S-136 as part of a battle between MTBs and 5th and 9th S-boat Flotillas. S-136 also sank. |
| June 11 | HMS *Halsted* | frigate | off Normandy | Torpedoed in action with 5th and 9th S-boat Flotillas—33 crew killed. Towed to Portsmouth, she was later declared a constructive total loss. |
| June 13 | USS *Nelson* | destroyer | off Normandy | Damaged by S-boat torpedo—24 crew killed |
| July 6 | HMS *Trollope* | frigate | off Normandy | Sunk in action with 2nd and 9th S-boat Flotillas—54 crew killed |
| July 26–27 | MTB 430 | MTB | off Normandy | Sunk in action with 2nd S-boat Flotilla as a result of ramming by S-182 |

## ATTACK ON ETM46

| DATE | VESSEL | TONS (TYPE, IF WARSHIP) | POSITION | ACCOUNT |
|---|---|---|---|---|
| July 27 | *Fort Perrot* | 7,171 | off Dungeness | Damaged by torpedoes from S-97 and S-114 and towed into harbor on fire |
| July 27 | *Empire Beatrice* | 7,046 | off Dungeness | Damaged by torpedoes from S-97 and S-114 and beached |

## NORMANDY

| DATE | VESSEL | TONS (TYPE, IF WARSHIP) | POSITION | ACCOUNT |
|---|---|---|---|---|
| July 30 | *Samwake* | 7,219 | S of Eastbourne | Sunk by 6th S-boat Flotilla (Dieppe). Also damaged: *Fort Dearborn* (7,100); *Fort Kaskaskia* (7,187); and *Ocean Courier* (7,174). Lloyd's War Medal awarded to 2nd Officer T. Pearson. Citation: "The ship was torpedoed and badly damaged while sailing in convoy. There were several casualties among members of the crew, some of whom were trapped in their quarters. Second Officer Pearson showed exceptional courage and leadership in difficult and dangerous circumstances. Although it was uncertain at the time whether the ship would remain afloat, he collected together a party of volunteers and led them to the rescue of their shipmates. Five bodies were recovered and two men brought out alive." |
| Aug 7 | *William L. Macey* | 7,176 | off Normandy | Damaged by G7e Dackel torpedoes fired by S-boats |
| Aug 8 | HMS *Frobisher* | cruiser | off Normandy | Damaged by G7e Dackel torpedoes fired by S-boats |
| Aug 10 | HMS *Vestal* | minesweeper | off Normandy | Damaged by G7e Dackel torpedoes fired by S-boats |
| Aug 10 | *Iddesleigh* | 5,208 | off Normandy | Damaged by torpedo G7e Dackel torpedoes fired by S-boats and later sunk by torpedo from U-438 while under tow from Normandy |
| Aug 11 | HMS *Albatross* | repair ship | off Normandy | Damaged by G7e Dackel torpedoes fired by S-Boats and later towed to Portsmouth— 66 crew killed |

## ATTACK ON FTM70

| DATE | VESSEL | TONS (TYPE, IF WARSHIP) | POSITION | ACCOUNT |
|---|---|---|---|---|
| Aug 18 | *Fort Gloucester* | 7,127 | off Dungeness | Damaged by torpedoes fired by S-boats |

## SUNK OFF OSTEND

| DATE | VESSEL | TONS (TYPE, IF WARSHIP) | POSITION | ACCOUNT |
|---|---|---|---|---|
| Nov 2 | *Rio Bravo* | 1,141 | Ostend Roads | Sunk by S-175—14 crew killed. Lloyd's War Medals awarded to Captain M. W. Thomas and Able Seaman J. O'Regan. Citation: "The ship was torpedoed while lying at anchor off Ostend and seriously damaged, the accommodation being completely destroyed. Fourteen lives were lost. Captain Thomas acted with outstanding courage and coolness in the face of great difficulty and danger. He was blown overboard by the explosion but succeeded in clambering back again, and although barefooted, he at once led a small party to the rescue of the trapped and unconscious officers. He then searched among the wrecked accommodation and debris for other members of the crew. After two hours the search was abandoned shortly before the ship sank. Able Seaman O'Regan displayed conspicuous bravery and devotion to duty regardless of his own safety. He was prominent in the rescue efforts and cleared a mass of debris to free an unconscious officer and took him to the foredeck." |
| Nov 2 | HMS *Colsay* | buoy tender | Ostend Roads | Sunk by S-207—36 crew killed |

## 1945
### LONE SINKING

| DATE | VESSEL | TONS (TYPE, IF WARSHIP) | POSITION | ACCOUNT |
|---|---|---|---|---|
| Jan 16–17 | LST 415 | LST | Thames Estuary | Beached after being torpedoed in action with 2nd and 5th S-boat Flotillas |

### ATTACK ON TAC114

| DATE | VESSEL | TONS | POSITION | ACCOUNT |
|---|---|---|---|---|
| Jan 22 | Halo | 2,365 | N of Dunkirk | Damaged by S-178 and S-175 and sank under tow the following day |

### ATTACK ON FS1734

| DATE | VESSEL | TONS | POSITION | ACCOUNT |
|---|---|---|---|---|
| Feb 22 | Goodwood | 2,780 | off Lowestoft | Sunk by torpedo in action with 5th S-boat Flotilla |
| Feb 22 | Blacktoft | 1,109 | off Lowestoft | Sunk by torpedo in action with 5th S-boat Flotilla—2 crew and 4 gunners killed. *Skjold* (1,345) damaged by S-204 in same engagement. |

### ATTACK ON FS1759

| DATE | VESSEL | TONS | POSITION | ACCOUNT |
|---|---|---|---|---|
| Mar 19 | Crichtoun | 1,097 | off Lowestoft | Sunk by torpedo in action with 6th S-boat Flotilla—20 crew and 1 gunner killed |
| Mar 19 | Rogate | 2,871 | off Lowestoft | Sunk by torpedo in action with 6th S-boat Flotilla—1 crew killed |

### COASTAL FORCES ENGAGEMENT

| DATE | VESSEL | TONS | POSITION | ACCOUNT |
|---|---|---|---|---|
| Apr 7 | MTB 5001 | MTB | North Sea | Hit by cannon fire and exploded—3 crew killed |
| Apr 7 | MTB 494 | MTB | North Sea | Rammed and sunk by S-174 (which also sank)—14 crew killed from the MTB and 5 from the S-boat, with the rest being captured. S-177 sank after collision with MTB 493, with the survivors being rescued by S-174. |

# NOTES

**PREFACE**
1. Alfred Thayer Mahan, *The Influence of Seapower on History, 1660–1783* (Boston: Little, Brown and Company, 1890); H. J. Mackinder, "The Geographical Pivot of History," *Geographical Journal* 23, no. 4 (April 1904): 421–37.
2. Cathryn Pearce, "Is Coastal History Maritime History," *Topmasts*, special issue, 2017, www.snr.org.uk/wp-content/uploads/2017/12/Topmasts-special-issue-rev.pdf, 25–28 (accessed December 16, 2017); J. R. Gillis, *The Human Shore: Seacoasts in History* (Chicago: University of Chicago Press, 2012).

**INTRODUCTION**
1. Alexander McKee, *The Coal Scuttle Brigade* (London: New English Library, 1973), 7.
2. James A. Williamson, *The English Channel: A History* (London: Collins, 1959).
3. Peter C. Smith, *Hold the Narrow Sea: Naval Warfare in the English Channel, 1939–1945* (Annapolis: Naval Institute Press, 1984).
4. J. P. Foynes, *Battle of the East Coast* (Isleworth: self-published, 1994).
5. Robert Jackson, *Churchill's Moat: The Channel War, 1939–1945* (London: Airlife, 1995).
6. Alan Burn, *The Fighting Commodores: The Convoy Commanders in the Second World War* (Annapolis: Naval Institute Press, 1999), 47–74.
7. Nick Hewitt, *Coastal Convoys, 1939–1945: The Indestructible Highway* (Barnsley, U.K.: Pen and Sword, 2008).
8. Lieutenant-Commander Peter Scott, *The Battle of the Narrow Seas: A History of the Light Coastal Forces in the Channel and North Sea, 1939–1945* (London: Country Life, 1945); Captain Peter Dickens, *Night Action: MTB Flotilla at War* (London: Book Club Edition, 1974). See also Harold Pickles, *Untold Stories of Small Boats at War: Coastal Forces Veterans Remember* (Edinburgh: Pentland Press, 1994).
9. Bryan Cooper, *The E-Boat Threat* (Oxford: Purnell, 1976); Donald E. Graves, "'Hell Boats' of the RCN: The Canadian Navy and the Motor Torpedo Boat, 1936–41," *Northern Mariner* 2, no. 3 (July 1992): 31–45; James Foster Tent, *E-Boat Alert: Defending the Normandy Invasion Fleet* (Annapolis: Naval Institute Press, 1996).
10. Gordon Williamson, *E-Boat vs MTB: The English Channel, 1941–45* (Oxford: Osprey, 2011), *Kriegsmarine Coastal Forces* (Oxford: Osprey, 2009), and *German E-Boats, 1939–45* (Oxford: Osprey, 2002); Leonard C. Reynolds, *Home Waters MTBs and MGBs at War, 1939–1945* (Stroud, U.K.: Sutton, 2000); Jean-Phillippe Dallies-Labourdette, *Deutsche Schnellboote, 1939–1945* (Stuttgart: Motorbuch Verlag, 2006); Hans Frank, *Die deutschen Schnellboote im Einsatz* (Berlin: E. S. Mittler & Sohn, 2006). Hrvoje Spacij, *Schnellbootwaffe: Adolf Hitler's Guerilla War at Sea, S-Boote, 1935–45. Rare Photographs from Wartime Archives* (Barnsley, U.K.: Pen and Sword, 2021), is the most recent example of this kind of work, which does not enjoy the quality (academic and illustrative) of the works of Williamson and others.
11. Jac J. Baart, *Schnellboote: Operaties vanuit Holland, Vlaanderen en Frankrijk, 1940–1945* (Emmen: Lanasta, 2006).

## NOTES TO PAGES 3–7

12. Lawrence Paterson, *Schnellboote: A Complete Operational History* (Barnsley, U.K.: Seaforth, 2015).
13. Richard Woodman, *The Real Cruel Sea: The Merchant Navy in the Battle of the Atlantic 1939–1945* (London: John Murray, 2004), 57.
14. A. J. Yeatman, Telegraphist, HMS *Pearl*, 1943–45, BBC People's War Website, A4189098, June 13, 2005, http://www.bbc.co.uk/history/ww2peopleswar/stories/98/a4189098.shtml.
15. See, for example, Stephen E. Ambrose, *D-Day, June 6, 1944: The Battle for the Normandy Beaches* (New York: Simon & Schuster, 1994); Joseph Balkoski, *Omaha Beach* (Mechanicsburg, PA: Stackpole Books, 2004). See also Stephen Badsey and Tim Bean, *Omaha Beach* (Stroud, U.K.: Sutton, 2004); Antony Beevor, *D-Day: The Battle for Normandy* (London: Viking, 2009); Simon Trew and Stephen Badsey, *Battle for Caen* (Stroud, U.K.: Sutton, 2004); Christopher Pugsley, *Operation Cobra* (Stroud, U.K.: Sutton, 2005); Steven J. Zaloga, *Operation Cobra 1944: Breakout from Normandy* (Oxford: Osprey, 2001); Stephen E. Ambrose, "Eisenhower's Generalship," *Parameters*, June 1990, 90–98.
16. Craig Symonds, *Neptune: The Allied Invasion of Europe and the D-Day Landings* (Oxford: Oxford University Press, 2014). See, for example, William B. Kirland Jr., *Destroyers at Normandy: Naval Gunfire Support at Omaha Beach* (Washington: Naval Historical Foundation, 2002); Adrian Lewis, "The Navy Falls Short at Normandy," *Naval History Magazine* 12 (December 1998), http://www.usni.org/magazines/navalhistory/1998-12/navy-falls-short-normandy; Adrian R. Lewis, *Omaha Beach: A Flawed Victory* (Chapel Hill: University of North Carolina Press, 2001).
17. Samuel Eliot Morison, *History of United States Naval Operations in World War II*, vol. 11: *The Invasion of France and Germany* (New York: Castle Books, 2001); Captain S. W. Roskill, *The War at Sea, 1939–45*, vol. 3, pt. 2 (London: HMSO, 1961).
18. Foreword by Rear Admiral T. B. Inglis to Grand Admiral Dönitz, "The Conduct of the War at Sea," January 15, 1946, http://www.uboatarchive.net/Admiralty/Admiralty MessageBigrams-Frame.htm.
19. Historical Section Admiralty, *The Defeat of the Enemy Attack on Shipping, 1939–1945: A Study of Policy and Operations*, vol. 1A, Text and Appendices, CB3304(IA), Historical Section Admiralty, 1957.
20. Historical Section Admiralty, *The Defeat of the Enemy Attack on Shipping*, 1.
21. Karl Dönitz, *Memoirs: Ten Years and Twenty Days* (London: Weidenfeld and Nicolson, 1958). For Dönitz's influence, see Edward P. Von der Porten, *The German Navy in World War II* (London: Arthur Baker, 1969). In his review of the book published in 1970, S. W. Roskill commented, "Some parts of the books are strongly tinged with . . . [Dönitz's] outlook and prejudices." "Review," *International Affairs* 46, no. 4 (October 1970): 781.
22. Theodore Ropp, "Review," *Journal of Modern History* 33, no. 1 (March 1961): 98.
23. See, for example, David Syrett, *The Defeat of the German U-Boats: The Battle of the Atlantic* (Columbia: University of South Carolina Press, 1994).
24. Vincent P. O'Hara, *The German Fleet at War, 1939–1945* (Annapolis: Naval Institute Press, 2004).
25. The website http://uboat.net/ identifies some 2,383 titles published in twenty-five different languages on the submarine war since 1998.
26. Ronald O'Rourke, CRS-RL33741 Navy Littoral Combat Ship (LCS) Program: Background, Issues and Options for Congress, Congressional Research Service, April 6, 2012.

27. Naval Postgraduate School, https://nps.edu/-/nps-faculty-researchers-stand-up-new-littoral-operations-center (accessed November 30, 2022).
28. Milan N. Vego, *Naval Strategy and Operations in Narrow Seas* (London: Frank Cass, 2003).
29. Vego, *Naval Strategy*, xv.
30. Milan N. Vego, "On Littoral Warfare," *Naval War College Review* 68, no. 2 (Spring 2015): 30–68.
31. Vego, "On Littoral Warfare," 39–41.
32. Charles Burdick, "The Tambach Archive—A Research Note," *Military Affairs* 36, no. 4 (December 1972): 124–26.

## CHAPTER 1. GERMAN NAVAL STRATEGY

1. Joan Cergol and Ellen Schafer, *Images of America: Oheka Castle* (Charleston, SC: Arcadia, 2012), 113.
2. Fabian Yates, "Commuters," *Nautical Quarterly* 17 (Spring 1982): 66–75.
3. Luerssen Defence, http://www.luerssen-defence.com/en/company/past-and-present (accessed February 6, 2016).
4. "Oheka II," *Die Yacht* 39 (1927): 22–25.
5. Holger Herwig, "The Influence of A. T. Mahan upon German Seapower," in John B. Hattendorf, *The Influence of History on Mahan* (Newport, RI: Naval War College Press, 1991), 70.
6. Admiral Viscount Jellicoe of Scapa, *The Grand Fleet, 1914–16: Its Creation, Development and Work* (London: Cassell and Company, 1919), 408–11.
7. Mark D. Karau, *The Naval Flank of the Western Front: The German MarineKorps Flandern, 1914–1918* (Barnsley, U.K.: Seaforth, 2003), x.
8. Philip K. Lundeberg, "The German Naval Critique of the U-Boat Campaign, 1915–18," *Military Affairs* 27, no. 3 (Autumn 1963): 106.
9. Karau, *The Naval Flank of the Western Front*, 225.
10. Guntram Schulze-Wegener, *Die deutsche Kriegsmarinerüstung, 1942–1945* (Hamburg: E. S. Mittler & Sohn, 1997).
11. Holger H. Herwig, "The Failure of German Sea Power, 1914–1945: Mahan, Tirpitz, and Raeder Reconsidered," *International History Review* 10, no. 1 (February 1988): 68–105. See also Keith W. Bird, "The Origins and Role of German Naval History in the Interwar Period, 1918–1939," *Naval War College Review* 32, no. 2 (March–April 1979): 52.
12. See Paterson, *Schnellboote*, 4.
13. See Erich Raeder, *Struggle for the Sea* (London: William Kimber, 1959), 12–14.
14. See Neustädter Slip-GmbH, Neustadt/Holstein (Werft und Motorreparaturwerkstatt), 1927, BArch, R 8135/383.
15. See Travemünder Yachthafen AG (Trayag), Travemünde: Bd. 1, 1927, BArch, R 8135/1890; Travemünder Yachthafen AG (Trayag), Travemünde: Bd. 2, 1928, BArch, R 8135/1908; Travemünder Yachthafen AG (Trayag), Travemünde: Bd. 3, 1928, BArch, R 8135/1891.
16. Raeder, *Struggle for the Sea*, 25–26.
17. Geoffrey Till, "Naval Power," in *Warfare in the Twentieth Century*, ed. Colin McInnes and G. D. Sheffield (London: Unwin Hyman, 1988), 81.
18. See "Sub-committee of the Committee of Imperial Defence on the Question of the Capital Ship in the Navy, 1920–21: Report and Proceedings," vols. 1–3, The National Archives (hereafter TNA): CAB16/37/1, CAB 16/37/2, CAB 16/37/3. For the draft report

see TNA: ADM 116/3610. In terms of public debate, see, for example, "Our Future Naval Policy," *The Times*, December 7, 1920, 13; "The Future of the Battleship," *Evening Telegraph and Post* (Dundee, Scotland), December 15, 1920, 3; "Battleship or Submarine," *Nottingham Evening Post*, November 23, 1920, 3; "Future of the Battleship," *Nottingham Evening Post*, December 3, 1920, 4; "Battleship Problem," *Nottingham Evening Post*, December 15, 1920, 6; "The Value of the Battleship," *Courier and Argus* (Dundee, Scotland), January 4, 1921, 5; "Testing the Value of the Battleship," *Evening Telegraph and Post* (Dundee, Scotland), January 18, 1921, 2; "Use of the Battleship," *Nottingham Evening Post*, February 4, 1921, 5; "Bucknill Committee-Interim Findings," TNA: ADM 167/116; "Second Report of the Bucknill Committee," April 25, 1942, TNA: ADM 116/4521; Admiral Sir Hugh Binney Papers, Imperial War Museum, IWM/PP/MCR/95.
19. Theodore Roscoe, *United States Destroyer Operations in World War II* (Annapolis: Naval Institute Press, 1953), 357.
20. Order from Raeder to various commands, February 10, 1932, Oberkommando der Marine Miscellaneous Documents (hereafter *OKM Misc*) RG242, T1022, roll 4082, NARA.
21. Inspektion des Torpedo und Minenwefens, April 2, 1932, *OKM Misc*, RG242, T1022, roll 4082, NARA.
22. Report by Kommando 1 Schnellbootehalbflotille, October 11, 1932, *OKM Misc*, RG242, T1022, roll 4082, NARA.
23. Report by Rear Admiral Kolbe (BdA), October 19, 1932, *OKM Misc*, RG242, T1022, roll 4082, NARA.
24. "Tactical and Staff Duties Division (Foreign Documents Section), German E-Boat Operations and Policy, 1939–1945, War Diary Schnellboote Command" (hereafter E-Boat Operations and Policy), TNA: ADM 223/28.
25. E-Boat Operations and Policy, TNA: ADM 223/28. See also Paterson, *Schnellboote*, 15–16.
26. Paterson, *Schnellboote*, 14.
27. Raeder, *Struggle for the Sea*, 40–41.
28. Thomas Hoerber, "Psychology and Reasoning in the Anglo-German Naval Agreement, 1935–39," *Historical Journal* 52, no. 1 (March 2009): 153–74.
29. Keith W. Bird, *Erich Raeder: Admiral of the Third Reich* (Annapolis: Naval Institute Press, 2006).
30. Erich Raeder, *My Life* (Annapolis: Naval Institute Press, 1960), 125.
31. Raeder, *My Life*, 135.
32. Paterson, *Schnellboote*, 24–36.
33. David H. Olivier, *German Naval Strategy, 1856–1888: Forerunners to Tirpitz* (London: Frank Cass, 2004), 1–6.

## CHAPTER 2. THE RISE OF THE S-BOAT
1. Board of Trade, *Statistical Abstract of the United Kingdom*, no. 82 (London: HMSO, 1938), table 272, 366–67.
2. John Marriot, "Smokestack: The Industrial Heritage of the Thames Gateway," in *London's Turning: The Making of the Thames Gateway*, ed. Philip Cohen and Michael Rustin (Aldershot: Ashgate, 2008), 22–23.
3. Clarence Winchester, *Shipping Wonders of the World* (London: Fleetway House, n.d.), 2:1328.
4. On the outbreak of war, these were deployed as follows: Firth of Forth 5; Portsmouth/Southampton 5; Dover 2; Scapa Flow 2; Liverpool 2; Plymouth 3. Michael Melvin,

NOTES TO PAGES 27–35   225

*Minesweeper: The Role of the Motor Minesweeper in World War II* (Worcester: Square One, 1992), 3.
5. Winston S. Churchill to Roy Harrod, January 4, 1940, First Lord Personal Minute 120, Churchill Papers (Churchill College Cambridge) 19/6.
6. War Cabinet minutes, February 1, 1940, TNA: CAB65/5.
7. S. W. Roskill, *The War at Sea, 1939–1945* (Uckfield: Naval and Military Press, 2004), 1:323.
8. Hewitt, *Coastal Convoys*, 7.
9. Dickens, *Night Action*, 28.
10. See Friedrich Kemnade, *Die Afrika-Flottille: Der Einsatz der 3.Schnellboot-Flottille im Weltkrieg* (Stuttgart: Motorbuch, 1976), 16–28.
11. Hans Frank, *Die deutschen Schnellboote im Einsatz*, 22–23. See also Gerhard Hümmelchen, *Die deutsche Schnellboote im Zweiten Weltkrieg* (Hamburg: E. S. Mittler, 1996), 24–28.
12. Hans Frank, *German S-Boats in Action in the Second World War* (Barnsley, U.K.: Seaforth, 2007), 21.
13. Entry for May 28, 1940, "Narrative Summary of S-Boat Operations May–December 1940," RG242, PG70979, roll 3125, NARA.
14. Survivors Report by Second Officer, V. P. Wills Rust, June 5, 1940, TNA: ADM 199/2132.
15. Entry for May 23, 1940, Narrative Summary of S-Boat Operations May–December 1940, RG242, PG70979, roll 3125, NARA; Baart, *Schnellboote*, 49; Dallies-Labourdette, *Deutsche Schnellboote*, 38.
16. "Motor Torpedo Boats," Admiralty Weekly Intelligence Summary, June 20, 1940, 4, TNA: ADM 223/146.
17. Walter Ansel, *Hitler Confronts England* (Durham, NC: Duke University Press, 1960), 317.
18. Ansel, *Hitler Confronts England*, 97.
19. On this point Fricke is supported by Kenneth Macksey, *The German Invasion of England, July 1940* (London: Arms and Armour Press, 1980).
20. Werner Kreipe, "The Battle of Britain," in Kreipe et al., *The Fatal Decisions* (London: Michael Joseph, 1956), 11.
21. Kreipe, "The Battle of Britain," 12.
22. Paterson, *Schnellboote*, xii.
23. Roskill, *War at Sea*, 1:329.
24. Dickens, *Night Action*, 28.
25. Note of the First Lord's Meeting with Ministers, July 16, 1940, TNA: CAB65/57/24.
26. Roskill, *War at Sea*, 1:330.
27. Captain Eric Wheeler Bush, *Bless Our Ship* (London: George Allen & Unwin, 1958), 197–98.
28. Entry for July 26, 1940, Narrative Summary of S-Boat Operations May–December 1940, RG242, PG70979, roll 3125, NARA.
29. Roskill, *War at Sea*, 1:323–24.
30. Entry for August 8, 1940, Narrative Summary of S-Boat Operations May–December 1940, RG242, PG70979, roll 3125, NARA. See also Hümmelchen, *Die deutsche Schnellboote*, 33; and Andy Saunders, *Convoy Peewit: August 8, 1940: The First Day of the Battle of Britain* (London: Grub Street, 2010).
31. Roskill, *War at Sea*, 1:325.

32. W. H. B. Court, *Coal* (London: HMSO, 1951), 87.
33. Sönke Neitzel, "Kriegsmarine and Luftwaffe Co-operation in the War against Britain, 1939–1945," *War in History* 10, no. 4 (October 2003): 448–63.
34. Neitzel, "Kriegsmarine and Luftwaffe Co-operation," 453.
35. Historical Section Admiralty, *The Defeat of the Enemy Attack on Shipping, 1939–1945*, vol. 1B (London: Admiralty, 1957), table 26.
36. Neitzel, "Kriegsmarine and Luftwaffe Co-operation," 456.
37. Entry for September 4, 1940, Narrative Summary of S-Boat Operations May–December 1940, RG242, PG 70979, roll 3125, NARA.
38. Paterson, *Schnellboote*, 81.
39. Kemnade, *Die Afrika-Flottille*, 32–33.
40. Paterson, *Schnellboote*, 83.
41. Entry for October 18, 1940, Narrative Summary of S-Boat Operations May–December 1940, RG242, PG 70979, roll 3125, NARA.
42. Court, *Coal*, 91.
43. On Operation Sea Lion, see German Plans for the Invasion of England, 1940, undated, OSS Files, https://www.cia.gov/library/readingroom/docs/GERMAN%20PLANS%20FOR%20INVASION%20OF%20ENGLAND%2C%201940_0001.pdf (accessed January 21, 2017).
44. "Appreciation of the Situation by FdT," July 5, 1940, TNA: ADM 223/28. *Schnellboote* flotillas were commanded by the Führer der Torpedoboote (FdT) until 1942, when a new post, Führer der Schnellboote (FdS), was created.
45. "Defensive Minelaying Policy in Home Waters," TNA: ADM 1/15815.
46. Court, *Coal*, 87.
47. Kemnade, *Die Afrika-Flottille*, 90ff.
48. E. R. Hooton, *The Luftwaffe: A Study in Air Power, 1933–1945* (Hersham, U.K.: Classic Publications, 2010), 88.
49. See testimony by Sergeant Pilot Harold Bennett (602 Squadron) in Richard C. Smith, *Hornchurch Offensive: A Definitive Account of the RAF Fighter Airfield, Its Pilots, Groundcrew and Staff, 1941–1962* (London: Grub Street, 2001), 35.
50. Hooton, *The Luftwaffe*, 88.
51. For their performance in the attack on Russia see Hümmelchen, *Die deutsche Schnellboote*, 47–50.
52. Baart, *Schnellboote*, 248–55.
53. Oostende 8 berths, Boulogne 12 berths, Rotterdam 16 berths, Ijmuiden 10 berths. See http://s-boot.net/sboats-kriegsmarine-sbb.html (accessed March 9, 2016).
54. Roskill, *The War at Sea, 1939–45*, 3:479.
55. See minute by Wing Commander Chamberlain, January 11, 1942, TNA: AIR 15/122.

## CHAPTER 3. THE CAMPAIGN IN THE BALANCE

1. Many of these were built in the smaller boatyards (such as Par, Looe, Dartmouth, and Grimsby) more used to the construction of wooden fishing boats. Melvin, *Minesweeper*, 28.
2. KTB Seebefehlshaber West (hereafter "KTB der SB West"), May 9, 1942, RG242, T1022, roll 3974, NARA.
3. KTB der SB West, May 11, 1942, RG242, T1022, roll 3974, NARA.
4. KTB der SB West, May 31, 1942, RG242, T1022, roll 3974, NARA.
5. 1941 Construction Programme, paper for the War Cabinet (41) 88, April 20, 1941, TNA: CAB66/16.

NOTES TO PAGES 45–54     227

6. British Embassy (Washington) to Foreign Office, May 2, 1941, TNA: FO954/29A/168.
7. KTB der SB West, June 15, 1942, RG242, T1022, roll 3974, NARA.
8. The New Construction Programme 1942, paper for the War Cabinet (42) 173, April 21, 1942, TNA: CAB66/24.
9. Historical Section Admiralty, *The Defeat*, 151.
10. Historical Section Admiralty, *The Defeat*, 152.
11. Historical Section Admiralty, *The Defeat*, 228.
12. Rear Admiral G. S. Ritchie, *No Day Too Long—An Hydrographer's Tale* (Edinburgh: Pentland Press, 1994), 30.
13. Commodore J. O. Rowlands, "Fifty Years at Sea" (unpublished paper, 2003).
14. Winston S. Churchill, *The Second World War*, vol. 2: *Their Finest Hour* (London: Reprint Society, 1951), 473.
15. SS *Aberhill*, SS *Afon Towy* (684), HMT *Agate* (627, armed trawler escort), SS *Betty Hindley* (1738), SS *Deerwood* (1914), SS *Gallois* (2687), SS *Oxshott* (1241), SS *Taara* (1402). Another vessel, SS *Paddy Hendley*, on her maiden voyage, also ran aground but appears to have been successfully salvaged.
16. Historical Section Admiralty, *The Defeat*, 29–30.
17. Vice Admiral Sir Peter Gretton, *Convoy Escort Commander* (London: Corgi, 1964), 21.
18. Burn, *Commodores*, 57–58.
19. Captain Augustus Agar, *Footprints in the Sea* (London: Evans Brothers, 1961), 143.
20. Eddie Griffiths (SS *Bandicar*) undated interview, Amble Social History Group, *A Time to Remember: Recollections of the Second World War by the People of Amble and District* (Alnwick: self-published, 2005), 84.
21. Jack Prior interview, http://www.merchantnavyunsungheroes.co.uk/jack-prior.html (accessed November 11, 2013); Fred Dent, DEMS gunner (SS *Methilhill*), Imperial War Museum Interview 22116, 2002 (accessed June 18, 2021).
22. See "Barrage Balloons for Convoys," October 24, 1940, film id 1059.16, British Pathé Archive; "Channel Passage, with the Mobile Balloon Barrage through the English Channel, 1940," *Blackwood's* 252 (November 1942): 273–82.
23. Burn, *Commodores*, 68.
24. Tony McCrum, *Sunk by Stukas Survived at Salerno: The Memoirs of Captain Tony McCrum* (Barnsley, U.K.: Pen & Sword, 2010), 84–85. On the bringing down of a Heinkel by HMT *Withernsea*, see Nowell Hall, "Towing Story," in *Wavy Navy by Some Who Served*, ed. J. Lennox Kerr and David James (London: George G. Harrap Co., 1950), 92–93.
25. Photo caption from an image released to the *Chicago Tribune*, April 24, 1942, author's collection.
26. KTB der SB West, August 31, 1942, RG242, T1022, roll 3974, NARA.
27. KTB der SB West, September 30, 1942, RG242, T1022, roll 3974, NARA.
28. KTB der SB West, October 31, 1942, RG242, T1022, roll 3974, NARA.
29. S. W. Roskill, *The War at Sea, 1939–1945* (London: HMSO, 1956), 2:255.

**CHAPTER 4. THE HUMAN DIMENSION**

1. See "Convoy Attacked in the Channel," July 18, 1940, film id 1051.07, British Pathé Archive.
2. See "Pathé Gazette Special: Shells across the Channel," August 26, 1940, film id 1053.55, British Pathé Archive.
3. "Swarms of E-Boats," *Evening Herald (Dublin)*, August 9, 1940, 6.

4. "E-Boat Alley Is 100 Miles of Danger," *Daily Mail*, November 5, 1941, 5.
5. "E-Boat Alley Is 100 Miles of Danger."
6. A. B. Seaman, "Bombed in a Convoy in the English Channel," *New Republic* 103 (November 4, 1940): 622–23.
7. Bartimeus, "Sweeping Death's Doorstep," *Atlantic Monthly*, August 1941, 288–94; Herbert W. Richmond, "Coastal Trade and Flotilla Warfare," *Fortnightly*, January 1943, 30–33.
8. "Our Miniature Destroyers," *Yorkshire Post*, February 9, 1942, 1.
9. "A Captured German E-Boat," *Yorkshire Post*, August 1, 1942, 1.
10. "Hunting E-Boats with Clubs and Cutlasses," *People*, April 4, 1943, 8.
11. "E-Boats Sign of Invasion Nerves," *Lancashire Daily Post*, June 11, 1943, 1.
12. "OBE for Seaton Sluice Captain," *Shields Evening News*, June 10, 1943, 3.
13. "E-Boat Twice Rammed by Navy Launches," *Shields Evening News*, September 27, 1943, 1.
14. James N. Minifie, "An Eastbound Channel Convoy," *Harper's* 182 (January 1941): 113–19.
15. Bartimeus, "Sweeping Death's Doorstep," *Atlantic Monthly* (March 1941): 288–94. M. Mulier, "In E-Boat Alley," *Newsweek* 20 (November 2, 1943): 24–26.
16. Contemporary publications on the Merchant Navy mentioned the coastal convoys in only a handful of pages if they mentioned them at all. See, for example, Warren Armstrong, *Battle of the Oceans* (London: Jarrolds, 1943), 103–7; and Sir Archibald Hurd, ed., *Britain's Merchant Navy* (London: Odhams, 1944), 52–53.
17. For example, *The Royal Marines: The Admiralty Account of Their Achievement, 1939–1943* (London: HMSO, 1944), 58–59, recounted the story of a Marine gunner decorated with Lloyd's War Medal for bravery in an action on a coastal convoy in 1940. Central Office of Information, *British Coaster, 1939–1945* (London: HMSO, 1947).
18. Ken Forrester, "If Only I Had Known," https://cfv.org.uk/research/personnel/memoir/if-i-only-had-known (accessed June 30, 2020).
19. *War*, issue 36, January 23, 1943, reproduced in Jennie Gray, ed., *"This Is War!": The Diaries and Journalism of Anthony Cotterell, 1940–1944* (Stroud, U.K.: Spellmount, 2013), 81–82.
20. See Gray *"This Is War!,"* 78–82.
21. Mike Farquharson-Roberts, *Royal Navy Officers from War to War* (Basingstoke, U.K.: Palgrave Macmillan, 2015), 187.
22. Lieutenant-Commander Robert Peverell Hichens, *We Fought Them in Gunboats* (London: Michael Joseph, 1944), 61–62.
23. C. Anthony Law, *White Plumes Astern: The Short, Daring Life of Canada's MTB Flotilla* (Halifax, NS: Nimbus, 1989), 16.
24. Entry for November 19–20, 1942, War Diary 7th MGB Flotilla (HMS *Mantis*), Suffolk Record Office (Lowestoft) 1678/1.
25. Hichens, *We Fought Them in Gunboats*, 149.
26. Nicolas Wolz, *From Imperial Splendour to Internment: The German Navy in the First World War* (Barnsley, U.K.: Seaforth, 2013), 1–17.
27. I am indebted to Hans Kolbe and Henriette Schlesinger for sharing their memories of their father, along with his memoir and other papers.
28. S-53 interrogation report, undated, TNA: WO 208/3243.
29. Baart, *Schnellboote*, 263–65.
30. Interview with S-boat man Karl Heinz Thiele by Thea Wrobbel for TVT productions, January 2014, forwarded to author in an email, March 31, 2014. Thiele spent four and half years in S-boats after volunteering for military service.
31. Ulrich Kolbe, private family memoir, 1997–98.

32. Ulrich Kolbe, private family memoir, 1997–98.
33. Ulrich Kolbe, private family memoir, 1997–98.
34. Ulrich Kolbe, private family memoir, 1997–98.
35. Ulrich Kolbe, private family memoir, 1997–98.
36. Interview with S-boat man Karl Heinz Thiele by Thea Wrobbel for TVT productions, January 2014, forwarded to author in an email, March 31, 2014.
37. See, for example, *Die Kriegsmarine*, June 20, 1940, 6.
38. *Die Kriegsmarine*, August 5, 1940, 6.
39. Bd. 4, BArch, RM 8/1529.
40. Bd. 12, BArch, RM 8/1537.
41. Bd. 13, BArch, RM 8/1538.
42. Bd. 35, BArch, RM 8/1560.
43. Bd. 42, BArch, RM 8/1567.
44. Bd. 44, BArch, RM 8/1569.
45. Georg von Hase, *Die Kriegsmarine im Kampf um den Atlantik: Erlebnisberichte von Mitkampfern* (Leipzig: Hase & Koehler Verlag, 1942), 295.
46. Hase, *Die Kriegsmarine im Kampf*, 298.
47. Hugo Bürger, *Schnellboote Vor! Ein Erlebnisbericht vom Einsatz einer Schnellboot-Flottille im Osten* (Oldenburg: Stalling, 1943).
48. P. P. Möbius, *Schnellboote* (Berlin: Carl Curtius Verlag, 1943).
49. Möbius, *Schnellboote*, 226.
50. Möbius, 226.
51. The newsletter started out as a relatively poorly produced newssheet, but by 1943 it had grown into a professionally printed mini-magazine (see Archiv Peter Schlichting).
52. "Wie weit reicht unsere Continent" and "Wir haben immer die bessern Waffen," *Feldpost Zeitung*, December 11, 1941, 3–4, Archiv Peter Schlichting.
53. "Narchrichten aus dem Betrieb," *Feldpost Zeitung*, March 1942, 2–3, Archiv Peter Schlichting; text of speech and 16-mm footage in Archiv Peter Schlichting.
54. Ritterkreuzträger Kpltn Opdenhoff besuchte die Werft, *Der Werftbote*, March 1943, 6–7, Archiv Peter Schlichting.
55. Baart, *Schnellboote*, 110.
56. *Der Werftbote*, March 1942, 2, Archiv Peter Schlichting.
57. For example, see visits by Werner Toniges, February 20, 1942, text of speech and 16-mm footage, Archiv Peter Schlichting.
58. Schlichting Werft friendship books 1–3, Archiv Peter Schlichting.
59. See, for example, Jack Prior interview talking about life on SS *West Town*, undated, http://www.merchantnavyunsungheroes.co.uk/jack-prior.html (accessed November 11, 2013).
60. Jack Prior interview, undated, http://www.merchantnavyunsungheroes.co.uk/jack-prior.html (accessed November 11, 2013). See also Lt. Commander Gurney Braithwaite (Conservative, Holderness), *House of Commons Debates*, July 14, 1943, vol. 391, cols. 236–38 (see esp. col. 237).
61. *War*, issue 36, January 23, 1943, reproduced in Jennie Gray, ed., *"This Is War!,"* 81–82.
62. See, for example, *Transactions of the Institute of Marine Engineers* 56 (1944): 94.
63. See C. H. Brown, *Nicholls Seamanship and Nautical Knowledge*, 18th ed. (1938; repr., Glasgow: Brown, Son and Ferguson, 1943), ix.
64. Patrick Campbell, "Come Here I Tell You: Sean Tar at Sea," *The Spectator*, July 23, 1959, 8.

65. Christopher Lloyd, *The British Merchant Seaman, 1200–1860* (London: Collins, 1968), 29.
66. See *House of Commons Debates*, June 21, 1938, vol. 337, cols. 875–77.
67. W. L. Shortland, "Defensively Equipped Merchant Ships," 2003, http://www.heroesofhull.co.uk/pages/memories/WW2/Lol%20Shortland's%20War.pdf (accessed February 25, 2014), 8.
68. James Goodchild interview, undated, http://www.merchantnavyunsungheroes.co.uk/james-goodchild.html (accessed November 11, 2013).
69. Burn, *Commodores*, 56.
70. Commodore J. O. Rowlands, "Fifty Years at Sea" (unpublished paper, 2003).
71. Amble Social History Group, 86.
72. See Lt. Commander Gurney Braithwaite (Conservative, Holderness), *House of Commons Debates*, July 14, 1943, vol. 391, cols. 236–38 (see esp. col. 237).
73. Fred Dent, DEMS gunner (SS *Methilhill*), Imperial War Museum Interview 22116, 2002.
74. Morris Beckman, *Flying the Red Duster: A Merchant Seaman's First Voyage into the Battle of the Atlantic 1940* (Stroud, U.K.: Spellmount, 2011), 14.
75. R. J. Scarlett, *Under Hazardous Circumstances* (Dallington, U.K.: Naval & Military Press, 1992): June 24, 1940, *Kingfisher*, LWM [and BEM] to Second Engineer W. Pybus; August 8, 1940, *Empire Crusader*, LWM [and MBE] to Chief Engineer J. E. Cowper, LWM to Able Seaman W. Robson; March 8, 1941, *Togston*, LWM to Captain L. Laurenson; July 30, 1944, *Ocean Courier*, LWM [and MBE] to 2nd Officer T. Pearson; November 2, 1944, *Rio Bravo*, LWM [and MBE] to Captain M. W. Thomas, LWM [and BEM] to Able Seaman J. O'Regan.
76. See Lt. Commander Gurney Braithwaite (Conservative, Holderness), *House of Commons Debates*, July 14, 1943, vol. 391, cols. 236–38.
77. See complaints from personnel aboard SS *Fulham*, SS *Colonel Crompton*, SS *John Hopkinson*, logged by Security Officer (Portsmouth), November 5, 1943, TNA: ADM 1/15815.
78. Report by Security Officer (Portsmouth) in Conversation with W. Johnston (First Mate, SS *Fulham*), November 5, 1943, TNA: ADM 1/15815.
79. Amble Social History Group, *A Time to Remember*, 87.
80. Hall, "Towing Story," 94–95. *Ilse* was one of four casualties sustained by convoy FN832 on October 7, 1942.
81. Emmanuel Adrien, Free French Merchant Seaman (SS *Daphne*) 1940–41, Imperial War Museum Audio Interview 20135, 2000.

**CHAPTER 5. DÖNITZ REPLACES RAEDER**
1. See Rahn's chapter on peak and decline of the U-boat war in Horst Boog et al., *Germany and the Second World War*, vol. 6: *The Global War* (Oxford: Oxford University Press, 2001), 379–404.
2. Jürgen Rohwer, *The Critical Convoy Battles of March 1943: The Battle for HX.229/SC122* (Annapolis: Naval Institute Press, 1977).
3. Führer Naval Conference, January 6, 1943, in J. Mallmann Showell, *Führer Conferences on Naval Affairs, 1939–1945* (London: Greenhill Books, 1990), 318–19.
4. Herwig, "Influence of A. T. Mahan," 73.
5. Jak P. Mallmann Showell, *Dönitz, U-Boats, Convoys: The British Version of His Memoirs from the Admiralty's Secret Anti-submarine Reports* (London: Frontline Books, 2013), ix–x.

6. Lieutenant Commander Peter Kemp, "Grand Admiral Karl Dönitz," in *The War Lords*, ed. Field Marshal Sir Michael Carver (London: Weidenfeld and Nicolson, 1976), 473.
7. Peter Padfield, *Dönitz: The Last Führer* (London: Gollancz, 1993), 495.
8. Eric C. Rust, *Naval Officers under Hitler: The Story of Crew 34* (New York: Praeger, 1991), 56–57.
9. Dönitz, *Memoirs*, 342.
10. Padfield, *Dönitz*, 284.
11. Padfield, 288, 495; Lieutenant Commander S. M. Ritchie, "The Effectiveness of the Leadership of Admiral Karl Dönitz," *Geddes Papers* (2003), 40.
12. Clay Blair, *Hitler's U-Boat War: The Hunted, 1942–1943* (London: Random House, 1998), 353.
13. Essay by Grand Admiral Dönitz on the war at sea, September 24, 1945, TNA: ADM 223/688.
14. Essay by Grand Admiral Dönitz on the war at sea, September 24, 1945, TNA: ADM 223/688.
15. Dönitz, *Memoirs*, 347–51.
16. Dönitz memorandum to Hitler, presented at the Führer Naval Conference, April 11, 1943, in Showell, *Führer Conferences*, 318–19.
17. Entry for June 3, 1943, *Kriegstagebuch der Seekriegsleitung* (hereafter *KTB der SKL*) (translation), Part A, vol. 46 (Washington: Naval History Division, 1948), 25, U.S. Naval War College Archives.
18. Entry for October 5, 1943, *KTB der SKL*, Teil A, Band 50, October 1943 (Berlin: E. S. Mittler & Sohn, 1994), 82–83.
19. Entry for October 25, 1943, *KTB der SKL*, Teil A, Band 50, October 1943, 508–11.
20. See table detailing number of boats in service January 16–31, 1942, *KTB 2nd S-Boat Flotilla*, January 1942, RG242, T1022, roll 3126, NARA.
21. See Schulze-Wegener, *Die deutsche Kriegsmarine-Rüstung*, 173–74, 167.
22. Report by FdS to Group West, May 25, 1944, in *E-Boat Operations and Policy*, TNA: ADM 223/28.
23. The yard was founded in 1898 by Johannes Schlichting (1872–1946). See Eike Lehmann, *100 Jahre Schiffbautechnische Gesellschaft: Biografien zur Geschichte des Schiffbaus* (Berlin: Springer, 1999), 432–33.
24. Report by FdS to Group West, May 25, 1942, in *E-Boat Operations and Policy*, TNA: ADM 223/28.
25. Report by FdS to Group West, May 25, 1942, in *E-Boat Operations and Policy*, TNA: ADM 223/28.
26. Entry for October 18, 1942, *KTB der SKL*, Teil A, Band 38, 359–62.
27. Report by FdS to Group West, December 31, 1943, in *E-Boat Operations and Policy*, TNA: ADM 223/28.
28. Rudolf Schlichting Diary, December 16–18, 1943, Archiv Peter Schlichting. My thanks to Peter Schlichting for this.
29. Information from Marcus Schlichting, February 12, 2012.
30. Schulze-Wegener, *Die deutsche Kriegsmarine-Rüstung*, 173–74.
31. "The Attack on the *Tirpitz* by Midget Submarines on 22 September 1943, Dispatch submitted to the Admiralty, 8 November 1943, by Rear Admiral C. B. Barry," *Supplement to the London Gazette*, February 11, 1948, 993–1008. See also Ultra decrypts relating to Operation Source in TNA: HW 1/2036, 2039 and 2041.

32. *"Tirpitz* Hit in Fjord Raid—Gallant Midget Submarines," *The Times*, October 12, 1943, 4.
33. C. D. Bekker, *Swastika at Sea: The Struggle and Destruction of the German Navy, 1939–1945* (London: William Kimber, 1953), 137. Bartels (July 5, 1910–July 31, 1945) had been granted the Knight's Cross of the Iron Cross on May 16 for his conduct in the Norwegian campaign as commander of Minesweeper M-1. Later he took on the responsibility of developing local forces, usually involving trawlers, to defend the coast. His success in improvising such forces brought him to the attention of higher command.
34. C. D. Bekker, *K-Men: The Story of the German Frogmen and Midget Submarines* (Maidstone: George Mann, 1968), 21–22.
35. Report by FdS to Group West, November 1943, in *E-Boat Operations and Policy*, TNA: ADM 223/28. Rudolf Petersen (June 15, 1905–January 2, 1983) entered the navy in November 1925 as a cadet; he reached the rank of Leutnant-zur-See (October 1, 1929), then Oberleutnant-zur-See (July 1, 1931), then Kapitänleutnant (September 1, 1935). He was then appointed head of 2nd S-Boat Flotilla (August 12, 1938–October 19, 1941), Korvettenkapitän (January 1, 1940), FdS (April 20, 1942–July 22, 1945), Fregattenkapitän (March 1, 1943), Kapitän-zur-See (March 1, 1944), and Kommodore (September 23, 1944). He received the Iron Cross 2nd Class in 1939 and First Class in 1940, the Knight's Cross of the Iron Cross in 1940 (with Oak Leaves in 1944), and the Fast Attack Craft War Badge 1942 (with Diamonds in 1944). He was in captivity on July 22, 1945, and released later that year.

## CHAPTER 6. THE 1943 TURNING POINT: THE EMERGENCE OF A MULTILAYERED SYSTEM OF DEFENSE

1. Ulrich Kolbe, private family memoir, 1997–98.
2. C-in-C Nore to Admiralty, December 30, 1942, TNA: ADM 1/15815.
3. HMS *Walpole*, HMS *Montrose*, HMS *Mackay*, HMS *Wivern*, HMS *Worcester*, HMS *Windsor*, HMS *Whitshed*, and HMS *Campbell*.
4. Report by Commanding Officer HMS *Walpole* enclosure 1 in Actions against E-boats on December 22–23, 1944: Recommendations for Honours and Awards, March 1, 1945, TNA: ADM 1/30193.
5. C-in-C Nore to Secretary of the Admiralty, October 16, 1943, TNA: ADM 1/15815.
6. *Introduction to Naval Gunnery (BR224)* (London: Training Department, Admiralty, 1960), 29, 100–101.
7. Führer der Schnellboote (hereafter FdS) war diary, April 22, 1942, TNA: ADM 223/28.
8. J. Lennox Kerr and Wilfrid Granville, *The RNVR: A Record of Achievement* (London: George H. Harrap & Co., 1957), 192.
9. Reynolds, *Home Waters MTBs and MGBs*, 46.
10. B. H. S., "Review of *We Fought Them in Gunboats*," *Naval Review* 32, no. 2 (May 1944): 169–70.
11. See, for example, the shooting up of MGB89 and the death of Lt. S. B. Bennett, RNVR, entry for April 20, 1942, War Diary 7th MGB Flotilla (HMS *Mantis*), Suffolk Record Office (Lowestoft) 1678/1.
12. Hichens, *We Fought Them in Gunboats*, 12.
13. Dudley Pope, *Flag 4: The Battle of Coastal Forces in the Mediterranean* (London: William Kimber, 1954), 31.
14. Pope, *Flag 4*, 35.
15. Bryan Cooper, *The Battle of the Torpedo Boats* (London: Pan, 1970), 76–79.
16. P. G. C. Dickens, "Narrow Waters in War," *Journal of the Royal United Services Institute* 114 (March 1969): 42–45, quote on 42.

17. Peter Scott, Wartime BBC Broadcast, April 1943, http://www.coastal-forces.org.uk/peter_scott.mp3 (accessed April 29, 2021).
18. Mike Whitley, *Deutsche Seestreitkräfte, 1939–1945: Einsatz im Küstenvorfeld* (Stuttgart: Motorbuch Verlag, 1995), 53.
19. S. W. Roskill, *The War at Sea, 1939–45* (London: HMSO, 1954), 1:500–501.
20. Scott, *Narrow Seas*, 36–37; Williamson, *E-Boat vs MTB*, 48.
21. "British Rout Nazis in North Sea Fight," *New York Times*, November 22, 1941, 5.
22. David Jefferson, *Coastal Forces at War: The Royal Navy's "Little Ships" in the Narrow Seas* (Sparkford, U.K.: Haynes, 2008), 153.
23. Hewitt, *Coastal Convoys*, 169. See also Charles Parham, Served MGBs and MTBs (Channel) 1943–45, Imperial War Museum Audio Interview 10719, 1989.
24. The forts were at the Nore, Red Sands, Shivering Sands, Tongue Sands, Knock John, Rough Sands, and Sunk Head. Frank R. Turner, *The Maunsell Sea Forts* (Gravesend: F. R. Turner, 1997).
25. Anthony Firth, *East Coast War Channels in the First and Second World Wars: A Report for English Heritage* (Salisbury: Fjordr, 2014), fig. 14.
26. Paterson, *Schnellboote*, 152.
27. Roskill, *The War at Sea*, 2:162.
28. "7 German E-Boats Blasted by British," *New York Times*, March 16, 1942, 1, 3.
29. Entry for March 15, 1942, War Diary 7th MGB Flotilla (HMS *Mantis*), Suffolk Record Office (Lowestoft) 1678/1.
30. Hichens, *We Fought Them in Gunboats*, 69–70.
31. Peter Scott, *The Eye of the Wind* (London: Hodder & Stoughton, 1961), 449.
32. Robert Hichens, *Gunboat Commander: The Biography of Lieutenant Commander Robert Hichens DSO, DSC RNVR* (Barnsley, U.K.: Pen & Sword, 2008), 289.
33. Scott, *Eye of the Wind*, 433. Official Admiralty Communique No. 826, April 13, 1943, announcing the death of Robert Hichens, is reproduced in Hichens, *We Fought Them in Gunboats*, 152.
34. Peter Scott, Wartime BBC Broadcast, April 1943, http://www.coastal-forces.org.uk/peter_scott.mp3 (accessed April 29, 2021).

### CHAPTER 7. THE 1943 TURNING POINT: THE ROLE OF INTELLIGENCE

1. See in particular John Winton, *Ultra at Sea* (London: Leo Cooper, 1988).
2. See minute by Admiralty Director of Plans, June 23, 1937, and following papers in TNA: ADM/111119.
3. See, for example, Vego's analysis of the British Command organization covering the English Channel and North Sea, which covers Coastal Forces but doesn't go into the role of the headquarters and the wider issue of sea control. Vego, "On Littoral Warfare," 47.
4. Patrick Beesly, *Very Special Intelligence: The Story of the Admiralty's Operational Intelligence Centre, 1939–1945* (London: Hamish Hamilton, 1977), 42.
5. Winton, *Ultra*, 3.
6. "Motor Torpedo Boats," Admiralty Weekly Intelligence Summary, June 20, 1940, 4–5; TNA: ADM 223/146.
7. "Motor Torpedo Boats," Admiralty Weekly Intelligence Summary, July 20, 1940, 5–7; TNA: ADM 223/147.
8. David Syrett, "The Infrastructure of Communications Intelligence: The Allied D/F Network and the Battle of the Atlantic," *Intelligence and National Security* 17, no. 3 (2002): 163–72.

9. "E-Boats in the Mediterranean," TNA: ADM 223/610 and TNA: ADM 223/611.
10. See "E-Boats in the Mediterranean," TNA: ADM 223/611.
11. Translated B-dienst Report Number 42 (1942) for October 12–19, 1942, TNA: HW 40/154.
12. Translated B-dienst Report Number 42 (1942) for October 12–19, 1942, TNA: HW 40/154. SS *Lysland* was towed to Immingham. *George Balfour* was towed to Yarmouth in two halves. See Foynes, *Battle of the East Coast*, 301.
13. F. H. Hinsley, *British Intelligence in the Second World War*, vol. 3, part 2 (London: HMSO, 1988), 453–54.
14. "Receipt of Special Intelligence in the Admiralty and Its Dissemination in the German Surface Units Section," TNA: ADM 223/209, 8; Hinsley, *Intelligence*, 454.
15. Hinsley, *Intelligence*, 454. See also Ultra decrypts July 1944, TNA: ADM 223/200.
16. Hinsley, *Intelligence*, 456.
17. Simona Tobia, "Invisible Violences, Interrogation and Representation in Post-war Germany," in *Liberal Democracies at War: Conflict and Representation*, ed. Andrew Knapp and Hilary Footitt (London: Bloomsbury, 2013), 118; Kent Fedorowich, "Axis Prisoners of War as Sources for British Military Intelligence, 1939–42," *Intelligence and National Security* 14, no. 2 (June 1991): 156–78.
18. See German E-Boat S-38 Interrogation of Survivors, February 1941, TNA: ADM 186/806.
19. "The Secrets of the London Cage," *The Guardian*, November 12, 2005, http://www.theguardian.com/uk/2005/nov/12/secondworldwar.world.
20. See German E-Boat S-53 Interrogation of Survivors, March 1942, TNA: ADM 186/807. See also undated report on interrogation of survivors from S-53, TNA: WO 208/3243.
21. The different accounts come from two members of the same boarding party. See A. G. F. Ditcham, *A Home on the Rolling Main: A Naval Memoir* (Barnsley, U.K.: Seaforth, 2012), 91–92; and commentary on the loss of S-53 derived from David R. on Die Schnellboot-Seite, http://s-boot.net/englisch/sboats-km-channel42.html (accessed July 14, 2022).
22. Maschinemaat Helmut Reimann.
23. See German E-Boat S-111 Interrogation of Survivors, March 1942, TNA: ADM 186/807.
24. Hichens, *We Fought Them in Gunboats*, 27.
25. Ulrich Kolbe, private family memoir, 1997–98.
26. Admiralty, *Light Coastal Craft Operating in the North Sea and English Channel* (BR834) (London: Admiralty, 1941).
27. See German E-Boat S-96 Interrogation of Survivors, November 1943, TNA: ADM 186/808.
28. See German E-Boat S-96 Interrogation of Survivors, November 1943, TNA: ADM 186/808.
29. Appendix B, German E-Boat S-96 Interrogation of Survivors, November 1943, TNA: ADM 186/808.
30. See German E-Boat S-88 Interrogation of Survivors, December 1943, TNA: ADM 186/808.
31. See German E-Boat S-141 and S-147 Interrogation of Survivors, July 1944, TNA: ADM 186/809.
32. See German E-Boat S-141 and S-147 Interrogation of Survivors, July 1944, TNA: ADM 186/809.
33. See German E-Boat S-141 and S-147 Interrogation of Survivors, July 1944, TNA: ADM 186/809.

34. See German E-Boat S-141 and S-147 Interrogation of Survivors, July 1944, TNA: ADM 186/809.
35. Beesly, *Very Special Intelligence*, 51.
36. Conversation with Captain Tony McCrum, signals officer HMS *Mendip* (East Coast 1941), Britannia Royal Naval College, December 11, 2015; McCrum, *Sunk by Stukas*, 98. During one engagement (presumably the attack on an East Coast convoy on February 19, 1942) the "headache operator" on board HMS *Mendip* confirmed that an S-boat had fired and "target is us." A similar incident took place on board HMS *Westminster* when one of the headache operators heard an S-boat request permission to launch torpedoes toward them. Michael Baron, HMS *Westminster* (Channel) 1942–43, Imperial War Museum Interview 34088, 2014.
37. FdS Memorandum on Torpedo Attacks, January 20, 1943, TNA: ADM 223/28.
38. Control Frigate and Coastal Force Action with E-boats, September 18–19, 1944, October 14, 1944, TNA: ADM 1/29955.
39. Enclosure 10 in Actions against E-boats on December 22–23, 1944: Recommendations for Honours and Awards, March 1, 1945, TNA: ADM 1/30193. See also Headache Intercepts by HMS *Curzon*, December 22, 1944, in Report of Action with Enemy E-boats in North Sea off the Netherlands Coast, night of December 12–23, 1944, C-in-C Nore War Diary, RG 38, A1823, NARA.
40. Hewitt, *Coastal Convoys*, 168.
41. Hewitt, *Coastal Convoys*, 152.
42. Alan Peacock, *The Enigmatic Sailor* (Caithness: Whittles, 2003), 19.
43. Jenny Nater, *Secret Duties of a Signals Interceptor: Working with Bletchley Park, the SDS and the OSS* (Barnsley, U.K.: Pen & Sword, 2016), 35.
44. Christian Lamb, *I Only Joined for the Hat: Redoubtable Wrens at War—Their Trials, Tribulations and Triumphs* (Malta: Bene Factum, 2007), 131.
45. Bush, *Bless Our Ship*, 198.
46. Hilda Hale interview, WREN, BBC People's War Website, A3130183, October 14, 2004, http://www.bbc.co.uk/history/ww2peopleswar/stories/83/a3130183.shtml.
47. Dickens, *Night Action*, 29.
48. See testimony of Derek Wellman (HMS *Onslow*) in Roderick Bailey, *Forgotten Voices of D-Day: A New History of the Normandy Landings* (London: Ebury, 2010), 51–52.
49. Jefferson, *Coastal Forces*, 164; Dickens, *Night Action*, 29–30; conversation with Captain Tony McCrum, signals officer HMS *Mendip* (East Coast 1941), Britannia Royal Naval College, December 11, 2015. During one engagement (presumably the attack on an East Coast convoy on February 19, 1942) the headache operator on board HMS *Mendip* confirmed that an S-boat had fired and "target is us."
50. McCrum, *Sunk by Stukas*, 99.
51. Michael Baron, HMS *Westminster* (Channel) 1942–43, Imperial War Museum Interview 34088, 2014.
52. Christopher Dreyer, Staff Officer Operations Division and to Captain Coastal Forces (Channel), Imperial War Museum Audio Interview 8984, 1985 (hereafter Dreyer interview, IWM 8984).
53. Hinsley, *Intelligence*, 454. See also use of Special Intelligence during Operation Neptune, TNA: ADM 223/267, 166.
54. *Bawdsey and the Development of Radar* (Felixstowe: Bawdsey Radar Trust, n.d.); Gordon Kinsey, *Bawdsey: Birth of the Beam. The History of RAF Stations Bawdsey and Woodbridge* (Lavenham: Lavenham Press, 1983).

55. Minute by Director of Local Defence, January 14, 1943, on file "C-in-C Nore: Proposed Alterations to Searched Channels," TNA: ADM 1/15815.
56. Minute by Director of Local Defence, January 14, 1943, on file "C-in-C Nore: Proposed Alterations to Searched Channels," TNA: ADM 1/15815.
57. The calculations assume (given the distance between radar site and war channel and S-boats launching torpedoes at more than five hundred yards) an effective radar range of fifteen miles between a convoy and an attacking force.
58. "Coastal Force Action of Night of 15–16 April 1943," April 25, 1943, reproduced in Peter Scott, *Eye of the Wind*, 434–36.
59. Original proposal in C-in-C Nore to Admiralty, December 29, 1942, TNA: ADM 1/15815. Confirmation in Herbert Morrison to C-in-C Nore, February 12, 1943, TNA: ADM 1/15815.
60. Vego, *Naval Strategy*, 39.
61. C-in-C Nore to Secretary of the Admiralty, October 16, 1943, TNA: ADM 1/15815.
62. Plymouth Command War Diary, July 2, 1943, TNA: ADM 199/656.
63. Historical Section Admiralty, *The Defeat of the Enemy Attack on Shipping*, 198.
64. Williamson, *E-Boat vs MTB*, 53.
65. Recommendation for immediate award Leading Seamen Edward Dowdall (radar), December 28, 1944, enclosure in Actions against E-boats on December 22–23, 1944: Recommendations for Honours and Awards, March 1, 1945, TNA: ADM 1/30193. Interestingly, FdS estimated the maximum range of ship-based radar at five miles in a report dated December 31, 1943. See FdS Observations on S-Boat Operations in the West during 1943, TNA: ADM 223/28.
66. Rob White 2014 interview with Lieutenant A. G. F. Ditcham, officer HMS *Holderness* (East Coast, 1941–42), privately held.
67. Prior to preparations for the D-Day landings, ship-to-ship vectoring does not appear to have been practiced very frequently; such was the perceived effectiveness of shore-based radar vectoring. This changed with the necessity of operations on the far shore of the narrow sea, with coastal units operating with heavier vessels to form anti-S-boat screens for the invasion fleet. Dreyer interview, IWM 8984.
68. See Donald Collingwood, *The Captain Class Frigates in the Second World War* (London: Leo Cooper, 1998).
69. HMS *Duff* K352, HMS *Riou* K557, HMS *Retalick* K555, HMS *Seymour* K563, HMS *Stayner* K573, HMS *Thornborough* K574, HMS *Torrington* K577, and HMS *Trollope* K575.
70. "Radio Equipment in Coastal Craft," Admiralty Signal Establishment Bulletin (Confidential), September 1944, 76, Museum of Royal Navy Radar and Communications (HMS Collingwood). See also T. Garth Connelly, *Vosper MTBs in action: Warships No. 13* (Ellijay, GA: Squadron-Signal Publications, 2000), 11, 18.
71. Derek Tolfree, Served HMS *Westminster* (Channel) 1942–45, Imperial War Museum Interview 31411, 2008.
72. Historical Section Admiralty, *The Defeat of the Enemy Attack on Shipping*, 196.
73. Williamson, *German E-Boats*, 33.
74. Chris Ashworth, *RAF Coastal Command: 1936–1969* (Sparkford, U.K.: Patrick Stephens, 1992), 66. Interestingly, the development of ASV eventually led to the abandonment of an airborne warning system that was the forerunner of the modern AWACs system. Vickers Wellington R1629 was fitted with a rotating antenna array. The intention was to use the aircraft over the northwestern approaches to give warning of Focke Wulf 200

maritime reconnaissance aircraft. R1629 was also trialed in an anti-S-boat role in May 1942. The success of ASV led the project to be discontinued, and on September 24, 1943, R1629 was written off after a crash with Wellington R1412 at Bramcote.
75. Report by *Führer der Torpedoboote* (hereafter FdT), December 1941, TNA: ADM 223/28.
76. Andrew Hendrie, *The Cinderella Service: Coastal Command, 1939–1945* (London: Leo Cooper, 2006), 174.
77. Hewitt, *Coastal Convoys*, 152. See TNA: AIR 15/122.
78. Air Commodore J. Constable-Roberts Papers, Imperial War Museum Documents 1183.
79. Minute by Director of Air Warfare and Flying Training, May 11, 1943, TNA: ADM 1/15815.
80. George McCracken Rutherford, 841 Squadron Fleet Air Arm, Imperial War Museum Audio Interview 12345, November 20, 1991.
81. Minute by Director of Air Warfare and Flying Training, May 11, 1943, TNA: ADM 1/15815.
82. Dennis Haslop, *Britain, Germany and the Battle of the Atlantic: A Comparative Study* (London: Bloomsbury, 2013).
83. "Radio Equipment in Coastal Craft," Admiralty Signal Establishment Bulletin (Confidential), September 1944, p. 78, Museum of Royal Navy Radar and Communications (HMS *Collingwood*).
84. Ida Steadman, WREN plotter Coastal Forces Base (Dartmouth), Imperial War Museum Audio Interview 27211, 2004.
85. Dreyer interview, IWM 8984.
86. C-in-C Nore to Admiralty, October 16, 1943, TNA: ADM 1/15815.
87. C-in-C Rosyth to Admiralty, June 16, 1943, TNA: ADM 1/15815.
88. FdS Observations on S-Boat Operations in the West during 1943, December 31, 1943, TNA: ADM 223/28.
89. Captain (Destroyers) to C-in-C Rosyth, June 13, 1943, TNA: ADM 1/15815.
90. C-in-C Nore to Secretary of the Admiralty, October 16, 1943, TNA: ADM 1/15815.
91. C-in-C Portsmouth to Admiralty, November 14, 1943, in E-boat Attack on Convoy CW211 on November 3, 1943: Complaints from Merchant Navy Personnel, TNA: ADM 1/15815.
92. Destroyers: HMS *Worcester*, HMS *Mackay*, HMS *Eglinton*, HMS *Campbell*. MTBs: 438, 440, 443, 444, 445, 689, 693. MLs: 112, 114, 250, 517. MGBs: 85, 86, 313, 327, 603, 607, 609, 610. See Admiral Sir John Tovey to the Admiralty, November 18, 1943, "Destroyer and Coastal Force Action with E-Boats on Night of 24/25th October 1943," published in *Supplement to the London Gazette*, October 15, 1948, 5500–5505.
93. Minute on file "East Coast Convoys: Protection against E-Boat Attack," November 1, 1943, Minute on file "Destroyer Reinforcements for Plymouth and Other Home Commands, 6 November 1943," TNA: ADM 1/15815.
94. Director Trade Division, November 28, 1943, TNA: ADM 1/15815.
95. Admiralty to C-in-C, Nore, Rosyth, and Portsmouth, November 25, 1943, TNA: ADM 1/15815.
96. C-in-C Nore to Admiralty, November 27, 1943, TNA: ADM 1/15815.
97. W. Stephens (Trade Division), November 15, 1943, TNA: ADM 1/15815.
98. Scott, *Narrow Seas*, 9.
99. On June 8–9, USS *Frankford* engaged S-boats using airbursts to keep them at bay. Roscoe, *United States Destroyer Operations*, 359.
100. Tovey, "Coastal Force Actions," 5505.

## CHAPTER 8. THE 1943 TURNING POINT: GERMAN FAILURE TO RESPOND EFFECTIVELY

1. See Die Schnellboot-Seite, http://s-boot.net/sboats-kriegsmarine-sbb.html (accessed March 9, 2016).
2. *KTB der SB West*, May 1, 1942, RG242, T1022, roll 3974, NARA.
3. Report by FdT, December 1941, TNA: ADM 223/28.
4. Report by FdS to Group West, May 25, 1942, TNA: ADM 223/28.
5. Baart, *Schnellboote*, 198; Hümmelchen, *Die deutsche Schnellboote*, 76.
6. Angus Konstam, *British Motor Gunboat, 1939–45* (New York: Osprey, 2010), 44, incorrectly lists this boat as scuttled by the British. Jak Mallmann Showell, *German Naval Code Breakers* (Hersham, U.K.: Ian Allan, 2003), 59, places this incident in 1940. See entry for September 11, 1942, *KTB der SKL*, Teil A, Band 37, 229; Remarks by FdS after Inspection of MGB 663, *E-Boat Operations and Policy*, TNA: ADM 223/28.
7. Showell, *German Naval Code Breakers*, 59.
8. Remarks by FdS after Inspection of MGB 335, TNA: ADM 223/28. See also "Report on Weapons Found aboard Captured English Speedboat," August 12, 1944, BArch, RM 45-II/227.
9. Report by FdS to Group West, May 25, 1942, in Tactical and Staff Duties Division (Foreign Documents Section), TNA: ADM 223/28.
10. FdS War Diary, September 10, 1942, TNA: ADM 223/28.
11. The G7a in use for U-boats had three settings, which allowed for variation in its range and speed. The three settings were 5,500 yards at 44 knots; 8,200 at 40 knots; and 13,700 at 30 knots. *Technical Staff Monographs, 1939–45: German Torpedoes and Development of German Torpedo Control*, BR.1972 (London: Admiralty, Underwater Weapons Department, 1952). 4.
12. *Technical Staff Monographs*, 3–4.
13. Entries for October 30 and 31, 1942, *KTB der SKL*, Teil A, Band 38, 645–46, 665–66.
14. Admiralty to Home and Mediterranean Stations, July 13, 1944, E-Boats in the Mediterranean, TNA: ADM 223/611.
15. Underwater Weapons Department (Admiralty), German Torpedo Documents, TNA: ADM 292/204.
16. Interestingly, in 1944 a further evolution of the S-boat design was developed. The S-700 class would feature the addition of a forward-firing 3-cm cannon and additional, aft-facing torpedo tubes to target any pursuing vessel. Although the hulls of several vessels were completed before the end of the war shortages meant that they would be finished to the S-100 specification.
17. S. O. Sichel to Speer, May 15, 1944, E-Boats in the Mediterranean, TNA: ADM 223/611.
18. Speer to Operations Group South, May 1, 1944, E-Boats in the Mediterranean, TNA: ADM 223/611.
19. *Technical Staff Monographs*, 23–24.
20. *Nauticus: Jahrbuch Deutschlands Seeinteressen* (Berlin: E. S. Mittler & Sohn, 1944), 71.
21. Scott report on Müller interview, Peter Scott Papers, Cambridge University Library (hereafter Scott Papers), NCUACS 87.8.99/B.31.
22. There were trials in 1944 to see whether S-boats could be rendered invisible to Allied radar using rubberized coatings (*Tarnmatte*).
23. Paterson, *Schnellboote*, 266.
24. Ulrich Kolbe, private family memoir, 1997–98.
25. Derek Tolfree, served HMS *Westminster* (Channel) 1942–45, 31411, 2008.

26. Frank, *German S-Boats*, 53.
27. FdS Memorandum on Torpedo Attacks, January 20, 1943, TNA: ADM 223/28.
28. Marcus Faulkner, "The Kriegsmarine, Signals Intelligence and the Development of the B-dienst before the Second World War," *Intelligence and National Security* 25, no. 4 (August 2010): 521–46.
29. Showell, *German Naval Code Breakers*, 59.
30. FdS War Diary, February 7, 1941, TNA: ADM 223/28.
31. Appreciation of the Situation by FdT, July 5, 1940, TNA: ADM 223/28.
32. See Neitzel, "Kriegsmarine and Luftwaffe Co-operation in the War." See also Sönke Neitzel, *Der Luftkrieg über dem Nordatlantik und der Nordsee, 1939–1945* (Bonn: Bernard & Graefe, 1995); Sönke Neitzel, "Die Zusammenarbeit zwischen Schnellbooten und Luftwaffe," *Militärgeschichte* 4 (1995): 55–63.
33. FdS Observations on S-boat Operations in the West during 1943, December 31, 1943, TNA: ADM 223/28.
34. Report by FdS, October 1942, TNA: ADM 223/28.
35. Report by FdS, April 19, 1943, TNA: ADM 223/28.
36. See, for example, FdS War Diary, April 23, 1942, TNA: ADM 223/28.
37. Note by FdS on Enemy Air Attacks, May 30, 1943, TNA: ADM 223/28.
38. See, for example, Speer to Operations Group South, May 1, 1944, "E-Boats in the Mediterranean," TNA: ADM 223/611.
39. Designs such as the BV40, HE162, HO229, FW Ta 154.
40. Leonard Reynolds, *Dog Boats at War: A History of the Operations of the Royal Navy D Class Fairmile Motor Torpedo Boats and Motor Gunboats, 1939–1945* (Stroud, U.K.: Sutton, 1998), 251.
41. Reynolds, *Dog Boats at War*, 251.
42. After Action Report by Lieutenant T. W. Boyd, May 29, 1943, TNA: PRO ADM 1/14391.
43. Report by FdT, December 1941, TNA: ADM 223/28.
44. Report by FdT, December 1941, TNA: ADM 223/28.
45. Cyril Hurcomb (Permanent Under Secretary at Ministry of War Transport) to Rear Admiral J. H. Edelsten (Assistant Chief Naval Staff), November 19, 1943, TNA: ADM 1/15815.
46. Cyril Hurcomb (Permanent Under Secretary at Ministry of War Transport) to Rear Admiral J. H. Edelsten (Assistant Chief Naval Staff), November 19, 1943, TNA: ADM 1/15815.
47. Defensive Minelaying Policy in Home Waters, TNA: ADM 1/15815.
48. One comment on the proposal (signature unreadable) stated, "It is likely that were every British mine in Home Waters to self-detonate to-night, we should find this less disadvantageous than their presence in the not too far distant future," July 21, 1943, TNA: ADM 1/15815.
49. The 2nd and 6th Flotillas were at Ijmuiden and the 4th and 8th Flotillas at Rotterdam.
50. Whitley, *Deutsche Seestreitkräfte*, 65.
51. Scott, *Narrow Seas*, 170.
52. Lieutenant J. O. Thomas to Peter Scott, October 22, 1943, Scott Papers, NCUACS 87.8.99/B.32. See also interview with Lieutenant J. Thomas and Lieutenant Seddon, September 28, 1943, Scott Papers, NCUACS 87.8.99/B.63.
53. Paterson, *Schnellboote*, 272.
54. Eric H. Whitehead, "MLs versus E-Boats," *Coastal Forces Veterans Association Newsletter* 122 (June 2005): 20.

55. Paterson, *Schnellboote*, 272.
56. "Nazi Trickery in Naval Clash," *Birmingham Post*, September 28, 1943, 3.
57. See maps in Report on Coastal Forces Action on Night of October 24–25, 1943, Commanding Officer HMS *Midge* to C-in-C Nore, October 28, 1943, TNA: ADM 1/3716.
58. Whitley, *Deutsche Seestreitkräfte*, 65.
59. Admiral Sir John Tovey to Their Lords Commissioners of the Admiralty, November 18, 1943, incorporated and published in "Coastal Force Actions," *Supplement to the London Gazette*, October 15, 1943, 5493–5523.
60. Report on Coastal Forces Action on Night of October 24–25, 1943, Commanding Officer HMS *Midge* to C-in-C Nore, October 28, 1943, TNA: ADM 1/3716.
61. Report on MGB 603 (radar) and MGB 609 (hydrophones) contained as enclosures to report on Coastal Forces Action on Night of October 24–25, 1943, Commanding Officer HMS *Midge* to C-in-C Nore, October 28, 1943, TNA: ADM 1/3716.
62. For German accounts of the action, see KTB entry for October 24, 1943, TNA: ADM 223/28.
63. Bryan Cooper, *The War of the Gun Boats* (Barnsley, U.K.: Pen & Sword, 2009), 170.
64. Reynolds, *Dog Boats at War*, 87–88.
65. Report to Commanding Officer HMS *Midge* from Commander MGB609 on Night Action of October 24–25, 1943, October 27, 1943, TNA: ADM 1/3716.
66. Whitley, *Deutsche Seestreitkräfte*, 66.
67. SS *Firelight* and MV *British Progress* were the two merchant ships damaged in the attack.
68. Paterson, *Schnellboote*, 276.
69. Paterson, 277.
70. Whitley, *Deutsche Seestreitkräfte*, 68.

## CHAPTER 9. S-BOATS AND THE SHIFT TO THE DEFENSIVE

1. Ulrich Kolbe, private family memoir, 1997–98.
2. Ulrich Kolbe, private family memoir, 1997–98.
3. See Thaddeus Holt, *The Deceivers: Allied Military Deception in the Second World War* (New York: Scribner, 2004); Roger Hesketh, *Fortitude: The D-Day Deception Campaign* (New York: Peter Mayer, 2002); Anthony Cave Brown, *Bodyguard of Lies* (London: W. H. Allen & Co., 1977); Michael Howard, *British Intelligence in the Second World War*, vol. 5 (London: HMSO, 1990); C. Bickell, "Operation Fortitude South: An Analysis of Its Influence upon German Dispositions and Conduct of Operations in 1944," *War and Society* 18, no. 1 (2000): 91–122; "Operation Fortitude: Cover and Deception Policy in North-West Europe," April–May 1944, TNA: WO 205/173; "Plan 'Fortitude': Fortitude South II, Section I—Preparation," June–August 1944, TNA: WO 219/2224; "Plan 'Fortitude': Fortitude South II, Section II—Implementation," July–September 1944, TNA: WO 219/2226.
4. In November 1943 it was estimated that deliveries of coal under the Bolero plan were three weeks behind schedule. See Director Trade Division, November 28, 1943, TNA: ADM 1/15815.
5. Admiralty to Commanders-in-Chief, Nore, Rosyth and Portsmouth, November 25, 1943, TNA: ADM 1/15815.
6. Dönitz, *Memoirs*, 395.
7. Frank, *German S-Boats*, 150.

8. Historical Section Admiralty, *The Defeat of the Enemy Attack on Shipping*, 200; TNA: ADM 239/415.
9. Views on Morale in the Kriegsmarine of a German Naval Deserter recently arrived in Spain and set down by Assistant Naval Attache, May 7, 1944, OSS papers, https://www.cia.gov/library/readingroom/docs/CIA-RDP13X00001R000100270007-8.pdf (accessed May 31, 2020).
10. Memorandum for President Roosevelt by William Donovan (OSS), March 21, 1944, OSS Papers, https://www.cia.gov/library/readingroom/docs/CIA-RDP13 X00001R000100270007-8.pdf (accessed May 31, 2020).
11. Notes to Memorandum for President Roosevelt by William Donovan (OSS), March 21, 1944, OSS papers https://www.cia.gov/library/readingroom/docs/CIA-RDP13 X00001R000100270007-8.pdf (accessed May 31, 2020).
12. Hümmelchen, *Die deutsche Schnellboote*, 156–75; Whitley, *Deutsche Seestreitkräfte*, 69–72.
13. The recovered dead from those sinkings are buried in Penzance, Cornwall.
14. Report of Action Between LST Convoy and Enemy E-Boats, Night 4/27–28/1944 in the English Channel, COMLST GR32, RG 38, A1061, NARA.
15. See Nigel Lewis, "U.S. Exercise Tiger and the Overlord Cover Plan," *U.S. Military History Review* 7, no. 1 (April 2021): 31–50.
16. See 5th S-Boat Flotilla, *KTB und Anlagen* for April 1944, and 9th S-Boat Flotilla, *KTB und Anlagen* for April 1944, RG242, T1022, rolls 3211 and 3150, NARA, which show that the attack on the T-4 convoy was at the time considered a routine operation.
17. HMS *Onslow* report of action, May 2, 1944, TNA: ADM 199/261.
18. Total number of vessels involved in Exercise Tiger: 29 LST, 35 LCI, 82 LCT, 31 British LCT Mk4, 62 LCM, 4 LCG, 2 LCT (R), 4 LCF, 3 LCT (A), 5 LCT (5), 3 PC Escorts, 13 ML, 4 LCC Misc. Craft, 9 RHF, 3 APA, 2 DE, USS *Augusta*. War Diary, COM-LANCRAB, 11th PHIBFOR, April 26–28, 1944, RG 38, 0906, NARA.
19. LST Group 30 Logs, LST51, 133, 134, 157, 285, 286, 502 towing Rhino Ferries 4, 5, 7, 8, 9, 12, and 15, NARA, via Dennis Hogan.
20. PC1232/1233 Logs, NARA via Dennis Hogan. HMS *Onslow* report of action, May 2, 1944, TNA: ADM 199/261.
21. "The Invasion and the German Navy," interview with Admirals Dönitz and Wagner, July 20, 1945, RG 338, ETHINT 28, NARA.
22. Tent, *E-Boat Alert*, 63–74.
23. Note on E-boat Operations in the English Channel, January–May 1944, TNA: ADM 223/172.
24. See transcript of interview between CTF125 and Commanding Officer (HMS *Scimitar*), April 29, 1944; Naval Commander (Western Task Force) to Commander-in-Chief (Plymouth), May 1, 1944; Commander-in-Chief (Plymouth) to Naval Commander (Western Task Force), May 5, 1944 Com LST GR32, RG 38, A1061, NARA.
25. USS *Baldwin* (DD624), Action Report for Night of June 8–9, 1944, RG 38, A1091, NARA.
26. Entry for June 2, 1944, *KTB der SKL* (translation), Part A, vol. 58 (Washington: Naval History Division, 1958), 23, U.S. Naval War College Archives.
27. Essay by Grand Admiral Dönitz on the war at sea, September 24, 1945, TNA: ADM 223/688. Dönitz's recollections were also confirmed by Vice Admiral Hellmuth Heye; see essay by Heye on the war at sea, October 15, 1945, TNA: PRO ADM 223/690.
28. See, for example, entries for May 5 and 10, 1944, *KTB der SKL*, Teil A, Band 57, 69, 163.

29. John Frayn Turner, *Service Most Silent: The Navy's Fight against Enemy Mines* (Barnsley, U.K.: Pen & Sword, 2008), 165.
30. Entry for June 3, 1944, *KTB der SKL* (translation), Part A, vol. 58, 32.
31. Entry for June 3, 1944, *KTB der SKL* (translation), Part A, vol. 58, 38.
32. Entry for June 3, 1944, *KTB der SKL* (translation), Part A, vol. 58, 33.
33. Entry for June 4, 1944, *KTB der SKL* (translation), Part A, vol. 58, 52.
34. Entry for June 5, 1944, *KTB der SKL* (translation), Part A, vol. 58, 62.
35. Entry for June 6, 1944, *KTB der SKL* (translation), Part A, vol. 58, 72.
36. War Diary *Schnellboote* Command, June 1, 1944, *E-Boat Operations and Policy*, TNA: ADM 223/28.

## CHAPTER 10. D-DAY FOR THE KRIEGSMARINE

1. Morison, *History of United States Naval Operations*, 11:170–75.
2. Entry for June 6, 1944, *KTB der SKL* (translation), Part A, vol. 58, 79.
3. Report by the Naval Commander, Eastern Task Force, August 21, 1944, 16, Walter Beddell Smith Papers, Eisenhower Presidential Library.
4. Whitley, *Deutsche Seestreitkräfte*, 72–74.
5. Entry for June 6, 1944, *KTB der SKL* (translation), Part A, vol. 58, 81.
6. Entry for June 6, 1944, *KTB der SKL* (translation), Part A, vol. 58, 80.
7. Entry for June 6, 1944, *KTB der SKL* (translation), Part A, vol. 58, 85.
8. Lawrence Paterson, *Dönitz's Last Gamble: The Inshore U-Boat Campaign, 1944–45* (Barnsley, U.K.: Seaforth, 2008), 22.
9. Dönitz, *Memoirs*, 396.
10. "The Invasion and the German Navy," interview with Admirals Dönitz and Wagner, July 20, 1945, RG 338, ETHINT 28, NARA.
11. Smith, *Hold the Narrow Sea*, 227.
12. Liberation of Europe (Operation Overlord) Operations of Coastal Command, Royal Air Force, from May to August 1944, TNA: CAB106/1042. Published as supplement 38111 to the *London Gazette*, October 28, 1947, 5125–29.
13. Collingwood, *Captain Class Frigates*, 110.
14. Christopher Dreyer, Staff Officer Operations Division and to Captain Coastal Forces (Channel), Imperial War Museum Audio Interview 8984, 1985.
15. Hümmelchen, *Die deutsche Schnellboote*, 175.
16. Within five days of daily operations almost every boat in the 9th S-boat Flotilla required significant levels of repair and maintenance, ranging from engine overhaul and replacement to deck damage. Amid the purpose-built Cherbourg *Schnellboote* bunker, the maintenance and repair issues were dealt with speedily. See Kriegstagbuch Abschnitt Machine, June 1–June 10, 1944, RG242, T1022, roll 3150, NARA.
17. E-Boats and E-Boat Shelters (Le Havre)—Narrative, Leonard Cheshire Papers, International Bomber Command Centre (hereafter IBCC Digital Archive), https://ibccdigitalarchive.lincoln.ac.uk/omeka/collections/document/16529, MCheshireGL72021-181210-020009 (accessed May 25, 2021). See also Interpretation Report, Le Havre, provisional statement of damage, IBCC Digital Archive, https://ibccdigitalarchive.lincoln.ac.uk/omeka/collections/document/16530, MCheshireGL72021-181210-020010 (accessed May 25, 2021); and Extract from Bomber Command Summary of Operations, Le Havre E-boat Pens—Effect of 12,000 lb Bombs, IBCC Digital Archive, https://ibccdigitalarchive.lincoln.ac.uk/omeka/collections/document/16541 (accessed May 25, 2021).

18. Bruce Johnson, 115 Squadron RAF, diary entry for June 14, 1944, http://lancasterdiary .net/June%201944/june_14_1944.php (accessed January 26, 2012).
19. "RAF Blow at E-Boats and U-Boats," *Liverpool Echo*, June 15, 1943, 3.
20. V. E. Tarrant, *The Last Year of the Kriegsmarine: May 1944–May 1945* (London: Arms and Armour, 1994), 69. See also Hümmelchen, *Die deutsche Schnellboote*, 175–77.
21. R. F. Delderfield, "Confidential Report on the Recent Bombing of Le Havre," *Canadian Military History* 20, no. 4 (2011): 69–74.
22. USS *Baldwin* (DD624), Action Report for Night of June 8–9, 1944, RG38, A1091, NARA.
23. Entry for June 6, 1944, *KTB der SKL* (translation), Part A, vol. 58, 135.
24. War Diary *Schnellboote* Command, June 1, 1944, *E-Boat Operations and Policy*, TNA: ADM 223/28.
25. Tarrant, *Last Year*, 67.
26. G. H. Bennett and R. Bennett, *Hitler's Admirals* (Annapolis: Naval Institute Press, 2004), 200.
27. Blair, *Hitler's U-Boat War*, 2:601.
28. John Terraine, *Business in Great Waters: The U-Boat Wars, 1916–1945* (London: Leo Cooper, 1989), 646–47.
29. Peter Padfield, *War beneath the Seas: Submarine Conflict, 1939–45* (London: John Murray, 1995), 429.
30. Corelli Barnett, *Engage the Enemy More Closely: The Royal Navy in the Second World War* (London: Penguin, 2000), 832.
31. Führer der Schnellboote War Diary, June 10, 1944, translated and reproduced in Frank, *German S-Boats*, 112.
32. *Die Kriegsmarine*, August 1944, 2–3.
33. *Die Kriegsmarine*, August 1944, 4–5. See also *Die Kriegsmarine*, August 1944, 8–15.
34. The Schlichting family maintained a diary of significant mentions of *Schnellboote* activity, which allows some understanding of the reports reaching the German public. On June 8, 1944, they had heard reports that thirteen landing craft had been sunk during the invasion or on the nights following. On June 9, they heard that *Schnellboote* had the previous night accounted for one cruiser, two destroyers, and five landing ships. Entries for June 8 and 9, 1944, Press and Scrapbook, Archiv Peter Schlichting, Travemünde. In the monthly newsletter of the Schlichting work, Rudolf Schlichting referred to the "blood drenched soil of Normandy" and "thousands drowned" in the English Channel when their landing craft/ships were sunk. "Arbeitskameraden an der Front under in der Heimat!," June–July 1944, *Der Werftbote*, Archiv Peter Schlichting.
35. Essay by Grand Admiral Dönitz on the war at sea, September 24, 1945, TNA: ADM 223/688.
36. *Defeat of the Enemy Attack on Shipping, 1939–1945*, 201, TNA: ADM 239/415.
37. Steven J. Zaloga, *D-Day Fortifications in Normandy* (Oxford: Osprey, 2005), 14.
38. Essay by Admiral Krancke on the war at sea, October 2, 1945, TNA: ADM 223/689, 197–98.
39. Vice Admiral Friedrich Ruge, "The Invasion of Normandy," in Hans-Adolf Jacobsen and Juergen Rohwer, *Decisive Battles of World War II: The German View* (London: Andre Deutsch, 1965), 327.
40. Neitzel, *Der Luftkrieg*, 221–26. Neitzel cites a figure of 4,407 mines laid by the *Luftwaffe* in the Seine Bight between June 6 and July 26, 1944; see p. 225. See also Sönke Neitzel, "Zusammenarbeit," 55–63.

41. Commander, U.S. Naval Forces in Europe, *Administrative History of U.S. Naval Forces in Europe, 1940–1946* (London: U.S. Navy, 1946), 5:443. The precise date of first deployment of the new oyster mines is a matter of some conjecture; F. H. Hinsley argues that "the date has not been exactly determined." Hinsley, *Intelligence*, 165.
42. Review of the German Mining Campaign in the British Assault Area, October 16, 1944, TNA: ADM 219/392. See also Sönke Neitzel, "Kriegsmarine and Luftwaffe Co-operation in the War against Britain, 1939–1945," *War in History* 10, no. 4 (2003): 448–63.
43. *Defeat of the Enemy Attack on Shipping, 1939–1945*, 200, TNA: ADM 239/415.
44. Tarrant, *Last Year*, 68.
45. Peter Croft (6th Minesweeping Flotilla, June 6, 1944), BBC Peoples War Website, January 23, 2006, article ID8763159, http://www.bbc.co.uk/ww2peopleswar/stories/59/a8763159.shtml (accessed February 7, 2012).
46. Brendon A. Maher, *A Passage to Sword Beach: Minesweeping in the Royal Navy* (Annapolis: Naval Institute Press, 1996), 180–82. While using an X-Sweep in Dutch waters in 1945, Maher received shrapnel wounds to head and body because one of the grenades didn't properly drop from the sweep.
47. Commander, U.S. Naval Forces in Europe, *Administrative*, 443–44.
48. On the performance of the *Schnellboote* in the English Channel on June 6–14, see Hümmelchen, *Die deutsche Schnellboote*, 168–75; Mike Whitney, *Deutsche Seestreitskräfte, 1939–1945* (Stuttgart: Motorbuch Verlag, 1995), 72–74. See also Fuehrer der Schnellboote Kriegstagbuch und Anlagen, June 1944 (U.S. National Archives Microfilm Publications, T1022, roll 3146); Records of the German Naval High Command, 1935–1945, RG242.
49. For example, S-130 became the last *Schnellboote* to vacate the Cherbourg bunker, at 2330 hours on June 23. Its destination was St. Malo. See 9th Schnellbootsflotille, Kriegstagbuch, und Anlagen Entry for 2330 hours on June 23, 1944, RG242, T1022, roll 3871, NARA; Records of the German Naval High Command, 1935–1945, RG242. See also entry for June 23, 1944, *KTB der SKL*, Teil A, Band 58 (Berlin: E. S. Mittler & Sohn, 1995), 319–24.
50. Tent, *E-Boat Alert*, 208.
51. On the K-Verband see Paul Kemp, *Underwater Warriors* (Annapolis: Naval Institute Press, 1996); essay by Heye on the war at sea, October 15, 1945, TNA: ADM 223/690.
52. Dönitz, *Memoirs*, 396.
53. Foreword by Admiral Hellmuth Heye to Bekker, *K-Men*, 6.
54. The *Hydraboot* were built at Krögerwerft (Warnemünde and Stralsund); Gebrüder Engelbrecht (Köpenick); Lürssen (Vegesack); Danziger Waggonfabrik; Karl Mathan (Berlin); Robert Franz (Hamburg); Karl Vertens (Winning); Hamburger Werft, H. Heidtmann, and Hinr. von Cölln (Hamburg); and Schlichtingwerft (Travemünde).
55. General Major von Gersdorff (Staff Officer 15th Army in 1944), "A Critique of the Defense against the Invasion," late 1945, Walter Beddell Smith Papers, Eisenhower Presidential Library.
56. Führer Naval Conference, December 3, 1944, in Showell, *Führer Conferences*, 420.
57. Führer Naval Conference, January 3, 1945, in Showell, *Führer Conferences*, 425.
58. Essay by Grand Admiral Dönitz on the war at sea, September 24, 1945, TNA: ADM 223/688.
59. Dönitz, *Memoirs*, 397.
60. Ruge, "Invasion," 323.
61. Ruge, 321.

## CHAPTER 11. THE LONG RETREAT

1. Baart, *Schnellboote*, 205–7.
2. Frank, *German S-Boats*, 159.
3. Frank, 159–60.
4. Frank, 161.
5. Frank, 115.
6. "OKM Interrogation Report," 1945, TNA: ADM 219/230.
7. Paterson, *Dönitz's Last Gamble*, 23.
8. FdS war diary, September 5, 1944, TNA: ADM 223/28.
9. Entry for October 2, 1944, *KTB der SKL* (translation), Part A, vol. 62, 39.
10. Report No. 183 Historical Section Canadian Military Headquarters: Canadian Participation in the Operations in North West Europe 1944 (Part IV: First Canadian Army in the Pursuit (August 23–September 23), 166–84, http://www.cmp-cpm.forces.gc.ca/dhh-dhp/his/rep-rap/doc/cmhq/cmhq183.pdf (accessed March 4, 2016).
11. FdS war diary, September 17, 1944, TNA: ADM 223/28.
12. FdS war diary, September 17, 1944, TNA: ADM 223/28, suggests that tons of supplies were to be landed. Paterson, *Schnellboote*, 299, indicates that eight tons of supplies were in fact delivered.
13. Headache operator log in After Action Report, Commanding Officer MTB724, September 20, 1944, Scott Papers, NCUACS 87.8.99/B.31.
14. After Action Report, Commanding Officer MTB724, September 20, 1944, Scott Papers, NCUACS 87.8.99/B.31.
15. Entry for September 19, 1944, *KTB der SKL* (translation), Part B, vol. 61, 396.
16. Paterson (*Schnellboote*, 299) suggests that sixty-seven men were rescued.
17. Dreyer interview, IWM 8984. The other officer with Dreyer who interrogated Müller was Peter Scott.
18. Scott report on Müller interview, Scott Papers, NCUACS 87.8.99/B.31.
19. Scott notebook on Müller interview, Scott Papers, NCUACS 87.8.99/B.35.
20. Scott notebook on Müller interview, Scott Papers, NCUACS 87.8.99/B.35.
21. Scott notebook on Müller interview, Scott Papers, NCUACS 87.8.99/B.35.
22. Colin MacFadyen (Naval Staff to Peter Scott), November 15, 1944, Scott Papers, NCUACS 87.8.99/B.33. See also Scott to Lieutenant Commander Dunstan Curtis, November 20, 1944, Scott Papers, NCUACS 87.8.99/B.33.
23. Circulation list, undated, see also Scott to Lieutenant Commander Dunstan Curtis, November 20, 1944, Scott Papers, NCUACS 87.8.99/B.33.
24. Press division to Peter Scott, July 5, 1943, Scott Papers, NCUACS 87.8.99/B.32.
25. See file of correspondence in Scott Papers, NCUACS 87.8.99/B.32.
26. Karl Müller to Peter Scott, November 3, 1944, Scott Papers, NCUACS 87.8.99/B.32.
27. FdS war diary, September 18, 1944, TNA: ADM 223/28.
28. Entry for September 19, 1944, *KTB der SKL* (translation), Part B, vol. 61, 11.
29. See Report No. 184, Historical Section, Canadian Military Headquarters: Canadian Participation in the Operations in North West Europe 1944 (Part 5: Clearing the Channel Ports, September 3–February 6, 1945), 166–84, http://www.cmp-cpm.forces.gc.ca/dhh-dhp/his/rep-rap/doc/cmhq/cmhq184.pdf (accessed March 4, 2016).

(Previous chapter, continued)
62. Bekker, *Swastika at Sea*, 207.
63. Howard Grier, *Hitler, Dönitz and the Baltic Sea* (Annapolis: Naval Institute Press, 2007), 181.

30. Entry for October 5, 1944, *KTB der SKL* (translation), Part A, vol. 62, 93.
31. *KTB der SB West*, November 14, 1944, RG242, T1022, roll 4073, NARA.
32. Scott lecture notes, Summer 1944, Scott Papers, NCUACS 87.8.99/B.92–93.
33. Scott lecture notes, Summer 1944, Scott Papers, NCUACS 87.8.99/B.92.
34. FdS war diary, September 18, 1944, TNA: ADM 223/28.
35. Situation report by FdS, September 16, 1944, TNA: ADM 223/28.
36. "Co-operation between A/C and Surface Vessels in Attacks against E & R Boats in the North Sea and English Channel," 1945, TNA: AIR 15/390.
37. FdS war diary, September 30, 1944, TNA: ADM 223/28.
38. Richard Brooks, *Walcheren 1944: Storming Hitler's Fortress* (Oxford: Osprey, 2011), 90.
39. See Bernard Griffiths, *MacNamara's Band: The Story of HMS* Duff (Sutton, U.K.: Severn House, 1976).
40. 4th Flotilla (Ijmuiden), 3 operational boats; 10th Flotilla (Ijmuiden), 2 operational boats; 8th Flotilla (Rotterdam), 2 operational boats; 10th Flotilla (Rotterdam), 2 operational boats.
41. Major L. F. Ellis, *Victory in the West*, vol. 2: *The Defeat of Germany* (London: HMSO, 1968), 230.
42. "End of the E-Boat Menace?," *Liverpool Echo*, October 24, 1944, 3.
43. 10th Flotilla (Rotterdam), 3 operational boats; 8th Flotilla (Ijmuiden), 3 operational boats; 9th Flotilla (Rotterdam), 5 operational boats. The 4th Flotilla had proceeded to home waters via inland waterways on October 19.
44. Ellis, *Victory in the West*, 2:127.
45. FdS war diary, November 29, 1944, TNA: ADM 223/28.
46. FdS war diary, December 15, 1944, TNA: ADM 223/28.
47. See also Hümmelchen, *Die deutsche Schnellboote*, 198–208.
48. 2nd Flotilla (Den Helder), 7 boats operational (1 nonoperational); 4th Flotilla (Rotterdam), 4 boats operational (3 nonoperational); 6th Flotilla (Rotterdam), 6 boats operational (1 nonoperational); 8th Flotilla (Ijmuiden), 5 boats operational (2 nonoperational); 9th Flotilla (Rotterdam), 4 boats operational (4 nonoperational). FdS war diary, January 1, 1945, TNA: ADM 223/28.
49. Frank, *German S-Boats*, 163.
50. Historical Section Admiralty, *The Defeat of the Enemy Attack on Shipping*, 202.
51. Paterson, *Schnellboote*, 305–9.
52. C-in-C Nore War Diary, "Report of Action with Enemy E-Boats in the North Sea off the Netherlands, 17–18 March 1945" and "Report by Commanding Officer HMS *Riou*, 19 March 1945," RG 38, A1823, NARA.
53. Situation report, March 22, 1945, OKM Miscellaneous Documents, 1942–45 (hereafter *OKM Misc.*), April 8, 1945, RG242, T1022, roll 4082, NARA.
54. No. 236 Squadron, Record of Events, TNA: AIR 27/1449/30.
55. FdS war diary, March 21, 1945, TNA: ADM 223/28.
56. FdS war diary, March 23, 1944, TNA: ADM 223/28; Situation report, March 23, 1945, *OKM Misc.*, RG242, T1022, roll 4082, NARA.
57. Ellis, *Victory in the West*, 2:233.
58. Ellis, 2:233.
59. Marine Nachrichten Dienst (Berlin), *OKM Misc.*, April 8, 1945, RG242, T1022, roll 4082, NARA.
60. Marine Nachrichten Dienst (Berlin), *OKM Misc.*, April 8, 1945, RG242, T1022, roll 4082, NARA.

61. Die Schnellboot-Seite, "S-Boats in the Kriegsmarine—Channel/North Sea 1945," http://www.s-boot.net/englisch/sboats-km-channel45.html (accessed July 1, 2021).
62. Marine Nachrichten Dienst, April 9, 1945, *OKM Misc.*, RG242, T1022, roll 4082, NARA.
63. Roderick Timms log, April 1945, 204, reproduced, along with other documentation relating to the incident, at http://www.rodericktimms.royalnavy.co.uk/the_nigh_of_7th__8th_april.html (accessed July 2, 2021).
64. "Wartime Memorabilia," http://www.rodericktimms.royalnavy.co.uk/war_trophies.html (accessed July 2, 2021).
65. C. D. Bekker, *Das Bildbuch der deutschen Kriegsmarine, 1939–1945* (Munich: Wilhelm Heyne Verlag, 1972), 237.
66. *Matrose* Fritz Wehrmann, age twenty-six (Leipzig); *Funker* Alfred Gail, age twenty (Kassel); *Obergefreiter* Martin Schilling, age twenty-two (Ostfriesland).
67. In the postwar period Petersen was tried three times for authorizing the executions. He was eventually acquitted and settled in Flensburg after marrying his long-term girlfriend. Petersen died on January 2, 1983, following a confrontation with youths in Flensburg, Germany.

## CONCLUSION

1. Vice Admiral Friedrich Ruge, *Der Seekrieg: The German Navy's Story, 1939–1945* (Annapolis: Naval Institute Press, 1957).
2. Ruge, *Der Seekrieg*, 13.
3. Ruge, 14.
4. Dickens, "Narrow Waters in War," 42.
5. DNOR, "On Some Features of E-Boat Warfare," June 15, 1945, TNA: ADM 219/220.
6. Interestingly, the operational rate of Royal Navy Coastal Forces was not far different. For example, in the Nore Command the operational rates for coastal force crews from May 1943 to February 1944 varied from a low of 3.1 in June 1943 to a high of 5.4 in January and February 1944. See DNOR, "Review of Coastal Forces (Interim Report)," 1945, TNA: ADM 219/242.
7. See, for example, DNOR, "Actions against E-boats in Home Waters," April 25, 1945, TNA: ADM 219/216.
8. "The War against E-Boats, 1945," TNA: AIR 15/390.
9. DNOR paper, "Review of Coastal Forces (Interim Report)," 1945, TNA: ADM 219/242.
10. "OKM Interrogation Report," 1945, TNA: ADM 219/230.
11. Roskill, *War at Sea*, 2:254.
12. See "Britain's Answer to the E-Boats—Exclusive Pictures," March 16, 1942, film ID 1320.26, British Pathé Archive.
13. Dreyer interview, IWM 8984.
14. Melvin, *Minesweeper*, 6.
15. Hervey Benham, ed., *Essex at War* (Colchester, U.K.: Benham, 1945), 89.
16. Hewitt, *Coastal Convoys*, 223.
17. SS *Alexander Kennedy* was sunk by U-1004 southeast of Falmouth on February 22, 1945. SS *Leonard Pearce* was sunk on January 11, 1940, in the Bristol Channel after a collision with MV *Queen Adelaide*. SS *Sir Joseph Swan* was sunk on September 4, 1940, by an S-boat off Hemsby; SS *New Lambton* was sunk by an S-boat in the same action. SS *Ambrose Fleming* was sunk by an S-boat off Cromer on April 28, 1941.

18. For the size of the Cory fleet, see Foynes, *Battle of the East Coast*, 238. SS *Corburn* was sunk by a mine off Le Havre on May 21, 1940. SS *Corhaven* was sunk near Dover by dive bomber attack on July 26, 1940. SS *Corbrook* was sunk by an S-boat off Cromer on September 9, 1940. SS *Corheath* was sunk by a mine off the coast of Kent on January 24, 1941. SS *Corduff* was sunk by an S-boat off Mundesley on March 7, 1941. SS *Cordene* was bombed and sunk off Mundesley on August 9, 1941. SS *Corfield* was sunk by a mine off Saltfleet on September 8, 1941. SS *Corhampton* was bombed on November 15, 1941, and later sank the following day off Spurn. SS *Cormarsh* was sunk by a mine off Blakeney Point on November 29, 1941. SS *Cormead* was sunk by a mine off Hopton-on-Sea on December 25, 1941. SS *Corfen* was sunk off Frinton-on-Sea by a mine on January 3, 1942. SS *Corland* was sunk off the spurn by a bomb on February 5, 1942. SS *Cormount* was damaged by a mine off Aldeburgh on November 13, 1943, and sank under tow.
19. Foynes, *Battle of the East Coast*, 238.
20. Foynes, 238.
21. Foynes, 238.
22. C-in-C Nore to Admiralty, October 16, 1943, TNA: ADM 1/15815.
23. C-in-C Rosyth to Admiralty, June 16, 1943, TNA: ADM 1/15815.
24. Vego, "On Littoral Warfare," 45.
25. Central Office of Information, *British Coaster*.

**APPENDIX**

1. Sources: *British Merchant Vessels Lost or Damaged by Enemy Action during the Second World War* (1947, HMSO; repr., Cambridge: Patrick Stephens, 1980); *Ships of the Royal Navy: Statement of Losses during the Second World War* (1947, HMSO; repr., Cambridge: Patrick Stephens, 1980); Scarlett, *Under Hazardous Circumstances*.

# SELECTED BIBLIOGRAPHY

### ARCHIVES, ONLINE REPOSITORIES
### NATIONAL ARCHIVES (U.K.)
Admiralty Papers: ADM 1/3716; ADM 1/14391; ADM 1/15815; ADM 1/29955; ADM 1/30193; ADM 116/3610; ADM 116/4521; ADM 167/116; ADM 186/806; ADM 186/807; ADM 186/808; ADM 186/809; ADM 199/74; ADM 199/261; ADM 199/303; ADM 199/567; ADM 199/656; ADM 199/697; ADM 199/2132; ADM 219/216; ADM 219/220; ADM 219/230; ADM 219/242; ADM 223/28; ADM 223/146–62; ADM 223/610; ADM 223/611; ADM 223/688; ADM 223/690; ADM 292/204
Cabinet Papers: CAB16/37/1–3; CAB65/5; CAB65/57/24; CAB66/16–24; CAB106/1042
Foreign Office Papers: FO954/29A/168
Royal Air Force Papers: AIR 15/122; AIR 15/390; AIR 27/1449/28–30
Security Services: HW 1/2036; HW 1/2039; HW 1/2041; KV 2/40; KV 2/42; KV 2/68; KV 2/69; KV 2/72; KV 2/73; KV 2/864; KV 2/4214
War Office Papers: WO 205/173; WO 208/3243; WO 219/2224; WO 219/2226

### CAMBRIDGE UNIVERSITY LIBRARY
P. M. Scott NCUACS 87/8/99

### CHURCHILL COLLEGE, CAMBRIDGE
Winston S. Churchill Papers

### ROYAL NAVY: MUSEUM OF THE ROYAL NAVY RADAR AND COMMUNICATIONS (HMS COLLINGWOOD)
"Radio Equipment in Coastal Craft," Admiralty Signal Establishment Bulletin (Confidential), September 1944

### SUFFOLK RECORD OFFICE
War Diary 7th MGB Flotilla (HMS *Mantis*), Suffolk Record Office (Lowestoft) 1678/1

### BRITISH PATHÉ ARCHIVE
"Barrage Balloons for Convoys," October 24, 1940, film ID 1059.16
"Convoy Attacked in the Channel," July 18, 1940, film ID 1051.07
"Pathé Gazette Special: Shells across the Channel," August 26, 1940, film ID 1053.55

### BBC PEOPLE'S WAR WEBSITE
Hilda Hale interview, WREN, A3130183, October 14, 2004, http://www.bbc.co.uk/history/ww2peopleswar/stories/83/a3130183.shtml
Thomas Sanderson, SS *Fulham* VII, A2877401, July 29, 2004, http://www.bbc.co.uk/history/ww2peopleswar/stories/01/a2877401.shtml

A. J. Yeatman, Telegraphist, HMS *Pearl*, 1943–45, A4189098, June 13, 2005, http://www.bbc.co.uk/history/ww2peopleswar/stories/98/a4189098.shtml

**BRUCE JOHNSON ARCHIVE**
Bruce Johnson, 115 Squadron RAF, diary entry for June 14, 1944, http://lancasterdiary.net/June%201944/june_14_1944.php

**IMPERIAL WAR MUSEUM (IWM)—AUDIO INTERVIEWS**
Emmanuel Adrien, Free French Merchant Seaman (SS *Daphne*) 1940–41, 20135, 2000
Michael Baron, HMS *Westminster* (Channel) 1942–43, 34088, 2014
Admiral Sir Hugh Binney Papers, IWM/PP/MCR/95
Air Commodore J. Constable-Roberts Papers, 1183
Fred Dent, DEMS gunner (SS *Methilhill*), 22116, 2002
Christopher Dreyer, Staff Officer Operations Division and to Captain Coastal Forces (Channel), 8984, 1985
Ray Lane, served HMS *Seymour* (Channel) 1944–45, 27050, 2004
George McCracken Rutherford, 841 Squadron Fleet Air Arm, 12345, 1991
Charles Parham, served MGBs and MTBs (Channel) 1943–45, 10719, 1989
Ida Steadman, WREN plotter Coastal Forces Base (Dartmouth), 27211, 2004
Derek Tolfree, served HMS *Westminster* (Channel) 1942–45, 31411, 2008.

**INTERNATIONAL BOMBER COMMAND CENTRE (DIGITAL ARCHIVE)**
E-Boats and E-Boat Shelters (Le Havre)—Narrative, Leonard Cheshire Papers, https://ibccdigitalarchive.lincoln.ac.uk/omeka/collections/document/16529, MCheshireGL72021-181210-020009 (accessed May 25, 2021)
Extract from bomber command summary of operations, Le Havre E-boat pens—effect of 12,000 lb bombs, https://ibccdigitalarchive.lincoln.ac.uk/omeka/collections/document/16541 (accessed May 25, 2021)
Interpretation Report, Le Havre, provisional statement of damage, https://ibccdigitalarchive.lincoln.ac.uk/omeka/collections/document/16530, MCheshireGL72021-181210-020010 (accessed May 25, 2021)

**J. O. ROWLANDS ARCHIVE**
Commodore J. O. Rowlands, "Fifty Years at Sea" (unpublished paper, 2003)

**NATIONAL ARCHIVE AND RECORDS ADMINISTRATION (NARA; COLLEGE PARK, MD)**
Via Dennis Hogan: LST Group 30 Logs, LST51, 133, 134, 157, 285, 286, 502 towing Rhino Ferries 4, 5, 7, 8, 9, 12, and 15 and PC1232/1233 Obstacle Convoy COMLANCRAB, 11th PHIBFOR, Apr. 26–28, 1944, A12, Record Group 38
Record Group 38: Admiralty War Diary, roll A2180; COMLANCRAB, 11th PHIBFOR, roll A906; Com LST GR32, roll A1061; Com LST FLOT10, roll A948; C-in-C Plymouth War Diary, roll A1088; C-in-C Nore War Diary, 1944–45, roll A1823; USS *Baldwin* War Diary 1944, roll A1091
Record Group 242 (T1022): Microfilmed German Naval Records (originals are now held by Bundesarchiv, Militärarchiv, Freiburg [BA/MA], and for cross-referencing their BA/MA file groups are also listed here)
*Fuehrer der Schnellboote (KTB und Anlagen)*—BA/MA RM55, Apr. 20, 1942–Oct. 15, 1943,

roll 3125; Oct. 16–31, 1943, rolls 3125–26; Nov. 1–Dec. 31, 1943, roll 3126; Jan. 1–31, 1944, roll 3145; Feb. 1–Aug. 15, 1944, roll 3146; Aug. 16–31, 1944, rolls 3146–47; Sept. 1–Dec. 15, 1944, roll 3147; Dec. 1, 1944–Jan. 31, 1945, roll 3864

*Fuehrer der Torpedoboote (KTB und Anlagen)*: BA/MA RM53, Nov. 30–Dec. 15, 1939, roll 2967; Dec. 16, 1939–Apr. 30, 1940, roll 4266; May 1–15, 1940, roll 2967; May 16–31, 1940, roll 4266; June 1–30, 1940, roll 2966; Jan. 1, 1941–Apr. 19, 1942, rolls 4266–67

*Marine Gruppe West*: BA/MA RM35 II, 1943–44, roll 2380

*Oberkommando der Marine Documents, 1942–45 (OKM Misc)*: BA/MA RM6 1942–45, roll 4082

*Seebefehlshaber Nord (KTB der SB Nord)*: BA/MA RM35 I, 1941–44, roll 2727

*Seebefehlshaber Nord See (various KTB Netherlands)*: BA/MA RM35 II, 1939–45, roll 2728

*Seebefehlshaber West (KTB der SB West)*: BA/MA RM35 II, May–Oct. 1942, roll 3974; Oct. 16–31, 1943, Dec. 1943–Jan. 1944, Jul. 16–24, Aug. 24–31, Sept. 25–27, Oct. 21–31, Nov. 23–Dec. 9, 1944, roll 2340; Jun. 12–30, 1940, Apr. 1–June 15, 1943, Aug. 1–31, 1944, Nov. 13–Dec. 31, 1944, roll 4073

*1st S-boat Flotilla, KTB and Anlagen*: BA/MA RM59 Sept.–Dec. 1939, roll 3254; Jan.–July 1940, roll 3208; Aug.–Dec. 1940, roll 3209; Jan. 1–15, 1941, roll 30891; Jan. 1–Aug. 31, 1941, roll 3207; Sept. 16–Dec. 31, 1942, roll 3208; Jan.–Aug. 1943, roll 3177; Sept. 16–Dec. 31, 1943, roll 3178; Jan. 1–July 31, 1944, Oct. 1–15, 1944, Jan. 1–15, 1945, roll 3255

*2nd S-boat Flotilla, KTB and Anlagen*: BA/MA III M362, Sept. 1939–Dec. 1939, roll 3255; Jan.–Mar. 1940, roll 3254; May–Sept. 1940, roll 3254; Oct. 1–15, 1940, rolls 3254–55; Oct. 16–Dec. 31, 1940, roll 3255; Jan. 1–Oct. 15, 1941, roll 3256; Oct. 16–Dec. 31, 1941, roll 3257; Jan. 1–Aug. 15, 1942, roll 3126; Aug. 16–31, 1942, roll 3120; Sept.–Dec. 1942, roll 3127; Jan. 1–May 15, 1943, roll 3209; May 16, 1943–May 31, 1944, roll 3210; June 16–July 30, 1944, roll 3864; Aug. 1–15, 1944, roll 3210; Aug. 16–Sept. 15, 1944, roll 3864; Oct. 1–Nov. 15, 1944, roll 3210; Dec. 1, 1944–Jan. 15, 1945, roll 3864

*3rd S-boat Flotilla, KTB and Anlagen*: BA/MA III M363, May 15–Dec. 31, 1940, roll 3089; Jan. 1–July 31, 1941, roll 3091; Aug. 1–Dec. 31, 1941, roll 3092; Jan.–May 1942, roll 3147; June–Dec. 1942, roll 3148; Jan.–May 1943, roll 3206

*4th S-boat Flotilla, KTB and Anlagen*: BA/MA RM59, Oct. 19, 1940–May 31, 1941, roll 3148; June–Dec. 1941, roll 3149; Jan. 1–Aug. 15, 1942, roll 3257; Aug. 16, 1942–June 15, 1943, roll 3258; June 16, 1943–May 31, 1944, roll 3259; June 16–Oct. 15, Nov. 16–30, 1944, roll 3259

*5th S-boat Flotilla, KTB and Anlagen*: BA/MA RM59 June 17, 1941–Aug. 15, 1942, roll 3178; Aug. 16–31, 1942, rolls 3178–79; Sept. 1–Dec. 31, 1942, roll 3179; Jan. 1–Feb. 28, 1943, roll 3210; Mar. 1, 1943–Dec. 15, 1944, roll 3211

*6th S-boat Flotilla, KTB and Anlagen*: BA/MA RM59, Mar. 1, 1941–Jan. 31, 1942, roll 3092; Feb. 1, 1942–Dec. 31, 1942, roll 3093; Jan. 1, 1943–May 31, 1944, roll 3124; June 15–July 31, 1944, roll 3866; Aug. 1–31, 1944, roll 3124; Aug. 16–Sept. 15, 1944, roll 3866; Oct. 1–15, 1944, roll 3124

*8th S-boat Flotilla, KTB and Anlagen*: BA/MA RM59, Nov. 8, 1941–Dec. 31, 1942, roll 3179; Jan. 1–June 15, 1943, roll 3259; June 16, 1943–May 31, 1944, roll 3260; June 16–July 15, 1944, roll 3866; Aug. 1–31, 1944, roll 3260; Aug. 16–Sept. 15, 1944, roll 3866; Oct. 1–15, 1944, roll 3260; Jan. 22–23, 1945, roll 3866

*9th S-boat Flotilla, KTB and Anlagen*: BA/MA RM59, Nov. 15, 1943–Mar. 31, 1944, roll 3149; Apr. 1–May 31, 1944, roll 3150; KTB Abschn. Maschine, June 1–July 15, 1944, roll 3150; KTB 1. Gruppe, July 7–31, 1944, roll 3871; KTB 2. Gruppe, June 16–July 4, 1944, roll 3871; KTB Abschn. Maschine, Aug. 1–31, 1944, roll 3150; Sept. 1–15, 1944, roll 3866; Sept. 16–30, 1944, missing; Oct. 1–15, 1944, roll 3150

Record Group 338: "The Invasion and the German Navy." Interview with Admirals Dönitz and Wagner, July 20, 1945, ETHINT 28

## NATIONAL ARCHIVE AND RECORDS ADMINISTRATION (BOSTON, MA)
Photographs of the First Naval District

## EISENHOWER PRESIDENTIAL LIBRARY (ABILENE, KS)
Walter Beddell Smith Papers

## CIA/OSS RECORDS
German Plans for the Invasion of England, 1940, undated, https://www.cia.gov/library/readingroom/docs/GERMAN%20PLANS%20FOR%20INVASION%20OF%20ENGLAND%2C%201940_0001.pdf (accessed January 21, 2017)

Views on Morale in the Kriegsmarine of a German Naval Deserter recently arrived in Spain and set down by Assistant Naval Attaché, May 7, 1944, https://www.cia.gov/library/readingroom/docs/CIA-RDP13X00001R000100270007-8.pdf

## U.S. NAVAL WAR COLLEGE
*Kriegstagebuch der Seekriegsleitung (KTB der SKL)* (translation) (Washington: Naval History Division, 1948–1958), U.S. Naval War College Archives

## KOLBE FAMILY ARCHIVE (CALIFORNIA)
Ulrich Kolbe, private family memoir, 1997–98; Ulrich Kolbe photographs; family memories and stories

## NATIONAL DEFENCE AND THE CANADIAN ARMED FORCES
Report No. 183 Historical Section Canadian Military Headquarters: Canadian Participation in the Operations in northwestern Europe 1944 (Part IV: First Canadian Army in the Pursuit (August 23–September 23), 166–84, http://www.cmp-cpm.forces.gc.ca/dhh-dhp/his/rep-rap/doc/cmhq/cmhq183.pdf (accessed March 4, 2016)

Report No. 184 Historical Section Canadian Military Headquarters: Canadian Participation in the Operations in Northwestern Europe 1944, part 5: Clearing the Channel Ports (September 3–February 6, 1945), 166–84. http://www.cmp-cpm.forces.gc.ca/dhh-dhp/his/rep-rap/doc/cmhq/cmhq184.pdf (accessed March 4, 2016)

## BUNDESARCHIV (GERMANY)
Neustädter Slip-GmbH, Neustadt/Holstein (Werft und Motorreparaturwerkstatt), 1927, BArch, R 8135/383

Propaganda Reports 1941–44, Bd. 4–70, BArch, RM 8/1537–70

Travemünder Yachthafen AG (Trayag), Travemünde: Bd. 1, 1927, BArch, R 8135/1890

Travemünder Yachthafen AG (Trayag), Travemünde: Bd. 2, 1928, BArch, R 8135/1908

Travemünder Yachthafen AG (Trayag), Travemünde: Bd. 3, 1928, BArch, R 8135/1891

## BUNDESARCHIV, MILITÄRARCHIV, FREIBURG (BAMA)
See elsewhere in the bibliography under National Archives and Records Administration (College Park, MD), Record Group 242 (T1022), for German Naval Documents microfilmed by the U.S. Navy, with reels held in Washington, DC, before the originals were returned to the Federal German archives.

## PETER SCHLICHTING ARCHIV (TRAVEMÜNDE, GERMANY)
Rudolf Schlichting Diary; *Der Werftbote* (works magazine); photos; films

## INTERVIEWS

McCrum, Captain Tony. Interview by author, 2015, with signals officer McCrum, HMS *Mendip*, East Coast, 1941

Thiele, Karl Heinz. Interview, 2014, by Thea Wrobbel, forwarded to author in an email, March 31, 2014

White, Rob. Interview, 2014, by Lieutenant A. G. F. Ditcham, officer HMS *Holderness*, East Coast, 1941–42

## NEWSPAPERS AND MAGAZINES
## (U.K. PUBLICATION UNLESS OTHERWISE STATED)

*Atlantic Monthly* (U.S.)
*Birmingham Post*
*Blackwood's Magazine*
*Coastal Forces Veterans Association Newsletter*
*Courier and Argus* (Dundee, Scotland)
*Daily Mail*
*Daily Mirror*
*Evening Herald* (Dublin)
*Evening Telegraph and Post* (Dundee, Scotland)
*Fortnightly Review*
*Hansard*
*Harper's* (U.S.)
*Die Kriegsmarine* (Germany)
*Lancashire Post*
*Liverpool Echo*
*Naval Review*
*New Republic* (U.S.)
*New York Times* (U.S.)
*Newsweek* (U.S.)
*Nottingham Evening Post*
*The People*
*RAF Journal*
*Shields Evening News*
*The Times*
*Transactions of the Institute of Marine Engineers*, vol. 56 (1944)
*Die Yacht* (Germany)
*Yorkshire Post*

## PUBLISHED PRIMARY SOURCES

Admiralty. *Light Coastal Craft Operating in the North Sea and English Channel* (BR834). London: Admiralty, 1941.

Agar, Captain Augustus. *Footprints in the Sea*. London: Evans Brothers, 1961.

Amble Social History Group. *A Time to Remember: Recollections of the Second World War by the People of Amble and District*. Alnwick: self-published, 2005.

Armstrong, Warren. *Battle of the Oceans*. London: Jarrolds, 1943.

Barrett, John. *Admiral George Dewey: A Sketch of the Man*. New York: Harper & Brothers, 1899. Reprint, London: Forgotten Books, 2015.

Barry, Rear Admiral C. B., to Their Lords Commissioners of the Admiralty, November 8, 1943.

"The Attack on the Tirpitz by Midget Submarines on 22 September 1943." *Supplement to the London Gazette*, February 11, 1948, 993–1008.

Beckman, Morris. *Flying the Red Duster: A Merchant Seaman's First Voyage into the Battle of the Atlantic, 1940*. Stroud, U.K.: Spellmount, 2011.

Benham, Hervey, ed. *Essex at War*. Colchester, U.K.: Benham, 1945.

Board of Trade. *Statistical Abstract of the United Kingdom*. No. 82. London: HMSO, 1938.

Brown, C. H. *Nicholls Seamanship and Nautical Knowledge*. 1938. 18th ed., Glasgow: Brown, Son and Ferguson, 1943.

Bucheim, Lothar-Günther. *U-Boat War*. New York: A. A. Knopf, 1978.

Bürger, Hugo. *Schnellboote Vor! Ein Erlebnisbericht vom Einsatz einer Schnellboot-Flottille im Osten*. Oldenburg: Stalling, 1943.

Bush, Captain Eric Wheeler. *Bless Our Ship*. London: George Allen & Unwin, 1958.

Campbell, Patrick. "Come Here I Tell You: Sean Tar at Sea." *The Spectator*, July 23, 1959.

Central Office of Information. *British Coaster, 1939–1945*. London: HMSO, 1947.

Churchill, Winston S. *The Second World War*. Vol. 2, *Their Finest Hour*. London: Reprint Society, 1951.

Dickens, Captain Peter. *Night Action: MTB Flotilla at War*. London: Book Club Edition, 1974.

Ditcham, A. G. F. *A Home on the Rolling Main: A Naval Memoir*. Barnsley, U.K.: Seaforth, 2012.

Dönitz, Karl. *Memoirs: Ten Years and Twenty Days*. London: Weidenfeld and Nicolson, 1958.

Drummond, John. *Through Hell and High Water: With the Men of the Little Ships of the Royal Navy*. London: Low, 1944.

Gray, Jennie, ed. *"This Is War!": The Diaries and Journalism of Anthony Cotterell, 1940–1944*. Stroud, U.K.: Spellmount, 2013.

Gretton, Vice Admiral Sir Peter. *Convoy Escort Commander*. London: Corgi, 1964.

Gröner, Erich. *Die deutschen Kriegsschiffe, 1815–1945*. Munich: Bernard & Graefe Verlag, 1994.

Hall, Nowell. "Towing Story." In *Wavy Navy by Some Who Served*, edited by J. Lennox Kerr and David James, 89–100. London: George G. Harrap Co., 1950.

Hase, Georg von. *Die Kriegsmarine im Kampf um den Atlantik: Erlebnisberichte von Mitkampfern*. Leipzig: Hase & Koehler Verlag, 1942.

Hichens, Lieutenant-Commander Robert Peverell. *We Fought Them in Gunboats*. London: Michael Joseph, 1944.

Historical Section Admiralty. *The Defeat of the Enemy Attack on Shipping, 1939–1945: A Study of Policy and Operations*. Vol. 1A, Text and Appendices, CB3304(IA), Historical Section Admiralty, 1957.

Hurd, Sir Archibald, ed. *Britain's Merchant Navy*. London: Odhams, 1944.

Jellicoe, Admiral Viscount of Scapa. *The Grand Fleet, 1914–16: Its Creation, Development and Work*. London: Cassell and Company, 1919.

Kemnade, Friedrich. *Die Afrika-Flottille. Der Einsatz der 3. Schnellboot-Flottille im Weltkrieg*. Stuttgart: Motorbuch, 1976.

Kreipe, Werner, et al. *The Fatal Decisions*. London: Michael Joseph, 1956.

*Kriegstagebuch der Seekriegsleitung (KTB der SKL)*. Teil A, Band 37, 38, 50, 57, 58. Berlin: E. S. Mittler & Sohn, 1993–94.

Lamb, Christian. *I Only Joined for the Hat: Redoubtable Wrens at War—Their Trials, Tribulations and Triumphs*. Malta: Bene Factum, 2007.

Law, C. Anthony. *White Plumes Astern: The Short, Daring Life of Canada's MTB Flotilla*. Halifax, NS: Nimbus, 1989.

Mackinder, H. J. "The Geographical Pivot of History." *Geographical Journal* 23, no. 4 (April 1904): 421–37.
Mahan, Alfred Thayer. *The Influence of Seapower on History, 1660–1783*. Boston: Little, Brown and Company, 1890.
Maher, Brendon A. *A Passage to Sword Beach: Minesweeping in the Royal Navy*. Annapolis: Naval Institute Press, 1996.
McCrum, Tony. *Sunk by Stukas Survived at Salerno: The Memoirs of Captain Tony McCrum*. Barnsley, U.K.: Pen & Sword, 2010.
Möbius, P. P. *Schnellboote*. Berlin: Carl Curtius Verlag, 1943.
Nater, Jenny. *Secret Duties of a Signals Interceptor: Working with Bletchley Park, the SDS and the OSS*. Barnsley, U.K.: Pen & Sword, 2016.
*Nauticus: Jahrbuch Deutschlands Seeinteressen*. Berlin: E. S. Mittler & Sohn, 1944.
Peacock, Alan. *The Enigmatic Sailor*. Caithness: Whittles, 2003.
Raeder, Erich. *My Life*. Annapolis: Naval Institute Press, 1960.
———. *Struggle for the Sea*. London: William Kimber, 1959.
Ritchie, Rear Admiral G. S. *No Day Too Long—An Hydrographer's Tale*. Edinburgh: Pentland Press, 1994.
Rodgers, Stanley. *Enemy in Sight*. New York: Thomas Y. Crowell, 1943.
*The Royal Marines: The Admiralty Account of Their Achievement, 1939–1943*. London, HMSO, 1944.
Ruge, Vice Admiral Friedrich. *Der Seekrieg: The German Navy's Story, 1939–1945*. Annapolis: Naval Institute Press, 1957.
Scott, Peter. *The Eye of the Wind*. London: Hodder & Stoughton, 1961.
Showell, Jak Mallmann. *Dönitz, U-Boats, Convoys: The British Version of His Memoirs from the Admiralty's Secret Anti-submarine Reports*. London: Frontline Books, 2013.
———. *Führer Conferences on Naval Affairs, 1939–1945*. London: Greenhill Books, 1990.
*Technical Staff Monographs, 1939–1945: German Torpedoes and Development of German Torpedo Control*. BR1972. London: Admiralty, 1972.
Tovey, Admiral Sir John, to Their Lords Commissioners of the Admiralty, November 18, 1943, incorporated and published in "Coastal Force Actions." *Supplement to the London Gazette*, October 15, 1943, 5493–5523.

**SECONDARY SOURCES**

Ambrose, Stephen E. *D-Day, June 6, 1944, The Battle for the Normandy Beaches*. New York: Simon & Schuster, 1994.
Ansel, Walter. *Hitler Confronts England*. Durham, NC: Duke University Press, 1960.
Ashworth, Chris. *RAF Coastal Command: 1936–1969*. Sparkford, U.K.: Patrick Stephens, 1992.
Baart, Jac J. *Schnellboote: Operaties vanuit Holland, Vlaanderen en Frankrijk, 1940–1945*. Emmen: Lanasta, 2006.
Badsey, Stephen, and Tim Bean. *Omaha Beach*. Stroud, U.K.: Sutton, 2004.
Bailey, Roderick. *Forgotten Voices of D-Day: A New History of the Normandy Landings*. London: Ebury, 2010.
Balkoski, Joseph. *Omaha Beach*. Mechanicsburg, PA: Stackpole Books, 2004.
Barnett, Corelli. *Engage the Enemy More Closely: The Royal Navy in the Second World War*. London: Penguin, 2000.
Bartimeus, "Sweeping Death's Doorstep," *Atlantic Monthly* (March 1941): 288–94.
*Bawdsey and the Development of Radar*. Felixstowe: Bawdsey Radar Trust, n.d.

Beevor, Antony. *D-Day: The Battle for Normandy*. London: Viking, 2009.
Bekker, C. D. *Das Bildbuch der deutschen Kriegsmarine, 1939–1945*. Munich: Wilhelm Heyne Verlag, 1972.
———. *K-Men: The Story of the German Frogmen and Midget Submarines*. Maidstone: George Mann, 1968.
———. *Swastika at Sea: The Struggle and Destruction of the German Navy, 1939–1945*. London: William Kimber, 1953.
Bennett, G. H. "Dockyard, Naval Base and Town: The Social and Political Dynamics of Plymouth 1800 to 1950." In *Kiel und die Marine, 1865–2015: 150 Jahre Gemeinsame Geschichte*, edited by O. Auge and D. Tillman, 113–36. Kiel: Ludwig, 2017.
———. "The Other Critical Convoy Battles of 1943: The Eclipse of the Schnellboote in the English Channel and North Sea." In *Decision in the Atlantic: The Allies and the Longest Campaign of the Second World War, New Perspectives on the Second World War*, edited by M. Faulkner and C. M. H. Bell, 225–51. Lexington, KY: Andarta Books, 2019.
———. "Schnellboote, Strategy and the Defence of Festung Europa, 1943–1944." In *The Sea and the Second World War: Maritime Aspects of a Global Conflict*, edited by M. Faulkner and A. Patalano, 115–42. Lexington, KY: Andarta Books, 2019.
———. "A Very Different Experience: Merchant Seamen on British Coastal Convoys, 1940–45." In *Allied Merchant Seafarers in the Second World War*, edited by Bjorn Tore Rosendahl, 47–74. Oslo: Cappelen Damm, Akademisk, 2018.
Bennett, Ralph. *Ultra in the West: The Normandy Campaign, 1944–55*. London: Hutchinson & Co., 1979.
Bickell, C. "Operation Fortitude South: An Analysis of Its Influence upon German Dispositions and Conduct of Operations in 1944." *War and Society* 18, no. 1 (2000): 91–122.
Bird, Keith W. *Erich Raeder: Admiral of the Third Reich*. Annapolis: Naval Institute Press, 2006.
———. "The Origins and Role of German Naval History in the Interwar Period, 1918–1939." *Naval War College Review* 32, no. 2 (March–April 1979): 52.
Blair, Clay. *Hitler's U-Boat War: The Hunted, 1942–1943*. London: Random House, 1998.
Bolitho, Hector. *Task for the Coastal Command: The Story of the Battle for the South West Approaches*. London: Hutchinson, 1946.
Boog, Horst, Werner Rahn, Reinhard Stumpf, and Bernd Wegner. *Germany and the Second World War*. Vol. 6, *The Global War*. Oxford: Oxford University Press, 2001.
Brooks, Richard. *Walcheren 1944: Storming Hitler's Fortress*. Oxford: Osprey, 2011.
Brown, Anthony Cave. *Bodyguard of Lies*. London: W. H. Allen & Co., 1977.
Burn, Alan. *The Fighting Commodores: The Convoy Commanders in the Second World War*. Annapolis: Naval Institute Press, 1999.
Capper, Douglas. *Moat Defence: A History of the Waters of the Nore Command, 55BC to 1961*. London: Barker, 1963.
Carver, Michael, ed. *The War Lords*. London: Weidenfeld and Nicolson, 1976.
Cergol, Joan, and Ellen Schafer. *Images of America: Oheka Castle*. Charleston, SC: Arcadia, 2012.
Collingwood, Donald. *The Captain Class Frigates in the Second World War*. London: Leo Cooper, 1998.
Cooper, Bryan. *The Battle of the Torpedo Boats*. London: Pan, 1970.
———. *The E-Boat Threat*. Oxford: Purnell, 1976.
———. *The War of the Gunboats*. Barnsley, U.K.: Pen & Sword, 2009.
Court, W. H. B. *Coal*. London: HMSO, 1951.

Dallies-Labourdette, Jean-Phillippe. *Deutsche Schnellboote, 1939–1945*. Stuttgart: Motorbuch Verlag, 2006.
Delderfield, R. F. "Confidential Report on the Recent Bombing of Le Havre." *Canadian Military History* 20, no. 4 (2011): 69–74.
Dickens, P. G. C. "Narrow Waters in War." *Journal of the Royal United Services Institute* 114 (March 1969): 42–45.
Ellis, Major L. F. *Victory in the West*. Vol. 2, *The Defeat of Germany*. London: HMSO, 1968.
Farquharson-Roberts, Mike. *Royal Navy Officers from War to War*. Basingstoke, U.K.: Palgrave Macmillan, 2015.
Faulkner, Marcus. "The Kriegsmarine, Signals Intelligence and the Development of the B-Dienst before the Second World War." *Intelligence and National Security* 25, no. 4 (August 2010): 521–46.
Fedorowich, Kent. "Axis Prisoners of War as Sources for British Military Intelligence, 1939–42." *Intelligence and National Security* 14, no. 2 (June 1991): 156–78.
Firth, Anthony. *East Coast War Channels in the First and Second World Wars: A Report for English Heritage*. Salisbury: Fjordr, 2014.
Fock, Harald. *Die deutschen Schnellboote, 1914–1945*. Hamburg: Koehlers Verlagsgesellschaft mbH, 2001.
———. *Schnellboote*. Band 1, *Von den Anfängen bis zum Ausbruch des 2. Weltkrieges*. Hamburg: Koehlers Verlagsgesellschaft mbH, 1974.
———. *Schnellboote*. Band 2, *Entwicklung und Einsatz im 2. Weltkrieg*. Hamburg: Koehlers Verlagsgesellschaft GmbH, 1974.
———. *Schnellboote*. Band 3, *Die Nachkriegsentwicklung bis heute*. Hamburg: Koehlers Verlagsgesellschaft mbH, 1974.
Foynes, J. P. *Battle of the East Coast*. Isleworth: self-published, 1994.
Frank, Hans. *Die deutschen Schnellboote im Einsatz*. Berlin: E. S. Mittler & Sohn, 2006.
Gillis, J. R. *The Human Shore: Seacoasts in History*. Chicago: University of Chicago Press, 2012.
Granville, William, and Robin A. Kelly. *Inshore Heroes: The Story of H. M. Motor Launches in Two World Wars*. London: Allen, 1961.
Graves, Donald E. "'Hell Boats' of the RCN: The Canadian Navy and the Motor Torpedo Boat, 1936–41." *Northern Mariner* 2, no. 3 (July 1992): 31–45.
Grier, Howard. *Hitler, Dönitz and the Baltic Sea*. Annapolis: Naval Institute Press, 2007.
Griffiths, Bernard. *MacNamara's Band: The Story of HMS Duff*. Sutton, U.K.: Severn House, 1976.
Hampshire, Cecil A. *Armed with Strings: The Saga of a Gunboat Flotilla*. London: Kimber, 1958.
———. *The Story of the Royal Navy Patrol Service*. London: Kimber, 1957.
Haslop, Dennis. *Britain, Germany and the Battle of the Atlantic: A Comparative Study*. London: Bloomsbury, 2013.
Herwig, Holger H. "The Failure of German Sea Power, 1914–1945: Mahan, Tirpitz, and Raeder Reconsidered." *International History Review* 10, no. 1 (February 1988): 68–105.
———. "The Influence of A. T. Mahan upon German Seapower." In *The Influence of History on Mahan*, edited by John B. Hattendorf, 67–80. Newport: Naval War College Press, 1991.
Hesketh, Roger. *Fortitude: The D-Day Deception Campaign*. New York: Peter Mayer, 2002.
Hewitt, Nick. *Coastal Convoys, 1939–1945: The Indestructible Highway*. Barnsley, U.K.: Pen and Sword, 2008.

Hichens, Robert. *Gunboat Commander: The Biography of Lieutenant Commander Robert Hichens DSO, DSC RNVR.* Barnsley, U.K.: Pen & Sword, 2008.

Hoerber, Thomas. "Psychology and Reasoning in the Anglo-German Naval Agreement, 1935–39." *Historical Journal* 52, no. 1 (March 2009): 153–74.

Holt, Thaddeus. *The Deceivers: Allied Military Deception in the Second World War.* New York: Scribner, 2004.

Hooton, E. R. *The Luftwaffe: A Study in Air Power, 1933–1945.* Hersham, U.K.: Classic Publications, 2010.

Howard, Michael. *British Intelligence in the Second World War.* Vol. 5. London: HMSO, 1990.

Hümmelchen, Gerhard. *Die deutsche Schnellboote im Zweiten Weltkrieg.* Hamburg: E. S. Mittler, 1996.

*Introduction to Naval Gunnery (BR224).* London: Training Department, Admiralty, 1960.

Jackson, Robert, *Churchill's Moat: The Channel War, 1939–1945.* London: Airlife, 1995.

Jefferson, David. *Coastal Forces at War: The Royal Navy's "Little Ships" in the Narrow Seas.* Sparkford: Haynes, 2008.

Karau, Mark D. *The Naval Flank of the Western Front: The German MarineKorps Flandern, 1914–1918.* Barnsley, U.K.: Seaforth, 2003.

Kemp, Paul. *Underwater Warriors.* Annapolis: Naval Institute Press, 1996.

Kerr, J. Lennox, and Wilfrid Granville. *The RNVR: A Record of Achievement.* London: George H. Harrap & Co., 1957.

Kinsey, Gordon. *Bawdsey: Birth of the Beam: The History of RAF Stations Bawdsey and Woodbridge.* Lavenham, U.K.: Lavenham Press, 1983.

Kirland, William B., Jr. *Destroyers at Normandy: Naval Gunfire Support at Omaha Beach.* Washington: Naval Historical Foundation, 2002.

Konstam, Angus. *British Motor Gunboat, 1939–45.* New York: Osprey, 2010.

Lake, Alan. *Flying Units of the RAF: The Ancestry, Formation and Disbandment of All Flying Units from 1912.* Shrewsbury: Airlife, 1999.

Lehmann, Eike. *100 Jahre schiffbautechnische Gesellschaft: Biografien zur Geschichte des Schiffbaus.* Berlin: Springer, 1999.

Lewis, Adrian. "The Navy Falls Short at Normandy." *Naval History Magazine* 12 (December 1998), http://www.usni.org/magazines/navalhistory/1998-12/navy-falls-short-normandy.

———. *Omaha Beach: A Flawed Victory.* Chapel Hill: University of North Carolina Press, 2001.

Lewis, Nigel. "U.S. Exercise Tiger and the Overlord Cover Plan." *U.S. Military History Review* 7, no. 1 (April 2021): 31–50.

Lloyd, Christopher. *The British Merchant Seaman, 1200–1860.* London: Collins, 1968.

Lundeberg, Philip K. "The German Naval Critique of the U-Boat Campaign, 1915–18." *Military Affairs* 27, no. 3 (Autumn 1963): 105–18.

Macksey, Kenneth. *The German Invasion of England, July 1940.* London: Arms and Armour Press, 1980.

Margaritis, Peter. *Countdown to D-Day: The German Perspective.* Oxford: Casemate, 2019.

Marriot, John. "Smokestack: The Industrial Heritage of the Thames Gateway." In *London's Turning: The Making of the Thames Gateway*, edited by Philip Cohen and Michael Rustin, 20–39. Aldershot: Ashgate, 2008.

Mayen, Jan. *Alarm—Schnellboote: Zwischen Kanal und Kaukasusküste ein Tatsachenbericht vom Einsatz der kleinen Boote.* Oldenburg: Gerhard Stalling Verlag, 1961.

McKee, Alexander. *The Coal Scuttle Brigade.* London: New English Library, 1973.

Melvin, Michael. *Minesweeper: The Role of the Motor Minesweeper in World War II.* Worcester: Square One, 1992.

Montenegro, Captain Guillermo J. (Argentine navy, Retired). "Alternative Naval Strategies." *Naval War College Review* 45, no. 2 (Spring 1992): 51–68.

Morison, Samuel Eliot. *History of United States Naval Operations in World War II: The Invasion of France and Germany*. Vol. 11. New York: Castle Books, 2001.

Neitzel, Sönke. "Kriegsmarine and Luftwaffe Co-operation in the War against Britain, 1939–1945." *War in History* 10, no. 4 (October 2003): 448–63.

———. *Der Luftkrieg über dem Nordatlantik und der Nordsee, 1939–1945*. Bonn: Bernard & Graefe, 1995.

———. "Die Zusammenarbeit zwischen Schnellbooten und Luftwaffe." *Militärgeschichte* 4 (1995): 55–63.

O'Hara, Vincent P. *The German Fleet at War, 1939–1945*. Annapolis: Naval Institute Press, 2004.

Olivier, David H. *German Naval Strategy, 1856–1888: Forerunners to Tirpitz*. London: Frank Cass, 2004.

Padfield, Peter. *Dönitz: The Last Führer*. London: Gollancz, 1993.

———. *War beneath the Seas: Submarine Conflict, 1939–45*. London: John Murray, 1995.

Paterson, Lawrence. *Dönitz's Last Gamble: The Inshore U-Boat Campaign, 1944–45*. Barnsley, U.K.: Seaforth, 2008.

———. *Schnellboote: A Complete Operational History*. Barnsley, U.K.: Seaforth, 2015.

Pearce, Cathryn. "Is Coastal History Maritime History." *Topmasts*, special issue, 2017, 25–28. www.snr.org.uk/wp-content/uploads/2017/12/Topmasts-special-issue-rev.pdf. Accessed December 16, 2017.

Pickles, Harold. *Untold Stories of Small Boats at War: Coastal Forces Veterans Remember*. Edinburgh: Pentland Press, 1994.

Pope, Dudley. *Flag 4: The Battle of Coastal Forces in the Mediterranean*. London: William Kimber, 1954.

Porten, Edward P. Von der. *The German Navy in World War II*. London: Arthur Baker, 1969.

Pugsley, Christopher. *Operation Cobra*. Stroud, U.K.: Sutton, 2005.

Reynolds, Leonard. *Dog Boats at War: A History of the Operations of the Royal Navy D Class Fairmile Motor Torpedo Boats and Motor Gunboats, 1939–1945*. Stroud, U.K.: Sutton, 1998.

———. *Home Waters MTBs and MGBs at War, 1939–1945*. Stroud, U.K.: Sutton, 2000.

Ritchie, Lieutenant Commander S. M. "The Effectiveness of the Leadership of Admiral Karl Dönitz." *Geddes Papers* (2003): 36–40.

Rohwer, Jürgen. *The Critical Convoy Battles of March 1943: The Battle for HX.229/SC122*. Annapolis: Naval Institute Press, 1977.

Ropp, Theodore. "Review of *Memoirs: Ten Years and Twenty Days* by Karl Doenitz." *Journal of Modern History* 33, no. 1 (March 1961): 98.

Roscoe, Theodore. *United States Destroyer Operations in World War II*. Annapolis: Naval Institute Press, 1953.

Roskill, S. W. "Review of *The German Navy in World War II* by Edward von der Porten." *International Affairs* 46, no. 4 (October 1970): 781.

———. *The War at Sea, 1939–1945*. Vol. 1. London: HMSO, 1954.

———. *The War at Sea, 1939–1945*. Vol. 1. Uckfield: Naval and Military Press, 2004.

———. *The War at Sea, 1939–45*. Vol. 2. London: HMSO, 1956.

———. *The War at Sea, 1939–45*. Vol. 3, pt. 2. London: HMSO, 1961.

Ruge, Vice Admiral Friedrich. "The Invasion of Normandy." In Hans-Adolf Jacobsen and Juergen Rohwer, *Decisive Battles of World War II: The German View*, 317–48. London: Andre Deutsch, 1965.

Rust, Eric C. *Naval Officers under Hitler: The Men of Crew 34*. New York: Praeger, 1991.
Saunders, Andy. *Convoy Peewit: August 8, 1940: The First Day of the Battle of Britain*. London: Grub Street, 2010.
Scarlett, R. J. *Under Hazardous Circumstances*. Dallington, U.K.: Naval & Military Press, 1992.
Schulze-Wegener, Guntram. *Die deutsche Kriegsmarinerüstung, 1942–1945*. Hamburg: E. S. Mittler & Sohn, 1997.
Scott, Lieutenant-Commander Peter. *The Battle of the Narrow Seas: A History of the Light Coastal Forces in the Channel and North Sea, 1939–1945*. London: Country Life, 1945.
Showell, Jak Mallmann. *German Naval Code Breakers*. Hersham, U.K.: Ian Allan, 2003.
Smith, Peter C. *Hold the Narrow Sea: Naval Warfare in the English Channel, 1939–1945*. Annapolis: Naval Institute Press, 1984.
Smith, Richard C. *Hornchurch Offensive: A Definitive Account of the RAF Fighter Airfield, Its Pilots, Groundcrew and Staff, 1941–1962*. London: Grub Street, 2001.
Spacij, Hrvoje. *Schnellbootwaffe: Adolf Hitler's Guerilla War at Sea. S-Boote, 1935–45 Rare Photographs from Wartime Archives*. Barnsley, U.K.: Pen and Sword, 2021.
Symonds, Craig. *Neptune: The Allied Invasion of Europe and the D-Day Landings*. Oxford: Oxford University Press, 2014.
Syrett, David. *The Defeat of the German U-Boats: The Battle of the Atlantic*. Columbia: University of South Carolina Press, 1994.
———. "The Infrastructure of Communications Intelligence: The Allied D/F network and the Battle of the Atlantic." *Intelligence and National Security* 17, no. 3 (2002): 163–72.
Tarrant, V. E. *The Last Year of the Kriegsmarine: May 1944–May 1945*. London: Arms and Armour, 1994.
Tent, James Foster. *E-Boat Alert: Defending the Normandy Invasion Fleet*. Annapolis: Naval Institute Press, 1996.
Terraine, John. *Business in Great Waters: The U-Boat Wars, 1916–1945*. London: Leo Cooper, 1989.
Till, Geoffrey. "Naval Power." In *Warfare in the Twentieth Century*, edited by Colin McInnes and G. D. Sheffield. London: Unwin Hyman, 1988.
Tobia, Simona. "Invisible Violences, Interrogation and Representation in Post-war Germany." In *Liberal Democracies at War: Conflict and Representation*, edited by Andrew Knapp and Hilary Footitt, 115–34. London: Bloomsbury, 2013.
Trew, Simon, and Stephen Badsey. *Battle for Caen*. Stroud, U.K.: Sutton, 2004.
Turner, Frank R. *The Maunsell Sea Forts*. Gravesend: F. R. Turner, 1997.
Turner, John Frayn. *Service Most Silent: The Navy's Fight against Enemy Mines*. Barnsley, U.K.: Pen & Sword, 2008.
Vego, Milan N. *Naval Strategy and Operations in Narrow Seas*. London: Frank Cass, 2003.
———. "On Littoral Warfare." *Naval War College Review* 68, no. 2 (Spring 2015): 30–68.
Whitley, Mike. *Deutsche Seestreitkräfte, 1939–1945: Einsatz im Küstenvorfeld*. Stuttgart: Motorbuch Verlag, 1995.
Williamson, Gordon. *E-Boat vs MTB: The English Channel, 1941–45*. Oxford: Osprey, 2011.
———. *German E-boats, 1939–45*. Oxford: Osprey, 2002.
———. *Kriegsmarine Coastal Forces*. Oxford: Osprey, 2009.
Williamson, James A. *The English Channel: A History*. London: Collins, 1959.
Winchester, Clarence. *Shipping Wonders of the World*. Vol. 2. London: Fleetway House, n.d.
Winton, John. *Ultra at Sea*. London: Leo Cooper, 1988.
Wolz, Nicolas. *From Imperial Splendour to Internment: The German Navy in the First World War*. Barnsley, U.K.: Seaforth, 2013.

Woodman, Richard. *The Real Cruel Sea: The Merchant Navy in the Battle of the Atlantic, 1939–1945.* London: John Murray, 2004.
Yates, Fabian. "Commuters." *Nautical Quarterly* 17, no. 2 (Spring 1982): 66–75.
Zaloga, Steven J. *Operation Cobra 1944: Breakout from Normandy.* Oxford: Osprey, 2001.

**WEBSITES**
http://s-boot.net/sboats-kriegsmarine-sbb.html
http://s-boot.net/sboats-kriegsmarine-types.html
http://www.german-navy.de/kriegsmarine/ships/fastattack/
http://www.merchantnavyunsungheroes.co.uk/
http://www.prinzeugen.com/SBOATIND.htm
http://www.wlb-stuttgart.de/seekrieg/km/sboot/sfl-frames.htm
https://uboat.net/
https://www.warsailors.com/freefleet/index.html

# INDEX

*Abukir*, SS (UK), 29
*Admiral Hipper* (Ger), 76
Admiralty (British), xii, 27, 29, 34, 46, 55, 90, 101–03, 111, 117, 121, 140, 174; Trade Division, 204
Adriatic, xvii, 18
Alsen Island (Denmark), 168
Amiens (France), 153
Amsterdam (Netherlands), 170, 176
Anglo-German Naval Agreement (1935), 21
Antwerp (Belgium), 106, 178, 180
Arctic, 77
Arras (France), 153
Atlantic, xi, xiv, xvi, 4–5, 27–28, 31–32, 38–39, 42, 48, 52, 55, 72–74, 76, 78, 89, 98, 122–24, 136, 161, 169–70, 176, 194–96
Atzerballing (Alsen Island, Denmark), 168
Aube, Admiral Théophile (1826–90), 17
*Azalea* (HMS), 150

*Baldwin* (USS), 159
Baltic, xiv, xvii, 11, 16, 33, 40–41, 60, 65, 85, 111, 132, 170, 183, 186, 188, 194
*Bandicar*, SS (UK), 49
Barents Sea, 76–77
Bartels, Kapitänleutnant Hans (1910–45), 84–86
Battersea (UK), 26
Battle of the Atlantic (1939–45), xiv, xvi, 55, 73, 76, 194–96
Battle of the Barents Sea (1943), 76–77
Battle of Britain (1940), 31, 35, 39–40
Battle of the Dover Strait (1940), 93
Battle of the River Plate (1939), 60

Bavaria (Germany), 9
Bawdsey Manor (UK), 116
*Beehive* (HMS), 184
Beeston (UK), 114
Belgium, xiv, 30, 51, 136, 153, 170, 176, 180
Berlin (Germany), 9, 55, 62, 77, 83, 87, 145, 165, 168, 182
*Bismarck* (Ger), 40
Black Sea, 8, 154, 187–88, 194
Black Forrest, 154
*Blanco Encalada* (Chile), 17
Block, Oberleutnant-zur-See Peter (1918–42), 108
Board of Trade, 68–69
Bonaparte, Napoleon (1769–1821), 192
Bordeaux (France), 32
*Boreas* (HMS), 35
Boulogne (France), 32, 41, 43, 46, 64, 127, 151–54, 156, 176
Bremen (Germany), 12, 107
Brest (France), 41, 43, 153
Breuning, Admiral Erich (1897–1978), 184
*Brilliant* (HMS), 35
Bristol Channel (UK), 28, 248n17
Britain: British Broadcasting Corporation (BBC), 96, 99, 152; cabinet war rooms, 102; war economy, 4, 15, 25, 28, 30, 40, 42, 78, 189, 195
British Army, xvi, 31, 50, 56–57, 95, 97, 101, 113; Army Bureau of Current Affairs (ABCA), 57
Brandi, Fregattenkapitän Albrecht (1914–66), 79
Britain trade, xiv–xv, xvii, 5, 24–27, 29–32, 36, 43–44, 53–54, 67–71, 88, 101, 122
British merchant navy, xix, 24, 57, 71, 114, 123; companies: Blue Funnel, 24;

Everards, 24, 68, 195; France Fenwick, 195; Horlocks of Mistley (Essex), 195; P & O, 24; Union Castle, 24; William Cory, 25–16, 195; DEMS (Defensively Equipped Merchant Ship) scheme, 50
British Pathé, 54
*Broke* (HMS), 93
Brown Ridge (North Sea), 59
Brunsbüttel (Germany), 37
Bundesmarine (West German Navy 1956–95), 184–85
Bürger, Hugo 65
Bütow, Kapitän-zur-See von (1894–1974), 62

Calais (France), 27–28, 146, 152–53
Cambridge (UK), 175
*Campbell* (HMS), 59, 107
Canada, 200
Cap Griz Nez (France), 153
Carls, Vice Admiral Rolf (1885–1945), 20
Cattaro (Montenegro), 154
Chartres (France), 153
Chatham (UK), 101–102, 114
Cherbourg (France), 32, 37, 41, 51, 87, 105, 110, 118, 127–28, 145, 149, 151, 153–56, 158–59, 193, 243n16, 244n49
Chile, 17
China, Sino-French war of 1883–85, 17
Churchill, Winston Leonard Spencer (1874–1965), xvi, 27, 31, 47, 59
Clyde (River, UK), 151, 205
CMB (coastal motor boats), xvii
coastal (littoral zone), 7–8, 18, 23, 25–26, 34–35, 47, 53, 55, 57–58, 85, 95, 98, 121, 127, 136, 147, 170, 185–189
coastal convoys/campaign, xi–xiv, xvii, 1–5, 8–9, 11, 23, 25–28, 31–34, 36–38, 40, 42, 44–52, 54, 56–58, 71, 75, 77–78, 81–82, 84, 87–89, 92, 96–97, 100, 101, 104, 106, 115, 118–24, 127, 131, 131–37, 140, 142, 146, 151–52, 167, 170, 177–78, 180–81, 189–92, 194–96; East Coast, xiv, xxi map, 1–2, 23, 26–28, 40–42, 44, 47–48, 50–51, 53–55, 57, 88, 90–91, 96, 97, 100, 105, 111, 114–18, 123–24, 136, 140, 143, 159, 170, 176–77, 184, 190–95 (*See also* appendix Vessels in English Waters Lost to Torpedo Attacks by S-Boats, 1940–1945); coastal convoys, South Coast, 23, 177, 147; Convoy routes, FN (Forth North), 28, 100, 123; FS (Forth South) FS, 28, 100; PW (Portland West), 28, 100; WP (West Portland) 28, 100 (*See also* appendix Vessels in English Waters Lost to Torpedo Attacks by S-Boats, 1940–1945)
convoys, individual:
CW8, 34, 35, 54, 137, 200;
CW9, 35, 54, 137, 201;
CW221, 72, 123, 143, 213;
FN11, 37;
FN426, 206;
FN434, 72, 205;
FN832, 51–53, 209;
FN1160, 125, 142, 212;
FS71, 37;
FS559, 47;
FS749, 44, 208;
WP183, 46, 118
Coastal Forces (British), 44–46, 53, 55, 58–60, 63, 82, 89–90, 92–100, 109, 112–115, 117–18, 121, 123–25, 129, 133–34, 136, 163, 172–73, 175, 175, 181–84, 186, 189, 190, 192, 194, 196
Combined Services Detailed Interrogation Centre (CSDIC), 107–09
Committee of Imperial Defence (CID), 101
Conflans (France), 153
Corbett, Julian (1854–1922), xii
*Cordruff*, SS (UK), 106
Cornwall (UK), 51, 93, 192
Cotentin Peninsula (France), 117, 152–53, 155
Covehithe (UK), 116
Cromer (UK), 47, 96, 105–06, 117–18, 171, 202–09, 212

Cross Sand (North Sea), 117
*Cubitt* (HMS), 182
Czechoslovakia, 21

Daimler-Benz (Company), 12, 19, 82
Danziger Waggonfabrik, 83
*Daphne*, SS (Fr), 72, 205
Dartmouth (UK), xix, 121
D-Day (Normandy Invasion), 4, 75, 76, 88–89, 102–03, 112, 119, 121, 124, 140, 144, 146–47, 149, 151, 155–67, 169, 178, 191, 236n67; Mulberry harbor, 160; Omaha Beach (France), 161; Force O, 151; Utah Beach (France), 149
Deben (River, UK), 116
Delfzijl (Netherlands), 170
Den Helder (Netherlands), 128, 130, 170, 181–82
Denmark, 83, 168, 185
Dreyer, Lieutenant Christiopher (1918–2003), 172–73, 194
Denning, Lieutenant Commander Norman (1904–79), 102
Dickens, Peter (1917–87), 3, 95, 186
Dieppe (France), 32, 145, 217
Distributed Lethality, 187
Dönitz, Gross Admiral Karl (1891–1980), 5–6, 22, 74–75, 77–85, 139, 144, 151, 153–54, 157, 159–60, 164–66, 169, 180
Dönitz, Leutnant-zur-See Peter (1922–43), 79
Dortmund (Germany), 62
Double Cross system, xvi, 146
Dover (UK), 26–27, 34–35, 92–93, 114, 120–121
Drake, Sir Francis (ca. 1540–96), 60, 192
Dublin (Ireland), 54
*Duff* (HMS), 177
Dungeness (UK), 35, 199, 205, 212, 214, 216, 218
Dunkirk (France), 27, 28–29, 33, 54, 60, 93, 128, 170–72, 174–76, 198

Eckernförde (Germany), 19, 61
English Channel, xi–xii, xv–xvii, xx, xxii; map, 1–4, 6, 8, 11, 14, 22–23, 26, 28, 31, 37–45, 47–48, 51, 53–55, 60, 64–66, 73, 75, 78, 80, 82–83, 87, 91–92, 94–95, 97–100, 102–04, 106–09, 111–12, 121–24, 126–28, 131–34, 136–137, 139–41, 147–50, 153–55, 157, 160, 163, 169–71, 176, 180–81, 184–86, 188–95, 200
Exercise Tiger (Force U training exercise 1944), 149–151, 193, 214

*Falke* (Ger), 156
Felixstowe (UK), 114, 184
Festung Europa, 4
Fimmen, Korvettenkapitän Kurt (1911–2001), 184
Finland, Gulf of, 154
Forth, Firth of (UK), 28, 47, 50, 191
Fort Southwick (UK), 102
France, xiv, 4, 16–18, 21–22, 24, 27, 29–31, 33, 60–61, 73, 76, 78, 84, 87, 91, 105, 136, 140, 148, 153, 155, 169–70, 176, 191, 200; French resistance, 63, 152–53
Franco, General Franciso (1892–1975), 20–21
*Frankford* (USS), 125
*Freedom* (USS), 7
Fricke, Admiral Kurt (1889–1945), 30
*Friedrich Eckoldt* (Ger,) 76
Frisius, Admiral Friedrich (1895–1970), 170
*Fulham*, SS (UK), 25–26, 72, 202, 125
Fulham Borough Council (UK), 26

*Garth* (HMS), 59, 107
Gelsenkirchen (Germany), 62
Geltinger Bay, 183
*George Balfour*, SS (UK), 105, 209,
Germany, xiii–xiv, xvii, 6, 9, 11–12, 14–16, 18, 20–23, 30, 33–34, 38–39, 41–43, 46, 61–63, 74–76, 78, 81, 84–85, 100, 127–28, 137, 139, 143–44, 147–48, 154, 162, 166, 173, 176–77, 180, 185, 188, 190, 194, 196 (*See also* separate entries for Heer, Kriegsmarine, and Luftwaffe); Oberkommando der Wehrmacht

266   INDEX

(OKW), 31, 33, 38, 75, 123, 144, 146, 165, 170, 173; war economy, 131
Gestapo, 61
Great Yarmouth. *See* Yarmouth
Gironde (France), 155
*Gneisenau* (Ger), 43
Godt, Admiral Eberhard (1900–95), 169
Gorleston (UK), 114
Göring, Hermann (1893–1946), 33, 35, 137, 162
Gosport (UK), 115
Grimsby (UK), 105

*Halsted* (HMS), 160, 216
Hamburg (Germany), 62
Harris, Air Chief Marshall (1892–1984), 158
*Harstad* (HMT), 110
Harwich (UK), 96, 177, 184, 207, 212
Hase, Fregattenkapitän Georg von (1878–1971), 65
Hearty Knoll (North Sea), 117, 207
Heer (German Army 1933–45), 30, 61–62, 76, 80, 144, 148, 151, 153, 157, 164–65, 169, 192
Hemsby (UK), 114
Heye, Vice Admiral Hellmuth (1895–1970), 85
Hichens, Lieutenant Commander Robert Peverell (1909–43), 92–100, 109
high frequency direction finding (HFDF), 101–103
Himmler, Heinrich (1900–45), 173
Hitler, Adolf (1889–1945), 16, 20–21, 30–31, 37–39, 41, 61, 76–80, 85, 109, 142, 161, 165, 171, 173, 188, 191
*Holderness* (HMS), 108
Hoofden (Netherlands), 177
Hoffmann, Admiral Kurt-Caesar (1895–1988), 153
*Hornet* (HMS), 115
*Horseferry*, SS (UK), 44, 208,
Hull (UK), 69, 200
Humber (River/Estuary, UK), 72, 182, 192, 206, 209, 213

*Hunter* (HMS), 21

Ijmuiden (Netherlands), 127–28, 141, 153–54, 170, 179–180, 208
*Ilse*, (Ger) 72
Imperial War Museum, 9, 172
information-centric warfare, xii
Ingenieurskantoor voor Scheepsbouw, 16
Inglis, Admiral Thomas (1897–1984), 5
intelligence, xi–xii, xv–xvi, 5, 34, 44, 89, 96, 101–26, 136–37, 146, 149, 167, 172–75, 192–94; enigma (Ultra), 101–02, 104, 105–07, 109, 115, 162; interrogation, 61, 102, 107–109, 111, 136, 151, 172–75, 190; photo reconnaissance, 102; radar. *See* separate entry; signals intelligence, 102, 104, 113–14, 119, 133, 177, 190; VHF (headache), 102, 112–19, 130, 133, 177, 190,
Irish Sea, 145
Italy, 28; MAS boats, 18

*Jaguar* (Fr), 29
*Jaguar* (Ger), 156
Japan, 17, 46, 189
Jellicoe, Admiral John Rushworth (1859–1935), 14
Jeune Ecole, 17
Jutland, Battle of, 14

Kahn, Otto Hermann (1867–1934), 12–13
Kaiser, Wilhelm II (1859–1941), 13–14, 61–62, 192
Kemnade, Korvettenkapitän Friedrich (1911–2008), 37, 62
Kiel (Germany), 61–62
Knock John (North Sea), 97
Knox, Frank (1874–1944), 45
Kolbe, Rear Admiral Hans (1882–1957), 19–20
Kolbe, Kapitänleutnant Ulrich (1917–2003), xx, 60, 62–64, 87, 110, 135, 145
Kriegsmarine (German navy 1933–45), xi, xiii–xiv, xvii–xviii, 1, 4–7, 9, 11, 16, 20–22, 28–31, 33–43, 46, 48, 52, 60–67,

73, 75–80, 82–86, 88, 98, 101–2, 106, 114, 122–23, 126–27, 129–32, 136–37, 139, 140, 144–45, 147–48, 152–55, 157–59, 162–69, 175, 177, 180, 183–85, 188, 191, 194; Beobachtungsdienst (B-dienst), 104–05, 118, 130, 136–37, 142, 149–50, 174; flotillas. *See* S-Boat entry for S-Boat Flotillas; Kleinkampfverbande (small battle units), 84–85, 165, 182; kleinkrieg, 14–15, 190; Kriegsschiffbau, 83; Naval Command North, 170; Naval Forces Netherlands, 171; Naval Group West, 146–47, 155–56, 169, 183, 185; Naval High Command (SKL), 20, 30, 41, 51, 77, 81–85, 117, 122, 126, 145, 151–53, 155–56, 159, 172–73, 175, 180, 188; Plan Z, 16, 18, 23, 85

Kriegsmarine ship types: Albatros, 186; Gepard, 186; Hydraboot, 164, 255n54; Jaguar, 186; minensuchboot, 81; pocket battleship, 16–17, 23; Seeadler, 186; Tiger, 186; torpedo boats, xiii, xvii, 3, 6, 13–14, 17, 32, 34, 37–38, 45, 54, 58, 64–65, 78, 81, 91, 100, 102, 145, 149, 155, 157–158, 160, 164, 168, 183, 189

Kluge, General Wolfgang von (1892–1976), 172

La Rochelle (France), 32
Le Havre, 32, 63, 103, 105, 118, 128, 156, 158–59, 163–64, 169, 248n18
*Lightning* (HMS), 17
Liverpool (UK), 70, 102
Liverpool Echo, 178
Lloyds War Medal, 71
Lohmann, Kapitän-zur-See Walter (1891–1944), 15–16
London, xix, 25–26, 28–29, 38–40, 47, 59–60, 63, 65, 70, 76–79, 92, 97, 102, 123, 166, 171, 175, 195, 199, 202–204, 206–08, 211, 213, 171, 175, 207
*Lord Hailsham* (HMT), 110
Lorient (France), 32, 40
Lowestoft (UK), 59, 62, 114, 142, 202–203, 207, 210–12, 219

Lübeck (Germany), 32, 40
Luppis, Giovanni (1813–75), 17
Luer, 13
Luftwaffe (German Air Force 1933–45), xvii, 28–29, 31–40, 46, 48, 50, 54, 75, 82, 118, 122–23, 127, 134, 137–39, 141–44, 152, 162, 165–66, 180, 191; aircraft: HE-111, 174; Ju-87 Stuka, 29, 64, 200–201
Lürssen Werft, 12–14, 21, 82–83, 107, 108
Lüth, Kapitän-zur-See Wolfgang (1913–45), 79
*Lützow* (Ger), 76
Lützow, Rear Admiral Friedrich (1881–1964), 29
Lyme Bay (UK), 87, 110, 149, 150, 211, 214
*Lysland*, SS (UK), 105, 209

*Mackay* (HMS), 134, 149
Mackinder, Halford (1861–1947), xiii
Mahan, Alfred Thayer (1840–1914), xiii, 13
*Mallard* (HMS), 59, 200
MAN, 19, 21
Marienfelde engine works, 82
MAS (10th Assault Flotilla), 84
Marine Korps Flandern, 14
Marschall, Admiral Wilhelm, (1886–1976), 51
Maunsell, Guy (1884–1961), 97
Maybach, 12–13, 19
Mediterranean, 12, 27, 77, 79, 84–85, 90, 104, 108, 123, 146, 188, 194
Memel, 168
Mercedes Benz, 19, 82, 109; engines: MB501, 21, 109; MB502, 19; MB508, 129
mine, xvii, 5–6, 17–18, 21, 26–27, 31, 34–36, 38, 44–48, 55–56, 63–64, 71–72, 83, 94, 97, 99, 102, 106, 112, 120, 125, 130, 133, 141–43, 147, 152–53, 162–63, 169–71, 177–78, 181–82, 192–94, 195, 197, 203, 209, 213–13, 248n18
minesweeper, 26–27, 44–47, 50, 55–56, 69, 78, 81, 93, 105, 145, 158, 163, 178, 189, 216–17

Ministry of Information, 56
Ministry of War Transport, 71
Mirbach, Kapitaenleutnant Götz Freiherr von (1915–68), 161, 173
*Modavia*, SS (UK), 110
*Moewe* (Ger), 156
Morison, Samuel E. (1887–76), 5, 155
*Moskva* (Russia), 8, 187
Motoscafo Armato Silurante (MAS), xvii
Müller, Leutnant-Kommander Karl Wilhelm Walter (1916–89) 149, 172–75

Narvik (Norway), 44
Nelson, Admiral Horatio (1758–1805), 60, 93, 100, 192
Netherlands, xiv, 30, 83, 86, 136, 170–71, 178, 180, 184
networked warfare, xii
Neugebauer, Oberleutnant-zur-See Kurt (1922–45), 182
Neustädter Slip-GmbH, 16
Norfolk (UK), 70, 114
North Sea, xi, xiv, xvii, 6, 8, 14, 22–23, 26, 28–29, 38, 41, 75, 80, 91, 94–95, 98, 102, 106, 111–12, 122, 124 169–70, 180–81, 184, 188, 194, 208–209, 212, 219
Norway, 22, 51, 78, 82, 84, 168–69, 188

Oheka II, 13
Obstacle (Convoy), 150
Oostende (Belgium), 29, 32, 41, 43–44, 97, 127, 154, 174, 177, 183, 218
Opdenhoff, Kapitänleutnant Hermann (1915–45), 66, 181
Operation Barbarossa, 194
Operation Bolero, 88, 123–24, 140, 143, 146, 149
Operation Cerberus, 43–44, 195
Operation Fortitude, 146
Operation Market Garden, 171
Operation Neptune, 4, 160
Operation Overlord, 4
Operation Sealion, 22, 30–31 38, 152, 192
Orford (UK), 116

Orfordnesss (UK), 205–06
Organisation Todt, 129, 165

Packard, 95
*Partridge* (USS), 160
Pas de Calais (France), 146, 152–53
Peter Paul Möbius, 66
Petersen, Korvettenkapitän Rudolf (1905–83), 62, 85, 92, 113, 122, 130, 135, 142, 159, 161, 170, 168–80, 179–80, 183–84, 190, 232n35
Philipp II (Spain), 192
Pitreavie Castle (UK), 102
*PLM14*, SS (UK), 38
Plymouth (UK), xv, xix, 78, 92, 101–02, 117, 119, 121, 167
Poland, 46
*Polperro*, MV (UK), 149, 213,
Popp, Oberleutnant-zur-See Paul (1916–42), 109
Portland, 149–50, 200
Portsmouth (UK), xv, 28, 46, 78, 92, 101–02, 121, 123, 146, 167, 210, 216–17
*Prinz Eugen* (Ger), 40, 43
*Pytchley* (HMS), 123

R-Boats, 6, 32, 81, 90, 99, 102, 128, 145, 162, 172, 194
radar, xvi, 82, 97, 102, 111–12, 116–121, 125–26, 130, 134–37, 142–43, 150, 174, 177, 179–81, 190–92; air-to-surface vessel (ASV), 112, 119
Raeder, Grand Admiral Erich (1876–1960), 16, 18–19, 21–22, 30, 39, 74–77, 85
Royal Air Force (RAF), xvi, 31, 37, 40, 45, 96–98, 101, 112, 119–120, 126, 157–58, 162–63, 181–82, 190; commands: Bomber Command, 158; Coastal Command, 41, 45, 56, 112, 119–121, 138, 157, 181; 16 Group, 119–120, 157, 177, 182; 19 Group, 157; Director of Air Warfare and Flying Training, 120; Fighter Command, xvi, 39; squadrons: No. 145 Squadron, 35; No. 236 Squadron, 181

## INDEX

RAF aircraft: Spitfire, 54, 97; Beaufighters, 143, 181; Lancasters, 162; Mosquitos, 182; Wellington, 177, 182, 237n74; Whitley, 120; Women's Auxiliary Air Force (WAAF), 114
Reichstag, 15
Reichsmarine (German Navy 1919–33), 13, 15, 16, 18, 20
Rhine (Germany), 12–13, 171
*Richard Beitzen* (Ger), 76
*River Trent*, MV (UK), 69
Rommel, Field Marshall Erwin (1911–1944), 153
Roosevelt, Franklin Delano (1882–1945), 30
Roskill, Captain Stephen (1903–82), 5, 34, 88, 190
Rotterdam (Netherlands), 32, 37, 40–41, 63, 127, 138, 141, 170–71, 176, 179–80, 246–47n48
Royal Navy, 21–22, 24, 34, 37, 41, 45, 49–50, 55, 57, 71, 73, 87, 89, 95–96, 100–103, 105, 110, 118, 122–24, 129, 136, 140–41, 146, 150–51, 163, 172, 181, 185–86, 188–192, 195–96
Royal Navy commands: 6th MGB Flotilla, 93, 109; 7th MGB Flotilla, 59, 97; 8th MGB Flotilla, 93; Naval Intelligence Department, 102–04, 107–09, 111–12, 172–73; Nore, 28, 88, 91–92, 95–96, 105, 117, 121, 123–24, 146, 191; Operational Intelligence Centre (OPIC), 103; Naval Operational Research (NOR), 188; Naval Staff, 5–6, 9, 34, 79, 81, 119, 124, 127, 153, 163; Rosyth, 90–92, 101–02, 122–24, 146; Royal Naval Patrol Service, 33–34, 51, 149; Western Approaches Command, 102; RNVR, 58, 72, 93; Y service, 112–16
Royal Navy Fleet Air Arm aircraft: Albacore, 120, 157; Swordfish, 120, 157
Royal Navy LCTs: LCT 314, 215; LCT 381, 110–111; LCT 875, 215

Royal Navy MGBs: MGB 20, 134; MGB 21, 134; MGB 64, 93, 96, 109; MGB 67, 96; MGB 76, 209; MGB 77, 99; MGB 87, 59, 97; MGB 88, 97, MGB 89, 59, 232n11; MGB 91, 97; MGB 335, 130; MGB 603, 111; MGB 607, 111; MGB 610, 142–43
Royal Navy MLs: ML145, 141; ML150, 141; ML197, 105; ML339, 51, 209; ML498, 105; ML499, 105; ML2220, 59; MTB28, 119; MTB430, 216; MTB448, 216; MTB482, 183; MTB484, 183; MTB493, 182, 219; MTB494, 182, 219; MTB724, 172; MTB5001, 219
Royal Navy ship types: Captain-class Frigates, 119, 182–83; coastal forces control frigates, 172, 177, 182–83 ; Elco, 45; Fairmile 'B', 45; Fairmile 'D', 45, 94; Hunt class, 123; LST, 149–150, 178, 214–15, 219; motor gun boats (MGB), 58, 63, 87, 91–92, 94–95, 97–98, 109, 114, 118, 123, 132, 134, 142, 157, 174, 178, 180–181, 183, 193–94, 205, 237n92; motor launch (ML), 91–92, 98, 132, 142, 178, 192; Town class, 90, 124; motor torpedo boats (MTB), 45, 59, 91–92, 94–95, 98, 114, 118–19, 123, 133, 142, 156, 172, 174, 180, 182–83, 190, 192
Royal Navy: Women's Royal Naval Service, 114–115
Ruge, Vice Admiral Friedrich (1894–1985), 162, 166, 185–88
Rumseld, Donald (1932–2021), 188
Russia, 17, 39, 63, 65–66, 75–77, 83, 131, 137, 170, 186–187; Russian Army, 75, 170; Russian Navy, xvii, 5, 187
Russo-Japanese War, 17
Russo-Ukrainian War, 8
*Rutherford* (HMS), 182–83

S-Boat:
  S-Boat armament, 19, 83, 103–04, 130, 143; torpedo, Dackel (TIIId), 131–217; G7a torpedo, 72, 131, 193, 238n11; G-7e electric torpedoes,

131; mine, oyster/pressure mine, 162–63; mines, 21, 64, 83, 94, 99, 106, 125, 130 147

S-Boat armoring, 111, 130, 138–140, 182, 193;

S-Boat bases, xxi map, 27, 32, 62–63, 87, 103, 105–06, 108, 118, 125, 128, 146, 151, 159, 169, 177;

S-Boat builders, xx, 12–13, 23, 66, 81, 83, 103, 245n54 (*See also* Danziger Waggonfabrik, Lürssen Werft, and Schlichting Werft); construction; 19–20, 42, 66, 80–83, 85, 103, 127, 193–94; engines (*See* Daimler Benz, MAN, Mercedes Benz); equipment, 83, 96, 107, 109, 129, 130, 134–35, 143, 159; intelligence, 106, 111, 118, 136, 146, 174, 177, 193; losses, 91, 138, 142, 147, 158, 172, 182; origins, 12–19; speed, 1, 12–13, 17–18; tactics, xvii, 9, 34, 53, 87, 92–100, 107, 112, 118, 134, 179, 192–93

S-Boat Command (FdS), 44, 46, 63, 82–83, 85, 92, 113, 128–130, 135–38, 142, 159, 168–69, 171, 173, 176, 179, 190, 226n44, 232n35. *See also* Petersen, Korvettenkapitän Rudolf (FdS)

S-Boat Command (FdT), 38–39, 46, 62, 129, 137, 140

S-Boat Flotillas:
  1st S-Boat Half Flotilla, 9, 188;
  1st S-Boat flotilla, 20, 22, 37, 40, 154, 194;
  2nd S-Boat Flotilla, 21–22, 37, 40–41, 43–44, 61, 82, 96–97, 105, 108, 118, 134, 142, 154, 168, 181–82, 209–10, 214, 216, 219;
  3rd S-Boat Flotilla, 37, 40, 85, 154, 194;
  3rd S-Boat School Flotilla, 183;
  4th S-Boat Flotilla, 40–44, 105, 118, 134, 141–42, 154, 156, 159, 181–82, 184, 209–10, 212, 240n49, 246n40 and n43;
  5th S-Boat Flotilla, 46, 51, 110, 143, 145, 149–50, 154–56, 159, 181, 213, 215–16, 219;
  6th S-Boat Flotilla, 134, 142, 154, 164, 181–82, 209–10, 217, 219, 240 n.49;
  7th S-Boat Flotilla, 104, 154, 194;
  8th S-Boat Flotilla, 141–42, 154, 170, 179, 183, 214;
  9th S-Boat Flotillas, 149–50, 154–57, 159, 161, 170–71, 181–83, 200, 215–16;
  10th S-Boat Flotilla, 154, 170–72, 176, 183;
  11th S-Boat Flotilla, 194;
  21st S-Boat Flotilla, 194;
  22nd S-Boat Flotilla, 194;
  24th S-Boat Flotilla, 194

S-Boats:
  S-1, 13, 19–20, 37;
  S-5, 20;
  S-6, 19;
  S-7, 19;
  S-10, 21, 37–38;
  S-11, 37;
  S-13, 37;
  S-14, 21;
  S-17, 21;
  S-18, 21, 37, 202;
  S-19, 19, 35, 40, 199–200;
  S-20, 35, 37, 40, 199–201;
  S-21, 37, 201–02;
  S-22, 37, 40, 202, 205;
  S-23, 52, 64, 203;
  S-24, 38, 40, 205;
  S-25, 21, 40, 202;
  S-26, 21, 200;
  S-27, 35, 37–38, 200–01, 204;
  S-28, 203–05;
  S-29, 21, 97, 204–5;
  S-30, 21, 202–03;
  S-31, 53, 204;
  S-33, 53, 184, 202–03;
  S-34, 29, 198, 203;
  S-36, 53, 199–200, 202;
  S-37, 21;
  S-41, 96, 109;

S-38, 111;
S-39, 108;
S-41, 96, 109;
S-43, 205;
S-46, 209;
S-47, 96;
S-48, 206, 208, 211;
S-49, 205;
S-50, 206, 208;
S-51, 206–07;
S-52, 149, 206–07;
S-53, 61, 111, 206–08;
S-54, 37, 207;
S-55, 205;
S-58, 202;
S-59, 203;
S-61, 204;
S-62, 208–09;
S-63, 208, 211;
S-64, 207;
S-65, 211, 213;
S-67, 208;
S-68, 211;
S-70, 208;
S-74, 212;
S-80, 209, 213;
S-81, 211;
S-85, 185, 186, 211;
S-88, 111, 141–42, 213;
S-96, 111, 141, 212;
S-62, 97, 213;
S-65, 112, 210;
S-75, 209;
S-81, 210;
S-84, 149;
S-85, 63;
S-86, 212;
S-88, 213;
S-90, 212;
S-96, 212;
S-97, 216;
S-99, 213;
S-100, 129, 132, 138, 212, 214;
S-101, 82, 129, 203–04;
S-102, 72, 203–05;

S-104, 44, 62, 97, 207–08;
S-105, 97, 206–07, 209;
S-106, 108;
S-108, 97;
S-109, 207–08;
S-110, 211;
S-111, 44, 55, 67, 97, 109, 111, 212;
S-112, 208, 210;
S-114, 134, 216;
S-115, 209–10;
S-116, 210;
S-117, 211;
S-119, 134;
S-121, 212;
S-130, xiii, xx, 9, 185, 214;
S-131, 129;
S-134, 129;
S-136, 149–50, 212, 216;
S-137, 129;
S-138, 129, 149–50, 212–14;
S-140, 150;
S-141, 149, 213;
S-142, 149–50;
S-143, 149;
S-145, 214;
S-147, 111;
S-150, 129, 214;
S-153, 104;
S-167, 129;
S-172, 215;
S-174, 182, 215, 219;
S-175, 215, 218–19;
S-176, 182;
S-177, 182, 215, 219;
S-178, 215, 219;
S-179, 215;
S-181, 181;
S-182, 216;
S-183, 172;
S-185, 113;
S-187, 215;
S-189, 215;
S-192, 113;
S-196, 179, 183;
S-199, 179;

S-200, 172;
S-202, 183;
S-204, 184;
S-205, 184;
S-207, 218;
S-218, 129;
S-227, 183;
S-702, 172;
S-703, 183 (*See also* appendix, Vessels in English Waters Lost to Torpedo Attacks by S-Boats, 1940–1945)
Saalwächter, Admiral Alfred (1883–1945), 44–45, 51, 128
St. Malo (France), 163
St. Nazaire (France), 32, 174
St. Peter Port (Guernsey), 32, 111
*Scharnhorst* (Ger,) 43
Scheldt (Belgium), 106, 170, 177–78, 180
Schveningen (Germany), 128
Schleswig (Germany), 61, 168
Schlichting, Werft, xx, 9–10, 66–67, 82–83, 107–08; *Der Werftbote*, 67
Scott, Lieutenant Commander Peter (1909–89), 94, 96, 99, 125, 175, 161, 164, 169, 285–9, 302
sea denial, xii
*Sea Mist* (HMT), 72
Seine Bay (France), 115, 117, 155, 159, 162
Sengwarden (Germany), 179
Sheringham (UK), 114, 203, 206, 208
Shipwash (North Sea), 117, 136
*Siroco* (Fr), 29
Smith's Knoll (North Sea), 70, 204
*Solstad*, SS (UK), 149
Southend (UK), 28, 50, 70, 205–06
Southwold (UK), 114
Spain, xvi, 20, 148, 185, 192; armada, xv, 44, 192; civil war, 21
Speer, Albert (1905–1981), 80
*Stayner* (HMS), 158, 172
Stuttgart (Germany), 62
Suhren, Korvettenkapitän Reinhard (1916–84), 79
Sunk Head (North Sea), 97
*Supremity*, MV (UK), 68

*Svenner* (HnoMS), 156
*Swift* (HMS), 93
Swinemünde (Germany), 63
*Szent István* (SMS), 18

*T28* (Ger), 156
Tambach (Germany), xix, 9
Thames (River/Estuary, UK), 25–26, 46, 70, 97, 117, 169, 177, 192, 219
*The Battle of the Narrow Seas* (Peter Scott), 94, 174
*Theodor Riedel* (Ger), 76
*Tide* (USS), 163
Timms, Sub-Lieutenant Roderick (1921–2003), 183
*Tirpitz* (Ger), 84–85
Tirpitz, Admiral Alfred von (1849–1930), 13, 15, 76
Töniges, Kapitänleutnant Werner (1910–95), 66
Topp, Korvettenkapitän Erich (1924–2005), 79–80
Travemünde (Germany), 16, 67, 82, 107
Treaty of Versailles, 11, 14–16, 18–20, 22
Trimingham (UK), 114
*Trollope* (HMS), 158, 216
Tyneside (UK), 50, 55, 196

U-Boat (submarine), xv, 4–7, 15, 17, 19, 22–23, 26–27, 33, 38–39, 42, 52, 60, 64, 66, 72–82, 85, 87, 101–02, 107, 122, 127–28, 131, 137–39, 141, 144, 154, 157, 160–161, 166, 169–70, 180, 189, 195–96
U-Boat Command (BdU), 33, 77, 169
U-Boat Types: VII, 32, 74, 161; IX, 74; XXI, 74–75; XXIII, 74, 76; electro-boats, 74, 78, 166; schnorkel boats, 157
U-Boats: UB-68, 77; U-954, 79
*Underwood*, MV (UK), 149, 213
Untertürkheim (Germany), 82
USA, xi, xiii, 4–5, 9, 42, 118; U.S. Army, 149–150; Civil War, 17; Cold Harbor Spring, 12; Congress, 30, 90; Lend

Lease, 90, 118; Neutrality Acts, 30; New York City, 12; *New York Times*, 97–98; press, 50
United States Navy (USN), xix, 155; United States Naval Intelligence, 5; Commander of U.S., Naval Forces, 162
United States Navy (USN) ship types: LCS, 7–8, 186–87, 307; PT Boat, 95; *Buckley*-class frigates, 118

Vegesack (Germany), 84, 107
Ventnor (UK), 117
*Vesuvius* (HMS), 17
*Vortigern* (HMS), 44, 208
Vienna (Austria), 62
Vlissingen (Netherlands), 37, 177

*Wakeful* (HMS), 29, 198
Walcheren (Netherlands), 178
Walsingham, Francis, xvi
*Wallasea* (HMS), 149, 213
Wash (UK), 192

*Wien* (SMS), 18
*Westminster* (HMS), 115
Wheatcroft, Kevin (1959–), xx, 9
Whitehead, Robert (1823–1905), 17
*Wildfire* (HMS), 102
Wilhelmshaven (Germany), 179
World War I, xiii–xv, xvii, 5–6, 11–15, 17–19, 26, 49, 60, 77, 93, 95, 131, 161, 168, 184, 193
Wintersdorf, Thuringia (Germany), 62

Yarmouth/Great Yarmouth (Norfolk, UK), 47, 56, 69, 105, 114, 181, 202, 203, 205, 207, 209, 213–214, 234

*Z29* (Ger), 76
*Z30* (Ger), 76
*Z31* (Ger), 76
Zandvort (Netherlands), 62
Zeebrugge (Belgium), 32
Z-line, 96–97, 100
Zymalkowski, Korvettenkapitän , Felix (1913–2004), 173